D1708123

FORTUNE'S FAVORITE CHILD

FORTUNE'S FAVORITE CHILD

THE UNEASY LIFE OF **WALTER ANDERSON**

CHRISTOPHER MAURER

UNIVERSITY PRESS OF MISSISSIPPI / JACKSON

A Mary Jayne G. Whittington Book in the Arts

www.upress.state.ms.us

Designed by Todd Lape

The University Press of Mississippi is a member of the
Association of American University Presses.

11 10 09 08 07 06 05 04 03   4 3 2 1
∞
Library of Congress Cataloging-in-Publication Data

Maurer, Christopher.
Fortune's favorite child : the uneasy life of Walter Anderson /
Christopher Maurer.
p. cm.
Includes bibliographical references and index.
ISBN 1-57806-539-9 (alk. paper)
1. Anderson, Walter Inglis, 1903–1965. 2. Artists—United
States—Biography. 3. Artists—Mental health—United States. I.
Anderson, Walter Inglis, 1903–1965. II. Title.
N6537.A48M38 2003
709'.2—dc21   2003010745

British Library Cataloging-in-Publication Data available

For María Estrella Iglesias

CONTENTS

ACKNOWLEDGMENTS

Through a generous subvention to the University Press of Mississippi, Ray L. Bellande made it possible to double the number of color reproductions in this book. With his thorough knowledge of the history of Ocean Springs and Jackson County, Ray provided an abundance of archival material and did everything possible to facilitate my work. Few biographers have been able to rely on such a source of constant help and information.

Additional funds for the color illustrations were provided by Maria T. Mavar of Ocean Springs. Her help is deeply appreciated.

It has been a privilege to work with Seetha Srinivasan, director of the University Press of Mississippi, who greeted my proposal with enthusiasm, helped me tell the story better, generously allowed me to write at greater length than either of us anticipated, and—a cause for even deeper gratitude—defended the book loyally, energetically, and with a sense of fairness to all involved. No one could ask for more from a publisher, and no one better exemplifies the ideals of an excellent university press.

I am grateful to Mary Anderson Pickard, best and most patient of teachers, for sharing her knowledge and her imaginative insights into the work of her father, for deepening my understanding of Walter Anderson's art, and for granting me the freedom to explore and write about every aspect of her father's life. I am also grateful to John G. Anderson for a trip to Horn Island and for many conversations, since 1997, about the meaning of his father's life. I thank Mary, María Estrella Iglesias, Leif Anderson, and Daniel Maurer for careful readings of the manuscript. Warm thanks, also, to Joan Gilley, curator, Family of Walter Anderson, who accommodated herself to my unpredictable schedule, led me straight to the materials I needed, answered my questions knowledgeably and efficiently, and showed steadfast support in every possible way.

The Anderson family has placed at my disposal source material unavailable to earlier researchers. Had it not been for the support, at crucial moments, of Mary, Leif, and Bill Anderson, this book would not have been published. Carolyn Anderson, Michael Anderson, and Patricia Findeisen shared family memories and papers and offered views which opened new doors. Pat Pinson, curator of the Walter Anderson Museum of Art, provided illustrations and other much appreciated help. Kendall entrusted me with information from her personal journals and from her talks with the late Agnes Grinstead Anderson and Margaret Sidney.

I owe a special debt to Patti Carr Black, who read the manuscript for the University Press of Mississippi and sent expert suggestions and much-needed words of encouragement. Carol Cox did outstanding work as copy editor.

I have received assistance during the course of my research from Marjorie A. Ashley; Ann Mulloy Ashmore, de Grummond Children's Literature Collection, University of Southern Mississippi; Curtis F. Barnett; David Beltrán; Theodore Barber, archivist at the Parsons School of Design; Calon E. Blackburn and Bruce McCall, U.S. Army Corps of Engineers, Mobile, Alabama; Dottie and Brad Burns; Burton Callicott; Julie H. Clark; William Creech, National Archives; Brent Funderburk, Mississippi State University; Gwen Dougherty, Tulane/DePaul Hospital; Suzanne Freeman and Sarah Falls, Virginia Museum of Fine Arts; Laura Frederick; Cyril Gardner; Kasha Mitchell Godleski, Director of Alumni Relations, Manlius Pebble Hill School; Sandy Hayes, Lauren Rogers Museum of Art; Mary L. Haynes and Burton Wright, U.S. Army; Erika Hichez, New York University; Patricia Kahle, Shadows on the Teche; Katherine Kraft, Radcliffe College Archives; Adele Anderson Lawton; Cheryl Leibold, Pennsylvania Academy of the Fine Arts; Wilbert Mahoney, Modern Military Records, National Archives and Records Administration; Nancy McCall, Alan M. Chesney Medical Archives, Johns Hopkins University; Genie McCloskey, archivist, The Isidore Newman School; Reb McMichael of the Mississippi State Hospital at Whitfield, who organized a fine symposium on Walter Anderson and helped me locate Anderson's records at Whitfield, Mobile Infirmary, and DePaul Sanitorium; Dr. James

Mead; Stacey B. Minyard, Friends Hospital, Philadelphia; Joseph S. Moran; Gene Morris, National Archives; Miriam Northrop; Francis V. O'Connor; Kip Peterson, Memphis Brooks Museum of Art; Norbert Raacke, New Orleans Museum of Art; Luise Ross; Frank E. Schmidt, Jr., M.D.; Harry J. Schmidt, Jr., M.D.; Cedric Sidney; Ellen Simak, Hunter Museum of American Art; Redding S. Sugg, Jr.; Barbara Thuet, who sent me the originals of letters by her uncle, Frank Baisden; Dennis Walker, Walter Anderson Museum of Art; Deborah Wythe, Brooklyn Museum of Art; Mary Wichmann; Maurice C. York; and many others.

I am grateful to Betsy Lerner, who took on this project as agent, and pursued it with persistence and enthusiasm, and to the editorial, marketing, design, and production staff of the University Press of Mississippi, especially Anne Stascavage. The University of Illinois–Chicago, has provided research funding.

This book was written in daily conversation with María Estrella Iglesias, who led me to Shearwater and to the Andersons, taught me more than I can say about a remarkable family, and opened my eyes to beauty I would have missed. To her it is dedicated, with gratitude for these and other gifts.

INTRODUCTION

The triumph of Walter Inglis Anderson—painter, writer, naturalist—was the momentary defeat of custom. He believed that custom destroys love, and although with love "man can see through a stone wall," without it we can only say *of course*. "Man begins by saying *of course*, before any of his senses have a chance to come to his aid with wonder and surprise. The result is that he dies, and his neighbors and friends murmur with the wind, *of course*! The love of bird or shell which might have restored his life flies away, carried by the same wind which has destroyed him."

There was nothing customary about his own restless life or about his best work. No American painter has ever drawn so close to the world of nature or returned with such abundant rewards. And few can have lived as dramatic and passionate a life as he did, on the edge of society, a voluntary exile from "the sordid thing most people call reality." Walter Inglis Anderson (1903–1965) is only now gaining wide recognition among historians of American art, partly because he spent almost his entire life in the isolation of a small coastal town, Ocean Springs, Mississippi, more intent upon understanding "natural forms"—the texture of pine bark, the curve of cloud or wave, the language of pelicans—than upon establishing his own place in the annals of painting. Afflicted with mental illness that baffled some of America's leading psychiatrists, alienated for long periods from his wife, children, and other family members, Anderson was a proud, fiercely independent soul, aware of the artist's debt to society but indifferent to fame and skeptical of ever receiving help from others. "The artist lives between assistance and opposition and is first overwhelmed by one and then both together—then is reduced to the ranks and is told that the gods help those who help themselves. So that he usually ends up living almost entirely on stolen fruit." Between "assistance and opposition," he left an astonishing abundance of work—murals and oil paintings, watercolors and drawings, block prints, essays, poems, and journals. Unsure whether others truly needed his images, he kept much of his work to himself. He seldom bothered to sign or date his paintings, took little interest in exhibitions and publicity, painted most of his watercolors on simple typewriter paper, and considered art, as one critic has written, "not a product but a process, a means of experiencing the world."

The work of Walter Anderson springs from the belief—uncommon in the twentieth century—that "in order to realize the beauty of man we must realize his relation to nature." Not that man is "a beast or an animal," he once wrote, "but [he] has a relation to nature as close as a dog or cat." The relation was one of mutual dependence: if humans need the natural world in order to find spiritual transcendence, nature requires the artist to fully "realize" the significance of its forms. "The man is only half himself," Emerson once wrote. "The other half is his expression." Walter Anderson would have extended that dictum to the natural world: it cannot be entirely "itself" without the intervention of the artist. Only when "realization" occurs—when art and nature become a single thing—do we feel a sense of wholeness and gratitude both for nature and for art. "To know that every movement you make is related to the movements of the pine trees in the wind, the movements of a man in a field plowing, the orbit of a star, or the spiral movement of the sun itself. To know that this was done through art by men, not gods, who named each gesture and posture and assumed each in its correct place and time, until they became perfectly related to the movements of the stars . . . [all this] is to accept man's inheritance. To deserve it is another thing. But the first step is to acknowledge the debt to those men who have numbered and realized and lived with art."

In taking nature for his master, Walter Anderson reminds one unmistakably of Cézanne (a painter he often invokes), though his manner of pursuing "realization"—both of himself and of nature—was uniquely his own. He not only roamed the pinelands, marshes, and barrier islands of the Mississippi Gulf Coast; he also pedaled his bicycle thousands of miles across the landscapes of New York, Tennessee, Texas, and Florida on adventures as unpredictable as those of Don Quixote. "Beware by whom you are called sane," he once wrote, in homage to Cervantes's knight, whose story he read and illustrated more than once. If his Spanish hero yearned for an idealistic, imaginary past, Walter Anderson asked for an inexhaustible present: the moment of "strange and transient unity," just beyond the reach of his hands and avid senses, when art and nature could become one. In *Don Quixote*, Anderson once observed, the road was everything, and so it was to him, as he biked and walked across the American landscape in pursuit of what he called "definite knowledge" of nature. Twice during his lifetime—first as an art student and again in the early years of his marriage—he attempted to paddle down the Mississippi River in a canoe. He trekked across war-torn China, feasting his eyes on rivers and mountains he had first encountered in old Chinese paintings. Many times a year, during the last fifteen years of his life, he rowed a tiny plywood skiff ten or twelve miles across the Mississippi Sound to a barrier island in the gulf, a wilderness where he fled "the dominant mode on shore" and drew and painted his own arduous vision of paradise. "So much depends on the dominant mode on shore," he explained, "that it was necessary for me to come to sea to find the conditional. Everything seems conditional on the islands. Out there, if I eat I live, if something stronger than I doesn't destroy me." Living under his overturned skiff, in the most primitive of conditions, he found that nature "loves to surprise; in fact seems to justify itself to man in that way, restoring his youth to him each time—the true fountain of youth." In innumerable sketches and watercolors he captured life and death on Horn Island, entering a different order of time, making birds and animals his "familiars," drawing closer to pelicans and gallinules than he ever had to humans. His long stays on the island, where he became as much a part of the natural world as any snake, coon, or migratory bird, were both a refuge from the tensions of family life and a mystical search for wholeness and completion. Despite the physical torment he endured on that windswept, sun-bleached piece of sand—walking "the back of Moby Dick, the white whale, the magic carpet, surrounded by inhabited space"—he felt himself in a sort of Eden, a land of "infinite refreshment," supplied by Providence with all that he needed as a creator. "A bleak dawn but the sun has come out. I took a walk and found a much-needed pair of shoes that fit me. Fortune's favorite child. Indeed, if man refuses to allow himself to be distracted—driven wild, mad, sick, raving—he would often realize that he was Fortune's favorite child, and not simply an idle ass with an empty saddle, begging to be ridden and driven. God knows there are plenty willing to ride him—professionals and the virgin youths full of confidence in their own skill."

Both on the island and on the mainland, his life was suffused with pain
and loneliness. In the midst of the depression, after long years of training at
the Parsons School of Design and the Pennsylvania Academy of the Fine Arts,
he struggled to make a living and had little time to paint. After the death of
his father, a discouraging setback in his work as a muralist, and a long, debil-
itating battle with undulant fever, he underwent an emotional crisis so severe
that he was confined for over two years to mental hospitals in Maryland and
Mississippi. The diagnosis was uncertain—schizophrenia, depression,
dementia praecox—and the treatment was grueling. He was a rebellious
patient, and more than once he escaped, walking home to Ocean Springs,
proving unable to cope with job and family but determined to get on with his
art. Regarded in the town as an oddity, he had few friends anywhere and
barely any contact with fellow painters. Remarkably, in his journals he hardly
ever speaks of suffering and often of joy—"the joy of imaginative life, the joy
of creative effort, the joy of being related to a loving and living body." Stub-
bornly, he held to his belief that "the normal or even fairly normal man has
to be almost knocked down physically to be anything but sublime" and to his
belief in the transcendent power of art, in all its forms.

"Decorator," rather than "painter," was the occupation he gave on his passport, and his prolific output and broad appeal as decorator further complicated
his reception as an artist, both during his lifetime and posthumously. During
the late 1940s and 1950s, when abstract expressionism began to dominate
American painting, few artists tried harder than he to "reestablish the relation
of art to the people" and to employ what he called "a common language of
forms." Walter Anderson's deep love of design and of the decorative drew him
to a variety of media. With equal enthusiasm he decorated ceramics, designed
figurines, furniture, clothing, and wallpaper, painted murals, carved in wood
and clay, and made some of the largest linoleum block prints ever pulled by an
American artist. He acknowledged no bounds between the "fine arts" and the
"lesser" ones: he knew that the distinction was a recent one in Western art, a few
hundred years old at best, and that no such hierarchy existed in other cultures
and periods. Without worrying about his artistic dignity, he turned restlessly
from one medium to another, learning from all of them, wishing on one occasion that he were "an Indian god," with arms enough to match his interests. "If
we are to develop a common language of forms in art," he wrote, "it must be
through the decorative." One of his lifelong concerns (he thought it the artist's
duty to the public) was to provide inexpensive handmade art—pottery, prints,

carvings—for "people who cannot afford to pay a great deal for works of art, but still have an appetite for beauty."

Underlying his unified vision of the arts, and further separating him from other painters of his day, was an appeal to a common imaginative and literary heritage. The notion of "pure painting," free from the influence of music and literature, art whose only "content" was the act of painting itself, was entirely alien to him. "Those who swear by purity destroy both it and themselves," he wrote, referring both to morals and aesthetics. He sought common ground in fairy tales and myth, cave paintings and cathedrals, and in a shared repertoire of stories and images—a wellspring of inspiration and poetry ranging from Hans Christian Andersen to Milton and Blake, from the *Ramayana* to Babylonian epic, from Greek myth to the *Arabian Nights*. When the Brooklyn Museum put on an exhibition of his block-printed illustrations of fairy tales in 1948, he hoped that those tales, "which people tell their children before they go to sleep at night," would produce a series of imaginative "explosions" more powerful than the threat of the atomic bomb: explosions "so identified with the life of man that they stimulate, without destroying, life." Characteristically, he did not attend that exhibition or a showing in a New York gallery, which might easily have served as a springboard in his career; he had chosen instead to visit China, a "strange and incredible place to an American who has not learned to accept resignation as the chief virtue."

Despite Walter Anderson's indifference to fame and to "career," his life and works have not gone unnoticed among critics, curators, and historians. In 1967, only two years after his death, the Brooks Memorial Art Gallery in Memphis produced the first comprehensive exhibition of his work, and its curator, Robert McKnight, ventured that Anderson would go down in history as the "South's outstanding painter." Reviewing the exhibition *Realizations of the Islander* at the Pennsylvania Academy of the Fine Arts almost twenty years later, the critic Edward J. Sozanski observed that Anderson's paintings were "like Van Gogh's in the way they bombard viewers with more visual information than they can handle comfortably. Even though modest thematically, they project a grandiose, intensely poetic interpretation of the natural world." John Russell of the *New York Times* spoke of "a quietly excellent power that puts them among the best American watercolors of their date." In the catalogue for the Philadelphia show, John Driscoll made the first serious attempt to bring Anderson out of critical and historical isolation and to place him within a broad European and American context. Anderson's interest in pattern and color, he wrote, "places him in the general sphere of Matisse and Picasso and an heir to the generation of American painters which included Charles Demuth, Charles Sheeler, and Stuart Davis." The "straightforward expression of his experience with nature" was comparable to that of John James Audubon, and "his isolation and mysticism" connected him with Albert Pinkham Ryder.

Five years later, the Walter Anderson Museum of Art opened its doors in Ocean Springs, one of a handful of museums in the United States dedicated to the work of a single artist. An exhibition at the Smithsonian Institution in the fall of 2003 brought renewed confirmation of both Anderson's originality and his place in the American tradition. For Susan C. Larsen, he "belongs with that wonderful and uniquely valuable group of artistic and literary visionaries who time and again sustain one of our deepest connections to the American natural landscape." Linda Crocker Simmons agreed: the "unifying thread which links Anderson to American art history" is his depiction of "the natural world . . . much as it must have been presented, fresh and wonderful, to newly arrived European eyes." In an essay for the Smithsonian exhibition catalogue, Anderson's daughter, Mary Anderson Pickard, a painter herself and a careful student of her father's work, summarized his ties to the art of his time: "He sought and attained the sensual acuity with which Georgia O'Keeffe explored the depths of flowers or used her brush to caress the nuances of form in bone or desert landform. He understood and used the magic of rhythm, of cycle, of pattern and synesthesia which occupied Burchfield. He shared a mastery of technique with Demuth, abstraction with Marin, the secret symbols of Dove, and the exuberant creativity of Picasso. Recognizing the validity of primitive art which sprang alive from a way of life, he evoked the same ancient rhythms that danced the paint onto Pollock's canvas."

In the thirty-eight years since Walter Anderson's death, a number of excellent books have examined different aspects of his creations: his depictions of animals and birds, his illustrations of tales of voyage and epic, his murals and block prints, and the journals he kept on Horn Island. In 1991, his widow, Agnes Grinstead Anderson, published a brave, poignant book of memoirs, *Approaching the Magic Hour: Memories of Walter Anderson,* covering the years between their meeting in 1929 and his death. In *Dreaming in Clay on the Coast of Mississippi: Love and Art at Shearwater* (2001), I gave an overview of the Anderson family and of Shearwater Pottery, the family business where Walter Anderson worked as decorator and designer. That book serves as background, and sometimes as source, for this one, the first documented biography, an attempt to explain his principal ideas on art and to narrate the drama of his life: his search for spiritual transcendence, his yearning to make of art and nature "a single thing," and his efforts to reconcile the demands of art with those of marriage and family. It has been particularly challenging to write about Anderson's protracted struggle with mental illness. Because I am neither a psychiatrist nor a historian of psychiatry, I have avoided offering a diagnosis of my own: I have simply described his behavior and the findings of those who treated him during his two years of hospitalization. Surely this material, culled from medical records and family papers and presented here for the first time, will be of interest to those interested in the interplay of mental illness and creativity. The pain caused by that illness—pain visited both on him and on his family—dominates many of the early chapters of this book, in contrast to the ecstatic feeling of unity and completion that he described so memorably during the later years of his life, when he had achieved greater control over his affliction.

While writing this book I have often thought of his dictum: "One single beautiful image is practically inexhaustible. Man is a wasteful fool." Those words, like so much of Walter Anderson's painting and writing, are an invitation to inquire more patiently into other worlds and to travel spiritually "on foot." In times when our relation to the natural world has become even more problematical than it was during Anderson's lifetime, it would seem foolish and wasteful to say *of course* to a life so passionate and so filled with grateful wonder.

University of Illinois–Chicago
26 March 2003

NOTE FROM THE PUBLISHER: *On 22 April 2003, members of the Anderson family (Mary Anderson Pickard, Bill Anderson, Leif Anderson, and John Anderson) met with representatives from the University Press of Mississippi (Hunter Cole and Seetha Srinivasan). At this meeting, John Anderson made clear his views on his father's illness and said that he would oppose publication of* Fortune's Favorite Child: The Uneasy Life of Walter Anderson *unless a statement of his views was included.*

AN ALTERNATIVE PERSPECTIVE

—John G. Anderson

Events are seldom clear when they are happening. We can look back now to get a fairly clear picture of who Walter Anderson was and what he was doing. We have most of the pieces of the puzzle. But the people in this book did not have all the information we now have. None of them had any idea of the scope, quality, and consistency of his art. The profound wisdom of his written words was unknown to them. They each saw just a little piece of who he was and were primarily concerned with how his abnormal life made their lives more difficult. This book has been written about the man those people believed Walter Anderson to be, not about the man we now know that he was.

Now we know that his life was not the terrible, tragic waste of creative potential that everyone believed it was until after his death. Looking back, we know his life was a celebration and a "realization" of creative potential. Now we know that he was not "hopelessly mentally ill" for most of his life, as they thought. Looking back, with all the information currently available to us, we can see his mental illness much more clearly than the people who had to look at it through a cloud of fear, anger, guilt, uncertainty and, occasionally, ignorance.

We know now that he was mentally ill for only about three years of his life. During the rest of his life he lived without medication or supervision and was much more productive and creative than most people. We also know that, during those three years, he was suffering from a form of Severe Depression

[xxi]

associated with transitory delusions and hallucinations. His delusions and hallucinations were apparently minimal and of short duration. He definitely did not have incurable Schizophrenia, as most of the people in his life believed. His diagnosis remained Severe Depression for the entire eighteen months of his treatment by Adolph Meyer and Norman Cameron at Johns Hopkins' Phipps clinic. Since they were two of the brightest stars to have ever shined in the fields of psychiatry and psychology respectively, they were far ahead of their time in the diagnosis of mental illness. Unfortunately, for others at that time it was common practice to diagnose everyone who had delusions or hallucinations as Schizophrenic. During the period in history in which he was ill, even many psychiatrists and psychologists did not recognize in their diagnoses that delusions and hallucinations occur in situations other than Schizophrenia, although there are many of these:

1. When normal people are deprived of R.E.M. sleep for two weeks, they become indistinguishable from Schizophrenics even though they are not suffering from Schizophrenia.
2. Some diseases can produce delusions and hallucinations. It is intriguing to note that Malaria and Undulant Fever, the diseases that Walter Anderson fought for more than two years prior to his breakdown, are two of these diseases. They also produce and exacerbate Depression.
3. Severe thirst and hunger can produce delusions and hallucinations.
4. Sometimes when normal people experience neurological injuries from accidents,they exhibit Schizophrenic symptoms. But this is not Schizophrenia.
5. When normal people take certain drugs, they hallucinate and have delusions just like Schizophrenics. But this is not necessarily evidence of Schizophrenia.
6. In almost all cases of Severe Manic-depressive illness, there are periods of schizophreniform symptoms but this does not change their diagnosis.
7. In some cases of Severe Depression, like my father's, the same thing happens without changing the diagnosis.

Lack of recognition or acceptance that delusions and hallucinations are produced by anything other than Schizophrenia eventually led to a belief that Walter Anderson was Schizophrenic. There were no effective medications then for Schizophrenia. So, if he had actually been Schizophrenic, his life would indeed have been as hopeless as his contemporaries thought it was.

Fortunately he did not have Schizophrenia. His mental illness was actually less of a handicap to him than the perception of him as "hopelessly mentally ill" which almost all the people in his life shared. This perception led to ostracism and extreme isolation. It sometimes even resulted in persecution.

If he was not mentally ill why was he so different? Certainly the isolation affected him. I can remember several incidents in which his efforts to socialize with his family were met with negative responses from us that must have been extremely painful for him. But I believe there is a much more cogent reason for his alienation. At a very early age Walter Anderson began seeking a more natural reality, a more human reality than the one most people live in. He referred to the thing most people call reality as the "dominant mode ashore," and wrote, "Man begins by saying 'of course' before any of his senses have a chance to come to his aid with wonder and surprise. The result is that he dies [a living death] and his neighbors and his friends murmur with the wind, 'of course.'" He went on to describe what his more natural reality was like. In his reality, "The bird flies and in that fraction of a fraction of a second man and the bird are real. He is not only King he is man he is not only man he is the only man and that is the only bird and every feather, every mark, every part of the pattern of its feathers is real and he, man, exists and he is almost as wonderful as the thing he sees." He also wrote, "In order to realize the beauty of man, we must realize his relation to nature. . . ." I believe he "realized" the beauty of man.

He found his more natural reality and tried to share it with his family and his friends. But we were too fearful. We wanted to be normal more than we wanted to be natural. So now we accept a world in which at least two heads of state, men under enormous pressure from global responsibilities, have buttons at their fingertips which can turn the only planet that we know of which can sustain human life into a nuclear inferno. It is a world where 99.9% of the damage ever done to the planet Earth by human beings has occurred within the past 50 years. This may be "normal" during the period of history in which we live. But I doubt that it is natural and I do not believe that it is actually human nature. Walter Anderson rejected it and chose to live in a more natural and more human reality. That is why he was not normal. That is why his paintings and words reveal a profoundly more beautiful world that tantalizes and inspires us.

No, we cannot all go live on Horn Island. But we can seek to learn, as Walter Anderson did, what being human means. We can each attempt to "realize" our own humanity. Perhaps if we are willing to accept being a little less normal and a little more natural something very wonderful will happen.

If you want to know who Walter Anderson was, look at his paintings, read his own words in context and with an open mind, or sail a small boat out to Horn Island for a two-week stay. Do not believe that I or anyone else can tell you who he was.

FORTUNE'S FAVORITE CHILD

TALENT AND TROUBLE

He was a "comical, adorable little ruffian," his mother wrote when Walter Inglis Anderson was a blonde-haired boy of six. "He is too rough, he is not obedient, he kicks, he even spits, he punches, he throws whatever happens to be handy at the offender." And yet, she added, "he is level-headed, he is quick to see when he *must* be good, and he is sweeter than anything in the world when he *is* good."

Reading those words when she was an old woman, Annette McConnell Anderson must have marveled at how early in life "Bobby was Bobby." An observant mother and a believer in writing as daily exercise, she had kept a journal of the sayings and doings of her three children—Peter, Walter (whom she called Bobby), and James. When they were grown, she returned often to those pages, trying to decipher the future in the past and pondering the early signs of talent and trouble. All three of her boys had become artists, and that was precisely the future she had planned for them when she married George Walter Anderson, a New Orleans grain exporter, in January 1900. She was thirty-three, and when she told her husband she felt too old to have girls—too old to attend to their social life until they were safely married—he replied that he had the secret for producing only males. He was as good as his word, and three were born: Peter in 1901, Walter Inglis on September 29, 1903, and James McConnell (Mac) in 1907.

It was no coincidence that 1900—the year of her marriage—was also the year Annette McConnell graduated from the art program of Newcomb College after years of trying to establish herself as a painter. "The will to do, the

[3]

soul to dare" was the motto she gave in her Newcomb yearbook, as though measuring herself for an adventure. What she hoped to do, whether or not she realized it at the time, was to raise a family in which art, in one form or another, would be a powerful, sustaining spiritual force, as normal a part of daily life as reading or prayer. It was a brave ambition for the daughter of a practical-minded lawyer, and it was nourished by one of her Newcomb professors, Ellsworth Woodward, a defender of the ideals of the Anglo-American Arts and Crafts movement, and by her own readings in John Ruskin and William Morris. Woodward taught his students that art wasn't merely something elaborated in schools and museums; it affected all that one did, saw, made, wore, touched. Art was more than "easel painting and unattached sculpture," and it had to be brought "into the limitless field of every-day contact." All of the crafts must acquire "the dignity of art," and all should contribute to an "appreciation of beauty." He instructed them, also, that if art were ever to prosper in the South, southern artists would have to stop painting northern scenes and capture the natural beauty that lay around them. And his third lesson was that, whether or not they became professional artists themselves, it was *women* who had to instill in their children the "ideality" that was "the foundation stone of taste." Woodward's advice came down to this: create art everywhere, not merely in the studio, and allow it to form character and foster truth. Art was simply "truth made visible."

There was much in Annette's family background and that of her husband, Walter, that chimed with what Woodward called ideality, but very little that related to art. Her father had encouraged her studies at Newcomb—a harmless enough "amusement"—but he made it clear, toward the end of his life, that he wanted his grandchildren to prepare themselves for "industrial pursuits." Both her father's family and her mother's were distinguished ones, known for public service, and had been involved for generations with the building and improvement of a great city. On her mother's side, Annette felt proudest of her great-grandfather, Samuel Jarvis Peters, who had come to New Orleans from Connecticut when the city was little more than a pestilent swamp, and helped found its public schools, pave its streets, and turn it into a great commercial emporium. Once a year, when Annette's three boys were little, the schoolchildren of the city honored her "Granpa Peters," the "Father of Public Education" by laying flowers on his grave. Among the family's most prized possessions was an elaborate engraved silver tea service which had been presented to Peters to honor his contributions to the cause of public education. At a ceremony in his honor, fellow citizens spoke of all he had helped make possible: the planning of the Garden District, the building of better wharves, and the city's first railway, library, and public schools. Annette carried his legacy of service close to her heart. Someone had once remarked that there was not a single important family in New Orleans to which she was not somehow related. But what mattered to her, and what she passed on to her own children, wasn't her family's social standing; it was the notion that their ancestors were kind, energetic, practical people, leaders of good sense and deep convictions, who had left the city better than they found it. She had not the slightest doubt that she and her children must go through life in the same generous, idealistic way.

The same public spirit characterized her father's side of the family. Annette's paternal grandfather—a friend of James Bowie, of Alamo fame—was a public benefactor and a celebrated surgeon at the Charity Hospital, and her father was president of the Law Association of New Orleans, chancellor of the Episcopal diocese, and a member of the board of administrators of Tulane University. Her father, the Honorable James McConnell, was the tallest of three lanky brothers—six feet, one inch, with a finely shaped head and prominent brow, and after he was gone Annette liked to remember his ruddy complexion, wispy grey hair, and big blue eyes, "kindly and interested in others," a curiosity she felt she had inherited from him rather than from her somewhat retiring mother, who was never much of a talker. Raised on a plantation below Baton Rouge, James McConnell graduated from Washington and Jefferson College in Pennsylvania and from law school in New Orleans, where he opened an admiralty law practice and, a few years later, married Delphine Angelique Blanc—eldest granddaughter of Samuel Jarvis Peters—who lovingly steadied his "naturally sanguine temperament" and calmed his "eager exuberance."

Annette's mother, Delphine, was a small, quiet, fragile woman, who often told her about her childhood at Buena Vista, an estate covering four city blocks, in the suburb of Bouligny, where the houses of several family members stood side by side, surrounded by rose gardens and sweet olive. Delphine's mother, Mama Blanc, whom Annette remembered as "a great lady of the old school," lived in a plantation house on Bayou St. John, where Annette paid her ceremonious visits as a child, pausing, in the parlor, before a glass-topped coffin containing a child that had died in infancy, from whom the mother could not bear to be parted. The marriage of Annette's parents was a happy one, and she liked to gaze at her mother's portrait, painted by Cecilia

Beaux, and open her Bible and read the words her father had inscribed in it: "The heart of her husband doth safely trust in her. She will do him good and not evil all the days of her life."

For the last ten years of her life, Delphine Blanc was an invalid, and spent long periods in bed, with Annette at her side. But McConnell was a devoted husband, grateful for all she had done for him. When Delphine was pregnant with their first child, McConnell went off to war, serving as lieutenant at the defense of Vicksburg, and later at Mobile, where he fell into enemy hands. The child died in infancy from her mother's deprivations, but Annette—and, eventually, her own children and grandchildren—grew up hearing how her mother boldly freed her father from a Union prison, smuggling clothes into his cell, pulling a pair of men's boots over her own tiny shoes, and sewing gold coins into her petticoats. After the war, she helped the family survive by making lampshades and painting porcelain. The McConnells and Peterses and Blancs harbored vivid, painful memories of the war years. The women of New Orleans had suffered especially, and Annette sometimes told her children stories of her mother's defiance of the Yankee general known as "Beast" Butler. Until the end of her life, Annette could not bear to hear the "Battle Hymn of the Republic." It was beautiful, yes, but "so damned self-righteous."

After four years in the Army of Louisiana, James McConnell served in the state legislature, enlarged his law practice, and rose to prominence in his profession. In one case, he helped defend the city of New Orleans against Myra Clark Gaines, one of the richest women in America, who had laid claim to urban real estate said to be worth thirty million dollars. It was one of the longest-running and best-publicized court trials in U.S. history, and the "Great Gaines Case" and others kept McConnell living for years at a time in Philadelphia, New York, and Washington, where he argued more than once before the U.S. Supreme Court. When Josephine L. Newcomb gave several million dollars for the founding of Newcomb, the first women's college within an American university, McConnell defended the bequest against her relatives (who alleged she had been mentally unstable at the time of the donation) and spent seven years in New York pursuing the case. He was in Princeton, in 1882, as legal advisor to his friend Paul Tulane, when Tulane gave over a million dollars to found Tulane University and named McConnell, who had been a schools supervisor as a young man, to the university's board.

Annette was at home in New Orleans at the time. But for long periods, she traveled with her father and ailing mother, living at hotels and rooming houses while McConnell prepared his briefs for northern courts, and she was able to turn his travels to her own use. In the late 1890s she appears to have studied at the Art Students League in New York, and at Branchville, Connecticut, with the American Impressionist J. Alden Weir. She may also have spent a summer at Shinnecock Hills, on Long Island, with William Merritt Chase. She had great admiration for Mary Cassatt, and she was on friendly terms with Cecilia Beaux, who had painted her mother's portrait.

But there was another reason, besides the Gaines and Newcomb cases, for her father's travels, one which hung like a cloud over the family and which they could not discuss in public: the supposed mental illness of Annette's older sister. When she was twenty-six, Delphine ("Dellie") McConnell, a beautiful girl, "with big dark eyes like shoes," fell in love and became more "excitable and talkative" than usual. Judge McConnell thought the young man "wasn't good enough" for his daughter, and did his best to prevent them from seeing each other. One night at dinner, McConnell's silver napkin ring fell to the floor, and instead of picking it up and returning it to him, Dellie threw it into the fire, along with other things he had given her. There must have been other such incidents, for in 1890, after consulting with the family doctor, Dellie's mother, father, Annette, and a cousin took her to Philadelphia to consult with a celebrated psychiatrist, Wharton Sinkler, who was associated with J. Weir Mitchell. "In those days," Annette remembered years later, "someone got sick, the matter was not discussed, and she would be back before too long, with no one the wiser." When Sinkler told McConnell he wasn't sure how long it would take to cure his daughter—perhaps months, perhaps a year—McConnell took his uncertainty as a sign of "incompetence." For over a decade Dellie was confined to northern asylums and sanatoria until at last, in November 1900, the year of Annette's marriage and graduation, McConnell decided to commit her—for life if necessary—to Friends Hospital in Philadelphia. There, doctors diagnosed "dementia praecox" and confirmed "a morbid sexual tendency, showing itself in undue fondness for men." Unlike Annette, who considered herself rather "plain," Dellie had always attracted suitors, including a son of the governor. In Philadelphia, an advance payment of ten thousand dollars, guaranteeing treatment for life, helped seal her fate and end a chapter in McConnell's life. Delphine had died four years earlier, Annette was now married, and in 1901 he married for a second time. According to the hospital records, Dellie "passed through a very long, stormy time, impulsive, destructive, noisy, and at times aggressive. After a period of about five years, she gradually became less difficult, with short disturbed episodes intervening, so that she was able to be transferred to accommodations for the quiet, continued-care group." McConnell would pray for his daughter every day, for the rest of his life. Annette was profoundly disturbed by the whole affair, and regarded it as an injustice she would, some day, redress.

While he traveled in the North, James McConnell left his law practice in charge of Annette's brother, Jimmy, a volatile, temperamental character with a practice of his own, to whom McConnell the elder directed more than one pained letter about punctuality, formality, and the need to develop good "office habits." Annette, who was more reliable, more like her father, felt a "deep bond" with her brother, partly because he had real artistic talent, which he had set aside in order to study law. She had to admit he was "somewhat unenlightened." He was intelligent, but often behaved like a fool with other people, including his wife, Lizzie, whom he antagonized—and finally lost—because of his habit of going home for sex in the middle of the business day. In all other matters, he was a procrastinator, a hotheaded threat to the family's reputation and fortune, quite impermeable to his father's advice and that of Annette, who was shocked by the way he treated his wife, and sent him snippets of Christian Science or inspiring thoughts from the pages of Tolstoy or her favorite minister, Henry Emerson Fosdick, of Riverside Church in New York. "I am not a credulous person," she wrote Jimmy, "but one thing I believe: the words, the promises of Christ. . . . Your mind must be clear as crystal, without resentment or anger."

Another major obstacle to Jimmy's "office habits"—besides sex—was chess. Both father and son were excellent players, and late in his life, one of the city's newspapers referred to McConnell, Sr., not only as the city's most prominent lawyer, its "Nestor," but also as the "Dean" of local chess, and praised him for playing that game the way he had conducted his life: "as a gentleman of the old school—courteous and considerate, kind in criticism, and strong in convictions." One of his favorite refuges, when Annette was growing up, was the Chess, Checkers and Whist Club, where he challenged visiting masters, held off the local competition, and took care not to be drawn into tournaments. In 1849, at the age of twenty, he defeated eleven-year-old Paul Morphy, whom he considered the greatest chess player in the world. Years later, he defeated Pillsbury, Mackenzie, and Zuckertort. Steinitz called one of his strategies "profound" and "clever." Jimmy, too, was greatly talented, but he was a gambler, and was so heavily in debt toward the end of his father's life that the latter had to pay his son's dues at the Chess Club.

At Newcomb College, Annette was a "special art" student, exempt from the requirements of the normal degree, and it took her eleven years, from 1889 to 1900, to graduate. During the entire period—part of which she spent traveling with her father—she was being courted by George Walter Anderson ("Wattie," she called him), an enterprising young man who worked on Canal Street as a grain merchant and who devoted far more thought to hunting, fishing, and golfing than to painting or art. He was a witty, fun-loving person, able to distract Annette from her family problems, allow her the freedom to which she was accustomed, and poke gentle fun at her "aesthetic" outlook on life. He, too, was proud of his ancestry and of his family's connection to New Orleans. His grandfather had won commendations for heroic service in the British navy, had gone to New Orleans to manage the mercantile house of Dennistoun, and had returned to Kirkcaldy, on the Firth of Forth, where he was twice elected Provost of the Burgh. In 1850 he retired from public life and bought an estate in Luscar, County Fife, where Walter spent happy days as a child. One of Walter's uncles had been a lieutenant-colonel in Her Majesty's Bombay Army, and another—a man of "singular boldness and independence of mind," according to his obituary in the *Glasgow Herald*—had been a managing partner in one of the flax-spinning mills of Glasgow and a Liberal member of Parliament before moving to Australia, where he was named Master of the Mint. There is less information about Walter's father. Born in Le Havre, France, Peter Anderson was a commission merchant who arrived in New Orleans around 1865, and formed a partnership there—Anderson and Simpson—but he seems to have lost his money and returned to Scotland before he died in Edinburgh in 1883. After Walter had made his way, like his father, through Kirkcaldy Burgh School, a secondary school in Bedford, England, and an international academy in Switzerland, where he learned French, he worked as a clerk in his father's firm. His father's death left him to care for his mother, Adele Byrne Briggs, and his sister, Adele (Daisy), as he advanced in the grain trade.

Despite his cheerful disposition, George Walter Anderson was subject to sudden bouts of depression and hypochondria which made Annette think long and hard about marrying him. In 1898, while she was traveling with her father, her brother, Jimmy, wrote that "Wattie" was suffering some sort of mental trouble. Judge McConnell was alarmed: "Tell him his marriage is a

George Walter Anderson, c. 1900   Annette McConnell Anderson, c. 1900

certainty, but merely put off until he gets well. To come north to see Annie in his present condition would increase his excitement and *might* lead to his permanent disability. By all means—all gentle and persuasive means—dissuade him from the thought of coming North. I want him, poor fellow, to have all the chances for recovery, and coming North at this time is not one of them. Recreation in the open air . . . is best for him." Given Walter's troubles, those of her sister, Dellie, the not quite rational behavior of her brother, and what she had glimpsed of the melancholia of Walter's mother, Annette thought it wise to consult both the family doctor and Sinkler, in Philadelphia, as to the advisability of having children. Neither objected. "Dr Sinkler. . . , knowing about both families, wrote that it was quite right. Dr. Elliott wrote that he did not know about the Andersons, but on my side it was entirely right." Neither of them dispelled her worries entirely, and for the rest of her life she would watch nervously for trouble in her own children.

Bob and Peter were born in a house given to Annette and Walter by her father, but in 1905 they built a comfortable new one on what Annette considered a "key lot" at 553 Broadway in the Garden District, not far from Newcomb, an easy walk from the levee and from the splendors of Audubon Park, one of the most beautiful public places in the country. It was a New England–style house, unlike others on the street; Annette had wanted it to look like the ones she had seen on her travels. Across Broadway, lined with live oaks, were some vacant lots with grazing cows that fascinated Bob and Peter, and the two of them often pretended, as little children, that they were cows, calves, or the cow man. Pecan and camphor and fig trees shaded the back yard. There was space for a strawberry patch, for the irises prized by Annette, and for her husband's huge collection of chrysanthemums—he had them sent to him from the North and got up at five o'clock each morning in the summer to tend to them: fifteen hundred single-stemmed plants, each tied to its own iron rod. In the house and yard, the Andersons cared for an ever-expanding menagerie of cats, cocks, hens, guinea pigs, rabbits, pigeons, and a lamb shipped in one Easter from the country. After three-year-old Bobby heard the story of Gerasimus, he asked his mother to enlarge the collection with a donkey and a lion.

Annette's father had a breezy, spacious vacation house down the coast in Bay St. Louis, and she and the boys went there for long periods in the summer: their first experience of the Gulf Coast. On weekends in the spring and fall, Walter, who loved the outdoors, took them to the Louisiana swamps, or on river trips on the *Wanda*, the forty-foot launch he had bought after a couple of "gorgeous" years in business. Duck hunting was one of his passions, and he once said he had "explored the Louisiana marshes of Lake Catherine and Lake Borgne more thoroughly than any other man [he had] ever known." The three boys accompanied him as soon as they were old enough to paddle a canoe.

A succession of nannies cared for the three children, and servants helped with the housework, but Annette was an attentive mother and recorded the boys' development in notebooks, along with precepts for parenting she had gathered here and there. "Make them dutiful, thoughtful, loving," said Professor Elliot of Harvard, and this from the naturalist Mary Treat: "Industry leads to skill, skill to love of work, love of work to helping others, helping others to unselfishness." Woodward had urged his students to give their children a love of beauty, and one of Annette's nieces remembered, years later, that "there was always something beautiful . . . on [Annette's] table. It wouldn't be a formal arrangement of flowers, but something she'd found in the garden. It might just be a bowl of magnolia cones with the little seeds in them, or [anything] she had found that was beautiful." As for discipline, a dose of castor oil corrected major offenses (using "bad words" or consorting with the wrong sort of children at the park) but neither Annette nor Walter was much of a disciplinarian, though Walter liked to remember his own Scottish father's favorite words—"There is a

Dionysus in His Boat, c. 1945

right way of doing everything, and if you don't know it, think it out"—and the razor strap his father used, at least once, to drive that lesson home.

What stands out in Annette's brief journal notes on Bobby is his interest in animals and, a little later, his love of gallantry. As a toddler he wakes up laughing, after a "happy dream—that some kind of animal was taking care of him," or decides he will be an angel when he grows up, so that he can "fly all about the sky and climb the trees and see the eggs in the birds' nests." Annette found him "a comical little monkey. . . . He has always amused us, from the time he was a week old. The way he let himself go when he cried, the faces he made when he tasted something new or something good. . . ." It seemed to her, when the boys were four and six, that Peter had more imagination and sensibility, and was a steadier worker than "Bobs," who had "more ingenuity and impudence" and worked only "spasmodically unless he is very much interested." As a small child his pet expression had been "'non,' pronounced as the French *non*. If you ask him to come to you, he says *non* with impudence and decision." He was a "ruffian," quick to lose his temper but equally quick to make amends, and he was drawn to anything that seemed noble and brave. "My little Saint Michael," she called him, for he had been born on September 29, feast of Saint Michael the archangel.

> He dreams he is a knight and spends his mornings making swords or flags. The other day he made a stick sword, decorated it with a blue bow begged from me, wrapped his strings of beads around it, and walked up and down with his back straighter than ever and his eyes shining. I said the first verse of [Tennyson's] "Sir Galahad"—all I knew. He said it after me, several times. "'My heart is pure,'" he said finally, because I have all these strings of beads."

Then, when he was a little older, and Annette and the boys were at the Bay St. Louis house together with their new little brother, Mac, there was a glimpse of the future naturalist: "Bobby today was catching minnows down in the O'Briens' ravine with Peter. When he came home he said Mr. Schafter had been there too, and caught hundreds. 'You know,' he said, 'all men have their *brutilities* and that is his. But that will wear away after a time and the fish will increase so it will be wonderful.'"

Bob and Peter learned to read at a small private academy on Aline Street run by the Finney sisters, friends of Walter's family, and Bob took an immediate liking to the Friday afternoon sessions devoted to stories, myth, and legend. When he was seven, Annette took him to an exhibition at Newcomb and found him curiously bored. He liked pictures of animals, he said, but there were none there. "When we were coming away, he said '*Mother*,' holding me back by the hand, 'Mother what are those?' pointing to the sphinxes at each side of the Art Building. 'Those,' I said, 'are sphinxes, half woman and half beast.' I began to realize how little I knew. 'Oh, yes,' said Bobby. 'I remember. Hercules told the maiden he had killed a sphinx.'"

By 1914–1915, Bob and Mac were enrolled at the R. M. Lusher Public School, and Peter at Isidore Newman Manual Training School, where he studied the usual academic subjects—history, English, geometry, Spanish—and woodworking. But Annette wanted something finer for her boys than New Orleans could offer, and in the summer of 1915, when they were eleven and fourteen years old, she escorted Bob and Peter to St. John's School, at Manlius, near Syracuse, New York, run by a son and grandson of Guido Verbeck, a "Christian hero" who had preached in Japan and whom Annette had probably heard about at St. Paul's Episcopal Church. Annette wanted her boys exposed to northern ways of thinking, with the opportunity to acquire some discipline and meet the right sort of people. Perhaps she also wanted more time for herself and for her painting: months earlier, Walter had built her a studio with a skylight on the top floor of their house, and although she was still taking an occasional class at Newcomb and exhibiting her work in the Arts and Crafts Club and other local venues, she had found little time to paint. Among her extant works from those years are an oil portrait of Walter smoking a pipe (*The Smoker*), a sketch of his sister, Daisy, and Impressionistic studies like *Sunlight, Against the Light*, and *At the Mouth of the Bayou*, showing Walter and the boys in a boat fishing.

"Manners Maketh Man" was the Manlius motto, of which Walter must have approved, though he found the whole idea of sending the boys north something of "a shot in the dark." Manlius was unmistakably a military academy, and its cadets were eligible upon graduation for commission as second lieutenant in the U.S. Army. Although Peter took at once to the regimented life, rose to the rank of lieutenant, and had to be discouraged by his parents from entering the army, Bob's grades, as junior corporal and corporal, were dismal. The officers in Troop A failed him in "enthusiasm" and "zeal" and barely passed him in "Saint John's Spirit." He managed to sound cheerful in his letters, although he sometimes stayed through Christmas and spring vacations. At Manlius, even during vacation periods, there was much going on: recitals of Kipling, an abundance of moving pictures, tea and cakes at the Verbecks', dances in dress uniform, and waves of patriotic oratory by professors who came over from Syracuse. But Bob said later that the school was like "four years of prison," and that the military part of it had nearly "destroyed" him. "I know what discipline is, having had four years of it. . . . I still suffer from it. The one great virtue [at Manlius] was conformity. You can imagine what a good thing that would be for a young boy who is just beginning to show individuality! Dad is a victim of that system. He went to an English Public school when he was very young, and he still believes in the good taste and virtue of the majority, just because it is the majority, and if so many peo-

ple believe a thing, it must be true, it's got to be." At Manlius, showing "individuality" led to demerits: for dirty boots, rifle, or saddle blanket, for "button
unbuttoned" or "bed not properly made," for "room not neat" or "laughing in
ranks." In February of his third year, he wrote his father he had been "reduced
to the ranks for engaging in a rough house with the rest of the Company." But
the place had its consolations. On Sundays, in religious processions, he carried the cross, after one of the teachers noticed "he needed a touch of the pic-
turesque to bolster him up." He had a few friends, and "special places" in the
woods where he went to read and draw or look at the nests of pheasants, cat-
birds, and partridges, including one with twelve large cream-colored eggs. An
older student who bred rabbits gave him a little one, which he kept for a while
in a box in his room.

In spring 1918, while Peter and Bob were at Manlius, their father suffered a
severe depression, brought on, in part, by the stress of his job. Annette had her
sister, also, to worry about. When James McConnell died in 1914, he had left
Annette a large sum of money and had asked her to care for Dellie. One of the
first things she thought about was how she might bring Dellie home from
Philadelphia and find her suitable living arrangements. In June 1918, pondering the future of the entire family—Walter, the three boys, and Dellie—she
made a life-changing decision. One afternoon she told her husband she was
going to look for a place to rent on the coast, perhaps for the summer. She
caught the train eastward, "over the lake," got off at Ocean Springs, Mississippi, and made her way to the offices of a real estate agent. Out came a long
list of town and country properties, from small lots to "fine pear and pecan
orchards under successful cultivation." One place in particular caught her
attention: Fairhaven, a twenty-four-acre tract of land jutting into the mouth
of the Biloxi Bay. Abutting the property on the northwest was a sleepy bayou
where a corn mill had once stood. The entire place lay on gently rolling terrain, with huge live oaks, towering pines and magnolias, pristine marshland,
and a narrow beach. At the end of a long, sandy, winding path was a large
white house (the "Front House"), built in the 1830s, with a view of Deer Island
and the glistening waters of the bay. Along the path, shaded by tall trees and
vines, lay a two-story carriage house (later known as the Barn) and a small
coastal cottage, nearly hidden in the woods. There was something almost
sacred about the stillness, broken only by the sound of birds.

As for Ocean Springs, it was a sleepy little town whose inhabitants felt
somewhat isolated from New Orleans and Mobile. There was no "industry,"

The Barn, 2003

The Cottage, 2003

except for a seafood cannery, and stores and businesses were confined to a few quiet streets shaded by live oaks festooned with Spanish moss. Cattle still wandered through the center of town, but the place was beginning to look prosperous. Land and labor were inexpensive, and for three decades the winters had been mild enough for growing satsumas, grapefruit, and oranges. The pecan business had gotten its start there, and off to the east, along the Pascagoula River, were lumber mills and a major shipyard, then turning out its first all-steel battleships. The beauty of the spot—the three-mile-long beachfront with its gazebos and piers and bobbing catboats, the graceful Biloxi schooners that plied the coast, the streets paved with oyster shells, and the sturdy, unpretentious white wooden frame houses—attracted summer residents from New Orleans and visitors from the North. There was a quiet optimism about the place, the proud feeling that it had been uniquely blessed by nature and offered a gentle, healthy way of life (the town was named for its mineral springs). Little had changed since architect Louis Sullivan had come down decades earlier from Chicago to build a cottage on the beach: "No 'enterprise,' no 'progress,' no booming for a 'Greater Ocean Springs,' no factories, no anxious faces, no glare of the dollar hunter, no land agents, no hustlers, no drummers, no white-staked lonely subdivisions." Annette had made up her mind—she always needed to be alone to think things through—and that evening when her weary husband asked her about her trip, she informed him that she had *bought* a place.

It had been a rough year for him, and it would be five more years before he was ready to retire. Either because of his "depressive breakdown" or because of business setbacks—perhaps both—the boys were called home from Manlius without being able to finish their studies. It was probably a relief for Bob, but a bitter disappointment for Peter, who expected to be made captain of his troop. In August 1919, he wrote the school to say he was not returning ("I doubt whether the condition of my father's business will permit me to do so"). From a camp in Highlands, North Carolina, where Bob and Mac were spending the summer of 1919, Bob wrote his father: "Please try to get me a job where I won't be cooped up in an office." Peter, too, was reluctant to enter his father's business—he had a brief stint there as an office boy—and in October he returned to Newman, which Bob entered for the first time. Both played football—Peter at tackle, Bob at guard—and neither was much of a student. Although Peter graduated (in 1921), Bob failed four of his six courses in 1919–1920 (Spanish, English, mechanical drawing, and plane geometry), and dropped out of school in January 1922, in the middle of his senior year, after failing French and chemistry. His highest grades were in woodworking and physical training.

At home, during Christmas of 1921, the family must have wondered what would become of him. Walter, at least, would have sympathized with his desire not to be "cooped up in an office." It was he who had had awakened his son's love of the water and of the outdoors, and for many years Bob would treasure memories of early-morning hunting trips with his father and Peter to the Louisiana marshes. At Lusher School, Bob had spent "all [his] time in class making maps of the lagoons where [he] used to hunt on weekends," and later, during his and Peter's years at Manlius, their father had sent them long letters about his adventures on the *Wanda*, beginning one of them: "My dear Kildee Pete and Greyduck Bob." By 1920, the two boys were learning to sail on their own, and one August afternoon that year, after his first hapless year at Newman, Bob ventured westward down the coast from Fairhaven, the new place, where he had been spending a few days with his mother. Late in the evening, after a squall at the mouth of the Pearl River, L. B. Charlton, keeper of the Lake Borgne lighthouse, peered through his spyglass and spotted a catboat, about a mile and a half out, anchored but empty. When he went to investigate, he found only the twelve-foot boat (the tiller was missing), an oar, and a khaki shirt with some money stuffed into the pocket. He took the boat back to the lighthouse and sent in a report. "Tide Sweeps Boy in Small Boat to Death," Walter read in the morning newspaper. When he went to question the lightkeeper, he saw to his horror that the empty boat was Bobby's, and offered a reward of one hundred dollars for his son's body. Two days later, his bedraggled son walked into the sitting room at Fairhaven and told his distraught mother and a reporter that his adventure had been "thriller enough" to last him a lifetime. When his tiller came loose, he plunged into the choppy water to retrieve it. The boat drifted away, and he swam two miles to a channel beacon. Lashed by wind and waves, clad in his bathing suit, he clung to it for twenty-eight hours. His voice was too weak to be heard by passing boats— one came within three hundred feet of him—and he grew so thirsty and so hungry that he "would have cheerfully given [his] front teeth for a drink of water," and "could have eaten the shadow of a bean." Finally, nearly unconscious, he was spotted by a passing fisherman, who gave him dry clothes and returned him to safety. He couldn't understand, a reporter wrote, why his parents had given him up for lost. "You knew I could swim," he said to his

mother. It was a sign of things to come, and a signal to Walter that his adventurous sons would never follow him into the grain business.

Perhaps, during the years at Newman, it had become apparent to Annette
that Bob's real vocation was art, and one summer she enrolled him in a course
on painting at E. Ambrose Webster's Summer School of Art in Provincetown,
Massachusetts, which offered instruction in "colour and sunlight effects, as
applied especially to landscape." Sometime in 1922, he carved a series of animals, pirates, and a wooden chest, adorned with elephants in relief, which—
according to family legend—he presented to his father, hoping to persuade
him to let him enroll in art school. Walter bowed gracefully to the inevitable.
That spring, the New Orleans Art Association, of which Annette was an active
member and Woodward was president, offered him a scholarship to the
Pennsylvania Academy of the Fine Arts. When the application was misplaced
by the school, he enrolled instead at the New York School of Fine and Applied
Art (now known as the Parsons School of Design), located in a five-story
building at Eightieth and Broadway, and founded in 1896 by Annette's old
teacher, William Merritt Chase.

The thought of her nineteen-year-old son living alone for the first time,
in so large and dangerous a place as New York, was a disquieting one for
Annette, but she had friends and relatives who could look in on him from
time to time. In October 1922 one of them reassured her that she had visited
Bobby in his "tiny little room on the fifth floor" of a boardinghouse on One
Hundred Twenty-third Street, on the Upper West Side, a block from Morningside Avenue, and that there was something "rather sweet and peaceful"
about it: it looked "like a hermit's cell." She found him a "very civilized
youth—charming to talk to—reminds me of you in his looks, especially in
his smile."

As for the New York School of Fine and Applied Art, Bob quickly learned
that the emphasis was on the "applied." In his biography of Tiffany designer
Van Day Truex, who studied at the school while Bob did, Adam Lewis reports
that its director, Frank Alvah Parsons, was an "arch-conservative in aesthetic
matters," and that the curriculum reflected his dislike of "all modern painting, architecture, design, sculpture and music," from the Arts and Crafts
movement through Cubism. In 1922–1923, only life drawing and lectures on
art history remained of the traditional curriculum. Courses in drawing and

painting had yielded to something known as the "Problem Method," inspired
by the ideas of Thomas Dewey: students learned only what they needed to
know of the fine arts by carrying out specific projects. During Bob's year in
New York, the school offered international training in architecture and decoration, landscaping, graphic and poster advertising, illustration, stagecraft,
industrial design, teaching art, and life drawing. The course for which the
school was best known—and the one which may have drawn Bob to New
York in the first place—was one taught by the painter Howard Giles, on Jay
Hambidge's theory of "dynamic symmetry," which Bob told his mother he
was "beginning to understand" in January 1923. The course offered a method
of geometrical composition based on classical Greek architecture and ceramics, and sought to "bring home with force the truth that the element of proportion or symmetry is fundamental in all types of art expression from painting to the lesser crafts." It was a theory to which Bob would turn again, with
renewed interest, twenty-five years later. On the whole, what Parsons and his
faculty of forty (half of whom worked in the professions) hoped to impart
were "the acquisition of taste (based on artistic principles)" and its application to "the trades and professions where art is a factor."

By the beginning of October 1922, in a "supercilious" and "cynical" mood,
Bob wrote Annette that his fellow students fell into two categories: first, "the
feminist—the one with affected ideals of art," and, second, "the commercialist, with no ideals, just frankly out to make money." He had decided to steer
clear of both. Although all of his courses were commercially oriented, it is
clear that he was developing an idea of himself as an "artist" rather than as a
designer. Finding the 1923 Independents Exhibition "very depressing," he
remarked to Annette: "If they simply want to be designers, let them say so,
and stop pretending to be artists." On the roster were, among others, Diego
Rivera, George Bellows (then much influenced by Hambidge), John Sloan,
Morris Kanter, and work by the pupils of Adolfo Best-Maugard, a young Mexican artist and educator whose theory of drawing, published that very year in
Mexico City, would, like Hambidge's, leave a deep mark on Bob's later work.

And yet, despite his distinction between "artists" and "commercialists," Bob's
year at Parsons and his pride in the work of his own hands—at Parsons and
perhaps at Newman—must have reinforced a principle he had learned from
Annette, who had absorbed it at Newcomb: that fine art was not incompatible
with fine design or the "lesser crafts." It was a message as old as Ruskin and as
new as Walter Gropius, who had insisted, in his "Manifesto of the Bauhaus" a

couple of years earlier, that there was no essential difference between the artist and the craftsman, and that "a foundation of handicraft is essential for every artist." Entering the world of business, of course, was another matter, and Bob must have known, as he worked in fall 1922 on an advertising poster for duck decoys, that he would never make his living that way.

If the Independents Exhibition disappointed him, there were plenty of others to write his mother about. In the Hispanic Society of America, he discovered the Spanish Impressionist Joaquín Sorolla and the colorist Ignacio Zuloaga. At an exhibition of the National Sculpture Society, German expressionists like Ernst Barlach and Matthias Eberle and Americans like Mahonri Young drew praise for their woodcarvings (rougher and less "rounded off" than the work of others). So did Eric Hudson—a painter of marine lifes—at a gallery on Fifth Avenue, and Boris Artzybasheff for his colorful murals at the Russian Inn. The watercolors of Winslow Homer in the Metropolitan Museum of Art were another revelation. On class outings to the American Museum of Natural History, only blocks away from the school, he drew skeletons and stuffed birds and looked at Indian totem poles, which would inspire his own woodcarving. All year, he turned out a succession of totem poles, pirates of all sizes, a "mammy," and other figures, until one day his chisel slipped, severing tendons deep in his right hand. As for painting, he was not using "oils at all at school, just tempera and water color."

In his letters to Annette he speaks as often of literature as of painting. Both of them were voracious readers and over the years books had become as strong a bond between them as art. The boardinghouse was only blocks from the New York Public Library's Harlem branch on East One Hundred Twenty-fifth Street, and he made a beeline for Brentano's whenever he had any extra money. Shaw and Chesterton were perennial favorites, but he was also reading drama that year—from Sophocles and Aeschylus to Dunsany, Masefield, Maeterlinck and especially Ibsen—as well as Rousseau and Schiller.

Parsons lay within easy reach of Riverside Drive and Central Park, and often he drew in the open air, or walked to the Bronx Zoo to draw the birds and animals. He loved getting about New York on foot, and only rarely, when it was raining, did he catch a streetcar. One day he spent the entire morning searching for white pine he could use for the totem poles, and walked one hundred blocks down the East River, from One Hundred Twenty-fifth to Fifth. Another, he took a ferry across the Hudson and trekked thirty-five miles along the New Jersey Palisades and back. Often he hiked to Greenwich Village to visit family friends, the Stockbridges. Dorothy Stockbridge, a distant cousin on his father's side of the family, wrote poetry and plays. She was well read and "very pleasant to talk to," Bob told his mother after helping her with the sets for one of her stage productions, although apparently his feelings ran much deeper. At Christmas 1922, the two of them attended a carol singing together and walked home through the snowy streets. Bob had no gloves, and as he put his hand inside her mitten, he realized he was "half in love with her." He had joked to his mother, a few days earlier, that he was planning to celebrate Christmas with a private one-man show: "by the artist, for the artist, and to the artist," including "woodcarving—figures and bas-reliefs—and enormous compositions both in transparent and opaque water color." Instead, feeling somewhat lonely, he opened his Christmas boxes from New Orleans and went to service at St. John the Divine, though he had told his parents, less than a year earlier, that they were "criminal in making him go to church."

In May, when Annette told him that the New Orleans Art Association had arranged at last for him to study at the Pennsylvania Academy of the Fine Arts, he jumped at the opportunity. By the time he returned from New York, in the summer of 1923, the family had moved to Fairhaven. Walter had sold the *Wanda*, was about to retire comfortably from the grain business, and was looking forward to golf, "a little shooting and a good deal of fishing." Mac, who was sixteen, had finished his first year at the McCallie School in Chattanooga, and was looking forward to a summer exploring the new place. Annette had bravely decided to turn her back forever on the social life of New Orleans. She would visit her relatives now only when she needed a break from life in the country, and if the family's public legacy was to continue it would have to do so on far different terms. Fairhaven seemed the perfect location for some sort of art colony, and she was planning to build a little studio, near the Front House, where Bob could paint. Peter seemed gloomy, even depressed, about leaving his friends in the city, but had occupied himself with painting and repairs at Fairhaven, and with trapping for mink and muskrat on a parcel of land his father rented for him in the pinelands of Pearl, Mississippi. A gift from Walter did much to lift his spirits: at a shipyard in Pascagoula they ordered the *Gypsy*, a twenty-five-foot, nine-foot-wide sloop with a detachable motor, perfect for exploring the coast and the barrier islands. He was also becoming interested in pottery. At an auction, Annette had bought a kick-wheel that had once belonged to the great Biloxi potter George Ohr, and one day she saw Peter digging into a little knoll at Fairhaven and building a brick, wood-burning kiln, three feet wide by nine feet deep. Pine knots were fed into one end, with the flue at the other, and there he fired his first pieces, experimenting with clay he dug himself from the nearby beach. Soon he was laboring at that kiln at all hours of the day and night, and one day he rowed over to Deer Island to ask advice from Joseph Meyer, the potter at Newcomb College, who had a summer home there. Walter wondered whether his oldest son's enthusiasm might be leading the family into a new business. Anderson Incorporated! Retirement would have to be put aside. It was clear to him now that, with a little help from Annette, the two older boys had found their vocations. Neither had taken up the "industrial pursuits" James McConnell had wished upon his grandchildren. But perhaps there was a way to marry art to industry and make of painting and pottery not only a "way of life," as Annette had wanted, but also a way of making a living.

AT THE ACADEMY

On the application form for the Pennsylvania Academy of the Fine Arts, Bob stated that he had a high school diploma but no previous training in art—he did not bother to mention his year at Parsons or his summer in Provincetown. Over the next few years, from fall 1924 through spring 1928, he would pursue a course of study designed to impart "a thorough knowledge of drawing, color, composition, modeling, construction, and perspective"—all this, the Academy's brochure promised, in "the heart of Philadelphia, within one square of City Hall" and "within easy reach of Fairmount Park and 3,000 acres of beautiful scenery."

Both the venerable Academy, founded in 1805, and the city itself had always had a reputation for conservatism. During the first two decades of the twentieth century, Philadelphia had awakened briefly to the latest currents of modern European painting, and collectors had begun to assemble their own private collections of modernist canvases. Music, too, was coming to life. The Curtis Institute of Music was founded in 1924, and at the *other* academy, just down Broad Street, Leopold Stokowski was winning enthusiasm for modernist composers like Berg, Mahler, Stravinsky, and Schoenberg. Apropos of a 1920 exhibition of modern French paintings, Stokowski urged Philadelphians to "recognize new painters as they had modern composers," and, in a lecture at the Academy, declared that music was far more advanced than painting.

By the time Bob entered the Academy, enthusiasm for European painting had waned, perhaps because of the war, and a period of openness and intellectual curiosity had all but come to an end. "Do Americans want their art to

be based on Picasso and Severini and their imitators over here?" a Philadelphia journalist asked scornfully in 1920. A few years later, when Alfred C.
Barnes persuaded the Academy to exhibit seventy-five of his European acqui-
sitions, including canvases by Modigliani, Lipchitz, De Chirico, Matisse,
Picasso, Derain, and Soutine, the city's journalists were moved to wrath. "It is
as though the room were infested with some infectious scourge," one of them
wrote. Another found that the pictures were "unpleasant to contemplate";
Modigliani was "very odd"; Soutine was "incomprehensible." It was "hard to
see why the Academy should sponsor this sort of trash." Not only modern
European but also the latest American painting sometimes came under fire.
In 1923, a year before Bob arrived in Philadelphia, the Academy's Committee
on Instruction considered Thomas Hart Benton for a faculty appointment,
but rejected him as an "extreme modernist." As a new student, Walter Anderson would have been the last person to complain about the school's conservatism, and if he enjoyed his visit to the Barnes collection, he never said so. "I
saw a lot of modern painting," he wrote his mother in 1925. "Cézanne, Renoir,
Daumier and a lot of others, most of them awful stuff."

A triumvirate of instructors—Hugh Breckenridge, Arthur B. Carles, and
Henry McCarter—would be responsible for changing his attitude and helping
broaden his interest in modern painting. Known as the Academy's "modernist"
faction and as the only instructors who had gone beyond Impressionism both
in their teaching and in their own work, all three tried to stimulate the individuality of their students. "An art school at its best is not controlled, and has no
relation to the usual school," Henry McCarter once wrote. "It has no books, nor
coddling, nor arranged entertaining, nor espionage. . . .The student has to find
his way and should be let alone. If they are no good—throw them out."

Bob had already had a taste of that lack of "coddling" in New York, and,
despite a shyness so pronounced that some of his classmates called him "the
Mystery Man," he soon became part of a circle of friends who identified
themselves with the modernist triumvirate, without, however, rejecting the
teaching of an archconservative like Daniel Garber. Two of Bob's earliest
friends were southerners: Francis Speight, a polite, easygoing painter from
North Carolina whose sister Tulie also studied at the Academy, and Frank
Baisden, who had spent most of his life in Chattanooga but had studied in
Breckenridge's school in Gloucester, Massachusetts. The judicious Speight,
son of a Baptist preacher and the youngest in a family of many children, was
probably a good source of advice and a stabilizing influence. He had always

thought of himself as a writer, not a painter, and didn't mind admitting that he had felt like a "chicken in a garden" when he arrived at the Academy, drawn there by the teaching of Garber ("If anyone had said 'shoo,' I'd have been right over the fence"). He was seven years older than Bob, had been at the Academy for four years by the time he entered, and was appointed to the faculty, as an assistant in Garber's drawing classes, during Bob's last three years. By then he had something of a "career" under way: in 1927 three canvases had been exhibited at the Carnegie International Exhibition. When Arthur B. Carles complained of the conservatism of the student body, he used to say that there were two sorts of painters at the Academy: those who went up the Delaware River, and those who went to Paris. In the years he shared with Bob at the Academy, Speight had gone not "up the Delaware," like Garber, but up the Schuylkill to paint, to the manufacturing town of Manayunk, chipped out of the rocky hillside "like a Cubist landscape" and captured by him in one oil after another for the next several decades.

Bob felt closer to Baisden, an affectionate, strikingly handsome student from Chattanooga, with whom he shared a love of the outdoors, a passion for music, and a strong sense of family. Baisden had entered the Academy in 1922, took several of the same classes as Bob, and for a while, in 1926, lived at the same boardinghouse at 1622 Summer Street, half a block from city hall, and a ten-minute walk from the Academy's awe-inspiring edifice at Broad and Arch. Years later, Baisden recalled that Bob "drank a good deal" that year, and impressed everyone with his "taciturnity," noticeable as far away as Ocean Springs. Annette puzzled over his long silences—"It must be something beyond mere dislike to writing." As for Baisden, he often felt "homesick" and hoped to "serve his apprenticeship up here in Decoration" and, after a few years, return home, to a region that was "growing growing growing." His dream, he told his family, was to help "*establish* the New South."

Both Baisden and Speight made friends far more easily than Bob, and drew him into their own circle of faculty members and fellow students: Garber and his wife; Leon Karp, who would later enter the world of advertising; Conrad Roland, a student from Norristown, Pennsylvania, who showed minor talent as an illustrator; Archie Bongé, an amiable six-foot, four-inch farm boy from Nebraska who spent only one term at the Academy (Bob thought him a bad painter, but the two would become lasting friends); and two brothers from Liverpool, England, Walter and Cyril Gardner, both close friends of Speight. Cyril often ate lunch with Bob and remembers the two of them arguing heatedly, over a bowl of corn mush, in a basement locker room, with students proselytizing for the Communist Party.

Cyril Gardner was a plucky young man who had left his family at the age of seventeen and was earning his way through the Academy by working part-time. What struck him, in retrospect, about the place was the absence of instruction in the techniques of oil painting and the general laxity of the faculty, who, with a few notable exceptions, were "paid to lend their names" but did little that might be described as teaching. The most any of them would offer, on looking at a student's work, was an unhelpful passing comment: "That leg is too short; that arm is too long." Nor did anyone take a regular look at the work students were doing, or failing to do; it seemed to Gardner that there was a "total lack of supervision."

Of the three "modernist" faculty members, the one who left the deepest impression—perhaps the only one Bob truly loved—was Henry Bainbridge McCarter (1866–1942), a rotund, cheerful iconoclast with a love of the "new learning in art" and a deep mistrust of the institution that paid his salary. McCarter was a year older than Annette, but there was something extraordinarily youthful about him, and his irreverence, his perpetual "succession of enthusiasms," his kindness and joie de vivre probably mattered as much to Bob as his painting or his advice on technique. He was "very amusing to listen to," Bob wrote Annette during his first year. "I don't agree with him in anything but I'd rather hear him talk than anybody else at the School."

There were few formal lecture courses at the Academy, but Cyril Gardner remembers that McCarter "held court" on decorative painting each Friday in an upper room where his own teacher, Thomas Eakins, had taught anatomy and dissection. Gardner and Baisden were in charge of projecting McCarter's magic-lantern slides at one time or another, and the two of them and Bob followed his lectures closely. For Gardner, the job of *projecting* the slides soon turned into *selecting* them; no easy matter, since the talks—not really lectures—meandered unpredictably, ending with a question-and-answer session on "artistic or personal problem[s]." McCarter had given himself some leeway in the catalogue—his course, "Decorative Design and Color Values," aimed to "encourage [the] student to express courageously and forcefully his own impressions and conceptions." Baisden remembered later that the course covered "everything that could possibly have bearing upon painting, drawn from his rich background and expressed with brilliance and wit." The nattily dressed McCarter would bound into the hall late—Gardner imagined him taking too long in front of the mirror—and launch into an entertaining causerie of informal art history, personal anecdote, and impish advice to his students on conquering the conventional. He taught them that there was an "unbroken thread of individual, robust art" extending from the ancient Greeks to the best of the moderns—Charles Demuth, Carles, John Marin— and that the enemy of that robust art had always been the academy. It didn't matter whether "the academy" was in Greece or Rome or Paris or Philadel- phia: any artist worth his salt would go there merely to have his hands trained and then leave it, "as a growing child leaves the nursery and its basic lessons." We must "all be academic for awhile," he liked to say, but the schools were full of stupefying prejudices, and eventually, any true artist had to "lock [his] academy and its traditions in a box" and throw away the key. Time was too precious to waste on "people with entirely closed minds." What the world needed was surprise, wonder, respect. "Surprise is good," McCarter told one of his classes. "There's emotion in it. The time is past when you can dare to laugh. Just go and look [at a picture] and presently that picture will have a great gift for you. If not, you simply respect it!" None of *his* disciples would ever sneer at modern art. It was too late for that, too late for "small talk." What mattered most was faith in one's own convictions and instincts. To "walk alone in untrodden ways" was a lesson that Bob took deeply to heart.

Like Breckenridge and Carles, McCarter had spent a long spell in Paris, decades earlier, when Cézanne, Seurat, and Gauguin were rebelling against "the patternless disclosure of Monet, Sisley and the early Pissarro." To Bob, and the rest of his students, he seemed to have met everyone. He could rem- inisce for hours about Pissarro, Degas, and Toulouse-Lautrec, who had taught him to paint only what truly matters. "When you paint," McCarter said, "you have to rise to a "sustained dramatic passion" to achieve anything memorable. The important thing was to organize one's work, do away with all but the essential, and not fall into the habit of failing. "Work carefully, deliberately, with the idea of success."

Maxims, anecdotes, advice on life were what he could best offer his stu- dents, along with this or that precious piece of advice on technique that Bob would put to work years later. In a letter written in 1985, Baisden remembered McCarter as "a startling and rather shocking 'modern' in the conservative fac- ulty" and recalled his "use of color 'radiation' on and around forms":

Walter understood this use of warm and cool colors to model objects and give them dimension and space. [In the 1920s at the Academy] Impressionism (as a color theory) was still considered revolutionary and the students were required to paint in 'broken color', as the Impressionist technique of applying color was then called. McCarter did not encourage students to use this 'broken color' technique, as did Hugh Breckenridge in his classes. . . . But McCarter . . . had the authority of one who had had first-hand contact with this then-startling movement. . . . Naturally, Walter . . . found McCarter's 'radiation' theory of color modeling much to his taste. Walter later developed this approach far beyond anything McCarter had propounded.

A notebook from one of McCarter's students in the 1920s records a few words of that advice:

How to make color vibrate:
For brightest vibration take blue.
❤ Blue in this quantity of red makes violent pulsation because it is a discord.
White canvas increases pulsation.
Cobalt violet and lemon yellow for warm grey.

One of McCarter's allies—another of Bob's favorite teachers—was Arthur B. Carles (1882–1952), an outspoken Philadelphian who shared McCarter's love of modern European painting and who offended academic sensibilities with his bold use of color, "flat art" without shadow, and rejection of realism. By 1924, Bob's first year, Carles was in the last, stormy days of his career as a teacher. The gossip was that he had tossed some plaster casts from the "pink antique" room down an elevator shaft to express his disgust with academic convention. Like McCarter, he believed in individualism, and his students responded with gratitude. In 1923, a group of twenty-three of them signed a petition asking that he be made full-time head of the life classes in place of the conservative instructor then assigned to them. In spring 1925, when he was finally dismissed from the faculty because of noncompliance with academic regulations and a growing problem with alcoholism, a group which included two of Bob's friends (Conrad Roland and Cyril Gardner) arranged to take private instruction from him. Like Breckenridge and McCarter, he was in love with color, and believed that "a loaded palette is often more lovely than a finished oil."

Another of Carles's peculiarities—one which was to leave a mark on Bob—was his interest in the harmonic correspondence of color and music.

Whistler had once written of his desire for "a living harmony of tones, a harmony not unlike that of a musical composition," and during the first two decades of the twentieth century the analogy between painting and music had been developed by Kandinsky, Robert Delaunay, and composers like Scriabin and Schoenberg. McCarter wrote in 1930 that for years he had wanted "to paint the fact and color and vibration of the sound of a chime of bells," and Carles, Breckenridge, and he were all interested in "vibrating color." One of Carles's cherished memories was "how Matisse had invited him to his studio to observe how colors in a painting vibrated at twilight," and he once thanked Breckenridge for having taught him that "color resonance is what you paint pictures with."

Relatively little survives of Bob's own work at the Academy, but his letters to Annette suggest that he worked intensively, sometimes for as many as nine hours a day, and that his deepest concern was learning to draw. In December of 1924, after a semester of antique cast drawing, he was painting a self-portrait (now lost) "with fair success," and beginning to attend Garber's night class in drawing, which trained students in quick sketching as opposed to the "hard drawing" done during the morning sessions. "It's good in one way," Bob wrote of the night class. "Very strong light and shade." The Academy's traditional insistence on a mastery of drawing seems to have frustrated more than a few students, impatient to devote themselves fully to painting, but Bob showed few signs of rebellion. In 1925, a year into his studies, he told his mother that he was *painting* in two courses (Breckenridge's portrait class and Henry Rankin Poore's on composition), and drawing in his other two (the life classes of Garber and Joseph Thurman Pearson): "I'll be a draftsman yet!" Many years later, Speight remembered Garber's cast-drawing sessions:

[Garber] would walk through the rotunda and on to his locker in the back hall, where he would put on his richly brown smock and then continue on down the hall tying the belt of his smock and on into one of the cast drawing classes. The students were more aware of his presence than they showed. He would walk over to where a student was drawing. The student would get up out of his chair, Mr. Garber would sit down in the chair, look at the cast that was being drawn and at the drawing. Meanwhile, he would take out his pocket knife while looking at the drawing, open the knife and put a very sharp point on the charcoal—sharper than the student could get with a sandpaper sharpener. Then he would make some clear and decisive lines of correction. Then he would talk to the student a bit, modulating his voice to suit the

merits of the drawing. Then he would go on to the next student while sometimes the student for whom he had just been criticizing would leave the class
for a breather, and sometimes, though rarely, to shed a few tears.

At skits performed by Academy students at the annual student dance, Cyril
Gardner "would imitate 'to the life' [the] abrupt penetrating voice with which
Garber sometimes chided his female students: 'Can you cook? You sure can't
draw, so you'd better learn how to cook.'" At which his brother Walter, "in the
part of a shrinking female student, would dissolve in tears."

Carles, too, gave a class entitled "Drawing from Living Models," on Saturday mornings, from nine to twelve, filling two rooms to overflowing; one had
to draw lots for a space. "Nowhere else in the School was there as much enthusiasm or a finer spirit," Speight remembered. "A draped model was arranged
for the students, who usually sketched in oil, but sometimes used charcoal,
watercolor or pastel. Carles would arrive to make comments after the work
was under way, and he would often stay after class to comment on work
brought from other classes."

Bob's painting of a girl dressed in eighteenth-century costume, *Portrait of a
Girl*, done in Breckenridge's portrait class or Carles's Saturday morning session,
perhaps in fall 1925 or spring 1926, is the only oil still extant from the Academy
years, though several others, including a still life (1927) and a scene reminiscent
of Breughel's *Tower of Babel*, done in composition class (also 1927), are reproduced in the Academy's annual catalogues in 1927–28 and 1928–29. Around the
time he painted *Portrait of a Girl*, Bob had written his mother that he had
"decided on [his] way of painting. First one flat tone, then draw in the most
important things wet with dark blue as accents, then model thick paint, very
dry." He had tried it "once or twice" and had found that it "works like a charm."

From his very first days in Philadelphia, he made frequent use of his yearly
pass to the zoo, filling his sketchbooks with careful charcoal drawings of elephants, geese, monkeys, ostriches, antelopes, and lions. At the end of his first
year those drawings won him the President's Prize in the Packard Competition for Animal Drawing, but he was far from satisfied with his own work.
Even in his third year of study, he told his mother that he and a friend, George
Hiltebeitel, were "going to nightly class regularly. By the end of the year I
should know something about drawing."

As in New York and, earlier, in New Orleans, he worked hard on his woodcarving. Philadelphia and its environs—from the new museum of art to the
Swedenborgian Church in nearby Bryn Mawr—were excellent places to see

Lions, 1924

religious statuary and carving, and spring 1926 found him carving a Gothic saint which "could be used as a candlestick." He had decided to "put gold leaf on it and then paint nice bright colors and then rub off the paint where I want the gold to show through." In 1927 he did a large carved panel of St. George and the dragon and an "overmantel" of some saints. As at Parsons, woodcarvings of pirates, which he sold to people in Philadelphia or New Orleans for twenty or twenty-five dollars a pair, brought him spending money. During summer vacations he worked on trunks—carved and painted in a style reminiscent of the Pennsylvania Dutch trousseau chests at the Philadelphia Museum of Art—which he left with his father to send to the New Orleans Arts and Crafts Club, and some carved angels for a dealer in New Orleans, an old Newcomb acquaintance of Annette, to sell at Christmastime. When no one bought them, she suggested he take them back "and put a dull antique finish on the gold and remove the screws and twine from the sides to back, and disguise the tacks or nails which, in one at present, stick so far out that they are really dangerous to handle." Though the dealer, Catherine Labouisse, assured him she appreciated the "crudity" of his style, "anything selling as high as these should have a more finished appearance." He worked, also, at lithography, and at one point told Annette that he got "more strength from it than from any other black and white medium."

Even by the end of his first year, it must have been clear to Annette that her "Bobs" was working as hard as any other student and, after his initial prize in the Packard competition, that he was headed for a career of distinction. She must have worried constantly about his loneliness, but his living arrangements seemed acceptable: at first, the rooming house on Summer Street, shared with Baisden and two other students at the Academy, and later, a studio with two large front windows, comfortably heated in the winter by radiators and a stove he purchased on his own. He made time for exercise—boxing or fencing with Gardner and others in the basement of the Academy—and he told her often of his reading, from his beloved Chesterton to Stevenson's *Vailima Letters*, which he read for a time while he ate lunch; it was "almost almost like having a conversation, rather one sided but I have [rarely] objected to the other person doing most of the talking." In Philadelphia he also read biographies of William the Silent and Richelieu and more dramas by Masefield, as well as Montaigne, Rabelais, *Tristram Shandy* (which he liked well enough to buy), and Bram Stoker's *Dracula*, which kept him up all night. Clive Bell's *Since Cézanne* reminded him of his distaste for art criticism—a dislike shared by McCarter, who "rarely ever used such words as 'impressionism,' 'expressionism,' 'pointillism,' 'cubism,' 'futurism,'" and replaced them with others, "like 'Monet and those people,' 'the Tahitian fellows,' or 'the silly dot men.'" Occasionally, he read from the Bible and—partly for his mother's sake, partly because of his own deep love of ceremony—went to High Mass, from time to time, at St. Clement's Anglo-Catholic Church, where this or that old lady shared her hymnal and prodded him to sing, and he remembered the drills at Manlius: "Each time I go there I'm more impressed with the forms, more precise and more regular than any sort of military exercise. It is as though the whole power of the Church from the time of Christ was behind each movement." Annette had always insisted on both the spiritual and the social importance of going to church. "We must lead orderly lives," she told Peter in 1926, when he was serving an apprenticeship to a studio potter in Wayne, outside Philadelphia. "Think it out if God means anything. He means everything. Don't go to anguish in prayer as I have so often. Go to praise and be thankful. Of course you should search your heart to see what is keeping you back and do it quietly. . . .You will find real friends in the church. People who are out to be friends for no reason but the love of humanity. They are solid people to tie to. Strange but you *will* find development in the line of duty."

For Bob, who was tired of "the line of duty," aesthetics and "form" mattered more than leading "an orderly life." Music, too, drew him to church. He had always enjoyed singing with his brothers, blending his baritone voice with Peter's tenor and Mac's bass, and in Philadelphia he sang not only at St. Clement, but also in the choruses of opera productions, and he also went as often as he could to the Philadelphia Orchestra. One program in particular moved him to ecstasy. "Handel, Debussy and Ravel, [and] a most extraordinary thing by J. S. Bach. He must have been possessed by demons when he wrote it. Hearing it, you had the sensation of being torn wide open and then thrown to the other end of the world, which may or may not be a good thing for the listener. This morning to St. Clement's again, with Frank Baisden, who had come down from Trenton for the weekend. He went back this afternoon, leaving behind him a great book of Blake's drawings. They seem to have a great deal in common with Bach's music."

There was something else, besides music, that drew him to the orchestra, and a few years later he was not ashamed to admit that, at the Philadelphia Academy of Music, he used to fall into a sort of reverie gazing down from his inexpensive seat at a certain young woman in the loge who seemed the epitome of loveliness. He would stare at "the shine of [her] hair, and the way it was coiled up the back" like his mother's. Each time he went to the orchestra, he said, all of his longing settled on that one girl—before long he had fallen in love with her, and hoped one day to meet her.

Besides music and literature, he often told Annette about the theater, film, and art exhibitions he saw in Philadelphia or on weekend excursions to New York: *Arms and the Man*; J. M. Barrie's *What Every Woman Knows*; *Porgy and Bess*; Gilbert and Sullivan; Mrs. Fiske in Sheridan's *The Rivals*; Eisenstein's *Battleship Potemkin*; Michel Fokine and the Ballets Russes; exhibitions at the Academy or at private galleries; the oil paintings and Chinese pottery in the John G. Johnson Collection of European Old Masters, then housed in a mansion on South Broad Street. Few of the exhibitions awakened any enthusiasm. One which did was a memorial exhibition of the work of George Bellows at the Metropolitan in New York, in 1925: "great stuff; [I] came away with my head going round."

Outings to the zoo, Fairmount Park, or the countryside to sketch with friends helped gratify his love of the outdoors, though not his wanderlust. When he thought of the sailboat, the *Gypsy*, which his father had ordered for Peter, he dreamed of sailing with his brother to the Isle of Pines, "seventy-five

Man with Hammer, c. 1925

miles south of Cuba. . . . One of the boys at school has just left for there in search of solitude and a place to paint." His favorite way of getting to Philadelphia or home to New Orleans was along the East Coast by ship, and he had some memorable voyages to tell his parents about. On one trip, a huge wave broke over the bow and washed him halfway down the deck. He saved himself by clinging to a chair.

Other trips hinted at adventures to come. In the spring of 1925, he won second place in the Packard competition, and used the prize money to hitchhike westward across Pennsylvania. To earn extra money, he decided to paint portraits, and somewhere in the rolling countryside a farmer agreed to let him paint his wife. He slept in the barn and ate with the hired help while he worked at it. In late June, near Coreopolis, he found a job on a work gang of the Pennsylvania Railroad, and earned enough money to begin his trip south. He found a battered old canoe with a hole in the bow, and put it into the Ohio with the intention of floating, bailing, and paddling into the Mississippi, and on to New Orleans. Along the way, he fed himself on green corn, which he picked in fields beside the Ohio, and after a few days of that diet, he fell violently ill, with a high fever and stomach pains. An old man came to his aid with the only "cure" that occurred to him: a bottle of Shane's Liniment. Without giving it much thought, he drank the entire bottle, and paddled on, in pain, toward New Orleans.

By the following year, 1925–1926, he had set his sights on Europe. Each spring, the Academy gave out up to twenty Cresson scholarships, awards of up to one thousand dollars for painters, sculptors, and illustrators, to be used "for traveling and other expenses in seeing some of the important galleries and art schools of Europe." Baisden, Speight, and Roland had already won Cressons, and for Bob the thought of Europe was enough to dispel any other plans. When he returned to the Academy in February 1926, after Christmas vacation, he was "painting like fury," his head "full of ideas," including plans for a large canvas combining scenes he had sketched the previous summer while working on the railroad. Months later, he was still going strong: "If I get the scholarship I go to Europe [this summer]. If I don't get the scholarship I go to New Orleans, locate near some convenient almshouse or orphan asylum and paint old men or orphans, as the case may be. I was going to make another cruise coming home along the coast but I can't spare the time; if I fail on the C[resson] S[cholarship] I'll need every spare minute to paint. I had the trip all planned. There is an inside route almost the whole way down. I could

have made it easily in three months but being an artist and not a bootlegger
I have given it up."

He did not win a Cresson that year, and by the beginning of spring semester 1927, he was thinking of Europe more vehemently than ever, for reasons
not strictly artistic. Two of his friends, Baisden and Schuyler Jackson, who
were now running an antique shop and interior decorating business in Trenton, had interested him in the teachings of the Armenian visionary George
Ivanovitch Gurdjieff, founder and director of the Institute for the Harmonious Development of Man, at Fontainebleau, near Paris. In a seventeenth-
century chateau, Gurdjieff was directing a program that promised to bring
into balance man's three principal faculties: body, intellect, and emotions. At
the institute, disciples were "shocked" into a higher level of self-awareness and
cosmic consciousness through hard physical labor, dance, music, and intellectual exercises, under the supervision of the master himself. For a number of
years, Gurdjieff's spokesman and fund-raiser in New York had been the brilliant English journalist Alfred R. Orage, former editor of *The New Age*. At
Socratic question-and-answer sessions attended by society people, "the intelligent middle-class," and, eventually, Baisden, Jackson, and Bob, Orage dealt
with a number of moral and ethical issues relevant to Gurdjieff's teachings:
the nature of love and of self-consciousness; man's relation to the natural
world and to the divinity; the proper use of time; and the way to live a well-
balanced life. A witness to one of Orage's lectures in New York, in the 1920s,
recalls the gist of his teaching:

> Briefly, what Orage has said is that man is a mechanical being. He cannot do
> anything. His organism acts without his concurrent awareness and he identi-
> fies himself with various parts of this victim of circumstances, his organism.
> There is only one thing he can try to do. He can try to observe the physical
> behavior of his organism while at the same time not identifying his "I" with it.
> Later, he can attempt to observe his emotions and thoughts. . . .The man who
> finally succeeds in developing the power of self-observation is on the path to
> self-knowledge and the actualizing of a higher state of consciousness. This
> higher stage, which Orage calls "Self-consciousness" or "Individuality," stands
> to our present waking state as the waking state stands to our state of sleep.

In January 1927, Bob informed Annette, who had always taken an interest
in alternative states of awareness, that he had gone to Trenton for a few days
to visit with Baisden and Jackson and to hear Orage, and that he was deeply

impressed. "[I] had the honor of meeting him. He is a very remarkable man but that isn't what strikes you; it is that he is possessed by something entirely separate from his personality. I'm going up tomorrow to hear him in New York. Afterwards I can tell you more about him. This week I do know that the whole business of the Gurdjieff clan with its enormous expense and time and trouble was entirely arranged by Gurdjieff for the training of this man Orage."

The thought of visiting Fontainebleau that summer—and perhaps meeting Gurdjieff himself—made him long even more for a Cresson, and in June 1927, he was awarded one of ten $750 traveling stipends for painters. He crossed the Atlantic on an aging Cunard liner, the *Carmania*, arrived in France in early July, and made his way to Mont-Saint-Michel, approaching it through the mist and marveling over the "marée . . . first as a noise that came nearer and nearer and then a wave about six inches or a foot high that came in faster than a man could run." From his room he could see "first, the sand and then the green plain with flocks of sheep and a few trees, and beyond that the hills," and on his meanderings through "miles and miles of crypts, vaults, cloisters and stairways, all apparently laid out haphazardly" he was struck by the absolute certainty of "one form from which the whole is made, not merely as the concept, however perfect, of one man or group of men. Everything was built under compulsion. If a stairway went up in a certain way, it was because that was the *only* way for it to go." In Paris, days later, he wandered through the Louvre. Later, taking to the country, he was impressed by the canals, vowing to explore them some day by canoe.

In early August, he arrived at the Chateau du Prieuré, the old mansion which had housed Gurdjieff's institute since 1922. Schuyler Jackson visited the institute that very summer, along with a couple of illustrious writers: Waldo Frank (who quarreled with the "master") and Jean Toomer, as well as Orage himself, but there is no record of Bob having met any of them. Into a French *cahier* he copied a few brief notes about Gurdjieff's system, but there is nothing in his letters home to indicate how long he lodged at the Prieuré, if at all. Later in his life he remembered his disillusionment on finding that only the wealthy could afford to stay there for any length of time. His interest in Gurdjieff formed part of a lifelong search for transcendence—a search shared, in different ways, by modern painters from Kandinsky to Pollock. But far from fostering the "harmonious development" of his faculties, Gurdjieff's ideas would come back to haunt him.

From Fontainebleau he headed south into Spain to visit the Prado and see a bullfight. He saw little of the Spanish countryside (he traveled by night) but upon reentering France, he was struck by the beautiful towns he could see from the train, between tunnels, in the Pyrenees. The "red roofs and the blue of the Mediterranean" lured him from the train at Banyuls, in southern France, where he "had a fine time in spite of [insect bites] and introspection. I went swimming, stole grapes, and painted watercolors." From Banyuls he traveled west to the caves of Les Eyzies, with their prehistoric renderings of hunters and bison: "extraordinarily good [but] very difficult to see owing to the space and lighting." He recalled later that he "got much more from seeing somebody's reproductions of them" in a nearby museum of prehistoric art. One way or another, the cave paintings—his first face-to-face encounter with "primitive" art—moved him deeply, and the lines of those "murals" and the notion of the artist who is "part of nature rather than just observing it"— were to affect his drawing, his pottery decoration, and his own painting. For the next few days he cycled along the Vézère, around Font de Gaume: "water-washed rocks on either side of a valley and plenty of places to look for arrow-heads." He did "a lot of watercolors and had a delightful emotional experience," but one day as he went up a hill he broke a pedal on his bicycle and came down hard against his crotch: an experience even more memorable, he said, than the caves. The Chartres cathedral was—with Les Eyzies—the other great highlight of the trip: it seemed to him, years later, that "Gothic was not simply a matter of a certain kind of architecture, but stopping at a certain point in building." It was "a mistake: somebody looked before the cathedral was finished." From Chartres, in late August, he went back to Paris, and then on to Honfleur, in Normandy, where he painted "boats with red sails," and to Bayeux, "to see the tapestry of the Reine Mathilde. I have changed boats for the return passage; instead of the Cunard, I come back on a French Line boat which lands me in New Orleans about the end of September." One of the things he brought back from France was a fresh vision of "public" art, the "art of the caves and the cathedrals," and the sense (developed in an essay, years later) of an art which seems to arise from the "will-spirit" of a people rather than from an individual—the idea that American art, in contrast to European, had been overtaken by the notion of "effectiveness" and utility. Perhaps also, the conviction that the distinction between "fine" and "applied" art was a very recent one: certainly it didn't apply to cave paintings and cathedrals.

Cresson fellows were obliged to spend at least two semesters at the Academy after their return from Europe, and in fall 1927 Bob moved into a new studio and began working harder than ever before, in hopes of winning a second scholarship. By January 1928, as his family celebrated the opening of Shearwater Pottery to the public, he was at work on an oil painting of two black men, seated at a table, their elbows resting on a red-and-white checkered tablecloth. White shirts, yellow wall, green bottle—"should be pretty effective," he wrote his mother. "The result is amazing, and I am having a great time doing it." The painting was done for the Charles Toppan Prize competition, which had called for "an interior with one or more figures in which . . . portraiture is not the leading motive." The canvas won second honorable mention and was reproduced in the Academy's 1929 catalogue, along with an excellent portrait study of a man in a top hat. But much to his disappointment there was neither a Toppan nor a Cresson for him that year, perhaps because he had missed a deadline or ignored the rules. He was awarded free tuition for the excellence of his work, but his career at the Academy came to an end. "No one can do their best work in a school," his mother had written him in May. "With your studio and the pottery you could go ahead wonderfully." As he returned to Shearwater, he hoped she was right.

LIVING ON AIR

During Bob's last two years in Philadelphia, his brother Peter had been "making and breaking pottery." It seemed to Walter that no one "could possibly ever have made before so many shapes only to see them crack, blister, craze, crackle and leak," and these Peter smashed to pieces and tossed bravely into the trash. With the rubbish from the workroom and the brightly colored shards of thousands of broken pieces, he had begun to pave a path through the marsh to the dock where he kept the *Gypsy*. The "Glory Road," someone called it, years later, in honor of his perfection and persistence. Annette had sent him in 1926 to serve an apprenticeship with Edmund DeForest Curtis, a studio potter in Wayne, Pennsylvania, and in the summer of 1927, he had taken a class from one of the country's best-known ceramists, Charles F. Binns, at the New York State School of Clay-Working and Ceramics in Alfred, New York. He had come home thirsting for simple, perfect forms and sumptuous glazes. In July 1927, while Bob was in France, Peter and his father signed a partnership agreement, and in January 1928, with ten thousand dollars in backing from Walter, Shearwater Pottery opened to the public. Within months Peter had a steady stream of customers, both at the showroom and at art shops in New Orleans, and Walter was so sure of his son's talent and determination that he hired an engineer at Newcomb to build him an oil-fired kiln similar to the one at the college.

Ocean Springs proved to be an ideal location for the fledgling business. Tourism and real estate were booming, the Illinois Central was promoting the Gulf Coast, and signs of "progress" were everywhere. A new highway, the

Peter, Walter, and Mac Anderson on the steps
of the showroom, Shearwater Pottery, 1934

"Spanish Trail," crossed Ocean Springs on its way from St. Augustine to San
Diego; the dusty old shell roads were being paved; bridges replaced ferries; and
a sturdy seawall now protected a clean, white sand beach. During the winter
months, from December to April, tourists came from all over the country—
especially Chicago and the Midwest—to attend conventions or bask in the
sun. They stayed at expensive hotels in Biloxi, played golf at a splendid new
resort, Gulf Hills, in Ocean Springs, and somehow found their way to the rus-
tic-looking showroom of Shearwater Pottery, which Peter had named for a
coastal bird, the black skimmer, also known as a shearwater. When Bob got

home that summer in 1928, the family adventure was in full swing. Annette decorated pots, produced lampshades and occasional molded pieces, and worried over aesthetics. After a year at Tulane, Mac was working as designer and decorator, and Walter was doing his cheerful best to keep his "artists" on an even keel—to balance the books, run the showroom, and promote Shearwater to anyone who would listen, including old friends from the grain-export business, people from local newspapers, and buyers for department stores and gift shops from New Orleans to New York. Bob was full of design ideas of his own, and within months they were being fired in the new kiln. There were pelican bookends, figures of angular cats, standing and *couchant*, horses inspired by Chinese ceramics, pirate figurines, and a Greek-looking horse and rider, along with the plates, bowls, and vases decorated with the "natural motifs" he loved.

The following spring—May 1929—two women from Gautier, Marjorie Grinstead and her daughter Patricia, stopped at the Pottery to look for a gift. When Patricia and Peter saw one another on the path at Shearwater, sparks flew. Later that month, or early in June, when Patricia's sister Agnes ("Sissy") was home from Radcliffe, the Andersons paid a visit to Oldfields, the Grinsteads' estate in nearby Gautier. Sissy, who had never met any of the Andersons, would never forget her first glimpse of them. Annette, with her lovely gray hair and beautifully poised head, asked her "erudite questions about the Philosophy Department at Harvard" and left her feeling "as big as a flea." Mr. Anderson, with his "walrussy mustache" and English accent seemed the epitome of British courtesy and kindness. Peter was amazingly handsome—golden curls, green eyes, and "a physique like a Greek god's." Bob was sitting on the porch steps, leaning against a pillar. He had dark, curly hair, rather narrow deep-blue eyes, a big nose, and a "mobile mouth," and she was struck by his charm and courtliness: he actually stooped to kiss her hand.

As he rose to meet her, it dawned on him that Sissy was the girl he had seen at the Philadelphia Orchestra while he was studying at the Academy. He was sure of it.

Within months, Walter was writing to a friend in New York that Peter was "engaged to marry one of the nicest girls (and prettiest) you ever saw and is grinding out pots as if his, and her, future happiness depended on [it], which is, of course, to a certain extent, the case." There was one obstacle to their happiness: the Grinsteads had planned for Pat to spend the year studying classical piano at a conservatory outside Paris. It was not until a year later, in April 1930, that they married.

The Grinstead sisters and the three Anderson brothers spent the summer of 1929 sailing, swimming, and playing tennis at Shearwater, sitting on the pier at Oldfields, or bouncing about the countryside in the Andersons' old Ford touring car. Sissy was about to begin her junior year at Radcliffe, where she was studying fine arts: a pleasant, attractive girl, according to her tutors. "Does fair work. Has definite tastes and well formed opinions. Hard to draw out. Reserved." She was less outgoing than her older sister Pat, who was used to making decisions for the two of them, and had directed Sissy's life for as long as she could remember. In fact, the decision to attend Radcliffe was the first time she had ever asserted her independence. The two of them had traveled in Europe in the company of their mother and Ellen Wassall, their adopted sister, and together they had studied for two years in France—first at the Institut des Jeunes Filles at Versailles and the following year in classes at the Sorbonne. Sissy had then spent a year at a private school in Bryn Mawr, near Philadelphia, and it must have been while she was *there*, Bob told her, that he had gazed at her during the orchestra concerts. She and Pat had spent their childhood at Oldfields, but returned now only in the summer, for the Grinsteads had moved north, a decade earlier, to Sewickley, Pennsylvania, a well-to-do suburb of Pittsburgh, where William Wade Grinstead worked as a trust officer at the Union Trust Company.

Methodical and deliberate, though not without a quiet sense of humor, Billie Grinstead had graduated from Harvard in 1889 and begun his career as a lawyer in his native Louisville, Kentucky. A few years later he moved to Chicago, where he helped manage the real estate business—worth millions—of Helen Culver, one of the city's first women entrepreneurs, benefactor of Jane Addams at Hull House. When health problems made him look for a milder climate, he moved to the South hoping to find an estate in which he, Culver, and a friend might invest. Ocean Springs had been blessed with abundant pecan and citrus crops, and Grinstead arrived there in May 1904, descending from the train, to the amusement of the locals, in top hat, striped pants, and cutaway. A livery man took him to Bay View, a boardinghouse run by Sissy's maternal grandmother, and before long he had fallen in love with her daughter, Agnes Marjorie Duel Hellmuth. Two years later, they married and moved into Oldfields. Built in the 1840s, with a design similar to that of The Briars at Natchez, the elegant house, with its eighty-five-foot gallery, stood on a bluff above the Mississippi Sound. Around it were four hundred acres of marsh, old pecan groves, virgin pine lands, and open fields. Having

Bob and Sissy on the gallery at Oldfields, c. 1930

"dropped out of the law," Grinstead turned his careful mind to growing pecans, satsumas, grapefruit, and oranges, convinced that he would "find as satisfactory an income in farming as in any city occupation, and probably more contentment." No doubt, he was remembering Horace's gentleman farmer and Cicero's notion of "leisure with dignity"— *otium cum dignitate*, he put it, in a Harvard alumni bulletin.

Pat and Sissy were born in 1907 and 1909, and were joined by their "almost-sister," Ellen Wassall, an intelligent, spirited fourteen-year-old whose movements were hampered by cerebral palsy but who had determined to live as normal a life as possible. Ellen's mother, a professional songwriter and singer, had paid little attention to her, and her father had hired Sissy's grandmother as her nanny. When the father drowned in Lake Michigan in 1909, Ellen herself petitioned a Chicago court to allow Sissy's grandmother to become her legal guardian, and a few years later, the two of them joined the Grinsteads in Gautier. In 1917, a year before Annette bought Fairhaven, Billie Grinstead headed north again and, after a while, settled in Sewickley and worked as a trust lawyer, advising wealthy clients on their investments. For years he had been able to visit Oldfields only in the summer.

It was the summer of 1930, a year after they met, that Sissy and Bob started to think of themselves as a couple. Years later, Sissy tried to remember the day he had first told her he loved her. She had spent the afternoon at Oldfields practicing hockey, "galloping around the calf lot," in hopes of making the team at Radcliffe, and had fallen asleep in the cool of the hall. Ellen had roused her from her nap: "Bob Anderson is coming up over the bluff from that boat. I think he looks queer. You better wake up." She remembered him asking her, in his extraordinarily low voice, to take a walk with him, and leading her on "quite a chase, dashing around the end of the house out of sight and cutting north, out on the road at a run. In the young pecan grove between the two gates, he stopped so suddenly that I ran right into him. He took me in his arms. Those arms were frightening in their hunger, and I gasped: 'Let me go. I'm all right.' 'Oh, but I'm not,' he said. 'I love you. I have to have you. Say you will marry me.'"

She remembered his stricken face when she pushed him away and told him she needed time to think. She was "a child," she wrote later. "Nothing grownup about me. I had progressed to the point of having a certain little plan for my life: a progression from college to job, my adored family very much part of it. A man, love, sex, had absolutely no place in it." She had dated boys at Radcliffe, but those encounters had been "casual and rather intellectual"—concerts at the Pops, skating on the Charles, football games, riding horseback with friends in Medford. Nor had she ever met an artist—not a real one, anyway, though she had imagined them as tortured souls, tragically at odds with the world, and this one seemed no exception.

By the pond at Oldfields, he gave her a cigaret—the first hand-rolled one she had ever smoked—and the two of them stared at the shimmering wings of the dragonflies, two of whom were coupling.

"Is that what you're afraid of?" he asked. "I would never push you, never."

On the way back to the house, he paused by a huge Japanese persimmon tree, and she "smelled the odor of burned flesh." When she picked up his limp hand, she saw that he had put out his cigaret against his palm. The ash was still glowing, embedded in his skin. She had never seen such a thing, and was horrified, but gathered it was a sort of "trial by ordeal," meant to show his love for her. After an uneasy supper with Sissy, Ellen, and Mrs. Grinstead, Bob climbed back into his sailboat and left for Ocean Springs. As she watched him pole the boat into deeper water, Ellen shook her head and sighed. "I certainly would never marry him. He's as crazy as a goat." Mrs. Grinstead felt otherwise. He *was* a bit strange, a bit too passionate about things, but he was perfectly charming. They liked each other at once.

Sissy and Bob were together constantly that summer, and as Sissy showed him her favorite Oldfields places and they tramped the dusty roads, he taught her to look at nature in a way unknown to her—not as beauty to be "appreciated" or as backdrop for conversation, but as a mysterious, inexhaustible world. They sailed to Horn Island on a new little sailboat, the *Pelican*, which she watched him make with the help of a local carpenter. They took the truck from Gautier to Vancleave to pick wildflowers, biked to Biloxi for ice cream, and went on family picnics in the country around Ocean Springs. He thought her "the nicest person in the world," a "pleasant, cheerful, sweet, normal" sort of girl, and told her gratefully that she made him "see things in their proper relation"; in her company there seemed to be "no danger of little unimportant things growing out of proportion." And yet, often they did. More than once, when they were alone, he told her he was lonely and desperately unhappy and that only her love could keep him alive. When he kissed her, she could feel his desire, but felt unable to respond. "I like quietness and tenderness and contentment," she told him. "You make for violence and storms." At the end of summer, on the night before her return to Ralcliffe he took her in his arms and told her, more vehemently than ever, that he loved her. What he felt like doing, he said later, was to put one hand in the fire and hold her with the other, "to see whether I'd mind the heat." Her reaction was unbearably sensible and a bit coy: she could not really say that she *loved* him, not yet. She liked him in a brotherly way, and she liked him loving her. But "she might like somebody else's" love better. The next morning, when she was about to leave for Boston, he cursed himself for his impulsive behavior. Pat and Peter were to take her to the station. Too distressed to join them, he scribbled a note and put it in Peter's hand.

> *Dear Agnes,*
> *I love you, and I'm going to miss you horribly. There is no reason for doing things without you here. You, my love, my darling. It's awfully hard to write it on paper when I want to tell it to you so badly, but Pete and Pat are leaving in five minutes, and I have to tell you somehow that I love you, and I think you're right not to love me. I'm not fit to be loved. I wanted you to go away liking me anyway, but after last night you can't even do that, can you, dear? That's why I'm afraid to come to you now. I love you. I'll always love you. And I can't help it.*
> *They're going now.*
> *My dearest, darling Agnes, I can't say goodbye. I love you.*

On the train, somewhere in Alabama, she collected her thoughts and answered his letter, asking him to calm himself, to try to be happy, and not to "live on air." He had been afraid she would "hate" him for his oddness and his passion:

Dear Bob:

You must know that no matter what happens you aren't capable of making me hate you. If I don't love you ever, I'll always like you tremendously, but I'll get very sad if you start calling yourself names. I think you can do anything you really want to, and I want you to want to make the most splendid plates and pots, and, if you want to, write and tell me about them. Pick flowers, too, and go on Pelican *trips when you aren't too busy. Don't live on air, and, when you start thinking I hate you, remember I like you. I'm only afraid you'll hate me some day, and we have such good times together. . . .*

Please, Bob, don't write me letters like the first one. Tell me the things you're doing, as if you liked me the way I like you, and wanted me to know.

You've been very very extra nice to everybody this last week. I want you to know it.

I wish you could see the forest of goldenrod. It's all out, here. Remember Horn Island and the nice walks we've had, and all the treasures we've found together.

Agnes

That fall, as he worked at the Pottery and tried to resign himself to her absence, he wrote to her several times a week, though not always as calmly as she wanted.

I have known what it is to be happy through religion and through art, and neither was enough, just ways of forgetting, of running away. Then I loved you and I thought that that was the answer to everything, and all that I wanted was a chance to make you love me. I had it, and failed miserably. I tried to show you how much I loved you, but you couldn't see. So you went north and I stayed here. . . . Dearest, darling, my love, how could you love me? I didn't ask much . . . just to see you now and then. Why should you rather be with other people who don't love you, rather than with me who do? And if you had rather be with me, why aren't you?

Despite his efforts to rein in his emotions, his letters that year are a muddle of suffering and tension—between his desire to have her with him, his longing to get on with his painting, and the need to make a living at the Pottery, where he modeled figurines, lamp bases and bookends, and experimented with slip painting and sgraffito decoration. Although it was a family business, Shearwater kept strict hours, and he could paint only in his spare time: early in the morning, after work, or on this or that rare holiday. Mostly, he had to store up his impressions and bide his time, and he was no good, he told Sissy, at playing a waiting game, either in love or in art. In October he wrote her that he had "given up painting altogether, for the present anyhow":

> It's impossible for me at any rate to shift from pots to painting and then back to pots in the flash of an eyelid, and that's what I've been trying to do. They both suffer, and as for me, it makes me hate them both. Which is hard just now because I have just found something really worth painting. Enormous cabbages, gorgeous big things. I'm going out tomorrow and get some. They are growing out on the Point-au-Chenes Road, just to look at them, even if I can't paint them. It is so seldom that you find things so perfect in both form and color, and when you do, and really receive an impression, it's worth holding on to.

Besides the routine at the Pottery, he blamed his own inconstancy and restless curiosity: "When I am doing mudpies [i.e., modelling], I want to be doing slip. Now that I am doing slip, I have an overwhelming desire to use wood, and nothing is as it should be." He wished he were "an Indian god" with one head and several pairs of arms. No doubt, pottery decoration influenced the painting he did find time for. That fall, for instance, he wanted to fire pots in "very intense high-keyed colors: Persian blue and lilac and green," or use "flat shapes of bright-colored slip, doing away with line altogether." In his painting, too, he thought of "reaching into the air and grabbing two big color notes and forcing them to work together" rather than "pussyfooting around using sequences, that is, several friendly colors together." He had been carrying around those ideas since his classes with McCarter and Carles, but somehow, he had lost the powers of concentration he had shown at the Academy. "Some day," he wrote, "I'm going [to] give up everything else and just paint for a while." But there was no telling what would happen:

> I'd probably burn out on the first day. It's happened before. It's not enough just to have a wild desire to paint. There must be a reason back of it and a feeling which is entirely independent of the means of expression. That is my great trouble. I go off half-cocked just for the joy that I have in handling the material. But if I waited for an emotion worthy of use, I might wait forever and it is fun just to play with paint until you let yourself be drawn into it, or rather, until you are dragged into it by the hair of your head. And then there is nothing for you to do but get out anyway, as well as you can, taking your wounded with you. The trouble is that each time it happens you leave something of yourself behind you until, by and by, you have nothing left to leave.

Ellen had given him a book on primitive art, and he found himself "flitting from one influence to another," in both his painting and ceramics: African, Mayan, Minoan, Persian, Greek—"pretty *late* Greek," when he was unhappy with the results. Some figures he carved in cedar and shined with wax had a "strong African influence," he told Sissy, adding that African sculpture might appear "a bit revolting at first sight" but had an "extraordinary amount of genuine feeling" behind it. A large oil on plywood, three by six feet, which he began in August or September 1930 turned into a palimpsest of styles and manners as he painted over one scene with another, ending up with his mother's cat: "I have finished the mural which began as a 'Colored Quarter, Ocean Springs' (Persian influence), then 'Horn Island' (slip decoration), then 'Horn Island II' (possibly Cretan) and finally ended up as a 'Symphony in Color or The Cat and the Flowers.' So whoever buys it will be getting four for the price of one, which is not bad when you consider the amount of ground covered and paint used." As in his slip painting, he had begun by wanting "to paint flat color, forms playing one against another, letting one color influence another directly without actually painting the influence," the action "tak[ing] place in the eye of the beholder rather than on the canvas. Sounds rather complicated, but it's really very simple as far as the theory goes; it's in practice that it's difficult."

As he worked on that mural, he dreamt of their life together and the house he would build for Sissy, one which would "suggest the nicest things that you have ever seen or felt or done. Horn Island and flowers and birds and boats all jammed into one small [place]." They would "make everything inside the house for ourselves, and then plant all sorts of wild things outside." Sometimes, at night, he designed furniture or imagined the frieze that would go around the walls of the main room: he would use "yellow, gray and black on big tiles . . . do *Don Quixote* or *Aesop's Fables*." There would be a fireplace and mantle in red, black and white slip tiles; on the front doorstep, two large red-and-black-and-white ceramic cats; and outside, a garden with vegetables and flowers transplanted from the surrounding countryside. He wanted to carry her off to an imaginary world, made from the landscapes they had shared that summer and others he had read about—above all, Horn Island ("quite a nice place if you are there with the right person"), but also the lagoons and marshes of Louisiana where he hunted with his brothers; a valley in Vancleave, to the north of Oldfields, where he had discovered the most astonishing variety of wildflowers; the marsh at Shearwater; and woods and fields

around Ocean Springs where you could walk for hours without seeing anyone at all. Often, he told her about the plants and flowers he gathered: blazing star, possum berries, the yaupon branches he sent her at Christmas, wood
lily ("the most perfect wildflower we have down here"). She was taking a
course on painting at Radcliffe, and he hoped that they could paint together
when she returned: "Come home and we will find a new art together, something that has never happened before, and fool the old men who say that there
is nothing new under the sun."

Until then, all he could offer was advice. Paint only what you truly care
about and remember that whatever takes place in the mind of the student
matters more than "the mere material result on canvas." A man or a woman
could be an artist "without ever even smelling paint, but very few of the
painters are artists." It had helped him, he said, to develop a "system": it could
save "a lot of wear and tear on the emotions," a good thing, "because feeling
is the most valuable thing we possess and we only have a certain amount of
it, which should be spent carefully." Certain little tricks could keep her from
going stale: "It does help a whole lot sometimes . . . to make some sort of pos-
itive gesture. . . . Sometimes it helps to deliberately paint out the thing that
you like best in your painting, just by way of giving yourself a vote of confidence: anything to change the atmosphere." Had she tried "throwing paint at
the wall? A good many people have tried throwing paint at their canvas. That's
no use at all." But all this he could show her better in person. He wondered
whether she would come home for Christmas instead of visiting her family in
Pittsburgh, and did his best to entice her. She had told him it was cold in Cambridge, and he answered that Winslow Homer—one of the watercolorists he
most loved, and whom Sissy had been looking at—could speak on his behalf:
"wind and water and hot sun against snow and hockey and horses." He envied
her the art she could see in Boston, cursed himself for wasting his opportunities in New York and Philadelphia, and saw what little he could in New
Orleans: some African wild cranes at the zoo, an exhibit of Mayan art which
the anthropologist Frans Blom had brought back from the Yucatán, and the
great Spanish dancer La Argentina, whom Sissy had just seen in Boston,
though in fact it was Russian dance Bob preferred: dance, music, "everything
except painting," where the Russians had "never done anything much."

When Sissy returned to Gautier for winter vacation in December 1930, the
Pottery was buzzing with plans, and Bob was hoping to persuade her father—
and himself—that he could support her. The depression had forced potteries

everywhere, large and small, into bankruptcy, and the Andersons had decided to diversify, to open an "Annex" specializing in figurines and decorative pieces, with Bob and Mac handling all aspects of the work, including the glazing and firing. Walter had built a new workshop and had installed a second new kiln—for months he had been thinking that Bob needed a kiln of his own—and Bob had already helped Annette design an extension to the showroom, inspired by Japanese architecture, with floor-to-ceiling windows opening onto the woods and marsh.

Making figurines was—and is—a laborious process. The figurine is modeled in clay, and a plaster mold is made. Liquid clay called "slip" is mixed and poured into the mold and allowed to harden. The mold is removed, and the figure is carefully trimmed, given a preliminary (bisque) firing, decorated, glazed, and fired again. And yet, despite that long, tedious process, the figurines promised to provide steadier sales at lower prices than the "art" pieces that had been thrown by Peter and decorated by Bob and Mac. Bob had been carving pirates in wood for years, and ceramic ones now went into production, along with a series—designed by the two brothers—of figurines of blacks which promised to satisfy a certain demand for humorous stereotypes of southern life. There were musicians and dancers and cotton pickers, the inevitable "watermelon woman" and "washwoman," a "chicken thief" and a "possum man," and a grizzled "Uncle Ned on mule"—about fifty characters in all, brightly colored, with graceful lines, none without a touch of humor. "Potboiler work," Bob called it. "Perfectly worthless."

By the time Sissy returned to Radcliffe for her senior year (1930–1931), he had come to the glum conclusion that only those figurines would ever generate enough income to allow him to marry Sissy. He would be "an old man of ninety," he moaned, "still trying to make enough little figures, to make enough money to get married on." Except for the initial designs, and the modeling in clay, he detested the work: the mold-making that seemed to fill his very brain with plaster (the molds wore out quickly, and had to be replaced, so that there were always 100 or 150 of them on hand); the "horribly monotonous" trimming; the supervision of the local women who had to paint the figurines quickly and consistently; the uncertainties of the firing (a process which Mac had not yet fully mastered, so that, at least once, an entire kiln load came out covered with "grey scum"); and the constant worries over sales and orders. Their father was a tireless, resourceful promoter, and soon found an agent in New York—an enterprising young man named Wilson—

who offered to get the figurines into department stores and other outlets. But the more time Bob devoted to them, the less time he had to paint, until he painted hardly at all. Even the decoration of Peter's plates and vases—which he had always enjoyed—had to be crowded into whatever time was left after the figurines.

By spring 1931, after Sissy had graduated cum laude from Radcliffe and had returned to Oldfields for the summer, something changed in their relationship. Bob told her, more passionately than ever, that he could not go on living unless she married him. She hesitated; years later she would remember feeling somewhat coerced by his veiled threats of self-destruction. But she had no doubt that he loved her, and as they became more intimate, her resistance crumbled. They went on excursions in the country and watched a meteor shower from the Oldfields pier. They made "heavenly" trips up the Pascagoula River in the *Pelican,* took moonlight sails, cuddled together listening to symphonies on the radio, and danced, at last, in the phosphorescent water of the sound. Pat and Peter had married the previous spring, their first child, Michael, had been born a little before Sissy's graduation, and Sissy sensed that Bob was beginning to envy their happiness, which "spilled over everyone and everything. . . . He sensed that his brother had found the wholeness he was seeking."

Toward the end of the summer, Bob made his way to Oldfields to ask her parents for her hand, and to assure a skeptical Billie Grinstead that he would soon be able to provide for her on his income from the Annex. At Grinstead's suggestion, he had brought a detailed list of his assets and his marketing plans for the figurines, which he dismissively called "widgets." Despite his misgivings, Grinstead blessed the engagement, and Bob gave Sissy a ring, that had once belonged to Walter's mother. Any talk of a wedding date was to be put off until Bob's finances were more certain. In early October Sissy accompanied her parents back to Sewickley, leaving him longing for her "sweet, steadying" presence to take the curse off the hated figurines.

A month later, in November, the fortunes of the Annex took a sudden turn for the better. A prestigious panel of judges, including Peter's old teacher Binns, the architect Alexander Archipenko, and William Sloane Coffin, curator of the Metropolitan Museum of Art, chose some of the "Negro" figurines to appear in an exhibition of contemporary American ceramics at W. & J. Sloane, a department store on Fifth Avenue. The exhibition brought publicity—and a few photos—in the *New York Times,* the *Christian Science Monitor, Ceramic Age,* and *Creative Art.* In Sewickley, Sissy spotted news of

Shearwater in *Home and Field, Arts and Decoration,* and *Town and Country.*
"Aren't you proud of yourself?" she wrote him. "You've had a triumph, sure
enough. Daddy is thrilled, because he thinks it's greatly due to your good
business head! Isn't it really too superb? I can hardly stand thinking about all
it means. Mamma is in a perfect fever. . . ." In the wake of those reviews,
which brought Bob little pleasure, the Annex grew to employ six people—
three full-time and three part-time—and the widget business became a
question of numbers. Once, in just two and a half days, the three decorators
trimmed 614 figurines, and at one point that fall, Bob calculated that the
Annex was ready to turn out four hundred widgets a week, sixteen hundred
a month, twenty thousand a year: enough to give him a "buried-alive feeling." Even in his room, upstairs at the Barn, the widgets were everywhere he
looked. From New York, the agent, Wilson, told them even more would be
needed—perhaps a thousand a week—and Bob reminded him that he wasn't
dealing with a "pretzel factory." There was some doubt, anyway, as to whether
those orders would materialize, and for a long time they did not, though the
figurines sold steadily at the showroom. After a few months of this routine,
Bob felt himself turning "spiritually, mentally, morally," into little more than
"a machine for the production of widgets . . . more and more specialized.
Soon I won't be good for anything else."

> I don't want to lead this sort of life after we are married. Right now I am a
> drudge. After I leave the workshop I am dead. I can't take an interest in any-
> thing and I am disgustingly dull, as you may have noticed. I don't mind hard
> work, but I don't think it should kill you for anything else. This world is really
> a rather amusing place if you have time to look around a little bit. . . . The
> truth is that I would like to do a little painting, just enough to make me sick
> of it. But I can't take time out. I'm supposed to devote all of my time to the
> business of making money. It wouldn't be quite as bad if I were making it, but
> I'm not, not much, anyhow. I suppose all this is the result of having been
> curled up in the kiln all afternoon. I'm just beginning to get the kinks out.

He had never worried much about money, and it sometimes felt humili-
ating. When Sissy's father gave her a watch for Christmas, he wished he
could give her something other than pottery or the precious stone that
Annette had plucked from her own jewelry box. "It is a rotten feeling," he
wrote her. "You made a great mistake falling in love with a poor man. I've
never really minded being without much money before. It's filthy stuff, but
rather useful at times, especially when you haven't got it." More than once,

he thought of dumping his figurines into the bayou and looking for another job, but finding one seemed unlikely, given the economic downturn. From Sewickley, Sissy told him not to bother:

> I don't think there's a chance in a thousand of your getting a job, but, if there was, I don't want you to. I like you as you are, and don't want you to work the way job-people do. There's something freer about pottery, even though you probably don't think so now when you're pretty much tied down. Oh, I wish you weren't, and it's my fault that you are, because, before, you could pick up and go off adventuring, and you must be tired, and I'd like to be there, because I can almost feel your head wanting my fingers to rub it, and make it quickly well, and I will be just as soon as I can because that's what matters, now and always. Why did the world have to get depressed just when you and I wanted it inflated? Anyway, I love you.

Bob at Shearwater, c. 1932

But he was no "potter," he told her—not by a long shot. And he didn't feel at all "free."

> Your intended is not a potter. He's a great many things, most of them bad, but not a potter. Just at present he is a manufacturer, with a small factory for the production of widgets in numbers. Don't you be bothered by any of this, just remember that discontent is one of the penalties of greatness. Continually driving and forcing us to greater heights of endeavor. Which simply means that I don't expect to spend the rest of my life making widgets. Also and in particular that I refuse to be thankful for the opportunity to make more and more widgets. That has no connection with our right to lead a happy life. We have no rights except those we acquire by our own unaided efforts.

The struggle was beginning to awaken tensions with Peter. Mac was much easier to deal with—"never complains and, better still, never worries." Dependable and calm, he thought of himself in those days not as a frustrated artist but, more humbly, as a "sort of handyman . . . production manager, moldmaker, slip-pourer, kiln-firer and general factotum." It was Peter who found Bob's complaints hard to swallow, for it was he who bore responsibility for keeping the Pottery afloat, and his own love of beauty, his passion for shapes and glazes, was no less threatened by "the business of making money" than was Bob's. Like Bob, he had a fiery temper, and one can imagine his reaction on finding his brother in the Annex, relieving his boredom and frustration by firing wads of his "perfectly good clay"—three cents a pound—at a knothole in the wall. Peter had never been enthusiastic about the figurines or any other sort of decorated pottery. It was Mac who had made him see that, if the business were to outlive the depression and support the family, it would have to offer something other than classical shapes in a variety of glazes.

And so it went for months, with Bob feeling "abominably lonely," and dreaming of the future, carving a blanket chest and making a hooked rug—"symbolic," he told Sissy, both of his "prostrate state" and of his "desire to have you walk on me." There were occasional trips to Horn Island with Archie Bongé to hunt alligators and duck-hunting excursions with Peter in the Lousiana marsh. It was maddening not to be able to live in the present, as he had always done, and happiness was always *elsewhere*. He and Sissy went on dreaming—both of them caught up in it now—of the trips they would take together. They would travel to Mexico and Guatemala to see Indian ruins, to Florida for arrowheads, to the Chandeleurs to watch the nesting of the pelicans and "dine on turtle eggs and raw fish." They would float down the Mississippi in a shanty boat or explore the Pascagoula River when azaleas and mountain laurels were in bloom. Or sail away to the Great Barrier Reef, or—a recurrent fantasy—Horn Island. They had already made a couple of trips there that summer, but he hadn't especially enjoyed them. "It was probably because I wanted you so much to myself, and there were always too many other people around. Or else there were too many restrictions, necessary perhaps but they don't go well with Horn Island. Anyhow, I hope you and I can go out there someday without them." With nobody else around, they could build a treehouse in some tall pine tree, make love, and forget about the figurines and "bridge and movies and radios and everything else. Live as the birds live, in the day, taking no thought for the morrow." Or make "some sort of shack . . . so that we can go out in any sort of weather." One way or another, it was *their* place and theirs alone.

They often wondered what their daily life would be like. He was aware of his own "beastly temper"—she had seen it that summer. "I'll probably hurt you over and over again with it in small ways," he wrote, "but it won't ever be because I've stopped loving you." There was something mysterious about their relationship, something that went beyond loving or liking, he said, and made her a permanent part of him, though he felt too stupid to explain what he meant. She knew that, compared to his, her life was an easy one—a sort of stagnation, though she kept busy enough not to think about it: she coached hockey and basketball, helped out at Girl Scouts and Sunday school; played bridge and shopped; rolled balls of yarn for the kitten. She sent him fudge or knitted him a sweater. When she felt especially nostalgic, she hunted for arrowheads along the river in Pittsburgh or lingered at the fishmarket, remembering the shrimps and crabs and oysters of Biloxi and Ocean Springs.

It wasn't long, however, before the Grinsteads too began to feel the effects of the depression. For a long time, Billie Grinstead had been listening sympathetically, twelve hours a day, to tales of woe from clients whose investments had been decimated. In March 1932, he began to behave strangely, hearing voices at night, and blaming himself unjustly for their problems. In March, Marjorie took him to Oldfields for a period of rest and exercise, but nothing seemed to help: he refused to follow the treatment doctors had prescribed, and threatened suicide. At first, Bob kept him company, sitting up all night with him, but in early April, Grinstead angrily accused him of "misbehaving" with Sissy and tried to run him out of the house. When it was clear he would not improve on his own, Peter and his doctor took him to the Sheppard and Enoch Pratt Hospital, in Baltimore, where, after months of mulling over his condition, doctors diagnosed "psychosis with cerebral arteriosclerosis."

As Billie Grinstead withdrew into himself, Sissy and Bob's marriage receded farther into the future. Marjorie remained in Baltimore caring for him, and in the spring of 1932, Sissy closed her parents' house on Melville Lane in Sewickley, returned to Ocean Springs, and moved into the Front House with Peter and Pat. They would delay the wedding until Grinstead was well enough to attend and give his blessing. It was a year before Marjorie was able to report that her husband approved of the marriage. She copied down his words verbatim in order to send them to Sissy: "don't be in too much of a hurry, because I would like to be there." The delay "must be hard on poor Bob," Grinstead had added, and Marjorie reminded Sissy that he wasn't

Bob and Sissy on their wedding day, 1933

"antagonistic at all," and had offered to send them more than the five hundred dollars Marjorie had suggested as a wedding gift. Within days, however, he was having second thoughts, and, at the suggestion of the doctors, they went ahead without him. They married on April 29, 1933, at St. Pierre's Episcopal Church, in Gautier, a special place for Sissy: her father had contributed to the construction, and the altar was given in memory of her grandmother. It seemed painfully ironic that neither of her parents was able to attend. As she prepared for the ceremony, she remembered Pat and Peter's wedding, three years earlier in the same church. Bob was best man, but he had been late for the reception. He had noticed the church had been built on the site of an Indian burial mound, and while others toasted the newlyweds, he was prowling about for artifacts and arrowheads. After a while, he reappeared in his blue blazer and muddy white pants and proudly showed her a handful of interesting shards. This time too, Sissy was nervous. She was dressed for the wedding and ready to leave for Gautier, but Bob was nowhere to be found. Mac told her he was picking up the ring in Biloxi.

There was no money for a honeymoon, and the two of them spent a week at Oldfields. Years later, Sissy remembered making up the bed and waiting for him to come to her. Neither of them had ever had sex before. Unbelievably, the night of their arrival, he was leafing contentedly through a pile of *National Geographics* he had brought down from the attic. When, at last, they made love, she was "repulsed," shocked, disgusted. It was "agony." After they had tried again, and she had tried "in vain to respond," he climbed out of bed and headed for the bluff. She wondered whether he intended suicide and it occurred to her—again—that perhaps she did not truly love him. The following morning, "rather cold and reserved," he told her that the night before he had swum far out into the sound. "There was a full moon. You should have come." Days later, he drove them to New Orleans, careening down the coast, as he always did, at speeds which terrified her, and they went to an art supplies store where he often bought his things. She watched him as he selected paints and brushes, and felt proud to be the wife of a painter. When they returned, he sent Sissy to speak with her mother about sex. Marjorie Grinstead sided with him, and reminded her daughter that wives must be "submissive." Bob went to Ocean Springs and told Annette of the tension he felt. He was a painter, and painting required constancy and devotion. But he couldn't live without Sissy, and neither of them could survive without his work at the Annex. Annette understood immediately—she had felt the same tension. There was a time in her life, after the children were born, that she felt she simply had to give up painting. With her, too, it had been totally absorbing, and it was too much of a "distraction" from the business of raising them.

Over the months which followed, the two women—wife and mother-in-law—came to know one another better, and Sissy did her best to accept Annette's extraordinary importance in Bob's life. "You and I should be friends," Annette told her early in the marriage. "We both want the same thing."

Three months later, on July 15, 1933, Sissy's own mother, only fifty-one years old, died suddenly of a cerebral hemorrhage, while her father was still in the hospital. The burial was to be in Ocean Springs, and the coffin was taken to Shearwater so that friends and neighbors could pay their last respects. Thirty years later, Sissy remembered the night before the burial. "I wanted to feel his arms around me with a comforting and understanding tenderness. Instead, he made love. I think I wished that I were dead: one of the few times I have wished that sincerely." The next morning, with doors and windows wide open and the coffin covered with flowers, a tiny wren flew through the window and alighted on the back of Sissy's chair, caressing her with its wing. It flew out through the door, perched in an oak tree, and sang, "loud and liquid and sweet," like a blessing. With her father ill and her mother gone, the world of Oldfields—the world of her childhood—had come to an end. All depended now on the unpredictable Andersons.

AFRAID OF THE DARK

One snowy winter night in Sewickley, a year before they were married, Sissy had written Bob that she wanted him near, to keep her safe. For as long as she could remember she had been unable to see at night, and afraid of the dark. When she was a child, her father had given her a special flashlight, a "coffee mill" she could crank by hand: the more nervous she became, the more light it gave. Now, she hoped, it was Bob who would protect her.

"You flatter my ego," he had written, "by being afraid of the dark and wanting my manly protection. You must know how much I want to give it to you. It's curious how much I want you to be dependent on me. The truth is, I suppose, that I want to own you, have absolute possession of you. That sounds alarming, doesn't it? But the trouble is that I can't be really sure of you until I know that you do need me, almost as much as I need you. And I do need you. . . . The Lord knows how much, and I'll try to make it clear to you when we meet."

Years later, thinking back on that "dependence," she remembered a night— perhaps during their courtship—when they were walking along a bluff overlooking the Pascagoula River near an old burial ground.

"Why are you so afraid of the dark?" he asked her.

"I'm not," she lied.

Suddenly, he slipped away, leaving her to find her way alone back to the car. Frightened and angry, she stumbled along the edge of the bluff, trying to remember the path, cutting her legs on the undergrowth and stubbing her toes on the burial markers. Finally, she took a step into the void and landed in "the narrow confines of an open grave."

"Come, get up. It's all right. I'm here," he said, reaching to pull her out.

When she thought back on it, the incident seemed to her a metaphor of their relationship: "Bob wanting desperately to give me his sense of wholeness in the universe, to strip away my fears, and make me see with my whole being, to give me inner light." It was a double symbol, really: the supposed "enlightenment," but also a sort of resurrection—from the "narrow confines" of that "open grave." There was a period, early in the marriage, when someone heard her exclaim, without realizing what she was saying, "Bob damn it!" instead of "God damn it!" To Sissy (at least to the Sissy who remembered the story many years later) he was a god, a demiurge, and she was there, or so she saw herself later, as a witness to the creation. To others—to Ellen, for example—she seemed "entirely submissive," placing herself at Bob's disposition "in every whim and purpose" that crossed his mind. When he didn't get his way, he fell into what Ellen described as a "very marked and prolonged sulking." By 1934 or 1935, things were headed for trouble.

As they learned to live with one another, all they had anticipated in their letters seemed to be coming true—voyages by themselves, the little house of their own. The Andersons had given them the two-room Cottage for a wedding present, and over the next two years, in the time he could spare from widget-making and pottery decoration, he built furniture, including a bedframe and tall desks for the two of them—desks they could only use standing up and that were flush with the floor, so that they would never have to sweep under them. He also made narrow curtains, painted with geometrical motifs, and two chairs, large and heavy as thrones, where they sat at night hooking rugs—some for themselves, others to sell at the Pottery—until he told her that her hooking was too tight to match his, and she began, instead, to read to him while he worked: Chesterton's essays and Father Brown books, Gibbon's *History of the Decline and Fall of the Roman Empire, Look Homeward, Angel,* or Yeats. He made a table from a single wide cypress plank they brought from a sawmill up the Pascagoula, and when it was done, both of them sanded and polished it, applying wax and rubbing it to the smoothest possible sheen. There was more than enough space for the two of them, but the possibility of children was seldom mentioned; too poor to support anyone but themselves, they practiced birth control, and Sissy tried to content herself with her nephew and niece (Peter and Pat's second child, Patricia, was born in 1933). They had a radio, on which they listened to live orchestra concerts, and a phonograph; they ordered records of classical music from Kroch's in

Sissy and Hellmuth cousins at Oldfields, 1931

Chicago. Sissy discovered that when her husband listened to music he connected "tone with color, and rhythm with pattern," and sometimes tried to record those impressions in watercolors—an interest awakened by McCarter and Carles at the Academy which would blossom more fully a little later. In the spring, Bob started a garden, planting flowers among the vegetables, and they ate homegrown produce and the shrimp, flounder, and crabs they caught in the bay.

The Cottage lay only yards from the Pottery and from the Barn, where Annette and Walter were living, and they liked to get away from time to time. Sissy's father had given her a little blue Chevrolet roadster with a convertible top when she graduated with honors from Radcliffe, but with no money for gas or repairs they soon sold it, and got around by bicycle. One of their favorite trips was the day-long excursion to Oldfields, to hunt for arrowheads at Graveline Bayou when the tide was low. There were Indian mounds there, middens or burial sites that had been eaten away by the tides, so that after stormy weather, artifacts of all kinds washed onto the beach—axes, knives, borers, shards of pottery, and the occasional carved bead. There had always been Choctaw Indians nearby; when Sissy was a little girl, they fished at Graveline and she and Pat had spied on them through the bushes, ignoring their mother's warning to stay away. But neither she nor Bob ever had much idea which indigenous people had built the mounds, centuries earlier. For him, the objects they found, and which he sometimes drew, offered a connection with the "primitive" at a moment in the history of art when "old" was "new," and

the avant-garde was seeking simplicity and directness in the creations of earlier periods or rural folk traditions. In the 1920s, African art, prehistoric cave
painting, cante jondo, and folk ballads offered a whiff of the instinctive, the
telluric, and the uncanny. They were also a humbling reminder that, long
before Shearwater Pottery or Newcomb or Ellsworth Woodward, *homo faber*
had existed on the coast. For Bob, indigenous peoples—whether the local
mound-builders or the creators of the totem poles he had admired in New
York—had a unique relationship both to nature and to art. "Art is a mysterious business," he wrote years later, "which only an artist can understand. A
man can have years of academic training and be a good draftsman, and have
perfect material, nude bodies and rearing horses and plenty of time to do
them in, and still not *realize*. A savage or a child with three tones will realize
what the man with perfect opportunities or the camera has failed to do." The
mounds were a palimpsest of coastal history: occasionally, among the Indian
bones and the shards with their geometrical incisions and mysterious symbols, they found French and Spanish items—pieces of marble, flints, silver
ornaments, coins—along with objects the mound builders had acquired
through their trade with others. For weeks on end, the year before they were
married, while Sissy was living with Peter and Pat, she and Bob "arrow-
headed" furiously against one another, turning them up in incredible abundance at Graveline and Old Fort Bayou, as many as two hundred a day
between the two of them, according to Bob's careful accounts in one of Sissy's
old copybooks. Sometimes Annette went with him in the Andersons' car, and
as her son drove forty miles an hour down the highway toward Gautier, she sat
beside him feeling "like a bird hanging from the roof of its cage." She wasn't
particularly good at finding arrowheads, but enjoyed poking through the
broken oyster shells and the tea-colored tide pools, and catching sight of the
mysterious characters who used the place to bring in bootleg liquor.

One of the few pieces of furniture in the Cottage which Bob had not built
himself was an old Victrola cabinet Annette had given them to house their
growing collection of butterflies. In contrast to Peter, who loved beekeeping
and had built his own frames and equipment and, for a while, sold his own
honey in little pots he himself had designed and thrown, Bob was fascinated
by moths and butterflies, and chased them at Shearwater, in the countryside,
and—in his imagination—in two great reference books on Lepidoptera: *The
Moth Book* and *The Butterfly Book* by William Jacob Holland, whom he had
met long ago in Pittsburgh, the summer he canoed down the Mississippi. One

night, near the bright lights of an amusement park, he had noticed hundreds of huge moths falling into the waters of the Ohio. Scooping up the ones that seemed unusual, he found his way to Holland's office at the university, where he got a kind, encouraging welcome. According to Holland, moths would come at night to tree trunks smeared with a mixture of beer, sugar, and molasses. Sugar was expensive, but Bob and Sissy made a big batch, coated the trunks with it, and ventured one night into the woods with kerosene-burning torch, net, and flashlight to see what had alighted on the tree trunks. A large shadow flitted by, and as Bob dropped the torch to pursue it, pine needles burst into flame. Out of the darkness came Peter's voice: "What the devil are you up to, you damned fool?"

As Sissy shone her flashlight on the tree trunks, they saw—to Bob's amusement—not moths but Peter's precious bees: "bees heartily inebriated, bees staggering about, bees bumping each other and picking fights." The fire was quickly extinguished, but Sissy would never forget the fight that followed, the "blows landing solidly, flesh and bone against flesh and bone," until both had had enough.

There would be no more moth-baiting at Shearwater, but for years Bob had dreamed of hunting for Lepidoptera and arrowheads in Florida, and late one summer they rigged up the Oldfields truck as a camper, with canvas sides and a mattress, and headed south. They chased butterflies across the elegant lawns of Miami and Coral Gables and drove still farther, over the causeway to Key Largo, until hurricane weather forced them to turn toward home. They returned to Shearwater with six or seven moths with "wonderful, beautifully shaped wings, like the bark of a tree with lilac eyes," Bob wrote Annette, and added proudly about Sissy: "This trip has added to my already great admiration for the young lady. If you could have seen her pursuing butterflies in the face of the Miami tribe, completely indifferent [to them] with her shirt-tails flying in the breeze!"

There were other excursions they had dreamt of in their letters. In August, the first year of their marriage, Bob declared that they would take a vacation and sail the *Pelican* to all of the barrier islands, from Dauphin to Cat. It was a marvelous odyssey, though between one island and another the engine puttered out and Bob remembered that motors required oil—another way he differed from Peter, who once told Pat he "would have liked to be a civil engineer": he could design, assemble, and repair whatever machinery he needed for the Pottery or for whatever task was at hand. On another occasion, Sissy's

Hellmuth relatives came down from Chicago, and the three Anderson brothers organized a fishing trip to the islands. It was spring or early summer, at a time of year when giant sea turtles come out of the gulf to lay their eggs and bury them in the sand, and Bob walked off alone down the beach, hoping to catch a glimpse of one and watch the egg-laying from a distance. Hours later, his wish was granted: a huge turtle came crawling onto the beach. And then, obeying some dim predatory impulse, he pounced on it and managed to turn it over onto its huge, scarred shell. The rest of the group came running, stared at the giant animal, and hailed him as a hero. Swept up in their approval and the general excitement, he decided to slaughter the turtle to make a stew so that his guests could taste its eggs and meat. Years later Sissy would remember with nausea that the senseless act had destroyed 125 unborn turtles. Bob said nothing, but the incident would haunt him for the rest of his life. He had slain the albatross.

As before they married, his work at the Pottery left him little time to paint, and most of his creative energy went into woodcarving, drawing, or the decorated and molded pieces he was turning out for Peter. The accident with a chisel, years earlier during his student days at Parsons, had permanently injured his left hand, leaving a lifelong scar, and since then he had perfected a new way of woodcarving—he would "block out" the figure roughly with a small, very sharp axe and finish it off with a wood rasp. Animals, figurines, and a finely carved wooden platter, copied from an Aztec one, show that he had lost none of his dexterity. At the Pottery, he created a large molded figure—shown lifting her foot in dance—which he called Rima, after the bird-girl and wood nymph of Hudson's *Green Mansions*. His daughter Mary would recognize it, years later, as an early portrait of his muse. Drawings from the early period (1929–1937) are mostly finely drawn plants and birds, but there is a series of "oriental" scenes, perhaps from the *Ramayana*. Of the extant watercolors, one of the most striking is *Birth of Achilles* (Memphis Brooks Museum of Art), for which there are a number of preliminary sketches: scenes from *The Iliad*. There are also four oil portraits of Sissy. Despite her constant prodding, he painted so little during the first years of their marriage that she remembered her tears of joy when he broke out his brushes and settled down to do the portrait now known as *Sissy with Scarf*, using a chair for an easel, a plate as palette, and brushes and canvas given to him as presents by Pat and his mother. He seemed pleased with the painting, but told her firmly, as he put away his brushes, that he would not paint again: it was something that

Sissy at Table, c. 1933

could not be done in his spare time. The meager surviving output from those years includes a few still lifes (*Mallows, Zinnias in a Shearwater Pottery Vase*), several other portraits (*Allison Sleeping, Adele Van Court*, and *Mr. Boots as a Boy), Man in a Boat*, and, a little later, *Horse and Rider*. Susan C. Larsen has pointed out that the "strong curves, vivid color and healthy impasto of *Horse and Rider* suggest familiarity with the Blue Rider paintings of Franz Mark and Wassily Kandinsky," and observes that his style had yet to define itself: there were also the "flat broad planes of color and curvilinear geometry in *Jockeys Riding Horses*."

If, as Sissy often said later, she felt guilty about having married him and subjecting him to the routine of making a living, she must also have felt some resentment over having given up a career of her own. Her cousin Julia Vaughan, whom she had always admired, was a kindergarten teacher in Louisville, and from an early age, long before she decided to major in fine arts, Sissy had wanted to follow in her footsteps. After graduating from Radcliffe she had been offered a job at a private school in Virginia, but the opportunity vanished when she married Bob and the depression worsened: not only were there no openings in Ocean Springs, schoolteachers were being paid in script. It occurred to her, also, that despite her own excellent education, she would never be able to fill a certain void in his intellectual life. Besides Annette, there was no one he could talk to about painting. Of his closest friends from the Academy, Baisden was living in Chattanooga, and Francis Speight had never left Philadelphia. The painter Weeks Hall, whom he had met in New Orleans and who was a close friend of Henry McCarter, had returned to Louisiana, and they visited him once in his ancestral home, Shadows on the Teche, in New Iberia. But the visit was not a good one; they found him drunk or ill, and the two of them fled when he asked, rather rudely, in a manner which struck Sissy as effeminate, to be left alone with Bob. Of the painters he knew, only Archie Bongé was living close by: after a single semester at the Academy he had gone to New York, where he had fallen in love with Dusti Swetman, an actress from Biloxi. Bob had been the best man at their wedding, and they were living, with their son, Lyle, in a charming little house and studio filled with paintings Bob thought quite worthless. When Bongé died in 1936, at a very young age, Sissy was already aware of her husband's growing isolation. There was only his mother, hungry for conversation about art or ideas or any form of spirituality. Since the beginning of the depression, she had been a leader at the Episcopal church in Ocean Springs, and had been helping feed the jobless, but, despite her good intentions, even *she* seemed "stand-offish," and it was only the outgoing Pat and—of the three brothers— Mac who had any real friends in town. Ellen observed, perhaps too harshly, that the entire Anderson family was "rather set apart as 'queer'" in Ocean Springs, and that when they wanted social life "they tend[ed] to return to New Orleans" where they could visit relatives. Both the Grinsteads and the Andersons had always held themselves somewhat aloof from others, with a pride in who they *were*. And in a town as small as Ocean Springs, it was impossible to forget that the Andersons were "artists." Years earlier, in the summer of 1926, Annette had organized a resident art colony at Shearwater, bringing in a painter from the Arts and Crafts Club in New Orleans, to give unconventional classes on plein air painting, and putting up her students at the Front House. And when the Grinstead women had paid their first visit to Shearwater, following a path of little tin birds—shearwaters—that Bob had nailed to telephone poles, someone had told them to steer clear, that there was a group of "crazy artists" on the property who ran around naked in the

Bob with one of his vases, c. 1934

woods. By now, the town had grown accustomed to the Pottery—no one had ever sighted a naked body there—but some of those early suspicions had persisted. In the casual way they dressed, Sissy and Pat looked rather like the *wives* of artists, and one day, when they went to town to buy eggs, an old friend of the Grinsteads peered out of the egg chandler's window, shook her head, and sighed: "You should have seen your great grandmother, the prettiest, sweetest little woman I ever saw, and your grandmother, as lovely as a picture, and your mother, the most beautiful woman that ever [lived] in Ocean Springs. . . . Now just *look* at you two!" Annette must have drawn similar comments. "Clothes, fashion, and shopping bored her," her granddaughter Mary remembered, "so she chose a classic dress and jacket pattern with simple, elegant lines that, she said, suited her style of beauty. She had it made in many fabrics for different seasons: serge, corduroy, light cotton, linen, dotted Swiss; altered slightly by changeable collars, a pin, or a flower in her lapel. It was her costume, a part of her recognizable self. Her hats, always the same—felt in winter, straw in summer—were purchased in the men's department and blocked to her order in a becoming shape. She used no cosmetics beyond eau de Cologne for her migraine headaches, took cold baths, and washed her long, thick grey-white hair in Packer's Pine Tar Soap."

Bob's loneliness and possessiveness, his frustrated desire to paint, and Sissy's need to adjust to a style of life vastly different from the one to which she had been accustomed were problems that were beginning to strain their marriage. There was a certain irony to their relationship. At Radcliffe she had majored in art history, and, at least at times, that was what she thought she was living through now. She was his helper, a witness to his art. Hadn't that been the purpose of her studies? And yet, looking back, years later, it seemed to her that she could never fully accept her husband's need for creative solitude or his unwillingness to spend time with people he didn't truly care about. She was shocked, for example, when he brushed off a visit from Edward Maxted, the minister who had married them, barely saying hello before he invented some urgent business and slipped away. Never mind art history—she had been brought up in a world where, as she put it, "the creative act was the giving of oneself to others in ordinary human intercourse." She was used to "a very, very conventional sort of family and home. . . . Everything went just so. . . . The thing that was important in the Grinstead family life was the people, and your reaction to them, and their reaction to you, and what you could do to make things better . . . , and to stay away from anything that *didn't* make things better. [In the Anderson family] the people, in a way, were not important at all." What seemed to matter to *them* was "the creative side of people" and the pursuit of beauty. It "didn't matter what kind of art, or what it [was]; but that was the thing that counted." Bob's father was different, of course—she had often heard him poke fun at "the artists in the family"—but Annette held firmly to her belief that *all* people had *some* sort of creativity: it was only a matter of helping them discover it, and she was extraordinarily good at that, drawing people into conversation on things that mattered—religion, art, spirituality, the latest novel—or into the little art and design groups she was forever organizing at the Barn. "Real artists," she wrote, "are just people who are on the right track. The track is there for anyone to use." The family grew accustomed to the way she greeted visitors: "And what do you do . . . ? Are you a painter . . . ? Do you draw . . . ? Do you write . . . ? Then you must be a musician."

As for Sissy's own creative urges, for the most part they barely mattered; she grew used to subordinating them to Bob's, and although she had painted at Radcliffe, she never picked up a brush after they were married. At least once, he welcomed her inside the Annex, gave her a lump of clay and invited her to model a figurine. She had been reading Browning, and made an attempt at the Pied Piper of Hamelin, but the figure sat for months in a crock pot, and she put aside any thought of playing a creative role herself in the Pottery or the Annex. Bob had always wanted her to write and she worked for a while on an epic poem about the Spanish conquistadors, taking up her manuscript from time to time—"like knitting," she said. Once, she wrote a poem about the two of them:

> You will come back,
> your lips will be stained with the red
> of dewberry.
> Your mouth will be
> sweet with the warm, ripe juice
> of dewberry.
> Your shoes will be
> white with the powdered dust
> of old shell roads,
> and your blue shirt,
> darkened and damp with sweat,
> will mold your body.
> You will come back
> full of the sun's hot brightness,
> clean with light,
> and I will be
> lonely because my mouth is pale
> and my lips cool,
> because my dress
> will be fresh with a fearful crispness
> in the shade.

She had written her senior honors thesis at Radcliffe on the interrelationship of literature and painting in seventeenth-century France, and *there*, at least, was an opportunity for collaboration. Early in their marriage she persuaded him to illustrate some of the verses she wrote, and for years they exchanged notebooks or clipboards, so that she could write verses for one of his drawings or he could illustrate one of her poems. They also worked together on plays. Drawing on his theater experience from his Parsons days, he put on an elaborate Christmas play that set the whole family's nerves on edge. When one of Sissy's college friends came for a visit, Bob kept the two of them busy for the entire length of her stay, making them heavy beaverboard "costumes," fitting them out as turtles, birds, crabs, enlisting them, and everyone else at Shearwater, in an elaborate Christmas drama: "Air, Earth, Fire and

Water—each claiming to be supreme as to strength and godhead, and all suddenly vanquished by the weakest of all things, the Human Babe." Neither Annette nor Sissy nor Pat managed to interest him in more conventional venues: there was a little-theater group in town, but he sat through the first meeting and never went back.

For years, since seeing the great cave paintings at Les Eyzies, he had been wanting to paint murals. The muralist movement in Mexico, which had gotten under way in 1921, coincided with his years at Parsons and the Pennsylvania Academy, and no matter what he thought of the ideology and style of Siqueiros, Rivera, and Orozco, he must have shared the latter's idea of the mural as "the highest, most logical, purest and strongest form of painting, [one which] cannot be converted into an object of personal enrichment [and] cannot be hidden for the benefit of [the] privileged." Much debated in the Europe of the 1920s, the issue of public art—and the Mexican experience in particular—had come fully alive in the United States in 1933 with the suppression of Diego Rivera's mural at Rockefeller Center (an event that troubled Bob profoundly) and with the formation, that very year, of the Public Works of Art Project (PWAP), financed by the Civil Works Administration. This was an unprecedented plan to engage thousands of unemployed painters, sculptors, craftsmen, and laborers in the embellishment of publicly owned buildings. Both PWAP administartors and artists were vividly aware—as Bob himself was, after his trip to France—that any European village, no matter how small, had its public art, and that in the U.S. such works, expressing the life of the community, were a rarity.

Ocean Springs was no exception, and the condition of the art world in the South, particularly in Mississippi, was dismal. Among the PWAP's sixteen regional directors who gathered for a three-day conference in Washington in February 1934, one of the most enthusiastic about public support for the arts was Annette's former teacher at Newcomb, Ellsworth Woodward, regional director for Alabama, Mississippi, Arkansas, and Louisiana. Woodward turned immediately to the Andersons for a series of murals in the Ocean Springs Public School.

"The South has no [art] museums or schools," Woodward told the other directors, with a touch of exaggeration (he himself was now director of the Delgado Museum in New Orleans). "Most of our artists have come from back districts and have worked on their own impulse without very much to guide them.

They've had no stimulating contacts, and many of them are little trained." With its insistence on local subject matter, the PWAP offered an opportunity to correct another phenomenon he had been criticizing since the time when Annette was his student: because southern artists felt inferior to northern ones, they went elsewhere for their subject matter, and those who remained in the South captured only its "superficial picturesqueness." All this was deeply discouraging to a romantic like Woodward: "I've spent 50 years in the South—I'm more Southern than Jeff Davis in some respects—and when I make these annual pilgrimages to various parts of the South in the spring of the year, and wake up on a Pullman in the morning, and see the lovely Southern scene with its incomparable trees and flowers, and hear the song of the mocking-bird, I think what masterpieces I could paint, if only I were a Southerner-born!"

The PWAP offered artists the chance not only to paint typical regional scenes but to search for an "American past" and to connect their creation more closely to the community. Inspired by the Mexicans' pursit of the indigenous, in the midst of the Depression American artists searched for a history that would be "therapeutic, a 'usable,' useful past that [could cushion] the shocks of a confusing, topsy-turvy now." Woodward marshaled his resources, and within months easel painters were working on canvases suitable for high schools and colleges, while muralists had begun large projects at the University of Alabama and the statehouse at Little Rock and a few smaller ones for public schools. Their subjects, he explained in Washington, were typical of the South: trapping, turpentine, the cultivation of cotton and sorghum. By the end of March 1934, there were eight muralists in his flock, and about twenty-three artists working on easel paintings.

In Ocean Springs, in spring 1934, Peter and Mac created two panels of ceramic tiles for the entrance hall of the public school. One panel ran along each wall, painted and glazed by Mac on tiles about six inches square and fired by Peter. The design is similar for both panels: large birds and fish (pelicans, terns, flounder, speckled trout) with a flock of birds or school of fish filling the spaces between them. The Anderson brothers were paid by the hour, as stipulated by the CWA regulations, and made a couple of hundred dollars for their effort, which barely covered expenses. But it was the only such public project ever undertaken by Shearwater and, as PWAP field coordinator Ann Craton pointed out on a visit to Ocean Springs, these were "the only [murals] of the kind installed in any public building in the South, and perhaps in the U.S., under the PWAP."

Bob's murals, which were painted on canvas and glued to two walls of the auditorium and both sides of the stage, were his largest paintings ever. He was overjoyed to get the commission. Entitled *Ocean Springs: Past and Present* and painted between February and April 1934, they capture ancient and modern periods in the town's history. Along one wall, in *The Chase*, some Biloxi Indians with bows and arrows hunt for deer. The next panel, *Feast in Camp*, depicts a village of dome-shaped houses with Indians growing corn, feeding chickens, caring for their children, and preparing food. On the opposite wall were scenes of Ocean Springs present: oyster tongers and men fishing with nets, yacht races, and a shore lined with stylized coastal cottages, where women are washing and cooking. Plying the coastal waters are catboats and the Biloxi schooners that had all but disappeared from use in the 1930s. The figures of hunters and animals, in particular, have a vague but unmistakably "primitive" look to them. They are as slender and gracefully drawn as those on ancient Greek vases and similar in theme to those of bushman art, though they also reminded Sissy of Egyptian friezes or Minoan murals, or cave paintings like the ones Bob had seen at Les Eyzies. Warm tones of ochre and terracotta, which stand out against subtle greys, blues, and greens, are a distinct reminder of the world of Greek ceramics. True to the PWAP guidelines, the theme is "American" and "local"—it suggests the place where Fort Bayou meets the bay in Ocean Springs and wood lilies brighten the pine savannah. But it is as far from regional realism as from the mockingbirds and azaleas Woodward had gazed at from his rose-colored Pullman window. Mediated by earlier traditions, this "past" was a boldly universal one, and the style of the murals is no more "southern" than that of the arrowheads at Graveline. A large vase, *Sea, Earth and Sky*, and another oil painting, *Indians Hunting*, are undoubtedly from the same period.

Within months after a workman glued the murals to the walls, Bob's subtle colors were competing with the bolder ones of a curtain hung in the stage of the auditorium by a local company advertising construction supplies. The "unimaginably tawdry backdrop" caught the eye of Melrich V. Rosenberg, a writer and connoisseur whom Walter had authorized to sell Shearwater pottery in New Orleans. "Write a letter," Annette told him when he complained— a letter she could forward to the perpetrators. And so he did, protesting the exhibition of "such flawless pieces of American art in conjunction with the crassest example of materialism." A sand and gravel ad beside a work of "native art"? "Ocean Springs present" had been too intrusive:

It is just that kind of curtain, and particularly hung in a school auditorium, that makes one apologize for being an American. For many, many years now there has been a large group of people interested in fostering a native art. The murals in the high school are a realization of the hopes of that group, and the agony is most acute at being forced to look from the subtleties of the mural coloring to the garishness of the curtain [with] the observation that the no doubt estimable J.O'Keefe sells sand and gravel. . . . News of the murals is certain to get around, and tourists will certainly be stopping off to see them. Unless the city of Ocean Springs wishes to attain an infamous reputation throughout the art and literary world, it would be well advised to substitute a backdrop that would show the murals to advantage and destroy the hideous blot that now serves to make it impossible to view them with any equanimity.

Bob chuckled over the letter, but put it away without sending it to anyone: "we all enjoyed it very much, but thought it a little too potent for any but home consumption." The project had been an exhausting one, and what he wanted now was a long vacation. He and Sissy had been listening each morning to Bach's Brandenburg Concerti and had decided to travel to Bethlehem, Pennsylvania, for the annual Bach Festival, and on to Louisville for a visit to the Grinsteads. They would float home, as he had done once before, down the Ohio and Mississippi rivers. The morning of their departure a mockingbird was singing in the Cherokee rose outside the Cottage and Bob remarked how silly it was to leave when home seemed "so much like paradise." The agent in Ocean Springs had been enthusiastic about Greyhound's reclining seats, but after enduring a sleepless first night, they left the bus and spent the second at Roanoke, Virginia, so that they could finish the trip by daylight. Annette had traveled through the Shenandoah Valley with her parents long ago, and Bob found that it lived up to her reports. Turning east at Winchester, they traveled through high hills covered with dogwood and found themselves, as Sissy said, "constantly catapulted back into Spring." Gazing at the blossoming redbuds, she thought nostalgically of her old Radcliffe song—"She wore a cherry ribbon in her hair"—but scarcely dared to hum it; she was an "atrocious singer," no match for her husband.

From Washington to Baltimore, he wrote his mother, "it was one tourist camp after another, without much else, and yet, strangely enough, that was almost the best of the trip [because the] two ladies who occupied the seats just behind us spent the entire time in discussing the characters of their friends." It was, he told her, like a scene from Dorothy Parker's *Laments for the Living*. In Baltimore, they took a taxi to the home of their host, Edwards A.

Park, the renowned pediatrician-in-chief at Johns Hopkins Hospital. Park, a Baltimore blueblood descended from Jonathan Edwards, shared a passion for classical music with his vivacious English wife, Agnes. Sissy's "almost-sister" Ellen, whom Edwards Park loved like a daughter, was staying with them on their estate in Garrison, in suburban Baltimore. It seemed to Bob that the doctor and his wife led "well-balanced lives," playing and working with equal intensity. Their circle of friends and dinner guests had always been a distinguished one—Alfred North Whitehead, John Dewey, and luminaries from medicine including the obstetrician Helen Taussig and psychiatrist Adolf Meyer had gathered round their table. Sissy didn't know whether she "felt more like Joseph or the donkey"—Park and his wife had "marvelous minds," and Ellen, who read widely and had an inquiring intellect, was "one of the few people with whom [Bob] was always able to really talk—to share an exchange of ideas on any subject, with the certainty that she was not only keeping up with him, but contributing." Park was an avid fly fisherman, and on his summer trips to the Cape Breton Islands had developed an interest in birds. He and Bob took to each other at once, and on a Sunday picnic in the countryside around Garrison they lagged behind Sissy, Ellen, and Agnes, the men sharing a pair of binoculars and talking of fish and birds, with Bob complaining that there was no acceptable guidebook to the birds of the southeastern United States.

Sitting at the piano, Agnes Park gave them a sample of the music they were to hear at the festival, and then drove the group to Bethlehem, hours away, terrifying Sissy whenever she passed another car on the narrow, hilly roads, driving with "perfect abandon, it being her sure and certain knowledge that the Lord was with her." At the festival, the music was extraordinary. "Sissy and I both feel that we will never be the same people again," Bob wrote Annette, deeply moved not only by the *Mass in B Minor* and *The Passion According to St. Matthew*, the first live choral music he had heard since Philadelphia, but by the way the entire community took part in each year's festival. On the return to Garrison, with Agnes back at the wheel, an exhilarated Bob found himself in "a state of levitation," hovering just above the hills.

On a quick visit to Baltimore, he and Sissy bought a book on Chinese art and some copybooks and he purchased a supply of plain parchment lampshades along with "a tremendous pack of colored construction paper, all colors, brilliant and muted," which he had shipped to Ocean Springs. He would make his own lampshades, he told her later over lunch. "It will be like doing stained glass windows. . . . Imagine cutting shapes and pasting them on parchment and the light shining through."

Louisville seemed anticlimatic to both of them. As Sissy visited relatives and they waited for the lapstrake canoe they had ordered from Wisconsin, Bob watched birds in Cherokee Park and Mockingbird Valley and marveled at the city habits of species he had seen in the South: in the nests he found in Louisville, a cigar wrapper or strand of toilet paper took the place of a snake skin. The sleek, green canoe was delivered on Friday, May 25, 1934, and he and Sissy loaded it at the foot of Second Street, with Grinstead relatives offering unneeded advice and maps. Into it went canvas-covered bedrolls, a large tin garbage pail to keep things dry, an orange crate of provisions, a dusty sack of pots and pans, a gallon jug of water, a huge bag of pancake flour, and a special gift from Sissy's cousin Julia: a pint of gin. Sissy's aunt Angie gazed sadly at her niece, who had changed into trousers for the trip. A drifter had offered to help them load the canoe, and when Bob gave him a tip, he turned to the boyish-looking Sissy and thanked "both you and your wife" for their generosity. They made an exciting getaway, paddling through the filthy water into the first lock, past paddle-wheeled tugs, ferries, and barges loaded with gasoline (Bob was smoking nonchalantly). Sissy sat nervously in the "crazy, tipping pea-pod," staring at the dark and dirty water, and tried to let "the thought of freedom settle into [her] mind with long, full breaths." She had never traveled by canoe before; learning to paddle this one was no easy matter, and the trip would sometimes seem more like a ritual of initiation than a second honeymoon.

She had always thought her husband had the instincts of a homing pigeon when it came to navigation, but somewhere below Frankfort, Kentucky, those instincts failed him and they paddled into one of the cutoffs the locals called a "chute." As the water started to turn stagnant and thicken with cottonwood fluff, they sliced through cobwebs and came to a barrier of riprap. After unloading the canoe, they threaded their way with their supplies through the huge boulders to the main channel. As they started back to bring the canoe itself, Bob announced he was going to chose the easiest path and that Sissy herself was to take note of it and lead them back to the main channel again. Thinking back on the incident many years later, when she was writing her memoirs, Sissy remembered it as a test—similar, perhaps, to the one he had given her on the bluff in the dark—and recalled that as she led the way back through the rocks, her eyes covered by the front of the heavy wooden canoe, she forgot the way and stumbled blindly from one block to another until her foot slipped painfully into a crack between them and she barely avoided falling. Not a word of thanks or contrition when they reached their goal, she wrote years later: "no *bravos*, no *did you hurt yourself*—nothing, just *Load up!*" There is no hint of any of this in an account which she wrote in the 1930s, a little after the trip. There, they deftly cross the rocks, "gradually work our poor thin boat up, across and over" and, "loading again, paddle out onto the wide river."

The trip fell into a routine of twenty-five miles a day. When they had a following wind, they would catch it in a big green-and-orange umbrella; she held the long handle while Bob paddled and steered. Once, they raced with some boys in skiffs who had caught on to the idea and were using branches for a sail. Each evening, around seven, when they stopped for the night, it was her job to write up the log, and she jotted down their position, the miles they had traveled, and their expenditures for food and cigarets, and made note of the weather, which grew stormy as they reached Cairo, Illinois, where the dark, clear Ohio water turned to the yellow mud of the Mississippi and the river doubled in width.

The riverbanks were deserted, quiet and beautiful: cornfields ran down to the willow trees along the shore and birds sang in the overhanging branches. For the rest of his life, Bob would remember those bright birds against the gray-green of the willows, the turtles they saw in the cutoffs, the patch of quicksand he stepped into somewhere in Missouri, the river's "mysterious turns and unexpected sight of towns and houses." They slipped by quietly enough to hear an animal eating a fish or drinking from the river, or the gurgle of a brooklet flowing into the main channel. "We were alone and close together and yet miles apart," Sissy recalled years later; when a "mood" came over him, he seemed almost like a stranger, though he always had something to teach her. In her memoirs, Sissy remembers him telling her one evening, somewhat mysteriously: "Water is the element of feeling." To explain what he meant, he invited her to take a swim with him. "You cannot see, you cannot hear, you cannot taste, you cannot smell," he said, placing his arm around her shoulders in the strong current, until she went under and began to gasp for breath and swallow water. "Don't you see what [happened out there]?" she remembered him asking later, when they lay exhausted on the bank. "It was like finding yourself, your primal self, knowing exactly where you come from. God damn it, even with you in my arms I am as alone as if I were the only man on earth. Water is the element of feeling. I become one with all things when I blend water and my sense of touch. No more alone. Everything is accomplished through the senses. Don't you see?" No use to be afraid of the elements: afraid of the water or afraid of the dark.

Summer caught up with them in the heat and glare a little north of Memphis. Far out in the river, they could see men in skiffs letting out lines for catfish, lying back in the boats, their faces covered by felt hats which they dipped from time to time into the river, bringing up drafts of water. Since leaving Louisville, Bob and Sissy had been drinking from their jugs—filling them at fountains in the little towns they went through—but now Bob scooped up a hat full and drank deeply. They had become "river drinkers," Sissy noted with pride in her journal on June 21, but quickly realized that the Mississippi was one vast drainage system, "almost, might one say, a sewer."

They paddled on, past the shoreline of Memphis, where the depression seemed to have hit harder than elsewhere, and people were living in every sort of dwelling imaginable: old buses, shanties, ramshackle houses, or packing boxes. As they drifted under the old Mississippi River bridge, a baby swallow fell out of its nest into the water, and Bob paddled hard to save it. "Steve Brodie," he named it, for the man who had survived after jumping from the Brookyn Bridge. They kept it alive for days in his hat, feeding it bugs and bread. At Greenville, Mississippi, in June in the heart of the Delta, they stopped for ice cream, but he felt "too cold" to eat it. Sissy looked at the thermometer—ninety-nine degrees—stared at him in disbelief, and realized he was ill. A few nights later, he went to bed, too sick to eat, in the middle of a lonely, swampy reach on the Arkansas side. When he awakened the next morning he felt like jelly, unable to walk or move, with a burning fever and delirium. Terrified, Sissy managed to get him into the canoe and paddled him to Lake Village, Arkansas, where he was diagnosed with malaria. Exhausted, shaken, short on funds, she managed to buy a dress, clean herself up, pay in advance for a hotel room, and telephone Bob's father. When it came to having malaria, she thought, no one did it more dramatically than her husband. The doctor had told her on the third day that he was out of danger, and probably conscious. But he lay in the hospital in silence for several days more, and was released after ten, looking "like a yellow walking skeleton." There was no hope of continuing. They cashed a money order from Walter, shipped the canoe home and traveled by bus to Jackson, where they caught the Illinois Central to Gulfport. Annette and Walter picked them up at the station. To

Sissy's amazement, Bob never spoke again about that trip. When the canoe reached the freight depot in Ocean Springs, he took it up the Pascagoula River to the Poticaw Fishing Camp and left it there until it sank to the bottom. Their lives were approaching a crisis. It was the last long trip they would ever take together.

QUICKSAND

The public school murals and Mississippi River trip brought welcome respite from the numbing routines of the Pottery, but Bob had not yet been able to devote himself fully to painting. A year later, in 1935, freedom seemed once again within reach. In Jackson, architect Emmett Hull—husband of the painter Marie Hull, a great friend of the Andersons, with a "grand passion" for Shearwater—had designed a new federal courthouse and post office. On the fourth floor, behind the judge's seat, was space enough for a mural twelve feet high by twenty-nine feet long. No less than $4,450 had been set aside for the mural by the Treasury Department's Section of Painting and Sculpture, which had taken the place of the old Public Works of Art Project. Even allowing for materials and labor, it was a princely sum, twenty times more than what Bob had earned from the Ocean Springs mural, and infinitely more than he could have made from decorating pottery at Shearwater: he and Sissy were living on ten dollars a week, and the entire annual income for the Pottery was about thirty-five hundred dollars. A commission like this one, with the attendant publicity, could free him forever from widgets and bookends, and he had been dreaming of that for the past six or seven years. Even the architect considered the amount "liberal, according to Southern standards." Was the Treasury Department sure that it didn't want *two* murals for that price? The answer from Washington was unequivocal: the government had set aside one percent of building costs to cover the embellishment of federal buildings, and "$12 a square foot [was] not too much to pay a mural painter. . . . Our purpose is to get work of the very highest quality, . . . paid for decently."

The announcement, mailed out in May 1935, invited artists to submit designs involving "justice, local history (past or present), local industry, pursuits, or scenery." The distinguished selection committee put together in Jackson included a former president of the Mississippi Art Association, a superintendent of education, two well-known art collectors, and Emmett Hull himself. The competition was publicized in newspapers throughout the South, in order to attract "the best artists in the whole Southern region," rather than merely local ones.

For Bob, the competition could not have come at a more trying moment. He had not yet fully recovered his strength from his battle with malaria, and in May his father's sister, Daisy, who had often cared for Peter and him when they were children and who had shown him affection and understanding through the years, had died at Shearwater after a long battle with the effects of a stroke. He and Sissy drove into the city one day to clean out her apartment on Foucher Street, and Sissy noticed the peculiar unjustified sense of guilt he felt over her death: he said he had never done enough for her; had he done more, "she might have lived." She had been a good pianist, sharing his own love of music, and had wanted her piano, an exceptionally fine upright, to go to him when she died. Bob and Sissy had it loaded carefully into a truck and drove it back to Ocean Springs, thinking they might find room for it in the Cottage. When they could not, he was distraught, and years later, to Sissy's amazement, he smashed it to pieces and pushed the sounding board under the Cottage where it remained for decades. Peter was going through a period of illness, self-doubt, and depression strangely similar to Bob's. He too had come down with malaria—though a less serious case than his brother's—and blamed himself absurdly for the death of his mother-in-law two years earlier, and for the illness of Billie Grinstead, who had moved with an attendant into a little house in Ocean Springs. Peter, Pat, and Sissy were doing their best to care for him, and Bob's refusal to have anything to do with his father-in-law was a source of tension and anger—one which erupted, at times, into fistfights between the two brothers.

On days when he felt well enough to work, Bob had been doing a series of watercolors unlike any he had done before. In March, Ned Park had sent him a copy of *Chapman's Color Key to North American Birds*, and he had begun to prepare the book on southeastern birds the two of them had talked about in Baltimore. Mac agreed to bring him specimens, and went out hunting for blue jays and meadowlarks, kingfishers and yellow-crowned night herons.

Kingfisher, 1934

Working with the dead specimens, Bob produced a series of careful, realistic pen-and-ink drawings with a watercolor wash, but before long, revolted by the killings, he abandoned the project and turned his attention to the mural.

By September 1935, he had prepared a huge cartoon in oil and sent it to the committee in Jackson. Twenty-nine artists submitted designs, but they were soon narrowed down to seven. The unanimous first choice was one by Lumen Winter: an allegorical representation of Law, Justice, and Mercy, "encircled by the all pervading rays of light of Progress." In second place was Frank W. Long, from Knoxville, who, like Bob, had studied at the Pennsylvania Academy of the Fine Arts and had several previous murals to his credit. Only the committee's chairwoman, Lucille N. Henderson, included Bob in her rankings, and he was her second choice. On September 18, 1935, she wrote officials in Washington that she liked Bob's "very decorative piece of design . . . with the exception of the central figure."

Edward Rowan, the opinionated, bureaucrat who was running the competition in Washington, had never hesitated to overrule his local committees, and by October he had decided to reject all of the top choices of Henderson's group, including Bob. It had "high merit as a design," he wrote, "but [we] consider that, if located in a Court Room, the subject matter would seem almost trivial." The design by Long—which had not been among the committee's top choices—seemed to him to have the most "artistic merit." Though unacceptable in its present form, Long could be asked "for new designs, perhaps a change of subject matter executed in the same extremely able manner." The committee detested this idea, and sent an angry telegram and several letters of protest to Rowan. At least one member threatened to resign. It wasn't merely that they been overruled; Long's mural memorialized "the white man's inhumanity to the Indian," and would never meet with public approval hanging in a federal courtroom. Henderson added that she was certain it had been "taken almost exactly" from a painting she had seen in the Corcoran Gallery. And if Long were allowed to submit new designs, the other top competitors should be allowed to do the same.

Sensing further trouble, Rowan acceded, and five artists were invited to submit new designs: Bob, Long, Winter, Xavier González (an art instructor at Newcomb), and Paul Ninas (director of the New Orleans Arts and Crafts Society). Rowan's assistant, Inslee Hopper, offered some special advice to Bob: "The local committee wishes the character of the subject matter stressed in the redesign. It is particularly anxious to have subject matter suitable for a court room. The Section of Painting and Sculpture admired the fine decorative quality of your design but we think that the color should be considerably changed, and the subject matter more dignified, considering the location of the mural in a court room. We understand, also, that some of the people in Jackson who saw the design objected to the use of a negroid type as the dominate [sic] figure in the panel."

Bob's revised design—still extant—is an elaborate pastiche of the southern and the indigenous. In the center of his cartoon, on an architectural ornament built into the wall, for which he was directed to leave space, sits a meditative child, of uncertain race, his legs folded in a yoga position: he had given blond hair to the "Negroid" figure that had offended the sensibilities of Henderson and Hopper. Over the child are his figurative parents, wearing the robes of Justice: a bearded male bearing a sword and a blindfolded female with a bowl of fruit. In the background, magnolia trees are in bloom and the Mississippi River meanders through the corn or cotton fields of the Delta. Arranged symmetrically on either side of the "family" are supplicants for justice: blacks, whites, and ruddy Indians, along with figures representing the worlds of law, education, industry, agriculture, and the military. To the left and right are two mythological beings who bring the past into contact with the present and the Americas into contact with Africa: to the right, an African deity holding a skull, and to the left, presiding over the Indian supplicants, a Native American with the head, or mask, of a bear, although this figure, too, reminds one of African cave painting of the sort evoked by the hunters in the Ocean Springs mural.

As head of the committee, Henderson was not entirely satisfied with the revision, but had no doubt that Rowan ought to award the commission to Bob:

> We feel that the work of No. 1 [Bob] or No. 2A [Winter] would be quite satis-
> factory, not only to the committee as a whole but to the general public as well.
> We also feel that, in as much as No. 1 is by a Mississippi artist, whom we feel is
> amply qualified . . . we earnestly request that [he] be awarded the contract. We
> feel that the original design submitted by No. 1 (Mr. Anderson) with changes
> as to the central figure will be more pleasing than the second design as a
> whole. We feel that local artists, tho equally qualified, have always been greatly
> handicapped in any competition with Eastern artists. We know that this is an
> important work, and we feel that it will be capably handled by the artist of
> our choice. Knowing already your high regard for his original design, I feel
> sure that you will concur . . . and that we will have a happy solution to our
> many problems. . . .

Her comments, and those added by Hull in a separate letter, reveal that regional pride was at stake; "everything being equal, a Mississippi artist should have preference." Hull's remarks are reminiscent of those made by Woodward at the PWAP meeting a year or two earlier:

> The southern states are apt to bemoan the fact that the young artists and oth-
> ers of exceptional talent and ability leave the South and locate in the large
> cities in the East, yet very little has been done to encourage worthwhile people
> to remain [here]. They are prone to use the local people for the lesser com-
> missions and bring in the outsiders to do the worthwhile things—things
> which would mean the making of a reputation for an artist and which the

successful artists of the North and East accept with more or less nonchalance. This is not right, and we think it should be corrected just as rapidly as we produce creative artists equipped to do work of a recognized standard of excellence, which certainly applies to Mr. Anderson.

An emphatic final paragraph dwells on Bob's qualifications:

Mr. Anderson executed some splendid murals in the Ocean Springs High School. This was done under the P.W.A. [*sic*] and he received the minimum wage, which I understand made a total of only $200 or $300 compensation for about eight large mural panels easily worth thousands. The work was carried through to successful finish regardless of the fact that he was practically donating his splendid work to the school. These murals have demonstrated Mr. Anderson's high order of ability. They have been greatly admired by artists qualified to correctly judge such work, and since he practically donated his services, it would seem right to reward him with a really worthwhile commission, now that we have the opportunity. I hope you and your associates will see this as we do, and agree that you can make no mistake in awarding this work to Mr. Anderson.

But Rowan had little sympathy for "regional" arguments and even less for Bob's design: "The Section feels that the color and the design are much more suitable to a textile pattern than to a mural decoration. The general approach of Mr. Anderson's design is not considered appropriate for a Federal court room. Following the first competition, certain suggestions were made to Mr. Anderson which we do not feel were taken into account in the submission of his second design."

The same damning words were repeated to Bob himself in a letter of June 4, 1936: "We all felt that your design was more that of a textile than a mural." And that was that. Over the strenuous objections of the Jackson committee, all five designs were rejected, including Bob's, and the competition was declared terminated. The Treasury Department would choose its own artist. In Jackson, Henderson and the rest of the committee protested, but finally acquiesced, and told Rowan they would be "good sports." Later in June, a Russian-born artist from Connecticut, Simka Simkhovitch, was awarded the commission. To Bob, the entire affair seemed an affront and an injustice. He had tried to follow the "suggestions" of a faceless bureaucrat and had redone his "decorative" design, only to see the contract awarded to an out-of-state artist who had never visited Mississippi. In a year of labor, he had not earned a penny. It was back to the drudgery of Shearwater, with no end in sight.

That spring, he and Sissy joined his cousin Dick McConnell and his wife, Virginia, for a trip to the bogs of coastal Louisiana to tag wild irises, one of his favorite flowers, to judge from a note written later: "The iris is a lilac flower. Blue lilac. Pink lilac. Veined. . . . It is the consummation of bursting green fire starting from the earth and water, and having paid its debt to the sun with a flower, it is rewarded with an almost invisible fruit." In 1936 New Orleans was pushing eastward toward Gentilly, transforming the landscape that lay in its path, and Bob and Dick had mounted a "two-man crusade" to save the wild iris, in its unforgettable shades of lilac, creamy white, wine- or brick-red, violent blue, purple, and terra-cotta. Each spring they would tag the plants they found especially beautiful—once Bob tore up a perfectly good blue shirt to do so—returning in the fall to dig up the plants and transplant them to boggy spots at Shearwater. In September 1936, Bob and Sissy climbed into the Andersons' old Ford and headed for their rendezvous with the McConnells, but went astray somewhere in the Louisiana countryside. When they stopped at a farmhouse to ask directions, an exuberant old Cajun, who was celebrating his fiftieth birthday with his numerous children and grand-children, invited them to join the celebration. Sissy never forgot the prodigious quantities of food that had been laid out for over a hundred guests: "steaming pots of gumbo and great bowls of rice; platters and platters of fried fish and fried chicken; cauldrons of beans and potatoes and onions all cooked together; bowls of potato salad cuddled up to huge plates of boiled shrimp, crawfish and crabs; trays full of biscuits and cornbread; saucers of sliced tomatoes and cucumbers."

For dessert, waiting under the table in the shade, there was cream-cheese ice cream, a local delicacy with a "delicate hint of nutmeg." Their mouths burning from the spicy food, Sissy and Bob gobbled down huge plates of it, and began to leave, though Bob lingered behind, doing pencil portraits of all who asked for them. Months later, around Christmas, he and Sissy began to feel feverish, with aching joints and strange chills. They thought at first it might be a new outbreak of the malaria both Bob and Peter had been suffering from, but Frank Schmidt, the family doctor, diagnosed them both with undulant fever, guessing it had been caused by the unpasteurized ice cream. Treating the disease would not be easy, but the doctor's brother, Harry C. Schmidt, who had been doing research on low-grade infections in the

Louisiana countryside, had developed an antigen which he administered, for six weeks, by injection, deliberately raising their fevers still higher. Bob was stricken harder than Sissy, and for many weeks, they sipped liquids and took aspirin, too weak to hold a pencil or climb out of bed.

When Bob finally did, he pushed himself hard, redesigning and renovating the Cottage with the help of Alphonse Beaugez, the old carpenter who had once helped him build the *Pelican*. Working with Beaugez and his son, Bob pulled down a partition and turned the two rooms into a single space about fifteen by thirty feet. He turned the northern wall into casement windows, from floor to ceiling, and built window seats underneath, with room for extra storage. He added bunks which could be used as additional seating along the side walls. Between the screened porch and the main room, he installed heavy sliding glass doors, so that the entire Cottage could be opened to the woods outside. At the Annex, he designed a new series of figurines—football players glazed in white enamel. By now, the ceramics of all three brothers had earned national recognition, and their carved vases and platters (glazed in alkaline blue or Peter's new copper red) were being included in the Robineau Memorial Exhibition sponsored, each year, by the Syracuse Museum of Fine Arts, a show which traveled to museums of art from Worcester to Seattle and to a series of European museums. Some of the pottery was shown, also, in the 1935–36 California Pacific Exposition. Not that the recognition meant much to Bob, especially when the old "Negro figures" were involved. When the Syracuse Museum wrote to him asking for permission to include his "delightful 'Nigger on Horseback'" in an exhibition that would travel to Denmark, it was Walter who answered: "I find to my disgust that my son, Walter I. Anderson, was in possession of a letter from you [of two months ago], to which he had never replied. Plain fact is, that he never answers any letter."

As a consolation prize for his labors in Jackson, Bob was awarded a commission for a small mural in the Indianola, Mississippi, post office: a twelve-by-four-foot panel over the postmaster's door. The prospective payment, $535, was dramatically less than that offered for the Jackson mural, but a tidy amount for a couple with no savings and no prospect of work outside the Pottery. As with the Jackson mural, the first installment was to be paid upon approval of the preliminary sketches, and the subject could be anything "appropriate to the locale of this particular post office," in a town between Jackson and Memphis in the cotton fields of the Mississippi Delta. In September 1936, still weak from undulant fever, Bob sent Rowan three pencil sketches. One of them, a study in motion, showed a mailman making deliveries on either side of a long street, an idea which struck the nattering Rowan—again!—as more appropriate for "treatment in another medium, such as the textile." The "abstractions and decorative qualities of the human beings are too extreme," he wrote, adding that he could not recommend it for formal approval to the director of procurement. Wasn't Anderson "capable of more factual drawing"? This was a bit "too extreme for the decoration of a Post Office visited by all classes of individuals, to each of whom the decoration should have some appeal. . . . I suggest that you use a more factual approach throughout. If, however, you feel strongly that you wish to do a purely decorative panel, may I suggest that you consider a landscape or more intimate design of foliage and similar forms for this mural?"

To Rowan, "decorative" meant a failure to engage fully with "history"—the past that bound Americans together—and a "factual approach" meant one as far as possible from abstraction, expressionism, the sort of regionalism that favored the "typical" over actual historical details, Mexican-style propaganda, or any other sort of "modernism." His assumption was that the American public was tired of academic tricks—it wanted, like Gradgrind, *the facts*, just the facts. In a defense of the New Deal art projects, Forbes Watson had written that in the past the pendulum had "swung too far toward purely intellectual painting. This time it has swung back to the facts." WPA muralists all over America went scurrying for history books.

It was three weeks before Bob felt well enough to mail off another five sketches, and by then he was coping with a sadness deeper than any he had ever known. His father had been diagnosed with stomach cancer and had taken to bed in his room at the Barn, cared for by Annette, who was convinced, as always, that faith healers and prayer and Christian Science would prove more effective than ordinary medicine. Walter, less of a believer than she was, thought back over his seventy-five years and told himself that he was not a quitter. Neither in golf nor in business had he ever "picked up a putt," and one project, especially, had to be carried to completion. For the past year or so he had been writing a book that seemed to him extraordinary enough to revolutionize the art of putting and "bolster up the Anderson fortunes, if only in a small way." It was the fruit of his Scottish heritage, his eighteen years on the greens, and a long period of careful experimentation. When the family moved to Ocean Springs, before the Pottery had opened, he had built a tennis court for his three sons, but he had also ordered a couple of truckloads of sand and had converted a space around the barn into a putting green. It was a delightful place, about a hundred feet long and fifty feet wide, with a large hickory tree at one end and a red oak at the other. There were benches and canvas lounge chairs for family meetings. In front of the Barn was the sandy path that led to the Front House, about 140 feet away, with the woods on either side. This he had converted into a narrow fairway where he could perfect his chipping. He calculated that, in the ten years since he had moved onto the place, he had played half a million shots and walked around the globe several times. The previous spring, while Bob was working on the Jackson murals, he had also tried out his method at local courses and he had been sending Mac out on special experimental missions to the links in Biloxi and Gulf Hills. Despite his shaking hands and failing eyesight, Walter had done some marvelous putting, perfecting his "pendulum swing" and long, slow roll. He had written up his insights with the humor he put into everything, and it was all a matter now of finding a publisher. He needed a well-known sponsor, and he had begun with Quentin Reynolds, sporting editor at *Collier's Weekly*, introducing himself as a serious businessman, a purveyor of "good hard common sense"—no madman, no quack, no builder of castles in Spain. After retiring from the grain business, he told Reynolds, "I found myself running an art pottery, knowing as little about Art or Pottery as any man in the world ever did. My three sons put me into this and, in their behalf, I had to find the right way, and must have come somewhere near it, as for eight years, in spite of the Depression, I have managed to make it pay dividends, and something in the shape of a decent living for the three boys, two of whom married and one with three small children. I had a sort of tiger by the tail and, on their account, could not let go."

On the Greens or *Diary of a Dub* was to begin with one of Reynolds's columns on putting and end with Walter's reply. The two of them would make golf history and split the proceeds. Who could tell? There were millions of golfers out there, and if the two of them could get their book into the hands of Bobby Jones or Gene Sarazen, it might turn into a best seller. As the cancer wore him down, Walter's thoughts turned more somber. Wasted by the disease until he looked nearly transparent, he drifted into delirium and thought that those around him, including Sissy and Bob, were trying to poison him.

For Bob, completing the mural began to seem an insurmountable task. Sometime that fall, Rowan wrote him again, approving one of the designs but admonishing him once more to stick to the "factual," despite his predilection

Pencil sketch for Indianola mural, 1936

for the purely decorative. By December 11, 1936, Rowan received a color sketch and found it neither equal to the theme nor appropriate to the building. The design accepted did, in fact, tell an easily intelligible story, but the "insistent pinks and pastel tones" seemed incongruent with the subject matter. "May I suggest that you reconsider your palette in this instance, and submit a design which you are confident will be in harmony with the interior of the building. May I also suggest that in the color sketch which you submit you indicate as far as possible the general appearance of the finished work."

What Bob had proposed was a triptych on one of the stock themes of post office murals: "good news, bad news"—except that here, the bad news prevailed. Both the pencil sketch (darkened by erasures and corrections) and the color sketch survive. In the central panel of the pencil sketch a woman opens a door, and Fate, in the figure of a mailman, hands her a telegram. In the left-hand panel of the sketch, a family, their heads bowed in prayer or mourning, gathers around the bed where a woman—perhaps a man—is dying. Someone in the group is reading from the Bible, and someone is pulling up the bedsheet, like a shroud. In the right-hand panel, a mother raises a newborn baby in her arms. Her husband stands beside her, hands resting lovingly on her shoulders,

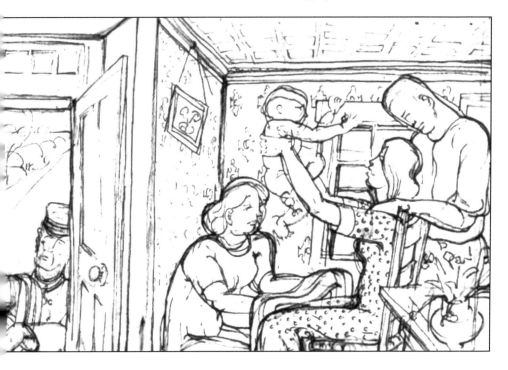

and another woman holds out a blanket, waiting to receive the infant. It is spring or summer: on a table is a bunch of irises in a Shearwater vase. It is a lugubrious scene, done from the depths of illness and despair. A note from Sissy to Rowan on January 3, 1937, asks for more time to complete the color sketch: "Mr. Anderson is still prevented by illness from going on with his work."

On January 15, sensing that the end was near, George Walter Anderson wrote out his will, leaving all of his possessions to his "dear wife Annette McConnell Anderson" and one hundred dollars apiece to his "three dear sons." Even then, Bob refused to believe how close he was to death. "He always feels the cold so," Sissy remembered him saying. "He'll be fine when the first warm days come." Toward the end of the month, Rowan notified Bob that the color sketch had been approved, with the exception of a minor criticism: "The criticism deals with the death room scene. The Supervising Architect felt that the message would be as potent if, rather than an actual death scene, you depicted someone ill with relatives grouped around the bed. Will you kindly give this your serious consideration."

Did Bob—perhaps Sissy—pause a moment to consider the irony? Mr. Edward B. Rowan, no painter himself but a friend of "the facts," was trying to help him with a scene of illness and death. Weeks later, Walter was gone, laid to rest in Evergreen Cemetery, overlooking Fort Bayou, with a few old business associates from New Orleans bearing the casket. Bob was overwhelmed with grief and with the feeling that he hadn't been "kind enough" to him. If his mother had given him art, it was his father who had awakened his love of the outdoors and a certain brave sense of adventure. Sissy noted that, as happened after the death of her own mother, he seemed to seek solace in sex and that he consoled himself by listening, over and over, to a record of "Jesu, Joy of Man's Desiring." One of his most striking early paintings dates from the same period: a tall, narrow oil on plywood of Don Quixote, a gaunt, expressionless "Knight of the Mournful Countenance," making his way through the depths of a ravine more deserted and gloomy than any ever imagined by Daumier, Sancho Panza trailing along far behind him. It is a vision of grief and loneliness, set perhaps in the Sierra Morena, where the Don is about to meet another character who seems as mad as himself. In the face of Don Quixote, Sissy saw the face of her father-in-law in death.

It was a while before Annette, now seventy years old, filed the inventory of her late husband's estate. There were $5,175 in stocks, bonds, and receivership certificates, but some of the stocks proved worthless. She had always left financial matters to her husband, but it was abundantly clear to everyone that from now on the entire family—seven adults and three children—would have to make do with the income generated by the Pottery. For Bob, there was little hope now of achieving any sort of independence. Sissy had noticed a change in him over the past few years: "little flare-ups, small explosions of unbearable intensity." One had occurred a year or two earlier, when she had surprised him with an expensive birthday gift she knew he would love: phonograph records of Beethoven's *Missa Solemnis*, ordered from Kroch's in Chicago. He listened to them for a while, and caught her up in a somber dance macabre, but he returned to "reality" with a crudeness that sent her running for the door. From outside the Cottage, through the window, she saw him throw the records to the floor and trample on the pieces. "Bobby is Bobby," said Annette when Sissy told her of the incident. His mother had shrugged off his behavior that way since he was a child, but this time there was a hint of arrogance in her voice, as though Sissy herself were partly to blame. Later that day, he had told her how sorry he was and how much he loved her, but now, a couple of years later, she found herself puzzling over his sudden changes of mood and her own role in his life, and wondering whether they could go on living together. In the time they had spent together, he had opened her eyes to countless things—in art, in nature, in all that lay within reach of his sharp and avid senses. But she sensed that he was less able than most people to deal with distractions and interruption. *Any* interruption always led to a half-finished work. Now that the Cottage had become a single open room, divided only by the tiled fireplace he had wanted there, it was harder than ever to keep out of his way. "As long as your shoes stick out like that I know you're here," she heard him say one day. She was tired, too, of trying to adapt: she had, after all, asked very little of him, and had done her utmost to adjust to the Andersons. Did he ever realize that?

One morning in early March, with Shearwater in full bloom, days after the two of them had scraped together the money to buy the canvas for the Indianola mural, she told Bob about two of her dreams. In the first, she was caught in quicksand in a place like Gentilly, where the two of them had dug irises, or their beloved valley in Vancleave where they often looked for azaleas to transplant to Shearwater. Struggling to escape, she had knocked over the azaleas. In the other, she was a large, grey Persian tomcat who belonged to the owner of a gift shop and charmed all of the lady customers. The owner was a shady character who skipped from one town to another without paying his debts and hardly ever allowed her any freedom. Bob's reaction alarmed her. When she had knocked over the azaleas, he said, she had shown him she didn't want them on the place, and was "laughing at him." He added that unless he died, none of the plants would live—hadn't she noticed that all of the bushes his father had transplanted had recently burst into bloom? Sissy's dream of captivity—the kept woman and jealous, unscrupulous proprietor—upset him still more, though it seemed obvious to her what had triggered it: the Pottery was now "precariously financed," and the day before she had been scouring the account books and trying to collect on bad debts. It occurred to her, as he became more agitated, that something had gone wrong with his mind; perhaps the "prolonged and constant fever had caused some sort of inflammation in his brain."

There was more. When Ellen returned from Paris that month, he asked her repeatedly whether she had been to Gurdjieff's institute at Fontainebleau. That Christmas—1936—Bob's old friend Frank Baisden had stopped to visit them on his way from Chattanooga to New Orleans. He was brimming with stories of the studio he had built with his own hands on Lookout Mountain and of his work with local residents, mountain people to whom he had taught

Gurdjieff as the tree of life, c. 1940

art, weaving, and other crafts, to help them eke out a living. The three of them had toasted with homemade elderberry wine, and when Sissy and Bob were alone, and the wine had loosened his tongue, Bob told her that a decade earlier, in 1927, on a rainy night at one of Orage's lectures on Gurdjieff at a camp in Trenton, Baisden had frightened him by crawling into his bed and putting his arm around him. For Bob, it was an agonizing confession, and when Sissy tried to comfort him by making light of it, he became very upset and ran out into the night. More of the story emerged over the next few nights, and from his troubled account Sissy gathered, somehow, that the love of other men was considered by Gurdjieff or by his followers to bring one closer to emotional, physical, and mental wholeness. The episode with Baisden loomed so large in her own memory, and was so hard to confront that, years later, writing her memoirs, she produced a number of different accounts of it. Bob hadn't mentioned the incident again—and it is now impossible to establish what actually happened—but much of his thought in March 1937 seemed to revolve obsessively around Gurdjieff. When the family went on a picnic with friends from Oldfields, the Hamills, who were visiting from Chicago, he kept gloomily to himself and told Sissy that not only Ellen but also Mrs. Hamill and Annette's maid were "secret agents" sent by the institute to humiliate him. They were "flagellating" him through praise: whenever they spoke kindly of him, they were really "applying the lash of the most terrible invective," something "superior" members of the institute did, as a matter of course, to help free ordinary ones from the "trammels of an ordinary, fleshly existence." Through humiliation of all sorts, including self-punishment, one achieved a higher level of consciousness.

On March 23, a month after his father's death, Bob sank into a strange sort of lethargy and his paranoia became even more acute. Peter found him in the bathroom with a razor in each hand, and when he pulled them gently away, Bob mumbled that he "thought that was what you wanted me to do." He told Sissy he was the "lowest of the low"; he had a venereal disease, he said, and should never have married. When a doctor reassured him he was perfectly healthy, he brightened up and told her he would like to have a child and begin a new life in the newly renovated Cottage. That night she took him into her arms, and they made love. By the next day, however, he was convinced, once more, that he was ill, and impotent, and began thinking again about ending his life. He thrust his hand into the living room fire—"to harden himself," he said—and rushed out the door. When he returned, a while later, he told her that he had wanted to throw himself under a passing car, but had not been able. One night he stiffened up in bed, his head hanging over the edge of the bedframe, and wept uncontrollably for the great sea turtle he had slain on Horn Island. She sensed that, besides his pain over his father's death, he was grieving for all that he had harmed, even in his imagination: butterflies, fish, the dead birds that Mac had brought him to draw, the ducks he had shot on his hunting trips with his brothers. For the first time in their marriage, he told her he wished he could believe in God, and asked her to pray with him—he felt too slow to formulate his own ideas. He told her also that he wanted to visit Baisden, the only person who could "straighten him out."

From there on, things changed rapidly for the worse. Against her better judgment, Annette agreed to take him to Chattanooga. Sissy would stay at home; she felt she was "bad for him," and that he was more likely to come to his senses without her. Just before leaving, he went to her with tears in his eyes, trembling all over, and said he had heard God. He took her into his arms but suddenly dropped to his knees, gamboled about the Cottage on all fours, and said he was six years old and perfectly happy. As he stood in the door, he asked her to leave him alone while he was gone, and explained that she made things worse: she was controlling him through hypnosis. Finally, Annette led him to the car, and they left for Mobile, where they could take the highway north. They had a flat on the way, and to his mother's amazement Bob sat in the car while she walked over a mile to get help. Desperate, she called home and asked Mac to come, and when they met in Mobile, the two of them took Bob to a doctor, who listened to him babble and noted that the patient was "psychopathic, manifesting religious and persecutory delusions, despondency, and suicidal impulses." In the afternoon Bob was allowed to visit a museum in the company of a trained nurse, and that night, in a hotel room, Annette, whose faith in art and literature remained unshaken, read to him from Thoreau and noticed that he wept at certain passages. Later, he went into the bathroom by himself, and swallowed the entire bottle of medicine the doctor had given him to help him sleep. By the next morning, when Annette took him back to the doctor, he gave them the diagnosis applied, long ago, to her sister—dementia praecox—and told them they had no choice but to commit him. There were frantic calls to the family in Ocean Springs, and from Ellen and Sissy to Baltimore. Through Ellen's friend Edwards Park—the pediatrician whom Bob had met on his trip with Sissy—it was arranged for him to be admitted to the Henry Phipps Psychiatric Clinic and entrusted to the care of Adolf Meyer. At Shearwater, Sissy stared at her account books and waited for news. Once again, her world had fallen apart.

Venus Panel (north wall), 1951
Community Center Mural
Oil and tempera on stucco,
12 ft. H

Sissy with Scarf, c. 1935
Oil on canvas,
29 x 22 in.

Leif Anderson, c. 1955
Watercolor on paper, 8½ x 11 in.

Child, date unknown
Watercolor on paper, 11 x 8½ in.

Mr. Boots, c. 1935
Oil on plywood panel, 32 x 26 in.

Ocean Springs: Past and Present (The Chase), 1934
Ocean Springs Public School Mural
Oil on canvas,
55 x 168 in.

Sun (east wall), 1951
Community Center Mural
Oil and tempera on stucco,
12 ft. H

Man on Horse, c. 1935
Oil on plywood panel,
16½ x 21 in.

Hunter Plate, c. 1935
Ceramic, 10 x 10 x 1½ in.
Thrown by Peter Anderson, decorated by Walter Anderson

Jockeys Riding Horses, c. 1935
Oil on plywood panel, 20 x 45 in.

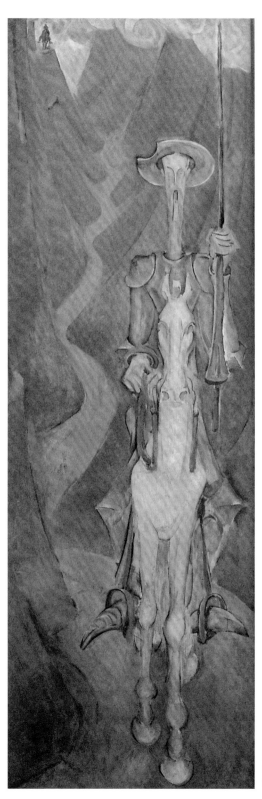

Don Quixote, c. 1936
Oil on plywood panel,
69 x 23 in.

James McConnell Anderson (Mac), c. 1935
Oil on canvas, 27 x 22 in.

Watermelon Eaters (detail), c. 1960
Oil on plywood panel, 24 x 24 in.

Horse Plate, c. 1935
Ceramic,
8½ x 8½ x 1¾ in.
Thrown by Peter Anderson, sgraffito
decoration by Walter Anderson

Vase with Horses, 1929
Ceramic, 6½ x 7 x 7 in.
Thrown by Peter Anderson,
decorated by Walter Anderson

Long Necked Horse, c. 1945
Tempera paints on paper,
48 x 19 in.

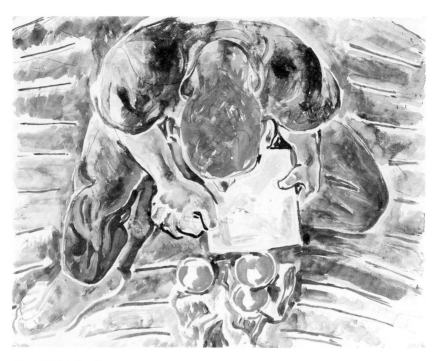

The Artist Painting Oranges, c. 1952
Watercolor on paper, 8½ x 11 in.

Broken Red Pot, c. 1955
Watercolor on paper,
11 x 8½ in.

Road to Oldfields, c. 1943
Watercolor on paper, 25 x 19 in.

Cat Teapot, c. 1955
Ceramic, 8 in. H.

Sheep and Pine Trees, c. 1943
Watercolor on paper, 25 x 19 in.

Turkey, c. 1944
Watercolor on paper, 24 x 18 in.

Blue Cat Vase, c. 1935
Earthenware, 5½ in. H
Thrown by Peter Anderson,
decorated by Walter Anderson

Man and Goat Vase, c. 1935
Ceramic, 5 in. H
Thrown by Peter Anderson,
decorated by Walter Anderson

Non-Competitive, c. 1960
Watercolor on paper,
11 x 8½ in.

Man Making Music with Cows, c. 1945
Watercolor on paper,
19 x 12¼ in.

Pepper Plant, c. 1950
Watercolor on paper, 8½ x 11 in.

Orange Fast (calendar drawing), c. 1942
Watercolor on paper, 11 x 8½ in.

Rotten Pumpkin, 1952
Watercolor on paper, 8½ x 11 in.

THE PHIPPS CLINIC

When doctors looked in on Bob for the first time on West I, they found him lying in bed, his head propped on his left arm, silently swaying from side to side. He seemed oriented as to time and place, was able to tell them his first name, though not his last, and answered questions in a low, thick voice that trailed off after a few words. Asked what his trouble was, he mumbled that he was feeling the separation from his wife and the effects of having eaten too many starches. Over the next few days he confessed in tears that he had been hearing voices: allegorical suggestions had been coming over the radio from some supernatural source, perhaps God himself, warning other people not to trust him. He said that he was revolted by the men on the ward. He thought all of them, especially the attendants, were homosexuals, and he defended himself by biting and kicking at them when they passed. Despite the hospital's efforts to calm and protect him, he was a storm of self-destruction. He ran his fist through the double pane of safety glass on his door, attempted to suffocate himself by aspirating water and food, bashed his head repeatedly against the walls and floor, and thrust a spoon down his throat. He refused food and drink and lost twenty-five pounds. Doctors noticed that nurses were better at calming him than the male attendants, and the staff learned to treat him cautiously. Even when he was weak from hunger, he was an exceptionally strong patient, "beautifully developed, muscularly," a physical threat to anyone who came near him. The hospital's immediate course of action involved sedatives and hypnotic drugs—sodium amytal and barbital—and two traditional forms of hydrotherapy: cold packs (in which the patient was cocooned in cold, wet sheets and strapped to a table until he began to perspire and relax) and continuous baths (which restrained him on a hammock in a tub of hot or cold running water). Both treatments were thought to improve circulation, relieve cerebral congestion, and ease tensions. Often, a doctor sat by the patient, waiting for him to become calm enough to talk.

Annette had always felt a profound distrust of doctors and, from the time her father had committed her sister to Friends Hospital, a deep suspicion of the way psychiatrists dealt with unusual people. The very notion of incarceration, even for criminals, she found repulsive. Her sister, Dellie, had been free for a long time now, and although she was far from normal—she flew into a rage whenever she remembered her "imprisonment" at Friends—no one could say she hadn't done better than expected. In 1919, a year after Annette had bought the property in Ocean Springs, she had gone up to Philadelphia to bring her home, on a personal "crusade against injustice, a protest against tyranny, and a triumph over the mental hospital." She had gotten Dellie settled with an attendant at her father's old house in Bay St. Louis, where she wrote lyrical little pieces for the local newspaper, *The Sea Coast Echo*, and she was living now in California, able to correspond with Annette and enjoy life. She had even been to Europe with a companion. In her sister's case, the doctors had been wrong. Mental states are contagious, she thought. To cure a disturbed person, you should place him among "normal" people, not among others who are disturbed.

As she settled into an apartment near Phipps, Annette wondered what psychiatry—in the person of Adolf Meyer—would have to say about Bob. She liked him immediately. Perhaps he didn't know what was wrong with her son, but, from the first, this kindly man, a year older than she, with his Swiss-German accent, his meandering speech, and sad, goat-like appearance, seemed sure that Bob could be helped. For a pragmatist and pluralist like Meyer, each person was a unique "experiment in nature," simple or complex, but never hopeless and almost always susceptible to therapeutic modification. Reacting against the physiological reductivism of those who "sought for exclusive salvation in the urine and feces" and against diagnosticians who "sorted out patients, not facts" under the rubric of easily recognizable pathological entities, Meyer taught his students, the families of his patients, and a wide audience at home and abroad that mental problems cannot be separated from the rest of a patient's "biological behavior," and that the mentally ill do not suffer from any one disease in particular, but react to a "group of facts and factors," some physiological, others behavioral and environmental. Psychiatric illness resulted "by and large from things people did (or did not do) rather than from something they *had.*" Lifelong habits and conflicts, family stressors, parental relationships—all these were at least as relevant as brain lesions or heredity, and the psychiatrist had no need to peer into the unconscious or Freudian "complexes" to discover "how the person thought about and responded to real-life experiences." Meyer believed that earlier psychiatrists, clinging to John Gray's maxim "No disease of the mind without disease of the brain," had too often associated mental illness with progressive, irreversible deterioration. On his weekly rounds, surrounded by some of the brightest—and most nervous—medical students in the country, Meyer did his best to dispel that idea. Every condition has a "multiconditional character," he taught them, and each diagnosis is but a working hypothesis. Even the best one was no substitute for holistic "understanding." One cannot get at the patient's problem without considering him as a unique set of assets and liabilities: "Few patients have but one abnormal factor working in them. That which is *one big calamity*, one disease, resolves itself usually into groups of facts, none of which is *the unique* and unequivocal cause or force 'back of it all.'"

Despite his imposing, rather gloomy appearance, Meyer was an optimist, or rather a "meliorist," who swept aside rigid nosologies, poked fun at his own terminological "word palaces" and those of other psychiatrists, and made others believe in the patient's capacity to grow, change, and modify his behavior. That optimism, and his reputation as the "dean" or "founding father" of American psychiatry, had helped him assemble one of the finest medical staffs in the country. Around him were Theodore Lidz, who was studying the relations of schizophrenics with their families in the South; Paul Lemkau, who was surveying the epidemiology of mental illness; Thomas A. C. Rennie, who had undertaken research on vocational therapy and on the recovery rates of manic depressives and schizophrenics, and who had treated Zelda Fitzgerald a few years earlier; Wendell Muncie, who would produce an influential textbook on psychobiology; and Alexander Leighton, on his first forays into the cultural contexts of disease and treatment. Two doctors, in particular—Henry Mead, an extern, and chief resident Norman Cameron—were to acquire special meaning in Bob's life. Cameron, who later wrote widely read works on schizophrenic thinking and personality development, was at the beginning of his career, learning to decipher the "language of madness, the truth in it, the devious truth." Although he detested much of Meyer's teaching, he admired his capacity to listen to his patients, rather than dismissing their words as nonsense or "word salad," and found the same sensitivity in his friend Mead. Mead, son of the famous pragmatist philosopher George Henry Mead, was older than the other interns and externs: forty-six, married, with children and a medical practice in Chicago. In midlife, he had become aware of the "growing shadow of the psyche [even] in the plainest of medical etiologies," and Meyer granted him reluctant permission to study with him at Phipps.

On May 8, 1937, after an attempt to speak with Bob and a long, careful look at the statements of Mac and Annette and letters from Sissy and Frank Baisden, Meyer called his staff into the Phipps library to discuss the life history of a "sensitive, intense, married artist" of thirty-three years, a rigid all-or-nothing personality, "tremendously impulsive, and with absolute disregard for himself or others, especially for himself."

There seemed to be nothing unusual in his birth, his childhood, or his schooling, and his marriage appeared to be a satisfactory one. Blood tests were normal, he was in good physical condition except for an appalling case of acne, stubborn constipation, and the migraine headaches from which he had long suffered. Neurologically, there was nothing of importance. No problem, either, with alcoholism; he had an occasional glass of wine or beer but never more than once a week. There were, however, "etiological factors," the first of which was the family history of depression and dementia praecox. Another was his sensitive, conscientious, perfectionistic nature and his "philosophy of personal physical suffering," fostered by his obsession with Gurdjieff, whose thought had taught him, apparently, that pain brought one to new heights of spiritual stamina and self-awareness. There were "situational factors" as well: "discontent with his enforced type of family work; disappointment at not winning a competition in his profession; deaths in the family; concern about sex" (including the incident with Baisden and a fear of impotence); "financial insecurity; and overwork."

"We can't really be sure what things count and what don't," one of the doctors remarked, early in the treatment. "I haven't been able to get anything from him, [except] for the first day or two he was in. He hasn't talked to us at all."

For Meyer, too, this case was, without a doubt, one of the most difficult the clinic had dealt with in many years. The diagnosis—like *all* of Meyer's diagnoses—would have to be tentative, a simple summary of symptoms:

The Alienado, c. 1939

hypothymergasia with homosexual panic and stupor. The term "hypothymergasia," little used outside the Phipps Clinic, meant a specific kind of depression in which the patient displayed feelings of guilt and inadequacy and the desire to harm himself. The "homosexual panic"—which Freud had associated with schizophrenia—was obvious and acute. During his initial attacks on male attendants and his persistent attempts at self-mutilation, nurses had noticed his dilated pupils, rapid pulse, and labored respiration. And although Bob had confessed to a fear of homosexuals, and Mead affirmed, without offering any evidence to support his claim, that "he was a straight homosexual at one time," Meyer reminded his staff that no one, not even Sissy, was certain that he had ever had "anything that we would look upon as an overt and sought homosexual relationship." As for the "stupor," the patient had spent much of April and the first week of May in a nearly catatonic state. Beyond that, there was little to go on, though the "Gurdjieff business" rang a bell. Muncie remembered that it was Phipps's second "Fountainebleau case," and that the previous patient, also, had been an artist who had mutilated himself. At a staff meeting, he read aloud from a clipping he had found in the archives.

> [At Fontainebleau] the life is very simple and uncomfortable, the food adequate, the work is extremely hard. The physical work indeed results often in a degree of exhaustion which perhaps exceeds anything that was produced even by a prolonged spell in the winter trenches of Flanders 1917. . . . Carried to extremes it creates increased capacity for effort. . . . Other conditions provided at the Institute—with an ingenuity that is almost diabolical—offer similar opportunities for the study of the emotional mechanism.

When a doctor wrote to Baisden, hoping he would have something to say on Bob's obsession with Gurdjieff and about their supposedly "homosexual" relationship, he replied that he was never very close to Walter Anderson at the Academy, and that his classmates had called him "the Mystery Man"—a "trait that has remained unchanged," someone observed. For weeks, he remained almost entirely mute, moving his head from side to side or lying in bed with his head held rigidly off the pillow—it amazed the doctors and nurses how he could keep it that way even after he fell asleep. His "alternating stupors and tremendous bursts of suicidal excitement" set the whole clinic on edge. Even when he himself asked for hydrotherapy, up to eight men were sometimes required to force him into the packs, and when he was in the tub he tried repeatedly to swallow water. When doctors questioned him, he sometimes took a full minute to produce an answer. The nurses struggled to get him to eat, led him to the toilet (he was now incontinent), gave him sedatives, and tried, often in vain, to bandage his self-inflicted wounds: he not only burned his hand on a radiator but pulled off the bandages and banged the raw wound

Man in Nullah, c. 1940

obsessively on the edge of his bed. For a couple of days in June he worked on a basket, but soon gave it up. When offered clay, in the hope that he would try to model something, he tried to eat it, and when someone gave him a pencil, to see whether he would draw, he broke it in two and swallowed it, pointing silently, a couple of days later, to his painful, distended abdomen. When doctors looked at an X ray, they spotted a piece five inches long with the words

JOHNS HOPKINS CLINIC. It was surgically removed. There were two distinct, equally discouraging groups of symptoms to report to Annette and Sissy: on the one hand, slowness, self-derogation, mood swings, and suicidal thoughts, and on the other, ideas of reference, feelings of persecution, and hallucinations.

Since the onset of his illness, Sissy had felt that her presence only worsened Bob's condition, and it was not until July, almost four months after he entered Phipps, that she came to Baltimore to see him and to elaborate on the information she had provided by letter and telephone. The day before her visit, he had been especially violent—had tried to choke one of the nurses—and Sissy's heart was pounding when she entered his room. With an attendant standing guard, Bob sat glumly through her visit, opening his mouth only to say goodbye. Moments later, in the doctor's office, he snatched a penholder from the desk, setting the doctor's nerves on edge, and while a nurse was taking his temperature the next morning, he grabbed the thermometer, bit off a piece, and swallowed. Sissy had come and gone without him noticing that she was four months pregnant.

By the end of summer, there were hopeful signs. He was asking more often for cold packs, explaining that "when tense he like[d] to feel helpless and protected." Later in his life he wrote that no one can explain the "magic" of water, that man sways back and forth from one extreme to another, from heat to cold, from hunger to satisfaction, like a "tormented worm," and that of all the elements, water alone seems to make the "pendulum" stop and time stand still. Another sign of improvement was that he had begun to trust one of the doctors, Alexander Leighton, and, for the first time, was able to joke about his condition and answer questions a bit more fully and politely. He had his cordial moments and his gallows humor. When he snatched another thermometer, and swallowed one and a half inches of the mercury part, he smiled and told the nurse she ought to use one of the large *bath* thermometers; he guessed that he had "a weakness for thermometers." Afterward, Leighton noted, "he was very pleasant and swallowed five slices of bread, three mashed potatoes and a large wad of non-absorbent cotton." In August, he dabbled in finger paints, and sang "Sweet Adeline" in his room with the attendants ("the first time he has said more than a word or two"), and by the first week in September he was working with pastels. But a day later he tried to strike Sissy and took another swing at an attendant. When a doctor asked him to explain what started it, he replied, "You did! Every damned one of you, but you wouldn't admit it," and added, smiling, that there was "too much egg-o in the cosmos."

By late September—his fifth month at Phipps—he was able to dress himself without prodding for the first time. When Sissy and Annette came for his thirty-fourth birthday, bringing a cake and ice cream, he dashed his mother's plate from her hand, and threw his own to the floor. "Spontaneous combustion," he mumbled later.

It was clear to the doctors by now that Annette was an "exciting factor." She was "very dynamic and emotional," Leighton noted. "[She] tells me she knows just how he feels [and] wants us to uplift him with fine books—Eastern philosophy and Thoreau. Thinks—and here with some justification—one of his big troubles is the other patients. I fear she is not a good influence. She has come to Baltimore to stay, and I look for storms ahead." When a doctor asked Bob how he had liked the visit from his mother, he answered that he *hadn't*, "not very much," and Leighton "couldn't help but correlate his mother's interest in Eastern philosophy with Mr. Anderson's interest in Gurdjieff." Annette's visits seemed, almost always, to provoke some sort of outburst. Hours after a brief, pleasant visit on October 10, he became combative again, and tried to bash his head against the floor and walls. After another, he rammed his head through a pane of glass.

When Leighton finally told him that his wife was expecting a baby in December, he showed no reaction, but that night he became violent again, and the next morning, when Annette came for another visit, and an attendant asked him why he was upset, he ran his hand, for the second or third time, through the double pane of glass on the door of his room. Through October, Leighton puzzled over the fluctuations in his behavior. He listened to the radio quietly as DiMaggio, Gehrig, and the Yankees took the Giants in the World Series, sang in a chorus with other patients, and spent quiet moments working carefully at the loom. He looked at books on natural history, and allowed himself to be drawn into conversation about coastal Indians and their boats, Chesapeake Bay log canoes, and his student travels in France and Spain. But not a week went by without some impulsive act of self-harm, and when he responded to the doctors' questions he did so in a quick, parrot-like voice, "the words run together and confused."

Since July, Sissy had been staying in the little apartment rented by Annette, who cared for her day and night during her pregnancy. Despite frequent visits from Ellen and from the Parks, she felt unutterably lonely. One November afternoon she lay alone in bed and stared dreamily out the window at the golden clouds. Pigeons flew by in a flock, and an airplane with sunlight on its wings, and she told herself that at such moments of peace and beauty, she *ought* to be happy, even in her solitude; after all, one could not be entirely alone with a baby kicking inside. She wondered about her "responsibilities" and Bob's. She had struggled at first with fear and with thoughts of ending the pregnancy, but now, with birth only a month or so away, she was no longer afraid. The child was "almost beyond me now, almost a little self." She knew that Bob would have loved to share the details of her pregnancy: "the whole process is so frightfully interesting, so much fun . . . it is a crime to have him miss it."

The baby arrived on December 8, 1937, a healthy girl, a "little dream of beauty," with Bob's eyes and mouth, and she yearned for him to see her. Her hospital room was not very far from his, and as she lay in bed, her head propped on her arm, she could look out the window and see the corner of Phipps. When Leighton told Bob that he had a baby daughter, he answered calmly that he was very glad. A while later, as he sat "quietly doing nothing," an attendant asked what he was thinking about.

"A name for the baby," he answered. "Mary Anne."

Over the next few days he began working on a basket for her, and when Sissy heard what he was doing she climbed out of bed and cried, longing for him to see what their love had wrought: she felt certain that he would be cured just by looking at his daughter. At times she grew weepy and homesick, but the hospital stay was a long one, and there were other moments when she felt blissfully spoiled, delighted with the cleanliness of the place, amused by the conversations of patients in other cubicles, with "letters galore," an enjoyable daily routine, excellent food, and visits from the Parks, from Ellen, and from a Grinstead cousin. It was more luxury and more relaxation than she had known in years, a far cry from bumpy, rustic Shearwater. Annette brought her letters from Pat, reading them over the telephone when she couldn't visit, and Leighton or one of the nurses—a Miss Rochmel—dropped in every few days with news of Bob.

Toward the end of December, the news took an unexpected turn for the worse. Annette had bought him a new grey suit and shoes for Christmas (he had gained more than fifty pounds), and though he took an interest in his gifts, and gave a few of his own, on December 26, after more than seven months of treatment, he suddenly became delirious, asking one of the nurses if she were his mother, dropping to his knees and begging her in tears: "Help me! I haven't lived right. When I was a kid, I played marbles for keeps. Did you ever kill anyone? I did. He was running around with my wife and I caught them. I hit him on the head with a mallet. They were playing croquet and they had done something they shouldn't have done. I was arrested and sent to Tulah, a jail, and my mother brought me out. His name was James Jones."

Alarmed by his delirium and by new outbursts of self-destructive behavior, Bob's doctors suggested convulsive therapy with Metrazol, a radical treatment which had been in use at Phipps for only a few months. At the beginning of January 1938, Leighton and Norman Cameron went to Sissy with articles about the treatment and an authorization form. "Of course, my first reaction is no," she wrote in her diary. "But I've got to have all the facts, and I've got to think it out. Oh, I feel as if I just plain couldn't have it done to him, couldn't. I can't believe it's necessary. I suppose I've never really believed in his illness. It's been a sort of interlude, like waiting for the baby. And now? Now it ought to be over too. I guess I had counted on that: the two being over together."

The "facts" about Metrazol were rather sketchy. Little was known of how it functioned, but it had been known to arrest, or send into remission, even the most severe forms of mental illness. A few years earlier, before the introduction of electroshock, the Hungarian physician Laszlo von Meduna had noticed the apparent incompatibility of schizophrenia with the convulsive stage of epilepsy. He reasoned that if epileptic convulsions could be induced artificially in schizophrenics, they might be shocked into improvement. Different agents were injected into patients' muscles or veins in order to bring about the convulsions. Two of the most common were Cardiazol and Metrazol (pentylenetetrazol). Within two or three seconds after the injection, patients went into convulsions severe enough to cause occasional spinal fractures, head injuries, and dislocated joints, and underwent a sort of near-death experience, passing through an "aura" that seemed to threaten them with "annihilation." For many, the experience was harrowing, a cataclysm or "catastrophe in the depth of the organism," a "falling into death," followed by rebirth and an odd sort of gratitude and euphoria. The psychology of the process was still a matter of speculation: the near-death experience of the convulsions and coma were thought to free the patient's psychic energy and renew his interest in life. As to the physiology of it all, no one really knew. Doctors compared the process to a "blowing asunder" of normal thought patterns, a "deep explosion in the brain," which, in the best of cases, brought relief to those treated and made them more accessible to their physicians. For Meyer there was something deeply troubling about the whole process, something that ran entirely contrary to his patient, holistic way of doing things. It was extremely hazardous, almost "brutal," he said, but he had to admit that it did, somehow, enable the patient "to start working on a much better basis." He wished, in Bob's case, that something else could be done: "You can throw anybody into a convulsion, you can throw anybody into a coma, but to get where we may be able to do it so that it is not a terrifying experience when it does not go perfectly well, will be a great achievement in psychiatry."

For Sissy, it was an agonizing decision, but by January 3, 1938, two days before her twenty-seventh birthday, she had discussed the matter with Annette, Ellen, and Leighton and Cameron, and both she and Annette signed the papers and stepped bravely into the unknown. Bob had told a nurse that he "wished they would find something to help him," and submitted "with the best possible spirit." Four days later, Sissy left for Ocean Springs, leaving Annette in Baltimore. The treatment would take a while to work, her stay in Baltimore was becoming expensive, and by now, despite the wonder of the new baby—a combination of possessing and feeling possessed—she was feeling preternaturally tired, with bleeding that never seemed to stop, constant back pains, and a sort of general "weepiness." It was time to go home, to check on her father, and be with Pat.

In January and February, Bob was given twenty-five injections, which produced a total of eighteen convulsions. On the whole his reaction had been a good one, though he roared with laughter when asked if he were optimistic. After the first few treatments, he had started to talk almost spontaneously, and was allowed to work in clay again. He drew "a very good picture of a horse with a man on it, very nicely done," and scribbled a note to Annette, "just to let you know that my condition is very much improved and I hope to start home soon." His impatience when one of the sessions was postponed prompted one of the doctors to wonder, with a smile, whether the treatments had indulged "his peculiar attitude toward self-inflicted pain." Before long, the entire staff had noticed an improvement in his spontaneity and affective relations. He had begun to feel especially fond of one of the female nurses, the Miss Rochmel who had visited Sissy and who now accompanied him after his treatments, and took him each day to the music room to give him piano lessons. He was "playing on the piano," he told a doctor, "or rather playing at it." In February and March he began to read again—not

Thoreau or Eastern philosophy, as Annette had suggested—but books on symphonies, *Nine Old Men*, about the Supreme Court, and books on natural history; and he was now able to talk about his readings with the doctors. He went back to working at the loom, modeled a "Brunhilda" in plasticine, and did some drawings (now lost): a man on a horse and "two excellent black and white pictures of a daffodil and of other flowers" which he presented to his nurses. On February 1, 1938, he asked for pen and paper and scrawled a note to Annette. In the throes of his illness, he had imagined that Sissy was about to divorce him.

> *Dear Mother:*
>   *Your flowers came this morning and were greatly appreciated. The whole room is more cheerful with them. I'm taking piano lessons hard; there is a music room with a piano in the other part of the house.*
>   *Please give my love to Sissy and my daughter and tell her that whatever she has done is all right with me.*
>   *That isn't the way I meant it—of course, if she wants a divorce, I don't, but I will agree to anything she wants.*
>   *Love from*
>   *Bob*

At Shearwater, Sissy had moved into the Front House with Peter, Pat, and the children. That summer, while she had been in Baltimore, there had been a new burst of activity on the place, this one from Mac, the youngest and last of the three brothers to heed Annette's—and William Morris's—advice: that "a man should be able to make all that he needs: his home and his furniture, his tools and utensils. . . ." He was engaged now, to a dark-haired, lively beauty from Arkansas, Jacqueline House, and was building a place for the two of them: a handmade shelter against family storms. That summer he had read a magazine article about the advantages of houses made of rammed earth; they were amazingly sturdy, cool in summer—up to ten degrees cooler than outside—and could be built for as little as five hundred dollars. The Department of Agriculture had published building instructions, and he sent away for them. Meanwhile, he fell to work, bringing in truckloads of earth from the highway department, lumber for the frames, and a bricklayer from Biloxi who helped him build a fireplace similar to the tiled one in the Cottage. With the help of two of the carpenters who had built the showroom, he laid a concrete foundation and topped it with wooden forms. Earth, strained clean of vegetable matter, was shoveled into the forms and tightly packed with an iron tamper in six-inch layers until it rang like stone. After each layer, the forms were unbolted and moved upward. When the walls reached the right height, he let them dry for two weeks and coated them with linseed oil and white paint. He married Jackie in Little Rock in September 1937, and by the time they returned from their honeymoon in Louisiana, the entire house— kitchen, bathroom, screened-in porch, and a large living area—was ready for its tin roof. He built furniture—cabinets and chairs, a long window seat, and a desk. The day the plans finally arrived from the Department of Agriculture, he was finishing up the porch.

For Sissy it was a reminder of the work Bob had done a year earlier on the Cottage. Long ago, she had written him that their house would be "the *ourest* house in the world." But the place seemed so much *his* now—desolate, empty, run-down in the winter sunlight—that she could not bear to live in it with-out him. Even going through the door gave her "an almost physical pain." In February, she gathered the strength to open doors and windows and air it out. As spring approached, Shearwater seemed "bliss in the sun, so peaceful and so divinely quiet," but there was nothing more troubling than the natural beauty she could not share with him. Looking at the Cherokee rose around the door "did something to [her] insides." There was little real sharing, either, with the rest of the family. Peter and her "wonderful old Pat" seemed totally absorbed by the children and the Pottery, buzzing now with people who wanted to sell figurines or represent Shearwater elsewhere in the country— one of them, she wrote Bob excitedly, was the wife of Jimmy Walker, the mayor of New York. Peter's copper-red glazes, the white-enameled football players, and some carved vases by Mac, who had developed into an outstand-ing decorator, were the order of the day. Mac was planning his future with Jackie, trying to interest commercial firms in his textile designs, and Mr. Grin-stead was still hearing voices, in the depths of his depression, although he brightened up whenever he saw Mary. Annette was doing battle with the pub-lic school PTA over the color of a new curtain to hang in the auditorium beside Bob's murals; the old one, with the advertisement for sand and gravel, had dropped suddenly to the floor, nearly killing three children. Despite the bustle, the whole family seemed lonely. All of them needed love Sissy felt too weak to give—she was overwhelmed with a sense of "futility," too depressed and too dependent to help them or get anything done or live "effectively." She told herself that much of her energy, her "ideas and vigor" had come from

Bob, and that she would not recover them until they were back together. As she drifted from one day to another and winter turned into spring, she had the sense that she was still in "hibernation," but needed that feeling of inertia and flatness to go on living; as she nursed Mary each night, or at odd moments during the day, she remembered a verse of Isaiah: "In returning and rest shall ye be saved: in quietness and in confidence shall be your strength." But something in her rebelled against that resignation: "In order to hide and quiet fears and sorrows, it seems to be necessary to squash everything flat, and this should not be so. It would almost be better to feel every minute than to lose one's whole self like this. Ordinarily, daily living is so easy, unless one wants to make an 'effort.' Oh, God, how I wish sometimes that I were only a little child."

Despite her weariness, she longed to write. Perhaps, she thought, it was simply a matter of discipline, of doing it every day. It was poetry that attracted her. Ideas, verses would come to her and linger for days; it was "funny how sometimes line after line will come, some half-formal, and ideas that one recognizes as the thing and that vanish without leaving anything but a memory that has lost the savor and can't be whipped into shape." What writing she did—in prose and verse—went into her journals, or into her letters to Bob. In April 1938, a year after his breakdown, she sat under the hickory tree beside the Barn, and tried to reassure him that all the things they had planted together were flourishing: the cucumber trees they had brought from Vancleave, the Philippine lilies in the side yard, a jack-in-the-pulpit, the Cherokee roses, and a beautiful blue morning glory she had planted by herself.

In Baltimore, Bob's Metrazol treatments had come to an end, and Meyer and his staff were pleased with his progress. He had been to the Walters Gallery in Baltimore, had written Sissy about the pottery he had seen there—some of it "put even the Shearwater in the shade. . . . Some of the glazes and decorations and shapes were marvelous." He was eating and exercising with the other patients, taking pottery classes and was eager to throw on the wheel. Above all, he had developed some affection for one of the attendants, a Mr. Hitchcock, whom he treated with courtesy and respect, a friendship that seemed to help him more than his contact with the medical staff. But even then, when things were going well, there were unaccountable relapses and new attempts at self-mutilation, including an attempt to gouge out one of his eyes, an especially horrifying act for a painter. He had yet to say a single word about his feelings, though one day, exhausted after a struggle with attendants, he declared, "I'm crazy as hell. As far as I'm concerned, I'll always be crazy as hell." In mid-April 1938, Dr. Louis Sharp confessed his frustration at a staff meeting:

> Although Mr. Anderson has been with us a year now, I do not believe we are nearer a diagnosis, nor do we know what was the cause for his marked improvement, except that life must have appeared much pleasanter when metrazol was stopped. . . .There is very little in [our] dead words of any sense at all of the real dramatic and terrible qualities of this man's psychosis, and the trouble he has been for the staff. It goes unchallenged, I think, to say that this man is certainly the most difficult case we have had in years, from the practical handling standpoint. . . .We know little more now then we did a year ago. Our chief efforts have been directed at the preservation of the patient.

Rennie concurred. It was remarkable how little anyone knew of "what is going on inside the man," and Meyer added, at another meeting in May, that the case had put the clinic itself on trial, had tested "to some extent what we stand for." Bob had been "the distress of the whole ward [and] I suppose it would have been a great temptation to have him go to another hospital, and a great relief for our personnel. [But] I do not want this place to be just a place for easy snaps."

One possible "way in" to Bob's mind was his drawing. For a time that spring he made at least two pencil sketches a day, refusing to be interrupted for any reason: a turkey admired by Meyer, birds, a horse, and numerous portraits of Mr. Hitchcock; a "very accurate enlargement of the two of hearts"; illustrations inspired by a children's book; the tulips, daffodils, and irises sent by Annette and Sissy. On a walk with his attendants, he asked, quite spontaneously, if he could do some outdoor sketching. Thorne had heard him humming and whistling cheerfully as he drew or worked at the loom, and was fascinated by his sketching: "When he draws from imagination, he makes a few sweeping lines first, and then fills in gradually, and then the form of the subject comes out. Composition appears to be more important than anything else." For Muncie, there was nothing particularly revealing about his drawing, "no clear indication of any content coming out unless it is in the repeated use of his male attendant [Hitchcock] as a model, but that seems fairly natural." Lemkau was stuck by certain characteristics of his art: "Most [of the drawings] have a cruel look about them. The faces are all exaggerated in that direction, it seems

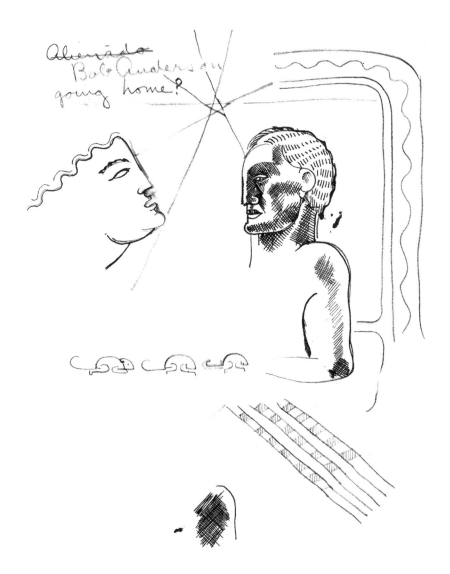

Bob Anderson Going Home, c. 1940

to me: very firm, nothing very pleasant about them. I have one up in my room which is a drawing of a face. You can hardly tell whether it is male or female— I don't know which it is—and it has a pleasant expression, but most of his stuff has no pleasantness about it, even though it is very good."

When interviewed by Henry Mead the following month, Sissy's beloved Ellen told him that for a long time—for the past six or seven years—she had noticed a change in Bob's art. His "earlier things" had seemed softer and more sympathetic. "She cites as an example a portrait of a fisherman which the patient did as a wedding present for his sister-in-law [Pat]. This does not have the harder characters which the patient's later work has. She likewise noted the 'cruelty of the eyes' which his later work has shown, and which has been noted here [at Phipps]. She is unable to state exactly at what time such a change took place, although she does feel that there has been a change."

It was July 1938, after they had spent spring and early summer at Shearwater, before Sissy and Mary were able to move back to Baltimore. Ellen had found her a vacant room—one of the doctors was on vacation—and, a little later, an apartment of her own. Ellen looked happier than she ever had, and when Sissy saw her "almost-sister" together with Henry Mead, she realized, with a shock, that they were in love. And so, she thought, was Bob. More than once in his brief letters, he had mentioned "Miss Rochmel"—the nurse who had brought her news of Bob, months earlier. She had led him back to music, helped him make a cradle for Mary, and had taken an interest in his rugs and drawings. "She was Russian," Sissy remembered in the 1980s.

> So she told me with a strange accent, a lilting blend with something of the orient in it. She was very beautiful, delicate and dark, lit by some internal fire. The morning after his treatments she would feed him his breakfast over and over until she succeeded in making one stay down. Then she would go with him to an upstairs hall or parlor of some kind where there was a grand piano. She was a truly accomplished pianist and she would play and play for him. "Music hath charms . . ." she told me. My goodness, I was jealous. I knew in my heart that they were in love. I do not even know if they ever knew it themselves, or what kind of love it was, or how far it went. Only a few years ago, I was still dreaming about her in an agony of resentment, an agony of gratitude.

When Leighton told Bob, sometime in August, that his wife and daughter had returned to Baltimore, he said he didn't want to see them, or rather didn't want *them* to see *him* in a place like the clinic. Over the summer, while Sissy was in Ocean Springs, he had done more complicated designs in weaving, and had produced a couple of rugs he felt proud of—a "yellow, green and black 'natural' man" and a design with dogs. Miss Rochmel had sent one of them to Sissy, and he had told Leighton he wanted to make another for Mary. He had already made her a little doll cradle, asking Sissy in a letter to "put it away until she gets older." His spirits were brighter, and one day, as though sensing he had come to the other side of his long ordeal, he happily kissed Mr. Hitchcock, two patients who were playing Ping-Pong, and one of the nurses on the cheek, and offered Hitchcock five dollars to "arrange a meeting with a woman with whom he could have sexual intercourse." Every day at mealtime he appeared at the kitchen door, offering to help serve the food, and several times, when he felt his tension returning, he asked for Metrazol treatments— which the doctors decided not to give him—for relief. At Annette's request, Meyer met with him on September 21 to assess the situation. Bob was silent at first, answering his questions politely, "with a great deal of reserve," but after a while he "developed some frankness" and told him that he resented having been held at Phipps for eighteen months, and that he wanted to go home, even if it meant being taken there by an attendant. He recognized that going home "might start the sickness again," but brushed aside Meyer's suggestion that he talk it over with the doctors or with an Episcopal priest who had been suggested by his mother. He had no realization whatsoever, Meyer wrote, of what had made the treatment unavoidable. But Meyer did not believe in "confronting" his patients: you shouldn't "order" them, he told his staff, you should only make suggestions and give them choices, and Bob seemed already to have taken a decision. The next afternoon, Annette, Bob, and Meyer met calmly in his office, and Bob turned to his mother and told her he was "sick of doctors" and wanted to leave. After she was gone, he took a piece of hospital stationary and wrote in a clear hand the required letter giving three days' notice. He told his doctor that he would stay in Baltimore, with two attendants, and come back to the hospital for treatment whenever it seemed necessary. On September 25, 1938, four days before his thirty-fifth birthday, Annette and an attendant came to get him and drove him to Sissy's apartment, where she was waiting to see him and planning a birthday celebration.

"I want to be with you all the time," she had written that day in her journal. "Sleep with you and cherish you and love you. Can I?"

THANKSGIVING

Two days after he left the hospital, Sissy made him a special birthday dinner and the two of them went off by themselves and talked about what to do. Bob thought it would help him to work outdoors on a ranch or a farm, but decided finally that he could get the same chance to do manual work at home. He would take things step by step. Within days, he picked up the phone, arranged to visit Meyer, and told him in person he had decided to return to Ocean Springs with his wife and mother. "He felt that in case anything happened there was a satisfactory state hospital not very far away, but he felt confident he was in good enough form. He spoke apparently with great ease, somewhat slowly but with perfectly normal modulation of voice, and it was obvious that he had the conviction of his capacity."

Meyer had deep misgivings about letting him go—there were "possible suicidal and homicidal tendencies and the danger of impulsive acts," and his patient had yet to emerge from the "mutism" he used protectively to "hold off the environment," but on October 1, 1938, Bob, Sissy, Annette, and an attendant boarded a train south. Annette had wanted to wait until they could find a private compartment, but her son was eager to be gone, and the little group settled for a semiprivate drawing room, with Bob in the upper berth. Annette told him that he was not to leave her sight, and followed him from car to car whenever he came down from his perch: "We are to be Siamese twins." But she soon realized that he could easily elude her, and she and Sissy let him sit by himself in the men's dressing room or in an unoccupied compartment. Annette held her foot in the bathroom door to prevent him from locking it,

[116]

and hovered about, in an agony of nervousness, when they took over an hour to serve him in the dining car. At night, Sissy and the baby curled up in the lower berth, and Annette sat dozing, with her eyes open, listening in the dark to the movements of her son. While the train was being shifted in Atlanta, he got down to walk about the platform. When they were nearly home, he seemed to want to talk, and Annette and he exchanged a few words about the family and about the new theory that most diseases have a mental cure.

Mac and Peter met the little group at the station and drove them back to Shearwater, where Bob walked about by himself, looking at the showroom, the Cottage, and Mac's new rammed-earth house. Over the next few days, he cut grass and cleared underbrush with an adze. He went off by himself to the studio, swept it out, and spread his drawings on the floor. He set up an easel and laid out his materials for block printing. In the Annex he listened to the World Series—the Yankees were at it again—while Mac fired a kiln load of figurines. Sissy was overcome with relief and gratitude: "Home, all of us! Bliss and heaven, and all the happiness!" She wrote less frequently in her journal and felt as if she would "never need to write in here again. Not in quite the same way, anyway. Blank pages that whisper of contentment when we riffle them." Once again, her thoughts turned to a different sort of writing. Poems? Prose? The fall air and northwest wind were invigorating, and everything she saw seemed to come together into musical harmony. Writing—if only she could keep at it—seemed a way to pull her life back together.

> Yellow butterflies today float upon the wind. Sometimes one thinks, is that a leaf, fresh from some Autumn tree? And then, veering . . . the creature lights upon some last fall flower. It's funny how the world sometimes will be bathed in a sort of poem: each sight, sound, taste smell will lead to a sort of rhythmic line of expression, and the whole will be sort of continuous, running from one thing into another, so that we see connections we have never seen or contemplated before. Now I hear the sound of a train starting up in the distance, and see the waving of yellowed leaves on a redbud tree, and a sort of repeat pattern of shadows on the screen, and it all goes together inarticulately to make the moment through which I am passing . . . that must be why it is so hard to catch it, to say just why we have a certain impression.

Mid-October brought a string of dry, sparkling, windy days of the sort Bob had always loved; even now they made him feel more energetic. Days after his return he did a pencil sketch of Sissy, and sometimes seemed so much *himself* that it was hard to believe he was ill. He brought in loads of wood, fixed the fire at night, and did little chores around the house. He would get up in the night—often around midnight, four o'clock at the latest—take a cold bath and have a sandwich and coffee for breakfast. Then he would draw, or look at books or art magazines, and, when it was light—around five—have a second meal and go to his studio, down a path he had made through the woods, so that he could slip away without being seen by visitors to the Pottery. Sissy wondered what he was working on there; she sometimes saw paint on his hands. He would reappear around eleven-thirty to eat, and then wash the dishes, and return to his studio until five or five-thirty in the evening, waiting for his meal until Sissy had fed Mary. Occasionally he took his daughter's hand in his and smiled. There was little room in his daily routine for Sissy and barely time for his seventy-one-year-old mother, who came to the Cottage every day at suppertime. She had wanted to eat with them every day, and Sissy sometimes prompted Bob to invite her in, but mostly he resisted. As for Sissy, she longed for his affection. "If he would just put his arms around me . . . just a wee hug. . . ." Only weeks after his return, she felt as lonely and helpless as she had when he was away: "I don't see [him] enough, and I don't seem to be able to do anything for him. It gives me such an inadequate feeling, and then it seems a strange thing to say, but I miss him so—he's here so little, and I've been without him so long. I'm starved for him. Not Mary or any substitute, but Bob." From Baltimore, Meyer recommended a "sound policy of non-interference": she should avoid any sort of "pressure that might increase his tension," and give him opportunities, without making demands.

In November she wrote Meyer that he treated her "part of the time, as if I were not present, and the rest of the time as if I were a piece of furniture. It is very rare that he speaks without being spoken to." He took little interest in the Pottery, and one day, after he had helped his mother arrange some flowers in the showroom, he picked up one of his own beautiful decorated pieces, carried it to the fireplace, and let it fall to the floor.

"That's too bad," he said. "I lost control of myself."

Caught up in their own problems, neither Bob nor Sissy—perhaps not even Annette—had any idea of the emotional turmoil that was going on at the Front House. On one of those bright October days, Peter had set out alone on a fishing trip in the *Gypsy* to think about a matter that would give him no peace. Five months earlier, at a time when Bob had relapsed into one of his silent periods at Phipps, glowering at the Easter packages sent by his family, an attractive twenty-four-year-old woman had come to Shearwater to work as an apprentice at the Pottery. Pat had offered to let her live at the Front House and she and the apprentice quickly became fond of one another. Later, on a warm August night when Pat was sitting alone on the lawn, Peter told her that he had "desired" the young woman; that in fact he had gone sailing with her and hadn't been able to resist putting his arm around her. When the apprentice left Shearwater, days later, Peter began to drink heavily, reproached Pat for having brought her on to the place, and behaved in such a bizarre, unpredictable manner that Pat wondered whether her husband might not be afflicted with the same psychosis as Bob. As for the "affair," there was no way to know for sure whether it had been a real one or whether Peter had imagined it. Bob's return to Shearwater, in early October, caught them in the midst of this crisis, and when Peter went to the station to bring his brother home, he was "horrified" by how little he had improved. While Peter's troubles grew more acute, Bob seemed to be getting better—or so it appeared to Sissy. Meyer had written her that it was best to leave him alone and avoid any sort of tension, and she was learning to suppress her desire to help him. That fall there were definite signs of progress, beginning with the many small, kind things he did for others. His mother was having problems with her teeth and although he had not said a word to her, he left a huge pumpkin flower one morning on her doorstep. A carpenter had opened the south wall of the Cottage in order to add a little room—about twelve by fourteen feet—to make a nursery for Mary, and, without a word to anyone, he did all of the painting by himself, and "made a very professional job of it." There were "no upsets at all," Sissy reported to Meyer.

> In every way, except seeing other people, there has been improvement. Perhaps the best thing has been his continued painting and drawing. He is consuming pencils, paper and paints at a great rate, and I have seen some of his sketches of the baby. She has begun to pose for him in the evenings, and the hasty things he has done are like his old sure work, that is, as far as I could see surreptitiously. He still never speaks to me—rarely answers, except for a nod. . . . Every now and then he does other little jobs around the house that need doing, never saying anything. He gets large quantities of wood and sees that the fire is supplied on cold days. He still washes all the dishes, and all his own clothes for me. He sleeps very much better at night. Usually goes to bed about 8:30 and gets up about 4:30. He is eating well and even regulating his own diet. I was so afraid he wouldn't eat that I had cakes and pies in the ice box to tempt him, but he very sensibly eats sandwiches and cereals and

apples. He reads aloud almost every evening, but spends the most of his time drawing or painting. Lately, I am sure he has been painting flowers. Sometimes he looks so happy, as though his work were going well. I told him that the wife of our retired minister had been to see us and had expressed a desire for a bracket to hang plants on the wall. He made ours and the next Sunday morning he brought me one for her, always without a word. You see he is thinking of other people, but his not seeing anyone worries me. The only time he has been in the least upset was when his brothers came back from a duck hunt, and gave us a duck. He ate a little, but took the rest out and threw it away. Duck hunts have meant a great deal to all of them since they were little boys, so I was a little worried . . .

From the time they were old enough to accompany their father on the *Wanda* into the Lousiana marshes, duck hunting had been a fall ritual for all three brothers. This year, Bob wanted none of it, and for Peter the trip had been harrowing. He had gone out with Mac and a seventeen-year-old boy from the neighborhood, towing canoes behind the *Gypsy*. Hidden in the reeds, he had shot with his usual skill, but Mac noticed uneasily that his brother had shot at ducks other than the pintail and mallard and teal they had hunted for in the past. That night, on the way back, the *Gypsy* crossed the beam of a searchlight from another boat and Peter became terrified that people were following him and that he was going to die. Mac tried to slap him to his senses, but when the *Gypsy* reached the dock Peter left the ducks behind, ran inside, and fell trembling into Pat's arms.

"This place is not glad," Sissy wrote on November 22, 1938. "Instead, it's just plain mixed, muddled and depressed." And the next day: "Peter is down in the depths. God bless him and lift him up." On Thanksgiving morning, at the Barn, Annette asked Peter to bring her wood. When he came back, moments later, his hand was dripping with blood. He had tried to sever his left forefinger, thinking—he said later—that the pain might shock him out of his agony. Pat bandaged the finger, and she and Mac drove him to the Veterans Home in Gulfport, where a nervous doctor interviewed him for a few brief minutes. Pat was shocked by what he told her: "Lady, I'm sure you want the truth. It is *dementia praecox*."

A day later, Mac, Pat, and Frank Schmidt—the family doctor—drove him, heavily sedated, to the Mississippi State Hospital at Whitfield, but Pat and Mac took one look at the place and at the crude-looking fellow who was to give Peter his admissions interview, and decided, without exchanging a word, that they couldn't leave him there. Whatever the expense, they would take him to Phipps. Back at Shearwater, matters grew still worse. Nothing, not even morphine, seemed capable of sedating him, and he made two attempts—one with a loaded gun and one with a razor—on his life.

In the early hours of December 1, 1938, while Bob worked on a high chair for Mary's birthday, Peter, Pat, Mac, a doctor, and a friend arrived in Baltimore, after a fourteen-hundred-mile trip by train. The admitting physician noted that the patient was drowsy and apathetic and that his mind was filled with thoughts of death. Asked what was troubling him, Peter said that he had "a seriously damaged conscience," had sinned against his wife, and deserved to die for it. Over the next two months, his self-destructive behavior seemed even fiercer than Bob's. He stabbed himself in the neck and abdomen with spoons and pencils, snatched a thermometer from an attendant and slashed himself with the pieces. When doctors bandaged his bruises, he ate the bandages. He swallowed plaster, potter's clay, and plasticine, tried, as his brother had, to drown himself in the continuous bath, and dashed his head in despair against the walls. By the end of the month he was confined to a room "denuded of furniture, with window guards and protuberances sawed off the walls, with only a floor mattress, guarded from the wall by another mattress, constantly attended, and with cardboard plates, cups and spoons." A doctor observed that such close but necessary incarceration must be "intolerable to one accustomed to such almost extravagant freedom." And Meyer, who remembered his experience with Bob as a trying one, told his staff that Peter's case had brought them to "the very center and climax, as it were, of the dramatic in psychiatry." The two cases gave "an exceedingly vivid picture of the destructive impulse at its worst," and Peter's was "quite obviously, one of the most difficult cases for psychiatric treatment."

Silent as ever, Bob made no comment on Peter's absence, and Sissy wondered whether he was even aware of it. Faced with a difficult choice, Annette decided to remain with Bob in Ocean Springs and follow Peter's progress through correspondence with him and the doctors. Did they know what sort of books he was reading? Had he seen a minister? It seemed to her that he had a "spiritual" problem, and that only the spirit could heal him. For the doctors, Annette's "Christian Science"—a belief that had sustained her through the years—was simply another element in a long family history of instability. The more Annette tried to help, the more questions she asked, the more clearly they perceived her as a threat to both of her children. When they had had the chance to talk with Pat, and Peter began to open up to them, it seemed to the doctors that Peter's feelings toward both Annette and Bob were deeply ambivalent, and that Pat felt the same ambivalence herself, at least toward Annette.

"Believe me when I say I am sincerely fond of her, and that she is truly very fine," she told one of the doctors at a tense, angry moment. "But she is *not* rational. . . . She is brilliant, too, very deeply religious, but unable to find a peaceful, comforting faith. A believer in miracles and far be it for *me* not to believe!

"There's never any peace in the place when she's there," she went on, and added that her mother-in-law had once reminded her that "you're only his wife. I've had him for thirty-seven years."

> She's the most disturbing element that ever drew breath. Why even Dr. Meyer described her as a pest. I was a little surprised, but he's absolutely right. There's nothing up to her standard; she's constantly criticizing what anyone does. She criticizes her sons fearfully. She's always urging them and talking of going round and making friends, but she herself has never done it in her life. Peter gets utterly sick and disgusted with her. She always gets her way. She'll burst into tears to get her way; that makes them give [in]. Peter doesn't. As a matter of fact, he's terribly rude to her, treats her like dirt, very often, yet he's fond of her. Oh, they're *all* fond of her. She's a very fine person. But she's a pest—it's the word—she won't leave them alone. She's always nagging at him, telling him he doesn't treat me properly. You can't get away from her. She's always flitting around from one house to another. Peter will say of Bob, "I don't like Bob. I suppose I *should*, we're brothers, but I just don't like him."

A young Oxford-educated psychiatrist, Maurice Aubrey Partridge, who had taken a keen interest in Peter's case and was better able than others to get him to talk about his problems, seized upon her remarks and wrote gloomily that it would be an understatement to say that Annette dominated the family: "she appears rather to have overwhelmed, and she still continues to rule her sons." Partridge showed little, if any, appreciation for Annette's efforts to help her sons find spiritual fulfillment through art. From his perspective, a rather chilly one, she had "ruled the children in their infancy and childhood," "overbore them in their school years," and even "decided their professions." She seemed "unconscious" of her favoritism for Bob—and Peter himself emphatically denied it—but no doubt this helped explain the feelings of intense aggression Peter felt for his brother. From his conversations with Peter he gathered that the two brothers had "fought over everything." Only months ago they were "engaged in angry physical combat over the question of a cigaret": Bob had angrily refused to interrupt his painting to give him one. As for Peter's marriage, it had been reasonably happy, though Pat had such an overwhelmingly strong personality, "she was such a leader, so lively" that Peter sometimes felt inadequate.

The medical staff pondered what to do. Sleep therapy, administered with sodium amytal, brought about dangerously low blood pressure and was soon abandoned. The Metrazol treatments that had helped Bob brought Peter occasional relief, but, unlike his brother, he hated them. They were preceded by anxiety attacks, and followed, almost immediately, by attempts at suicide or self-mutilation; after one of them, attendants took forty-five minutes to wrestle him into a pack. Shock treatment with insulin seemed to work better, giving him up to five hours of peaceful daily activity. But clearly, the prognosis was poor, worse even than for Bob, although Peter spoke more readily of his troubles.

At Shearwater, Sissy did her best to cope both with Mary and with the never-ending correspondence at the Pottery, and vowed not to burden Pat or Annette with her worries over Bob; there was already too much strain on everybody. Meyer had always been troubled about the two brothers marrying two sisters: it was a "sin against amphimixis," he thought, a symptom of their "lack of outgoingness into the world." But, however reluctant they were to add to each other's strain, the two sisters had become closer than ever. They shared their daily tribulations, compared their husbands' characters, symptoms, and treatments, coped in different ways with their mother-in-law, and gathered information that might prove useful to the doctors. As always, it was Pat who took the lead. One day that winter, when Peter had been at Phipps for over two months, and Pat had returned to Shearwater, she wrote Partridge that she had gone into New Orleans and had learned much that might prove relevant: information that her mother-in-law might already have given privately to Bob's doctors, but which she had concealed from the rest of the family. She had been "in complete ignorance," she told Partridge, of much of her husband's—and Bob's—family history, but would try not to let it disturb her. In New Orleans, friends and relatives had told her that when her engagement to Peter was announced, members of Annette's family had approached a friend of her mother and asked whether "the Grinsteads knew of the peculiarities of *both* sides of the family" into which Pat was marrying. Not only had Annette's sister, Dellie, been sent away to an asylum in Philadelphia, but her mother, Delphine Blanc, was also "very strange"; a cousin of Annette— another Blanc—was now in an asylum; and Annette's brother, James, was delightful but "unstable": before his father died, he had given Jimmy eighty thousand dollars with the understanding that he would get back together with his estranged wife. Instead, he gambled it away at the track. As for Walter's family, "his mother came from decidedly queer stock and died in an institution in New Orleans. She was violent at times and had a dreadful fear of not being clean." The doctors knew already about Walter's depression and his "terrific unreasoning fears" about his health. She was mentioning all this now, she said, because she had the feeling that all of these unsubstantiated rumors of mental illness had floated about Bob and Peter when they were growing up in New Orleans, and may have added greatly to their troubles.

For Sissy, too, these were troubling, though not unsuspected, revelations. Before she and Bob had married, she had dreamt of being taken care of, and of caring for a family in all of the ordinary ways. Often, now, she resented the role that life had handed her. Pat seemed to have done much better as a caregiver. There was a brief period, in December, when Peter seemed to be emerging from his psychosis and Sissy reproached herself for not having taken Bob to the hospital herself and not having stayed with him through his illness: "Why couldn't I have been like Pat? I am convinced that she has done it, and it's all my fault that Bob didn't come out in the same way." One day she wrote ironically about her own responsibilities and about love and care that had gone to waste.

> I should have lived one hundred years ago
> or more—at least when women knew their duty
> and in that simple walk of life
> where knowing equaled doing,
> I would have made so excellent a wife.
> A baby always at the breast
> and all my soul wrapped up
> in feeding my beloved all the ways
> that women can feed man to his delight—
> with food, with love, with flattering.
> I would have made so excellent a wife.

But the past—at least in her own family—seemed no less painful than the present. Going through some papers, she came upon some letters her mother had written to her during Billie Grinstead's hospitalization in Baltimore. "I could weep, now, with her pain and my own," Sissy wrote. "Why is it always the men?" Why was it always the men who made women suffer?

Toward the end of January 1939, at a time when the news of Peter had grown worse, and Bob had been home for more than three months, Sissy wrote Meyer again and told him he had made some "pretty big strides in the right direction." After some initial hesitation, he had gone to a movie, and he had made a "tremendous effort" to say hello to Sissy's uncle Ted, who was visiting from Chicago, coming into the room, shaking his hand, and bolting back to his studio, without saying a word.

There is to be a big Pageant here on the Coast later in the Spring, and we have been talking about a poster to advertise the Pottery. His mother was trying to do one which she brought to show him. He said, "Do you want me to do it?" Of course, we said, "yes," and day before yesterday he came in with the most perfect one, which he had done in two days' steady work. He never even comes in to dinner when he is working hard. The poster is done in oils on a big piece of plywood, painted a beautiful gray. The colors are beautiful. I will try to enclose a little sketch of it, as it might interest you. We are pretty sure it represents the three brothers at work in the pottery. Aside from the failure to talk at all, all this seems pretty normal, doesn't it?

Now, on the other hand, there are still things that worry me, and new ones. I told you that he never came near me. About a month ago, he was looking very sad, and every night he would get up as soon as I came to bed [on the porch of the Cottage], and go inside to sleep on the floor. One night, I had to get up with the baby, and when I passed him he suddenly reached out and grabbed me. I could not help feeling that he really loved me as well as just wanting me, and I think I showed him that I was terribly pleased. Anyway, we stayed inside [the Cottage] together and when I asked him if he were happy, he said "No." A few nights later he came to me himself, and said that he was happy afterwards. It seemed to me that that started him off on the up-grade. Now things have not gone altogether smoothly. I suppose I am not a very articulate person. It is hard for me to tell him in words what I feel. The next few times that he came to me it seemed to me that his lovemaking was not very normal, but I tried to talk to him. I had the feeling that if we were to live together as husband and wife we ought to have some sort of understanding. The result of that was he thrust his foot into the fire, pushing it into the red hot coals. I gave him stuff to put on it, and he used it. He has done it twice before, and also burnt his hand. He never gives any reason. The question of children comes up, and I am making as sure as

Treehouse, c. 1940

possible that we have no more for the present, but that may be just what he wants. How am I to know if I can't talk to him without having him hurt himself? I am trying just to leave him alone . . . but am I doing it too much?

He has picked out the tallest pine tree on the place and has nailed cross pieces up it to a height of a hundred feet or more. Up there, he is making a platform or treehouse. He has always, before his illness, wanted a treehouse, and been most interested in what he describes as levitation. It has something to do with height, and he used to say that he attained it once when he was nearly drowned. He could get close to it by listening to Bach's music, particularly the *B Minor Mass*. Also a slight degree of drunkenness. It's something like flying, as far as I can make out. Perhaps that is what he is after in the tree. I think he is after some sort of religious experience, even if he doesn't call it by that name. I suppose he has to find it for himself, but I wish someone could help.

He asked for the [phonograph], and as soon as I got it for him he played the little Bach record "Jesu, Joy of Man's Desiring." When his father died, the playing of that record made him cry. Does that belong to some experience of his, or am I just letting *my* imagination run? Since then, he has played it twice, and last night, we listened to a Gilbert and Sullivan program.

He reads aloud now and then, but still abuses his eyes [as he did in the hospital]. His mother brought a book called *The Simple Life*, by Charles Wagner, but he chose for himself last time *The Crock of Gold,* by James Stephens.

He sleeps much better now, since I moved both myself and the baby inside. Usually all night, from eight-thirty to five or six. He is eating fairly well, and losing weight. He gets his own breakfast. A half a sandwich, a piece of pie or some cookies, coffee with milk and sugar. Then, he usually skips dinner. He may take a sandwich and apple with him. For supper he eats a tomato, half a sandwich, and a glass of milk and some dessert. I suppose he has enough. I don't want him to get too thin. He only sees the baby for a minute before she goes to bed. He usually shakes her hand and says good night. The things he made for Christmas are fascinating: a wonderfully constructed chest full of animals made of wood. The horses are fitted together, eight pieces. The others are similar. There are birds, bulls, cats, and some I have never been able to do. He won't show me. He made an angel, too, and brought in a Christmas tree planted in a pot.

My sister told you, I think, about the carved cedar pelican he gave to her little boy [Michael]. He has also given him his precious set of Audubon books. I try to tell him things that seem to make life worthwhile after all, and I happened to tell him how Michael, when he first went to school, came home without a coat. When questioned, he said he had another, and a friend of his had none, so he had given it to him. Bob liked that, and I think that's why he gives him things.

I hope Peter soon will be able to help you with himself, and perhaps with Bob too: at least he talks. We have not had such good news lately, but all our trust is in you, and we hope and hope. My sister and I both think there ought to be some sort of clinic for poor wives. Somebody ought to teach us something. I feel so terribly inadequate.

Thank you, Dr. Meyer, for all your patience with me. I shall be anxious to learn if you do not agree with me that we should be encouraged.

It was a hopeful moment when she wrote that letter, despite all that troubled her about his behavior, and there were additional signs, in the days ahead, that he was coming out of his solitude. Though he barely spoke a word to anyone, he was carving a series of birds from cedar. He presented one of them to one of Michael's playmates and nailed another—beautifully cut from plywood—to the door of Mary's room. He also carved one with a bird feeder on its head, and began making a garden under Mary's window in the Cottage, planting it with violets and other wildflowers. He had made his way up the tree—fours steps higher each day—finished the narrow platform, and perched there like an eagle, keeping an eye on the Cottage and showroom and gazing out over the water.

"I'm going to heaven," he told his mother, and asked Sissy whether she would accompany him.

"I'm terribly afraid I won't be able to," she wrote Meyer; she had always felt shaky in high places, and "it must be two hundred feet up and the cross-pieces are nailed to the tree-trunk far apart." She knew it was an awesome accomplishment for a single person without help from anyone. Somehow she found the courage to join him. Pat, too, was relieved by his improvement, and wrote Partridge that he looked "pretty well—definitely not normal, or whatever we ever approach of that state." One night, when she had been calling seven-year-old Michael to dinner, Bob heard her booming voice and bounded out of the woods to tell her he hadn't seen him. Later, when Michael turned up in the Cottage, Bob spoke "a super-long sentence": "Young man, your mother has been calling you for a long time."

By the beginning of February 1940, however, after he had been home for four months, Sissy acknowledged that Pat was right—the "slight ups do NOT make up for the frequent downs" and his behavior was placing an unbearable strain on both of them. Pat was standing in the showroom one afternoon, surrounded by customers, when he entered, pale and distraught, and fell to his knees before her.

"Hello, Bob," she said.

"Oh, my God . . . ," he began.

"I think that is enough now, Bob."

He took her hand, rose quickly, and went out, and the "ladies"—the customers—"were very fine about it."

There had also been attempts at self-mutilation, many of which seemed to spring from the desire to "punish" himself after having sex with Sissy.

> Music seems to have a decided effect upon him, and to increase his tenseness beyond his control. Just this noon, I went to call him for dinner, and found him chopping wood for my sister. He came in in about ten minutes went straight to the phonograph and played one of Bach's *Brandenburg Concertos.* The slow movement of the third—to which he danced a perfectly beautiful

Dance No. 1, c. 1940

dance—mostly movements of the arms—ending with a very decided death, falling to the floor, etc. He sat down to dinner, and did not take any of the meat dish. About half way through dinner, he looked at the baby in a very strange manner, half rose from his chair toward her, and, suddenly, picked up the dish of meat and crashed it to the floor, just missing her. He has been digging in the garden all afternoon and seems to have calmed down.

He refused to talk to me, as usual, and I did not press him, feeling that I was in a rather agitated state myself. A few days ago, he played the first *Bran-*

denburg Concerto, and stopped it about half-way through, immediately going into the bathroom to bathe and wash his trousers, although he had just finished his usual evening bath and change of clothes. He continues to be very much upset, whenever he has been with me. Usually burning his feet, hands, or face in the fire. The other night, it was very warm and there was no fire. He picked up a bottle which was marked POISON and drank it down. It contained turpentine, and only made him very sick. He joked about it, saying he could [not] paint without a medium. Then, the other day in a storm he took off all his clothes and ran out to climb up into his tree. The other day, while washing the dishes, he stood for at least three minutes with the point of the carving knife against his throat. He hurt his head in some way. It is bloody and he conceals it from me, leading me to think that it may be self inflicted.

There were things she could not bear to tell Meyer. One day he had taken a blanket and covered Mary's head with it, as though he wanted to suffocate her. On another occasion, he had asked Sissy to bring him some large spikes. When she asked what they were for, he told her, with a smile, that they were to crucify her. "How wonderful," Annette said later, dismissing her son's words as a joke. "It means he's going to build something!" Sissy and Annette went to a hardware store, and when Annette saw the size of the nails her daughter-in-law had bought, she told her they were useless: "Bobby never uses nails that large." A few hours later, he was at work on the treehouse.

Sex sent him into an almost "animal-like frenzy," and, to her horror, he punished himself afterward more and more severely, leaving her with no choice but to send him back to the hospital. Phipps was out of the question. There were no empty beds and, anyway, it would be unthinkable to have the two brothers on the same ward. Meyer recommended Highland Hospital, in Ashville, North Carolina, and wrote to its director, Robert Carroll, though no one could imagine how the family would pay for it.

Once again, Pat took charge, and drove by herself to the Mississippi State Hospital at Whitfield, ten miles east of Jackson, the hospital she and Mac had fled from one night when first seeking treatment for Peter. Now, in the daylight, it seemed less frightening. Situated on three thousand acres, it was the size of a small town, larger than Ocean Springs, with over three thousand patients and nearly five hundred employees, but there was order there, and a certain melancholy beauty. As she drove toward the red-brick Georgian Receiving Building down a two-mile avenue lined by oaks, crepe myrtles, and scarlet roses, she could see, behind the fences, a formal garden with a lake and

Profile, c. 1940

geometric walkways that reminded her vaguely of Versailles. Fields, orchards, and gardens stretched away toward the pine trees in the distance. The hospital grew all of its own food, and it occurred to her that Bob would enjoy working on its farm. "Work is a balm and cure for mental ills," the brochure noted. "Every patient who is physically able should have some type of occupation and recreation." After consulting with the doctors, she drove back to Shearwater, and found, to her disgust, that Annette and Sissy were still undecided about committing him. It took both of them another couple of days to resign themselves to the inevitable. On Saturday, February 25, 1939, almost five months after Bob had returned from Phipps to Shearwater, the three women summoned Frank Schmidt and another family physician—Dr. Welch—to the place, and told Bob as gently as possible that they were taking him to Whitfield. "Which of you is God?" he asked, dropping to his knees. They told him about the hospital, and heard him say that he would go, though he didn't think it necessary. He was fine, he said, "except for a bad case of piles," but he promised to cooperate and begged them not to sedate him. He changed his clothes, and was silent with Sissy and Dr. Schmidt on the long drive down the coast and northward from Gulfport to Jackson. In the Receiving Building, he signed a paper committing himself voluntarily.

On Sunday, Sissy found him "beautifully quiet," neither speaking nor moving. When she returned on Monday to Shearwater, she entered his studio. There was a neat stack of pencil drawings, on typewriter paper, about six inches high. Some were the most beautiful she had ever seen from his hand. "He isn't just gifted or talented," she wrote Meyer. "He really is an artist, a genius. I hope I have not done wrong, or spoiled things by shutting him up again." For a while, she was haunted by the thought of having betrayed him, of having taken him away from work that seemed to show he had started down the path toward recovery. Pat, too, stared at the drawings, and wrote a separate letter to Meyer:

> It was a most difficult decision to make, and seemed so unfair to him. Today we have been looking over a few of the tremendous pile of drawings he has done. They are arranged in sequence since his return here, and are very very fine. I would like to bring them to show you when I come up, as they are speech in drawing to a great extent, many self-portraits of his daily occupations. I can't help believing that there must be a place where he can find expression and give some of his genius to others. I feel very sure that place is not with a family. I would like to found a colony for him. . . . It is a wonderful relief to have him not here, but in one way we feel lost, though why I should, I hardly know.

"ARTIST OR SOMETHING"

"Artist or something," Bob wrote on the admissions form at the Mississippi State Hospital when asked for his occupation. The admitting doctors knew he had done "very notable and unusual work" at Shearwater, but found him negativistic and mute, with a sad, dream-like expression and sluggish cerebration and movements. They noticed that he had cut several crosses on his arm, with a piece of glass or a razor blade, and found "a distinct mark around each arm, looking as though he had been corded [with] a shoestring or necktie for some purpose unknown to us."

By the time she first visited him in the hospital, in March 1939, Sissy found him somewhat better. They walked down to the lake near the Receiving Building, and he took a drink of water—"the only thing he seemed to do impulsively"—and on the way back picked two pansies, one for her and one for his mother, a detail that delighted Sissy: it was as though "he had a share in the hospital and could give us something." He seemed gentle and more companionable than he had been for months, didn't protest about being left there, and told her that, as a matter of fact, he was "not very violent" at the moment, and that what he most wanted was to paint outside. The hospital consented, and Annette hired an attendant to take him out on the lawn twice a day to sketch. He also asked to leave the grounds to see the mural that had gone up, instead of his, in the Jackson courthouse and post office. There is no record of whether Bob ever saw it. But it did occur to Sissy—and she suggested it to the superintendent—that her husband could do a mural for the hospital.

If she was expecting the same sort of reports from Whitfield, a huge state institution, as she and Pat had been receiving from Phipps, she was soon disillusioned. After Bob had been there for a month or so, the superintendent reported that the staff had studied the record from Phipps and could add very little. The diagnosis was "dementia praecox, catatonic type," and the prognosis quite uncertain:

> Catatonic praecox [sic], we find, simulates a type we know as manic depressive type of psychosis. They have excited stages and later stages of moroseness, even mutism, restiveness, impulsiveness, combativeness—all of these go with that type of psychosis. Usually, they do not deteriorate mentally [and] while they appear to take no interest at times, they never miss anything. After they have returned to a normal state of mind where they cerebrate normally and release ideas readily, they can always recall practically everything that occurred during that period of illness. The majority of patients of this type have distinct remissions, remissions of such length of time that they appear to be perfectly well. Some patients never have a recurrence, others have them regularly and do not deteriorate until they do so from age.

As for his "conduct and demeanor," it was "somewhat varied": "There are times when he is quiet, cooperative, has absolutely nothing to say, apparently taking no interest. At other times he is just the opposite, and it looks as though he were coming out of his semi-stuporous condition." He was looking better physically, and had been violent on only one occasion, after a visit from the Episcopal bishop, Theodore Bratton, an old friend and neighbor of the Grinsteads, whose daughter was a patient at the hospital. Bob himself had asked to see the bishop, and all had gone well: he had told him of his desire to return home and get a job. Hours later, however, appearing "mad with the whole world," he jammed his fist through a window, picked up a piece of the glass, and scratched a cross on his forehead. There was a mystery there that no one could quite fathom. Sissy had noted that religion seemed to be "one of the things most confusing and troubling" to her husband. Despite his egotism, there was something "upright, almost saintly" about him, she once said, and doctors both at Phipps and at Pratt had noted how at times, for no apparent reason, he would suddenly kneel and cross himself. Later in her life, Sissy wrote that he had been impressed by the conversion of his beloved Chesterton, and, like Chesterton, felt attracted to Catholicism. But except for his love of form and ceremony he seemed to have little interest in organized religion. Whether his uneasiness with the Episcopal Church was an attempt to distance himself from the world of his mother is impossible to say with certainty.

An uneventful month went by, as though he were gathering strength, and one night when Sissy and Annette were preparing to visit him again, he made his move. He tied together some bedsheets, removed the grating from the window of his room, lowered himself to the ground, and disappeared. The bishop's daughter told Sissy that in the morning she and other patients had gathered around Bob's building, gazing at the walls beneath his third-floor window. On the red bricks was a creation that delighted all but the staff: he had adorned them with drawings of birds—"great birds in flight"—drawn with Ivory soap. He had done his mural after all.

The hospital searched the area, notified the highway patrol, and sent word to Annette, who came for his clothing and sketches, and made the hospital promise they would turn him over to her as soon as he was found. She would return him to the institution, she said, "provided he did not strenuously object." No doubt, she was already considering alternatives.

At Shearwater, Pat was packing her bags for a return to Baltimore. Peter had been at Phipps for four months, but it had been a while since his last self-destructive episode and he had told the doctors that he wanted to return home, now that it was within his power "to be a good husband and a good father." Being a good son and brother would pose a far greater challenge. Absorbed almost totally by Bob, Annette had *not* gone to visit Peter, though she often sent him cheerful news of the Pottery, the children, and the grounds at Shearwater, and asked him to describe the doctors and nurses: "just see if you cannot write about them so that I can see them as you do." That spring, with narcissuses blooming everywhere, she wrote him that she wanted to plant hundreds more: "We want the place to be more and more beautiful and peaceful and alive. You can do your part now, where you are, to make it so. By patience, by loving thoughts of all of us. I wish I could send you peace and joy. I can only send you love. That must help." When they were all back together, she promised, they would "work out problems together." His stay in the hospital was an opportunity for "courage and patience and hope."

Unimpressed by her drumroll of cheerful advice, Dr. Partridge was as convinced as ever of her harmful influence and of the favoritism she had shown for Bob. Patients at Phipps were often shown passages of texts they could "identify" with, and one day Partridge copied some verses from a new play by

Man Holding Head, c. 1940

T. S. Eliot, *The Family Reunion*, and wrote beneath it, in his fine British hand: "Peter Anderson, on Mrs. G. W. Anderson." Every line seemed apropos: "The rule of conduct was simply pleasing mother; / . . . /What was wrong was whatever made her suffer, / And whatever made her happy was what was virtuous— / Though never very happy, I remember. That was why / We all felt like failures, before we had begun." If Peter felt insecure and "unworthy," Partridge told the staff, it was partly because "Mrs. G. W. Anderson, Sr." had made him feel that way during his childhood.

When she reached Baltimore, Pat was pleased by her husband's improvement. His hands and wrists were a bit paler and weaker than she would have liked—they no longer looked like the hands of a potter—but his complexion was ruddy, his eyes had a clearer, more self-confident expression, and he was able to talk about things other than himself: baseball, war news, the Pottery, the family, and his relationship with Pat. There were moments when he seemed to be emerging from a dream. He believed he had been brought to Phipps by Annette, appeared surprised to learn that she hadn't been to see him, and felt sure she had told him he would no longer be welcome at home.

"You're not a little boy any longer," Pat answered. "Now it's just you and me."

In April 1939, when Pat was still in Baltimore, Bob turned up at Shearwater—someone found him fast asleep on the bare springs of his bed in the studio, exhausted by the two-week 180-mile trek from Whitfield. For an entire week he rested, ate, and slept until Annette was able to report that he "looked beautiful" and was "almost ready to go out and meet people." The struggle to get home had been good for him, she thought, though his presence created almost unbearable tension for Sissy, who was sleeping with Mary in an upstairs room at the Front House, leaving a babysitter downstairs to watch over Peter's children. As always, it was his mother who saw him every day, tapping on the door of the Cottage and coming in to read to him in the evenings. He would put away his drawings and work on a hooked rug as she read to him. Annette felt "desperately responsible for everything," knew that Sissy had even less control over him than she did, and wrote to Meyer again, begging for advice. Was there "any possible way of caring for him in Baltimore"? She said she would "go anywhere" to help him.

At Phipps, Partridge was confronted with an unexpected problem. Despite Pat's attempts to calm him, Peter was now obsessed with returning home the way his brother had once done: by working his way down the Mississippi in a canoe. He had always felt "inadequate," Partridge noted, "a feeling which has persisted since the first invidious discriminations made between [him and Bob] in childhood." The canoe trip seemed a way of "getting even with his brother, to reassure himself that what the brother has done he can do himself." Annette's idea of bringing Bob back to Baltimore made the situation still worse, at a time when the hospital was "trying to overcome [Peter's] last doubts and give him every confidence in himself and in the future." Meyer had offered Annette a range of alternatives for Bob: a return to Whitfield; an "exchange" of brothers when Peter was well enough to leave; admission to Highland Hospital in Asheville, North Carolina, or perhaps to the Louisiana

State Hospital (he was not a resident of Lousiana, but given the McConnells' importance in New Orleans, "influence could be brought to bear" to get him in). Despite those suggestions, Partridge wrote, "Mrs. A. Sr. is determined to bring him to Baltimore. We need not concern ourselves with her curious plans, but the net result of them is to be that [Bob] goes to Sheppard Pratt."

Getting him there was no easy matter. By the end of April, he had told Annette he knew he was sick ("My mind is a perfect mess. I can't think") but begged her not to put him back in a hospital: "You can tie me up and take me there, but I will never go willingly." On the first of May, four men forced him into handcuffs, and Frank Schmidt, accustomed, by now, to the routine, gave him a sedative and put him on the train, with two attendants to watch him. Hours into the trip, Annette and the attendants relaxed their vigilance. As the train pulled out of Charlotte, North Carolina, they looked up and he was gone. At the next stop, Annette telephoned back to Charlotte, where police found him walking south down the highway, and held him in jail until the next train. At Sheppard Pratt, on May 4, doctors got their first careful look at Bob and his mother: a "well developed and well nourished male of athletic habitus" with burns on both his feet, and "an elderly, thin, wiry lady who expressed a great deal of concern for her son and showed a distressing tendency to try to manage everything for him." She had called Mr. Hitchcock (who was now caring for Peter) and a second attendant down from Phipps to meet the train, and "quite an argument" erupted in the lobby of the hospital, with Bob insisting he would be better off in a boardinghouse, coming to see the doctors when he needed them, and Annette and the two men urging him to "try it in the hospital." Over the next few days he told the doctors he thought he had an "incurable illness," but did not wish to be incarcerated. Not that he had any criticism of the hospital—it was just that he had undergone treatment for over two years, and did not believe it had brought him any closer to recovery. He said that his chief difficulty was his inability to get along with people—"perhaps it's an inferiority complex"—and admitted to having had delusions, but all that was in the past, and he didn't want to go into details; they could look at the record, if they wanted more information. Annette, too, was tired of explaining: all they had to do was request the records from Phipps. Her son did talk, but only about his escape from Whitfield, his journey home, and his hope to work on a farm—there, at least, his labor would be worth something, and "payment for it would be much more reassuring to him than the opportunity of working on art, with its uncertainty of income." He would give it another try, but he wasn't at all sure his art was "really saleable."

When she had settled Bob at Pratt, Annette visited Peter for the first time in six months. Pat noticed that her husband was "nervous, tense and ill at ease" during his mother's visit, but he got through it without incident. Within days, though, his "doubts began to crowd back in on him again," his behavior became suicidal, and Partridge began to suspect that the visit had precipitated a "regression." He thought his mother "knew all about his indiscretions," though Partridge noted for the record that she did not. She did, however, sense the *moral* dimension of his suffering, and reminded Meyer that she still felt very strongly that what Peter needed was "some affirmative religious thought" and the right sort of books. "There are books that change the current of your thinking," at least when they are "deeply experienced" and read with understanding. On May 8, 1939, believing that their patient had undergone more stress than he could bear—both from Annette's visit and from his own stubborn sense of guilt—doctors decided upon another course of insulin treatments, and a new attempt to get him to recognize his "true feelings toward his mother and brother." Earlier comments—and T. S. Eliot—notwithstanding, "he said merely that he had a high regard for his mother, that she had been a good mother to him, and that he did not feel he had been a very good son to her, though he could not say in what way he had failed. It was put to him that it would be unique if he did at no time entertain any slightly critical feelings toward his mother, but he absolutely denied any such, though he said he had occasionally had rows with her—over *what*, he could not recall. After some general conversation, the topic of his brother was introduced and the patient soon became tense, restless, changing his posture, fidgeting with his hands and, finally burying his head in his hands, he said, 'I don't want to talk about Bob.'"

If Peter didn't, Annette did, phoning Sheppard Pratt for news of Bob and relaying it by letter to Meyer, expressing "deep concern . . . that our stay here will not hurt Peter." There was another, equally urgent matter that she wanted to ask him about. Sissy was pregnant. What should she do? Did he think that Bob's "mental condition at the time would affect the child"? The question struck a deep chord with Meyer, who had written and lectured widely about birth control and "mental hygiene"—a phrase he had invented—and knew that, at that very moment, in Nazi concentration camps, the mentally ill were being slaughtered and their children sterilized or put to death. To Annette he replied that he "would not want to say that there *must* be any inevitable dire result" for the child, but that the interruption of the pregnancy would be justified, "for one does wish for a child freedom from an avoidable cloud of sorrow." As for Peter, he had inferred from something he had said to a nurse "that he feels that he does not rank in your affections with his brother." Annette should return to Ocean Springs, he said, lest there be any "appearance of partiality or difference." Days later, at Shearwater, Sissy noted tersely in her journal: "Mère [Annette] and Pat are home. They have little encouragement to report. We are low, low on finances. Do not know what is going to happen. Life is rather useless." It had now been two years since the onset of Bob's illness. Before returning to Baltimore with his mother, he had told her, very clearly, that he did not want another child—that he feared for its sanity and for Mary's. And yet, unable to control himself, he had done nothing to prevent a pregnancy. Despite those indelible words, despite Meyer's tacit advice and her own depression, fear, and weariness, she had decided to carry the baby to term.

Over the next few months, the doctors treating Bob at Pratt reached a diagnosis of "schizophrenia," but felt quite unable to say whether or not it was chronic or curable. Helping him would be exhausting, one of them said at a staff meeting: anyone who took a real interest "would have his hands quite full over a long period of time." He had given no sign at all that he wanted to talk about his problems, and that made it "pretty hard on the doctor." When he spoke to Pratt doctors, or to Meyer, whom Annette had persuaded to visit him, it was simply to insist that he needed to be outdoors; he said that he knew he was sick, and that hard physical work—perhaps on a farm or on the hospital grounds—would be his salvation. He added cryptically, in his conversation with Meyer, that he "sometimes felt like Napoleon," and Meyer was not sure exactly what he meant, or whether he was describing a delusion. Days after his admission, he began to draw, offering a new opportunity to the staff. "I think he has a chance," a doctor wrote, "if someone were smart enough to be able to interpret what he expresses in his art. I don't think he can verbalize his things." For the most part, "the pictures were not particularly remarkable," though by the middle of May they were "rapidly improving in character." He was doing wallpaper designs, in hopes of selling them and of helping the family through a difficult moment. When a nurse saw him sketching them directly onto the wall of his room, she taped up a large sheet of paper, but he carefully lifted it, went on drawing underneath, and "never defaced the paper." When the staff told him that wallpaper designs would be hard to sell and suggested he learn something more useful in occupational therapy, he simply ignored them. And some of his work seemed significant: "There is one fairly striking drawing showing a hunter shooting a stag which is looking back at the hunter. An angel is descending from heaven to push aside the hunter's gun so as to disturb his aim and another angel is descending as if to help the stag escape. Another picture shows a kneeling figure being blessed by an erect figure dressed in robes. It is impossible to tell whether the erect figure is a man or woman. The kneeling figure is a man. Both figures are without heads."

The drawing of the hunter would have given the staff some insight into his thought had they taken a closer look at the records sent from Phipps. During the onset of his illness, Bob had agonized over all of the living things he had killed, in particular for the great sea turtle slain on Horn Island. And there was a moment, at Phipps, when he stopped eating meat and eggs. Then, a little after his return to Shearwater, and before entering Whitfield, he had surprised Sissy by refusing to eat the duck Mac and Peter had brought back from a hunting trip. It seems clear, in retrospect, that during his long illness he was undergoing a change in the way he saw his own relation to nature. There would be other signs of that change—a rejection of the idea of man as hunter and predator—in the months ahead.

By June, he was drawing less, and told the doctors it was hard to concentrate amid the noisy antics of some of the other patients on South I. One in particular, who called on God to save him for hours on end, drove him to such distraction that he jabbed his hand—as he had done so many times—through a pane of glass, deeply cutting his fingers. Others produced the opposite response. One approached him and "kissed him soundly and repeatedly. Mr. Anderson apparently enjoyed this since he returned the compliment and this morning danced about the ward" with him. The hospital's excellent library provided a quiet refuge, and he spent much time there, watched by the special attendant the hospital had assigned to him, getting out books on epic and voyage, and planning, perhaps, a new voyage of his own. When Annette wrote again to Meyer, she barely mentioned Peter, still under his care, but peppered him with questions about Bob. Before leaving for Ocean Springs she had seen some of the drawings—perhaps the drawing of the hunter—he had done at Pratt. Didn't he think that her son's beautiful work meant an improvement mentally? One of the doctors at Pratt had told her that Bob's

"sickness was entirely apart from his art, that no matter what he did in drawing or painting it would not be a sign of improvement." She wondered
whether Meyer agreed. And whether he might know of a family that could
board Bob with two assistants in or near Baltimore. She was willing to live
nearby, hiding her presence from Peter if that was what the hospital thought
best. And how much money did Meyer think would be needed to give him
"the best possible environment"? By now, the Andersons' resources were
strained to the limit. Annette was getting to the end of the bonds left to her
by Walter, and, with Shearwater's bank balance "in one figure," Pat agonized
over whether to ask for Peter's signature, so that she could sell one of *his*
bonds. Instead, she sold a precious family heirloom—the silver tea set that
had been presented in 1846 to Annette's grandfather, Samuel Jarvis Peters. The
four hundred dollars she received for it would pay for another four months
of treatment for Peter.

By the time Meyer replied to Annette's letter, Bob had taken matters into
his own hands. On June 30, he called the attendant to whom he felt closest
and asked him to accept one of his pencil drawings. It was a farewell present:
the next morning, he asked the attendant to take him to the library, and when
no one was looking, strolled quietly out of the room. He walked calmly
through the kitchen, where a cook asked him what he was doing ("Nothing!"), sauntered to the door, ran down a flight of stairs and cautiously
opened the outside door. The hospital records tell the rest:

> He strolled across the grounds, down toward Charles Street. He passed Mr.
> Crowe (the mechanic) who saw nothing strange in his behavior. Again, Mr.
> Crowe did not know who he was or that he was a patient. About this time the
> attendant who was supposed to be specialling him started rushing frantically
> around the library looking for him and the hunt was on. We sent a good
> many men out who searched mainly between here and the City line. An hour
> after he left, one of the nuns from the Sisters of Mercy at the Corner of Bel-
> lona and Charles . . . asked if we had an escaped patient, saying a young man
> had called at their back door some time before. After an hour's search of
> something over twelve men, we notified the City and County police.

The "special attendant" was summarily dismissed, but Bob was free,
dressed nattily for the occasion in a gray summer coat, blue tie, white shirt,
cream-colored trousers, and white tennis shoes, all of which bore his name.
Word was sent to mental hospitals in the area and to Whitfield, in case he

Man Covering Ears, c. 1940

should turn up among the new admissions: the staff at Pratt warned that he was "rather preoccupied, appeared confused, brusque in his manner, frequently irritable and at times combative. He is much interested in drawing and painting and would undoubtedly soon call attention to himself because of his talents."

At Phipps, doctors told Peter nothing of the escape. The insulin treatments had brought about some improvement, and he was being seen now by a doctor whom he seemed to trust—Theodore Lidz, a twenty-nine-year-old resident from Yale who was studying the familial environments of schizophrenic patients from the South. Pat, too, struck a bond with Lidz, writing him weekly from Ocean Springs and humorously promising him "a folio" on the Andersons. He jumped at the chance, and asked her to send him some of Bob's drawings: "not only is [the Andersons'] an unusual story, but it would be of great value to psychiatry." With Bob's whereabouts and condition unknown, and the family living once again behind locked doors, "in constant terror of his return," Sissy had asked her sister not to leave Ocean Springs. "If only the problem of Walter would solve itself!" Pat wrote Lidz. "[B]ut it is possible for it to be long in the solving, if ever solved. I do worry so over the effect hearing of his brother may have on Peter. Here we have a feeling of apprehension which, most of the time, we disguise pretty well. . . . Do you think that even when Peter is discharged it will be possible to talk over the differences in his and Walter's illness with him, so that he is not disturbed and possibly made to feel that Bob has done something he feels he should have had the courage to do?"

With the family caught up in "continuous apprehension about [Bob] and a pretty continuous struggle for weekly wages," Shearwater seemed "a wretched place for [Peter] to come home to." Sissy tried to calm herself for the sake of her baby, which was due in October, though one night she awoke trembling, with a vision of her husband "crouching and running among the rushes and willows." Only Annette seemed to be praying for his return, promising her daughters-in-law that she would care for him herself, but prodding Sissy to give him another chance. Pat couldn't stand to listen to her. She was determined not to let her own husband come home unless he was well, had vowed to raise her children to be "normal persons," and wanted to set an example for her sister and mother-in-law. A couple of months after her return to Ocean Springs, she had made another agonizing discovery. When her husband had told her a year earlier about his affair with the apprentice, she had not quite believed him, and had wondered whether it was one of his delusions. But one day in August, going through some things in his room, she found incontrovertible proof that he had been telling the truth. It was a profoundly troubling experience, but she told Lidz that she had "not let it bother her, except for a moment." She told him, and later told Peter, that she felt responsible for the situation, for it had been she who had invited the apprentice to Shearwater: "My innocence was stupidity." Peter's long illness had given her "a steady kind of love" she had never known before. She felt closer to him than ever, mindful both of his weakness and of her own, and determined to adjust to his needs and to help him get well. When she returned to Phipps in mid-August, Peter had already been told of Bob's escape, and Lidz had reassured him that Bob's illness was very different from his. Told that his brother's condition was probably incurable, he had hardly reacted. He knew that the family was having trouble making ends meet, and wanted to return home to bring in some money again. Despite her misgivings about his condition, and the uncertainty over Bob, Pat took him back by train to Shearwater. The doctors' final diagnosis, which she was not allowed to see, was a deeply sobering one: "depression in a schizoid personality with symptoms of depression, self-deprecation, ideas of reference, numerous suicide attempts, mutilation, panic, and suspicion." As he got his things together and helped Pat with the packing, he "carefully included all of [her] letters, as if he intended to keep on living."

It had been a long time since the Pottery had produced anything sizeable or beautifully glazed, and that summer, when the business seemed likely to run aground, Sissy had gotten together with some women from town to do hand-blocked fabrics for upholstery and drapery, charging by the yard, at a "reasonable" price. After a couple of nervous half-days, Peter fell to work with a vengeance, going out early to work each morning and showing that he had lost nothing of his old craftsmanship. By late September he has fired his big kiln—a fifteen-hour job. Pat's news to Lidz was mostly good. She felt proud of Peter, of Phipps, and of herself. Nobody at Shearwater knew exactly how to speak or act around him, but that was all right—*she* didn't either. He was "looking splendidly, sleeping perfectly, eating well," playing tennis, and "still a fisherman." Only to her did he confide his anguish over Bob's illness, and all his other problems: he couldn't forgive himself for the previous summer, and doubted she could either. He spent a good deal of time in Bob's studio and rowed over to Deer Island with a pair of bad oars, just as his brother was accustomed to doing. When Pat saw him dipping into the "bee-savings" basket and heard him say he thought "he should go away," she could "feel Bob in every thought."

"Like Bob?" she asked.

"Yes. I think I should do the same things he does."

And then, suddenly, Bob was back. Food had been disappearing from the Front House, and for days Pat had been hearing someone in the woods outside. On the night of October 5, Sissy looked up from her reading and saw him standing silently before her—"very thin, bearded, bowed head, abrupt movements," and as silent as ever. Sissy guessed he must have followed the railroad tracks from Baltimore to Ocean Springs. Pat noticed fish hooks on his coat lapel, and road maps in his pockets. There were drawings done on squares torn from bags or wrapping paper and held together with string—an improvised logbook. He was wearing "all the clothes he started out in, but a pair of shoes gotten somewhere." Even Annette was appalled by his lack of improvement. He went off by himself all day, and prowled around the place at night, keeping to himself, in his studio. Peter went there to cook for him, and tried in vain to get him to talk. When Annette had resigned herself to taking him back to Whitfield, he sailed off by himself, out into the gulf, toward Horn Island. After he had been gone for three days, the Coast Guard picked him up, with instructions to turn him over to police: under *no* circumstances should they return him to Shearwater. But the message was somehow ignored, and when Bob got to the dock he ran away into the woods, with Peter and Mac in pursuit, until they were able to coax him into the Front House. Dr. Schmidt—back again—gave him a hypodermic, and his two brothers returned him to Whitfield. It was an "unbelievable week," Pat wrote Lidz. "I could write on for ten novels!" Sissy had taken refuge at the Barn, afraid to confront her husband. "Once again I must swear to myself that he *will* be well," she wrote in her journal. Days later, on October 26, 1939, their second child was born: William Walter Anderson, a healthy baby boy.

It was obvious, within days of his second commitment to Whitfield, that Bob had no intention of staying. He escaped on October 23, 1939, but was apprehended within minutes, and in early December, while helping clean some mops in the hydrotherapy department, he shoved out a window, and disappeared for several days. "God damn it all to hell!" Sissy wrote in her diary on a cold December day at the Barn, while Billy wailed for food, and Annette puttered helplessly about.

> I am selfish and I don't blame me. I've had all I can stand. That's that. It took
> him 17 days to get back last time. 17 + 11 = 28. He'll be late for Christmas unless
> he hurries. He had no coat, even. Just trousers and shirt. Do I love him still?
> I suppose so, but I am so tired of the constant strain. Sometimes I think I'll
> crack; in fact, I do. But oh dear God, I can't, I *can't* live with Mère [Annette].
> What shall I do? She ruins everything for me immediately, children and all.
> I ruin everything for *her*. I've got to go home. I will go crazy.

Days later, the police picked him up "on a complaint," somewhere between Terry and Crystal Springs, thirty miles south of Jackson, and "immediately recognized [him] as a lunatic." He had slept in the woods and that morning had been "chasing Negro school children," throwing stones at them, hitting one with a sack. His hands and forearms were scratched and swollen by briars and brush, his right eye was "somewhat contused or reddened," and his nose was packed full of tissue paper, a habit he had acquired on the thousand-mile trip from Baltimore to Mississippi, when he slept out of doors and was afraid that bugs would crawl up his nostrils.

Until his escape in December, he had been staying in one of the more pleasant buildings at Whitfield, the Receiving Ward—an area exposed constantly to public view—but after he was brought back by the police, the superintendent spoke of him as "a source of trouble at all times," "quite a care and strain on all of us," and transferred him to Chronic Service, also known as the "Disturbed Ward," where there would be less opening of doors, and much closer supervision. In a note for the record, he added that ten shots of Metrazol had not really brought about any improvement. "We understand he has been in this condition for several years, and we doubt very much if he ever gets well." Annette was aware that his condition had begun to deteriorate—he had burned his hands again, perhaps on a hot pipe or radiator—and felt she had "no choice but to make a change," along the lines of what she had done with her sister, Dellie. Annette felt older than her seventy-two years, and knew that her struggle was far from over. In late December she telephoned Sissy and asked for all of Bob's "painting paraphernalia" and on Christmas Eve got him discharged from the hospital and settled with him into a little cottage on Moss Avenue, a quiet crescent-shaped street of bungalows, close to the Jackson Zoo. She hired a six-foot, two-inch attendant, a Mr. Peavey, who had been dismissed from Whitfield for a drinking problem but who seemed strong enough to intercept Bob when he wanted to escape, and she told the family that she was going to carry out an "experiment" she had been thinking about since the beginning of his illness. Given an environment free from family stress and the chance to work uninterruptedly on his drawing, painting, and carving, her son would be more likely to recover than in any hospital. Whitfield lay within reach, in case of a crisis, and, though she was close to the end of her savings, she scraped together enough to hire a "colored woman"—a Mrs. Going—to come each day to cook, sew, and clean, though Mrs. Going soon found herself involved in the same "experiment" as Bob. "You've got to *do* something," Annette told her one day, handing her a lump of clay and pointing to something she could model. "You must be creative!"

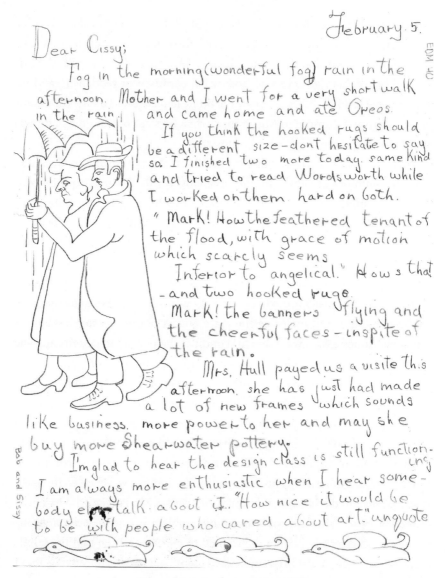

February 5.

Dear Cissy;

Fog in the morning (wonderful fog) rain in the afternoon. Mother and I went for a very short walk in the rain, and came home and ate Oreos.

If you think the hooked rugs should be a different size—dont hesitate to say so. I finished two more today, same kind and tried to read Wordsworth while I worked on them. hard on both.

"Mark! How the feathered tenant of the flood, with grace of motion which scarcly seems Interior to angelical." How's that —and two hooked rugs.

Mark! the banners flying and the cheerful faces—inspite of the rain.

Mrs. Hull payed us a visite this afternoon. she has just had made a lot of new frames which sounds like business. more power to her and may she buy more Shearwater pottery.

I'm glad to hear the design class is still functioning. I am always more enthusiastic when I hear somebody else talk about it. "How nice it would be to be with people who cared about art." unquote

Bob and Annette, from a letter, 1940

Meanwhile, Bob drew her in pencil, in ink, and did at least one large painting, though he couldn't achieve a "likeness" to his satisfaction. "She has beautiful hands and [a] beautiful face," he wrote Sissy. "It's much easier to realize the beauty in a colored person's face, and I think it is because of the one tone or value, that is when it isn't all broken up by highlights." For a month, Annette cared for her son's burnt and swollen hands, and did her best to create a peaceful daily routine for him. Twice a day he went for a walk with Mr. Peavey, lingering at the zoo to watch and draw the animals. He slept very soundly—up to nine hours a night at first—and spent much of the day reading and drawing. Annette found it hard to know when to stop him; he would work too long, "and then be upset." At times he would start to dash away, as though to escape, but as time went by, his thoughts seemed more and more on his work. Often, the two of them visited Marie Hull, who encouraged him to paint and draw with her. The large oil *Androcles and the Lion* is probably from this period. If so, it would be another sign of his changing relation with the natural world. It is one of his most forceful early works, in thickly applied oils and bold, flowing lines. The runaway slave—perhaps he felt like one himself—is face to face with the lion, about to remove the thorn from the animal's outstretched paw. He rests his hands on the lion's neck, and the lion stares at him in wide-eyed pain.

In the quiet of the small bungalow in Jackson, Bob spoke very little, but Annette had the sense that he was somehow finding his way back to language and overcoming the obstructed thought processes doctors had noticed in the hospital. "When I hadn't written for a long time," he wrote Sissy, "I thought that nothing could be more fun than just playing with words . . . and now I am as constipated as ever, almost. I'd hate to say that. Anyhow, it's real work to get them out, even just writing a letter, not even in ink. I think we will give up writing for radio. Words mean so much more when you get the sound with them. Soon as I've said that, I think of all the different meanings you could give to any word by rearranging the letters all the way from a literal meaning to a complete abstraction, and I think radio will have to wait, and on and on, far into the night. When I think of what could be done by a real writer, with just the few words in the paragraph I have just written, it makes me want to write. Doesn't it you? Still love, Bob."

"A nice letter from my darling," Sissy told herself. "Such a nice one, and drawings. I try to steel my heart against him, but I can't. I love him, want him still." The letters he wrote to her were illustrated with the people and animals he had seen on his daily walks, the snow-covered bungalows on Moss Avenue, an album of birds he had seen at the zoo, some statues from the battlefield at Vicksburg, which he had visited with his mother, a drawing of himself—"too fat"—sitting before his food, his back turned to the viewer. In almost every letter there is a nostalgic scene from the life they had once led at the Cottage and to which he hoped to return: cows, birds, the cat, scenes of himself digging in the garden, while Sissy looks on—a reaffirmation, perhaps, of his virility. In one of the drawings, she rises up like a vision behind the Cottage, larger than the house itself, holding a bunch of zinnias (his favorite flower) in her outstretched hands. Several of the drawings offer an aerial view—the Cottage as seen by a dogris on the wing, some Canadian geese over the statue of William Penn on city hall in Philadelphia. Over the past year or so, he had done a number of drawings from a birdlike, aerial perspective. There is no mention in the letters—and barely a glimpse in his imaginary idyll—of the children, as though he did not want to acknowledge their existence. Knowing it would help him, Annette had insisted on his writing frequently, and not only letters to Sissy but recollections of his school days and of his travels in Europe in 1927. The important thing was writing every day—750 words a day, she had always told herself, and him. Years later he would note that writing had "a cleansing effect, and although it is easy enough to keep the body clean, the mind seems to grow clogged." Once, when she felt him "getting away in his thoughts," she spoke to him about it and he pointed silently at the frame for hooked rugs, as though recognizing that it seemed to calm him. He did many, in hopes of selling them at the Pottery, and he also came up with a new idea for the women in Sissy's little design group, and asked her to get some heavy linoleum in Biloxi and send it to him.

> I have an idea. It is to get your girls and block print dresses any style, any color. Design the dress and fit the printed design to the particular dress. I can think of lots of objections, but I would enjoy doing it so much that they sort of fade away. And fill in with costume jewelry from the ten-cent store. Anyhow, the girls could have a good time without spending too much money and incidentally delight the eye of the beholder. And just think of them on colored people. . . . Something like these, and made of some washable material (unbleached curtain?) And sell them for as little as you could. Not just for young girls, either. Suit them to all ages and conditions. (They would have to be the right material). Anyhow, it would be fun trying it out on you and Pat.

By February, the "experiment" seemed to have reawakened his wanderlust. The state was in the midst of one of the coldest winters it had ever known. "Icebergs on the Mississippi!" he wrote Sissy. "Wouldn't you love to be in a canoe coming down from Vicksburg? It gives me goose flesh just to think of it!" Even more powerful was his longing to be back at the Cottage. As he sat with Annette hooking rugs one evening, some lines of Wordsworth ran through his mind, and he wrote beneath a pen-and-ink sketch of the Cottage:

What lovelier home could gentle fancy choose . . .

"For the Meuse," he added, "we can substitute the Mill Dam Bayou"—the little stream that trickled by the Pottery. He was "cookoo," he said. "Hooking rugs and Wordsworth are a rich mixture, and Canada geese from the Zoo. I am living high. Just the same, I crave home. Strange isn't it?" There was beauty at the zoo and on his daily walks, and he wanted to record and share it, though he could not always do so as eloquently as he wished: "A cardinal and a blue jay in a bare pear tree against a grey sky, and then you feel your pulse and you can tell how much you have overeaten. A red bird and a blue one, both crested in a tree, a pear tree, limbs upward-reaching, a bird, a complete bird realized in a pear tree, not just two spots moving against the sky. I say I have seen a bird a settlin' in a tree that was very lovely—lovely to me, only it wasn't. I was thinking how cold it was, and how long before I could go home, the same one I came away from."

From his letters, drawings, and paintings, Annette was certain that he was improving, but was not quite sure what to do next. "I have only limited amount of money," she wrote a doctor at Whitfield, "and this experiment of course is very expensive, so I do not want to waste time." Would he tell her, please, how she would know he was well enough to go home? What signs should she look for? For Bob, the time had already come. On February 7, 1940, he went out with Mr. Peavey, slipped away into the pinewoods around Jackson, and headed south toward the coast.

SEPARATION

Three weeks went by without news of him, and one night Pat thought she heard him again outside the Front House. When she called, he went crashing away into the brush beyond the studio. Then, after a week or so, two-year-old Mary sat up in bed and stared, wide-eyed, at the thin, bearded wraith of her father. To Sissy, always ready to believe the best, he seemed vastly improved. He was "a different person," she wrote on February 27, 1940. "Talks, works every day at the workshop. It is like a miracle. The kind you feel as if you weren't being thankful enough for. There are little things, but they will vanish. He asks for 'a little time.'" Within days she found him working "like a lion" on dresses and linoleum block prints to sell at the showroom.

Once again life seemed to be straightening out. With Peter back in the workshop, the showroom was doing big business daily, and Bob seemed delighted by much that he saw: he told Sissy that Billy looked beautiful when he was sleeping, and he rushed over one afternoon to tell her their peach tree was "a mass of blooms." Azaleas, too, were in flower and the two of them went on a bird walk to their special valley in Vancleave. Sissy moved back into the Cottage—the first time all four members of the family had ever lived together—and they planted the garden he had imagined in his letters, and watched a pair of thrashers build a nest in the Cherokee roses outside their door. But happiness was as fleeting as always. As Bob recovered his energy, Sissy noticed a sudden uptake in his desire for sex, and that spring and summer their relations were terrifyingly rough and frequent. In May, she and the children moved into Walter's old room at the Barn, and there was fresh talk of divorce. In June 1940 she wrote that he was making her hate him, "just as he made me love him. . . . I believe he is doing it on purpose to get rid of me! But I don't know. Every time I start to pick up and skitter, 'for richer, for poorer. . . . In sickness and in health.' . . . Of course it's *me* weighed in the balance and found wanting. This 'super-sex' business does something to one. It deteriorates one. I know it. I have put it up to him, really. Asked him to leave me alone for a week. Perhaps the absence might work the trick. If not, I think I will have to go. Anyway, I must call it separation."

For a long time now she had been longing to get away, and in July 1940 her uncle Ted (her mother's only brother) and her aunt Hulda, who had a big, elegant house in Winnetka, on the North Shore of Chicago, invited her to visit them, together with Mary and Billy. Sara Lemon, a young woman who was working at the Pottery, offered to accompany her and to care for the children. Sissy wanted to rest, to think calmly, far from the turmoil of Shearwater, to "get a long view, without all the emotions and petty angers that make me see criss-cross." She had already decided, when she set out in mid-July, that she would not return home until Bob was completely well—perhaps not at all. But there was no point in alarming him until she could develop plans for financial independence. Her aunt and uncle had often visited them in Ocean Springs, and Sissy knew that Theodore Hellmuth, in particular, sympathized with her predicament. He was fond of her, had the means to back her in whatever she decided to do, and—over the protests of his wife, who told him not to meddle—he had made no secret of his own opinion, that she ought to leave Bob and get on with her own life. He was a small, determined man, who had left Ocean Springs after high school, worked his way through John Marshall Law School, and was now a claims attorney for the North Shore and Milwaukee Railroad. If it came to divorce, he would know how to help.

Sissy, Sara, and the children caught the train on July 17, 1940, listening on the way up to talk of war and of Roosevelt's nomination. Sissy tried to steel herself against the thought of her husband—it seemed to her at times that he *could* control himself when he wanted to, and that his "madness" had been allowed to become a disguise for his selfishness. Meyer had advised her to leave him alone, and not to create stress. But perhaps that policy of "nonintervention" was making matters worse. He *was* egocentric; the whole place revolved around him.

In Chicago, however, her decisions "floated in the air." After so many months of tension and dashed hopes, the Hellmuth household seemed an "island of peace and sanity," a little like a return to her childhood at Old-fields. She felt "beautifully taken care of [and] surrounded by quiet love." And yet even in that calm, sane atmosphere escape was impossible. In Chicago all that she saw—plants and butterflies, birds and books, painting and ceramics—reminded her of him, and of all he had taught her to see and to love. Somehow, the separation and the yearning to share things reminded her of their engagement, a decade earlier, when she had written to him wistfully from Cambridge and Sewickley. On a long car ride with the Hellmuths and with Mary, she saw "everlasting fields of wheat," yellow as gold, being harvested by big combines, and couldn't wait to write him about it: "It is beautiful. Indiana is full of sand dunes as big as hills. Michigan is all flowers and fruit trees and berry patches. Gladiolas by the mile, blooming along the road in long rows. We passed a gully full of brilliant ironweed. The florist shops here are simply running over with blazing star, used in every imaginable combination."

Especially welcome were the culture and good conversation. People talked "politics and war," she wrote him. "Everyone does. In many ways people seem more alive here than at home, except for your mother." There were trips to the parks and to Ravinia with a Hellmuth cousin who she wished were Bob, and excursions to the beach or the Field Museum with the children. She wrote him about the butterflies and new flowers she had seen; the procession of "little aristocratic dogs" that went down the tree-lined street in front of the house; the strange way the locals dealt with the heat, letting in the cool air at night and keeping the windows shut during the day. She wrote him about an exhilarating night at the Democratic National Convention, where Eleanor Roosevelt had a "very fine presence, at least from thirty flights up, through the opera glasses." She told him she had spoken with her "almost-sister" Ellen, who must have sided with Uncle Ted and urged her to leave him. She visited old friends—Stephen Gregory and his wife, with whom Bob shared a passion for birds (he was director of the Illinois Audubon Society), and the Hamills, neighbors at Oldfields, whose Chicago house was a "museum of beautiful things." At the Gregorys' she spotted the Holland moth book and a big plate of arrowheads, and gazed at a collection of birdskins said to be the second largest in the country. She knew Bob would have loved it. One day she took a bus into the city to Kroch's, the book dealer from whom they had always ordered their records and special books. Bob had asked her to check for new volumes of *Summa Artis: Historia general del arte* by the Spaniard José Pijoan, an ongoing multivolumed history of art published in Barcelona, beginning in 1931: a leisurely journey from children's drawings and aboriginal art through the Egyptians, Greeks, Assyrians, and onwards—they did not know how far—toward the present day. Bob had been feasting on the first four volumes, with their excellent photographs (some in color, one to three to a page) of carvings and ceramics, tattoos and totem poles, clothing and architecture. No art book had ever been so lavishly illustrated and none contained so much information about all of the things that had helped shape the work

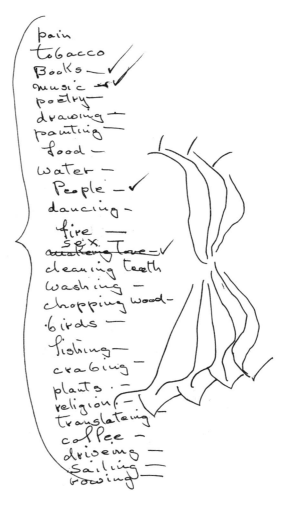

List, c. 1940

of his own hands. Even more interesting than the historical data were Pijoan's abundant comments on mythology and on specifics of technique. In Ocean Springs, Bob was translating the book into English. Although he had not studied Spanish since his days at Isidore Newman, he translated hundreds of pages with surprising accuracy, leaving occasional blank spaces when the dictionary failed him. He was recovering his command of language and retraining his drawing hand, and he often paused from translation and drew the illustrations in the volume in front of him, his way of fully savoring the work and reaffirming his belief in continuity of art. "To ignore the art of the past," he once told his mother, "is to refuse one's heritage." The project went on in his spare time for over a year.

Sissy gathered from his letters, and from Pat's, that he was working steadily and probably doing better without her. Peter had taken Bob and a couple of friends out on a fishing trip, and Bob had "plunged overboard in the middle of the sea." "All of Bob's queer and super-strange actions Pete takes as personal insults to himself and to the Shearwater Pottery," Pat wrote. "He says that he hates Bob at times, but Bob says he loves just three people: his wife, mother and Peter." Croquet, a game Peter had "introduced with a vengeance," seemed to break their tension. "We manage some quite exciting family tournaments," Pat wrote to Lidz, Peter's doctor at Phipps, who had recently visited the Andersons on his honeymoon. "Quite a crowd has joined in, so we have fun. It's a fine mental game [though] I suppose it wouldn't be good for a hospital!"

Sissy was impressed and touched by the gifts Bob sent her: a set of decorated plates for the Hellmuths, some figurines for her, and a little brass bulldog he had cast for Mary. He was working hard both on his rugs and on his pottery: slip-decorated pieces in black and white that Pat and Annette found very beautiful, Annette insisting on a high price because of their "intrinsic value," and Pat reminding her sharply that it was *market* value they had to worry about, and not simply aesthetics. A couple from Memphis, Louise and John Lehman, who would soon acquire importance in his life, had commissioned some rugs from him, and he was also doing linoleum block prints: some Mother Goose rhymes, a children's alphabet book, and a picture book entitled *Robinson: The Pleasant History of an Unusual Cat* (one who learns to play the piano, performs at Carnegie Hall, and opens a conservatory for animals). As he cut the blocks, he must have remembered his own discovery of the city—the orchestra, the zoo, Morningside Park—while he was a student at Parsons.

At the end of August, with the season winding down, Peter closed the Pottery and took a vacation—his first since returning from Phipps. Pat was relieved to see her husband doing things about the house and going over his boat "in his old careful way." He was not completely himself, of course, and she was still "being bawled out steadily," but in the seven months he had been home, she had learned to respond to his complaints and "recriminations" by balancing sympathy and sternness. As for Annette, she was busy with "plate classes"—art lessons for friends and acquaintances at which she handed out cardboard plates or blank circles of paper, and invited the "class" to try their hand at design in the hope that the best of them would be used at the Pottery. Sometimes, she persuaded Bob to join them.

Everywhere in Chicago, Sissy was looking at pottery—in Marshall Field's, the Merchandise Mart, the Art Institute of Chicago, and at stands by the side of the road—and more than once she wrote Bob about her discoveries. There was an ulterior motive to her pottery-hunting, though she was careful at first not to mention it to him. Uncle Ted had suggested that she open a gift shop of her own, perhaps in Florida, and sell Shearwater pottery and other items. He was willing to back her, and she spent much time in Chicago trying to get an idea of the sort of things most likely to sell. In August, she finally broached the idea in a letter to Bob, presenting it not as a possible business of her own, but as a family enterprise.

> We've always, even in the best days, felt the need of some other outlet than on the place. I don't mean just a pottery sales outlet but a place the family could take turns using for a vacation from too monotonous living. Well, I'm going to try to establish the outlet. As the winter season is approaching, my first idea is to start in Florida, but, with luck and care, the affair could be moveable, going to North Carolina or New England in summer. I have all sorts of flights of fancy in connection with it, and see the various families rotating in the management of the shop and, mostly, having a wonderful time. Of course, it would be plenty of work, too. But couldn't you and I have fun if we got Maine some year? Anyway, while you are getting entirely well, I would at least feel that I was doing something useful, and would not be so terribly far away.

As for returning to Shearwater, she couldn't come back to the kind of life they had been leading, and would never return at all until she was sure that he was better, and that they could be, "as we were, the happiest people in the world. . . . You must know that, by living as we have in the last four or five months, we were losing something so precious that I, for one, would leave it a hundred times, rather than lose it . . . which may sound rather like something out of Chesterton or the Bible and is just as true when you examine it. Talk it over with your mother, and let me know."

It was more than he could bear. Sensing she was about to leave him, he set out for Chicago, and appeared suddenly one day, with no advance warning, at the front door in Winnetka. Many years later, Sissy recalled how her aunt Hulda, who had always had a weakness for Bob, and who was tired of her husband's attempts to bring about a separation, had ushered him into the room where Sissy was resting. "I was startled, but, oh, what a feeling of belonging swept over me when I saw him." He went into the bathroom, opened the tap, scooped her into his arms, and dropped her into a tub of cold Lake Michigan water. "Wake up!" she remembered him saying. "For God's sake, wake up before it's too late! I had to talk to you. You must understand. No matter what happens, there is a trust that must be recognized. You and I belong together. We are one in a rare and special way. You have to wake up and see it. It's impossible to separate us. I am not sick any more. I promise to behave. Promise that you will come home. Promise!"

"So ended my family treat, and all my scheming seems to have gone for naught," she wrote dejectedly in her journal, two weeks after they had all returned to Shearwater. They had sent Bob home alone, and, the third week in September, she, Sara, and the children followed. She moved back into the Barn, aware that her husband was "tremendously well in many ways," and determined, as she had been in Chicago, "not to spoil it all trying to live with him" in the Cottage until he had recovered more fully. As usual, Shearwater was a "turmoil of conflicts," but she had not yet lost hope; with an effort, she might be able to achieve a sort of detachment, an "impersonal" love that transcended her feelings for him: "I must get back to my old affirmative principle. Love must hold a one-ness . . . not married love alone but the understanding of everyone. The desire not to criticize; not just to see faults so personally that anger comes, but to keep out of difficulties, to lead the middle life of happiness. Not the self but the whole. Escape doesn't do it. Florida was that as I see it now."

What dashed her hopes, as before, was his inability to control himself sexually. In October and November, he began again to prey on her, punishing himself, the way he always had, by burning himself in the fireplace, and letting off tension by ramming his fist through windowpanes. This time, however, there was a cruelly ironic new accusation: he denied having fathered the two children. Years later, Sissy tried to imagine his predicament; he remembered "only the early days of our marriage. He expected things to be the same. Instead, now the house was full of babies, the devoted wife preoccupied with children; there was literally no place for him; no place for his work. He still did not accept either child as his own. He had no reason for this belief except for his delusion of impotence at the time of their conception."

Fall brought its redeeming moments. On a family trip to Horn Island—another of their sacred places—she lay on the beach, gazing up at the sky, and felt overwhelmed by beauty: "geese, geese, all day, hundreds of gangs went over quite low and thrilling to the north. All was exhilarating, and everyone well. In many ways it seem[ed] as though old times were returning." In the cool October air, monarch butterflies, on their way south, were feeding on the goldenrod. But moments like those were overshadowed by truly horrific ones. Anything could set him off, and when he lost his temper he lunged at her violently. Once, when they quarreled and he was beside himself with anger, he picked up a knife and flung it in her direction and the baby's. It grazed her neck and landed, trembling, in the wall behind her, so deep that she could not pull it out. "I have to confess it—I cannot stand it," she wrote. "It seems *too* dreadful, but I shall have to escape somehow. *How?* That is the constant question and prayer." Mortified when others found out about the incident, she told herself that she was "a bitter failure. The hard part is knowing it, and still trying to go around kidding yourself that it is not so. If only I could hold on to my calm." In November, she thought harder than ever about divorce, and, encouraged by her uncle Ted, went to a lawyer, but found that Mississippi law left her in somewhat of a quandary. The mental illness of a spouse *was* grounds for divorce, but only if the spouse were considered incurable, and who could say *that*, with any certainty, about Bob? Left to himself, he seemed almost normal. Much else was holding her back: above all, her reluctance to separate the children from their father, but also the thought that her own "vile temper" had driven him to violence; the memory of past happiness; the belief that his work might be important enough to justify her struggle. For the moment, it would have to be separation. It was the painter Dusti Bongé, widow of one of Bob's old companions from the Academy, who made it possible, offering to share with Sissy and the children two rooms in her little apartment in Biloxi and to keep their whereabouts secret. She was away during the day, and they could have the place to themselves. They moved in at the end of November 1940, and as Sissy watched Billy learning to walk and listened to Mary's persistent question—"When do we go home?"—she reproached herself for taking the children away from all they loved, and for having behaved "like a beast"; she would have liked to have been more patient with both Annette and Bob. Within a day or so Pat brought her the first of a series of plaintive letters from him, in which he apologized for his behavior and begged her to take him back. Fearing she might be pregnant again, she tried to fend him off.

Dear Bob:

You know that I have long since forgiven and forgotten what you call your "recent behavior." I might well ask for the same charity from you. I do. I know myself and I knew that it would happen. It did. I see very little use in our trying to see each other at present. However, if I could trust you to make no effort to find me or come to me or force me to live with you, I would be willing to call it a separation, and not bring suit for divorce immediately. That would obviate the necessity for remarriage later if we should ever both want that.

I am perfectly sure that we have tried it often enough now. As for my helping you to get well, you must see as clearly as I do that quite the reverse is true. In the first place, the frequency of our conjugal relations is enough, according to all authorities, to ruin a well man, let alone what it does to a woman, as I have tried to explain to you. Also, it is absolutely necessary for a woman to be able to ask for and get rests when she knows she needs them. There are certain periods in the month when conception is much easier than at other times. I have tried to prevent your coming to me at these times, unsuccessfully, with your uncontrolled appetite, you have not always used proper precautions . . . and I am, right now, wondering if I will have to have either another child for you or an abortion. Neither alternative is exactly pleasant for me to contemplate, as you can imagine. Your talk, under the circumstances, of the children not being yours seems too silly for comment. If I should come back to you in your present condition, it would be the worst possible thing for you. You might be forced by my nervousness and ill-temper, into a display of temper that would result in much worse injury than a black eye or a bruise and that, in turn, would, naturally, result in hospitalization for you. I would not write you all this if I did not consider you perfectly sane enough to understand it, and perfectly capable of throwing off your "craziness." It is all too evident that, as long as you have what you want, you are content—even happy—in your pose. I am tremendously sorry for you, almost as sorry for you as I am for myself, and am terribly unhappy, as you must have guessed, and I'd like to help you if I could. You have thought that I could, and I have now tried your way a good number of times. Perhaps you would like to try mine. Do you remember my telling you of a place called "Spring Lake" in Vermont? It's a place that might enable you to stand on your own feet again. After the first month or two you would with proper effort be earning your tuition. It is not a hospital and [you could] go voluntarily, alone.

A year earlier, when he was at Whitfield, she had consulted with friends in Boston and had gathered information on farms and dude ranches willing to

Letter to Sissy, 1940

take in patients like him, allowing them to take part in the chores and earn their keep as they worked toward recovery. Spring Lake, in Cutlersville, Vermont, was one of them. But for now he wanted none of it:

Dear Sissy:

The place in Vermont sounds like a penal farm. I hope I won't have to go there. I have missed you today, and love you. I don't understand my behavior. I went to church this morning with Mother. How soon may I see you? Love from BOB

P.S. I love you. That may be why I seem crazy.

A day later he wrote again, begging her to "let me see you as soon as you can stand the sight," and again she did her best to keep him at a distance.

> *It's too bad that you can't make the effort to cast me out of your mind and heart—at least for a little—so that I might come back in less exclusive possession, as that is a decided hindrance to a normal life, in spite of your feelings to the contrary. As for my running away because you lose control "a little bit," as you call it, that is not the case, as I tried to explain. It is not the loss of control, but the lack of control that drives me away. . . . You ask how soon you can see me. My answer is that I would much prefer not to see you now, nor until you have learned that you are not a child leading a protected life according to his desires, but a grown man whose duties are numerous and who needs to face his life as it is, not as he might like it to be. Give my love to your mother, and tell her I still feel dreadfully about deserting her when she was so ill.*
> *SISSY*

By the middle of December, after two weeks of separation, he sent her a page of sketches of his daily activities—"I've been decorating pots and bow shooting"—and promised to be good to her if she came back. Before she left, she had told him of a story she wanted to write, and him to illustrate, "The Lord of the Lesser Peak," and he asked her now for the first installment. But as far as she was concerned, nothing had changed:

> *You ask me to write, and I do. I do not mean to be unkind, but there is very little for me to say to you, now. Until you can show me, in your letters, that you have lost that dreadful willingness—even pleasure—in remaining just as is, I cannot give you false hope of me, because I cannot live with you in that state. Don't you see that if I do everything you say in order not to make a scene, or not to be struck, or whatever it may be, that there will be no reason for you to want to change? It would be right nice to have one's life made to order, but I still doubt if it is good for one. Give me some idea of what you want to see me about. I have tried terribly hard—you just don't know how hard—not to seem contrary, but I haven't changed any. I would still like to be able to say when I wished for solitude, and know that I would get it. I should still lose my temper. I'll let you know if I get better control.*
>
> *I'll send you the story or part of it as soon as I get it started. Haven't had time yet.*
>
> *Don't think that I don't still love the you that could be.*
> *SISSY*

He replied a day later, promising her "any assurance that you like," that she would be "safe" from him if only she would return and live with him. At the bottom of his letter he sketched the four of them, setting out on a family excursion, himself in the lead, with a walking stick and a picnic basket. Sissy has her arm around him, and Mary and Billy trail behind, as though to tell her that he accepted the children as his own. When she failed to answer, he wrote again with all the pathos he could muster, ending the note with a sketch of the two of them, their heads enclosed by a sort of halo:

> I love you. I'm dying of thirst. If I don't see you soon I will miss you even more than I do now. And that's a lot. I know you have a lot to forgive and forget. Please try. I need to touch you and see you smile. Everyone else has somebody. I am alone. Let me see you soon. Many days have passed since you left. You have had plenty of time to love me. Come home soon. I [am] tired of living alone. Love, Bob.

Finally, on December 19, with Christmas approaching, she set down conditions for her return, and softened the letter with a touch of humor and some poems for him to illustrate.

> *Dear Bob,*
>
> *I have thought and thought, and tried to consider from every angle, and still I feel that it is much better for me to be away, I mean for you—from your point of view. You say you will give me any assurance that things will be right. But, old pessimist that I am, I want it first. Here's how. No more horrible wads of toilet paper in the nose. Hair grown out and decently cut by a barber and hat no longer worn all the time. Pants buttoned (all buttons, even that last one), care taken of your appearance. You know those things may seem like silly little trifles, but if they don't exist, it would be an indication that something else had ceased to exist too, and that you were aware of a you worth taking care of. Oh, and a little matter of fireplaces and panes of glass might be considered. Don't think I am just full of cranky notions. As I told you before, there is only one thing I want, and that is that you should be completely well.*
>
> *I haven't gotten to the "Lord of the Lesser Peak." In fact, try as I may, I find it hard to write when I am feeling rather low. . . . I did write [a poem] for Mary, but too poor. I don't see why I can't do better:*
>
> *Smiling, smiling, hard and bright,*
> *Small dancing waves in the sunlight,*

Cov'ring the shallows with your silly grin,
Daring the deeper waters to come in.
You, childish ones, then, don't you know
The tide will turn, however slow,
Or is it that you're being brave,
Waiting for the greater wave?
Let but the wind turn to the South,
He'll eat you all with his great mouth,
Or roll you up to the white sand
And leave you stranded on dry land.
Then I'll find you, smiling still,
Rigid on the low beach hill.

When the unexpected happened, and Pat and Annette told her he was actually trying to fulfill her "conditions"—no hat now, and all buttons fastened—she wrote to tell him she was not yet ready to return, and wouldn't be until he had proven he could live without her.

> You must not think that I am staying away only for myself. You are right in wanting to fulfill the conditions, but as long as you have that violent feeling of the necessity of being with me, you are not being straight in your own mind. No person can be wholly dependent on another. It is bad for you. Each time, you see, it comes back to that. I know, when I am clear-headed and disinterested (that's what you must try for) that it is not right for us to be together. I am not deserting you, I am thinking about you and with you all the time. As far as I myself am concerned, I must ask you for a little more time. Now I know I am still in that disturbed state that might lead to angry words, and that is wrong, and far better avoided. You say you are having a hard time and need me to help you. I wouldn't be a help. You don't need help. You are perfectly able to do it yourself, as I have said before right there the conditions may not be perfect—there is too much of a concentration on you.
>
> Please let me regain my confidence in you by being utterly patient, working on those things I have told you of, and forgetting me (putting me out of your mind, for a time). That is the way in which we will both find happiness in the end.

On Christmas day, 1940, as she opened presents with the children, she thought back wearily on the past few years. The Christmas before, he and Annette had called from the little house in Jackson, and he had sounded sweet and well, though it wasn't long after that, that he escaped. "Pick up the fragments of your life," she had told herself, and remembered wondering what sort of mark he would leave as an artist: "All day I have been thinking, 'If I should be alive in 100 y[ea]rs, what will he be?'" So many possibilities: "honor—shame—beast—or prophet—The world changed—or?" The year before that, on Christmas Eve 1938, she had wept out of loneliness and joy. He had brought her a little pine tree for Mary—planted in one of his own pots—with a single candle, and a box full of wooden animals he had cut out himself. And then, without a word, while she was filling Mary's stocking, he had suddenly wandered away by himself. A year earlier, in 1937, she was lying in the maternity ward in Baltimore, with Mary in her arms, listening to carols on the radio, staring at the little tree festooned with "icicles" from the big one in the lobby of Phipps, wondering if he would ever get well. And the year before? Walter was dying, Bob was struggling with his mural. Pain and despair. This year he had sent gifts to the children and a new fountain pen for her—an invitation to write.

A new year, she thought, should begin on a questioning note, and on the first day of 1941, after more than a month away from home, she prayed for patience and self-control, "that I may, without losing myself, do all that is best" for him. "What now?" she asked in her diary. "Oldfields? With him?" She knew that Frank Baisden and a friend—Schuyler Jackson, probably—had visited him at Shearwater during the Christmas holidays, and remembering earlier turmoil, she wondered whether the visit had been good for him. He had been unusually busy lately, drawing, decorating pottery—as many as twenty-eight pieces per day—and working on a series of block prints of butterflies, for which he had asked her to do some verses—an appeal to earlier, happier times at the Cottage. "Please tell me, God, if I may go back," she wrote in her journal.

Placing her faith in the power of prayer, Annette was on the lookout for anyone with the spiritual insight to help her troubled son. Lately she had found someone who "specialized in demons," Roland J. Brown, a Chicago minister associated with Glenn Clark, the leader of a pietistic prayer movement (Clark had "asserted that mental illness was actually demon possession and that exorcism was the only cure"). Brown was probably in Biloxi or Mobile for a prayer meeting, and on January 12 Annette reported that he had met with Bob and had done "wonders." Sissy was in bed with the flu—part of a nationwide epidemic that Brown thought "symbolic" ("that's the way he [sees] most things"), but determined to consult with Brown herself as soon as she was feeling better. Bob had talked to him "as he had talked to no one else" and had "agreed to all sorts of conditions." When Sissy went to Shearwater to see if there had been a change in her husband, she found him "well, as far as I can see." But *one* of his demons seemed as uncontrollable as ever: "He put me down on the bathroom floor, and had me. I'm not going to count that, though. At least I'm going to try not to. But it does make a difference. I wish I could make him see and feel it." Four days later, she moved back to Shearwater, promising herself to be "good tempered and patient," and the two of them agreed to "try through prayer." And for Sissy, at least, it seemed to help. She felt much steadier than she had for years. "Very happy, too, perhaps because I am acting a little better. Not much, but a little. Anyway, I have sort of taken God back into my life and am more willing to accept, less apt to think about my *dues*."

One of the first things she did upon returning to Shearwater was to take Mary and Billy to visit her father, who was still living in a little house in Ocean Springs in the care of an attendant. She knew he was intensely unhappy. From the sidewalk, she could see him through the window, rocking back and forth in his chair, mumbling to himself. The screen door was locked, and he refused to let them in. The attendant who was supposed to be taking care of him poked his head around the corner of the house, reeking of whiskey, and she felt a spasm of guilt. By the time she reached Shearwater, pushing Mary and Billy home in the stroller, she had made a decision. For years, the house at Oldfields had been empty. She would take the children and her father back to the place he most loved. She had no money, but she was sure her father would help—he had invested wisely and there was more than enough to meet expenses. Eventually, she would build a couple of cottages she could rent to paying guests. If Bob wanted to join them, fine. If what he really wanted was to work on a farm, perhaps this was the solution. It had been three years since the onset of his illness, but it was too soon to abandon hope entirely. She would try again.

"I'm going to Oldfields to live," she told him. "I've bought a car and a cow. I'm going back to the land. Would you like to come?"

GEORGICS

At nine o'clock one morning, the last week in January 1941, Bob and Sissy left Mary and Billy at Shearwater and sailed off in a new little boat—the *Dos*—to Oldfields, to take a good look at the place and see if they could live there together with the children and with Billie Grinstead. They spent the day on Deer Island, where they waited for the wind, and Sissy wrote some verses. At suppertime they departed, took turns rowing against the wind, and got to the Oldfields pier at two-thirty in the morning. For her, it was truly a homecoming. As she caught sight of the moonlit bluff where she had played as a child, she rejoiced to return to a place entirely her own. For almost four years, she had lived everywhere and nowhere, feeling like a "driven cloud": Baltimore, Winnetka, the little apartment in Biloxi. Much as she loved the Cottage at Shearwater, it had been years since she had felt at home there. Bob's illness or absence had kept her at the Barn or the Front House, living with Pat and Peter or with Annette. Oldfields was hers; the very name had always given her peace.

> *This was my home.*
> *Its narrow, secret places*
> *are bursting with my happiness, my pain.*
> *My childhood house*
> *of sweet protecting faces*
> *into whose rest I may not come again . . .*

Oldfields, Gautier, Mississippi, c. 1925

Empty, closed, mysterious, the old house awakened a part of her she had long ago surrendered to Bob and to his family. A caretaker, Lem Yocum, and his family lived there now, milking the cows, airing out the house, and caring for the horses and barnyard fowl. For years, the Andersons had come over on picnics or to check on the place. That January day in 1941, Sissy found it "crowded with joys." She and Bob set up camp, with a couple of lamps and a wood-burning stove, in a room in the carriage house where, long ago, Mr. Grinstead had had his office. They stayed for a week, with barely a contentious moment. They rode horseback, explored the woods and fields, and went arrowheading on the beach at Graveline. In the evening, by lamplight, they wrote in their journals, Bob sketching the day's activities, with a couple of hawk feathers in his detestable grey felt hat. One afternoon, as Sissy watched Yocum feed and milk the cows, she listened to "the long sizz of the milk stream and the contented munching, and looked out with momentary joy to the long line of Horn Island and over the closer open grassland to the great beauty of the house." Bob sketched whatever caught his attention— guinea hens, palmettos, pelicans—and collaborated with Sissy. She provided verse they could share with the children, and he, the drawings.

> In the sun, on a spit,
> the sea birds sit.

Poem written by Sissy and illustrated by Bob, c. 1942

The terns face the sun
where the small waves run.
The pelicans spread
their wings, having fed,
and clap their bills
having had their fills.

In the course of a week, they were interrupted by Annette and Mac, who came twice, to bring them food and news of the children, and by Pat, who had brought Billie Grinstead to talk to Yocum and a local businessman, Fred Moran, about cutting some of the pinewoods, which had been damaged by fire. Bob and Sissy did deep-breathing exercises on the gallery, staring up at the orange-colored nests of the mud daubers and breathing in the sea air. On the gallery at night, Sissy read aloud from the Bible. The two of them invented some reminders to hold themselves in check: "Bob says VT (=vile temper), and I say LN (=lower nature)."

An escort of porpoises accompanied them back to Shearwater, and the family was waiting for them on the dock. Sissy had felt a little uneasy about leaving Billy and Mary for a week with Annette, an ingenious but somewhat absented-minded babysitter. She always found the children amusing, and for a while she could interest them in drawing or reading or looking at natural things, but once, when she wanted to get on with her own work or her own book, she found some clothesline and tied Billy to a tree on a long leash. The children were fine, but within weeks Bob had another relapse, became violent, and attacked both Peter and Sissy. In April she took the children to Oldfields, and began to get the place ready for her father. Robert Andrews, who had grown up with Pat and Sissy and had been cooking for Mr. Grinstead in Ocean Springs, went along to help, as did Suzy, their cook. Electricity was installed, a refrigerator went into the kitchen, screens were repaired, and the old rooms swept out. For a while, Bob remained in Ocean Springs, going over on weekends on his little sailboat, but after a few weeks he, too, moved in, occupying a bedroom of his own and fixing up the huge attic as a studio. "Nerves are untangling, love is coming back, the children are fine," Sissy wrote hopefully on April 26, 1941, as she had so many times before, and added that they were to have a visit that weekend from the Hellmuths and from Ellen and Henry Mead. Days later, Mead, who had treated Bob at Phipps and had never felt much sympathy for him, sent a bulletin to Paul Lemkau, another of the Phipps psychiatrists. There *had* been a change in Bob, Mead reported, but it was clear that he posed just as much of a danger as ever and that Sissy was deeply ambivalent about his behavior.

I think you will be interested with respect to the situation in Mississippi. Bob (Walter I.) Anderson has definitely changed. There is no longer a shuffle in his gait, he seems assured in his manner and looks like a person who seems to know what he is about. Do not, however, misinterpret me. I do not know what he is about. Some of the most extraordinary things you have ever heard of. For example, he knocked out his brother and explained it by saying that he felt he had to beat somebody up. You will remember how powerful a man he was when he was at Phipps; he is maybe a little more powerful now. He is reported by his wife to hear "religious" voices. I got no information as to whether he sees anything. Some ten days ago he throttled his wife *nearly* to death. One has the impression, however, that he hasn't wished to go to that limit so far, because it seems to be a pretty reasonable opinion that stopping him would be well nigh impossible. A change has definitely come over him. He sailed around one day to the house where the Hamills live and, soaking wet from wading ashore in a heavy rain and covered with mud from climbing up a bluff which the cattle are not able to get up—ten or twelve feet high—came in during dinner time to present himself to Dr. Ralph Hamill, the psychiatrist who has known him and his case for some time, to see what a change there had been. I have not seen or spoken to Dr. Hamill, but others who were present told me that Dr. Hamill's comment was that he had rarely seen such a change in a man and that "something seems to have gone out of him." Whatever it was that made him shuffle and seem to slink about and to mumble for eighteen months at Phipps to avoid saying a word is not present now. There is a change in the motifs of his work. There is a new style of bird, which is to say, a new style of design. His work is, if anything, better than it has been. I believe that we now have a first-flight artist and a homicidal in one and the same man. There is no one in Ocean Springs who at the present time would undertake or consider his commitment for various reasons which they gave. I believe fear is the ruling motive, which I believe to be well considered.

Peter mumbles, appears quite shy, but I was surprised that during the evening he came up and discussed a volume of photographs with me, put in his oar in a discussion of the war and aside from a mumbling enunciation seems like any quiet, normal person. He did not look awfully well to me. He works continuously putting out a large amount of pottery for his brother to decorate day by day. He is said to hate his brother, and I think this is probably well justified. . . .

Bob's wife is like a bewitched woman. Almost in the same sentence she will tell you that no one knows what Bob may do next, and that murder would not be unreasonable to expect, and then she will say "but he would not do that now." She refers to his change, which I have described as a "recovery." I should have told you that Peter's wife said that Bob told her that he was "crazy" and that nothing could cure him, and he said this with no trace of apparent regret. Indeed, he said it with some apparent satisfaction.

I hope that this information may be of some use in Bob's record. I have no content to add although I believe some might be elicited from his wife if one were to go after it carefully. I shall not be a particle surprised to hear or read that a tragedy has taken place, how big, how great it will be difficult to say.

Ralph Hamill, the psychiatrist to whom Mead had referred, corroborated with a note of his own:

The Anderson boys were seen the latter part of March. Peter was very quiet, diffident as usual, and seemed to be doing his work fairly well. Bob seemed as psychotic as I have seen him. A few days before I saw him, he had knocked Peter over with a right to the jaw as Peter was recovering from an attack of illness. However, he did not attack Peter's wife when she came to Peter's aid. One night Bob surprised me by dropping in from a moonlight sail in a skiff as I was at dinner. Apparently he merely wanted to take a look at me, perhaps to reassure himself that he was not afraid of me.

Gloomy reports, to be sure. But something was going on in Walter Anderson that neither Mead nor Hamill was able to fathom. He had begun to emerge from himself, to recover the use of language, and to turn toward the outside world. At Oldfields he was drawing more than he ever had before, carrying a clipboard and bottle of ink with him everywhere, sketching whatever he saw, with a growing rapidity that seemed like magic to his daughter Mary. "Billy and I watched, impressed by his skill and speed with a dip pen and a bottle of ink. Magically, chickens, cows, cats or zinnias appeared on the white paper as he passed his hand over it." Since leaving Whitfield, his drawing had grown more stylized and symbolic, as though he were seeing people and things as types, or archetypes, and concentrating more on universals than particulars. Part of the change in style was attributable to his reencounter with a little book entitled *A Method for Creative Design* by Adolfo Best-Maugard, a little-known Mexican artist who had reformed art education in Mexican grade schools in the early 1920s. In "primitive" Mexican art, brought to light in the years after the Mexican Revolution by German ethnographer Franz Boas, Best-Maugard had discovered a set of seven basic graphic motifs: a grammar of primitive design. The nationalistic message of his book, which aimed to turn Mexicans away from the imitation of European models and encourage them to take pride in the creations of their pre-Columbian ancestors, was entirely absent from the English-language adaptation published by Alfred Knopf in 1926 and reread—perhaps only remembered—at Oldfields by Walter Anderson. In the English adaptation, the seven motifs—zigzag, half-circle, circle, straight line, s-curve, wavy line, and spiral—are said to be present in *all* "primitive" art, not merely that of Mexico, and together they form a universal visual language that even a child can learn easily, taking his first steps in art without having to copy objects from life in a realistic way. For Bob, with his classical training in realistic life-drawing, the motifs were a break with the past and a major discovery: a Rosetta stone that seemed to decipher both art and nature. Over the next few years, as he recovered his mastery of the line, they formed an intimate, easily recognizable part of his sketches and watercolors. Often, he would "warm up" by jotting the motifs in a neat square at the top of the page, reminding himself, perhaps, that his little grid contained all possible forms of creation. The motifs were not only the basic elements of design but were a springboard to metaphor and analogy, leading him from one natural form to another:

The beauty of a shell is found in a succession of small waves in rapids:
and in a plowed field on the top of a hill.

    Best-Maugard had associated each of the motifs with a characteristic emotion, and Bob elaborated on his suggestion, linking each to a particular natural form, activity, emotion, or region of the earth. The zigzag, for example, reminded him of walking, fear, mountains, earth, and Africa; the half-circle of sitting, fatigue, sunrise and sunset, clouds, rain, and the South Seas; the circle of hunger, sun, and Japan; the straight vertical line of standing and boredom; and the horizontal one of flatness and the Aztecs. The s-curve meant bending, love, and beauty, and the spiral meant saluting, acquisitiveness, and growth.

    In a little poem, Sissy joked about what it was like to accompany him on his walks, and see the world through the eyes of Best-Maugard. When she saw human forms in cypress knees, he saw only "symmetries," and she too was fatigued by them. "What do I see when I walk with thee? / My love, o my love o! / Straight lines below / spirals above, / the s-curve in a dove."

    Mary Anderson has written that her father used the motifs both as creative mantra and as crutch, and that when he arrived at Oldfields they steadied his trembling hands as he drew. Like his drawings from Pijoan, the motifs mattered both physically and psychologically, retraining his hand and offering a sense of unity and wholeness at a time when his life seemed fragmented and broken. For Best-Maugard, the motifs themselves are parts of a larger whole, "phases or aspects" of the "whirling spiral" or "whirling vortex," the source of all art and all life, a phenomenon observable throughout nature "in atmospheric phenomena, as in the vortical movement of the air and of water, . . . in whirlwinds, movements of all gases and liquids, clouds, flames of fire; the arrangement of leaves and branches, the growth of trunks and stems, the arrangement of petals in flowers, the structure of pine cones and pineapples; in animal life, in antelope-horns, arrangement of feathers in birds, scales of fishes, structure of nests and spider-webs, and in many other forms of natural growth."

For Bob, the motifs seemed to draw together all previous art, from the incised pot shards he picked up on the beach at Graveline Bayou to his own drawing, reminding him, as he once wrote, that "there are constant qualities in art and music which go through all paintings or music regardless of the name underneath." In his "psychology of creation" Best-Maugard promises the artist nothing less than a consciousness of universal harmony: after reconciling thought and feeling, the masculine and feminine principles, the artist can reach "what has been called by philosophers 'the musical state' or 'the lyric state,' or what is known as 'ecstasy' in the language of mysticism." The search for wholeness, and the attempt to reconcile thought and feeling—conundrum of modern art—must have reminded Bob of Gurdjieff, whom he had studied earlier with such troubling effects.

Several other books which he had read years earlier but remembered or studied at Oldfields helped him redefine the relations between art and nature. First, the photographic albums of the German sculptor and art teacher Karl Blossfeldt, *Art Forms in Nature*: clear, stark, black-and-white close-up photographs of plants which reminded readers of art's debt to the natural world. More arduous reading than Best-Maugard and Blossfeldt were two books by Jay Hambidge (Bob always called him "Hambridge"), whom he had first studied at Parsons: *Dynamic Symmetry: The Greek Vase* (1920) and *The Parthenon and Other Greek Temples: Their Dynamic Symmetry* (1924). Dynamic symmetry was a set of design principles which Hambidge claimed to have discovered in classical Greek art: principles of Euclidian geometry deduced from Greek architecture, sculpture, and ceramics which could be used by modern painters and designers in the composition of their own work. It was a study of areas, of inner spaces and their relationships, based on various possible configurations of the square and its diagonal and the application of the golden section. Numerous sketches and diagrams from the 1940s and 1950s testify to Bob's attempts to apply Hambidge's geometry to problems of design. What delighted him more, however, was the idea that there are certain common morphological principles present in both art and nature. Hambidge taught him that the composition of a drawing can correspond to the way a cell grows or a fern unfolds because the same geometrical principles—for example, the spiral generated by the golden section—is found in a variety of natural phenomena, from snail shell to a ram's horn, from the spray of an ocean wave or falling meteorites to the tail of a comet or the seed head of a sunflower. Like Pijoan and Best-Maugard, Hambidge seemed to reaffirm the continuity of art: the same organic principles could be found in a Greek temple or a painting by George Bellows. Hambidge believed in another sort of unity which Bob must have found reassuring: that of the fine arts and of *all* design. The two concepts had sometimes been in tension in his life, and Hambidge's writing on nature and art, and on the weakness of modern design and architecture, must have struck a deep chord, planting the seeds of a notion that would accompany Bob through the remainder of his life in art: "realization." The "lesson modern artists must learn," Hambidge wrote, is "that the backbone of art is formalization and not realism."

> Art means exactly what the term implies. It is not nature, but it must be based on nature, not upon the superficial skin, but upon structure. Man cannot otherwise be creative, be free. As long as he copies nature's superficialities he is an artistic slave. No craftsmen ever so thoroughly understood this as the Greeks. When they used a flower or a plant as a design motive the superficial or accidental aspect of the thing was eliminated.

While Blossfeldt's emphasis was on the way art has *imitated* nature, both Best-Maugard and Hambidge were idealists who shunned realism and recommended that the artist attempt to discover the underlying principles of nature in order to use them in his own work, allowing nature to perfect or "realize" itself. According to Hambidge, the goal of art is the "realization of nature's ideal." The artist must "anticipate nature, to attain the ideal toward which she is tending, but which she can never reach." For Walter Anderson—at first during the years at Oldfields and later on Horn Island—the process of "realization" was a way, as the motifs were, of finding order and meaning in the world around him. One of the first times he uses the word is in 1941, not long after leaving Whitfield, in a note where "realization" means the awareness that a form in art or nature is a *significant form* (a term he had borrowed from Clive Bell). Given the importance which the idea of "realization" was to acquire in his work, the passage is worth quoting in full. In it, he makes clear that "realization" gives meaning to one's own life, as well as to one's surroundings.

> The object in being is realization—to realize everything, from the smallest object in nature to the most casual acquaintance. Considering that we are

Pelicans, c. 1942

receiving something like 500 stimuli of various kinds at the same second in time, this will probably always remain an object.

Blake says that success is the mark upon the brow of a small desire.

Anything that helps the individual in the realization of his life, that is, taking it away from the dream state we are continually falling into, is good to us. Someone said that life began with form. That is, the realization of the reason of the shape of an object. In this sense, form does not mean shape and weight, but what in modern language is referred to as "significant form." As soon as perception and the realization of the reason for the form of a chair or house occur simultaneously, then realization has begun. That means that

Gobbler, c. 1943

thinking has been a means to an end, and that the end has been reached. This is the opposite of "taking for granted." The realization precludes the possibility of that.

In another fragment, he emphasizes the role of the senses in bringing about the "consciousness" that keeps us alive:

The realization of form and space is through feeling. When I feel the beauty of a flower or the trunk of a tree I am at once inducted into a world of three dimensions and have a sense of form which is the opposite of artificial forms and conventions. I live and have my being in a world of color and shape. Consciousness of this means being alive. You arrive at that consciousness through the five senses: smell, sight, hearing, touch and taste.

In the company of Best-Maugard and Hambidge, and drawing upon his own wide knowledge of world art, Bob was finding his way toward a new freedom in drawing, one which reflects joy and gratitude for his new surroundings. Looking back, several years later, he remembered the feeling that, at some point in his life, things had somehow gone wrong: "It was as if I had lost my flower and my chance of fruit, and what was left of the stem was being eaten by caterpillars. It's true that some of them would turn into butterflies, and I should try to be comforted by that thought. But it would take a good deal of effort."

That effort began to bear fruit at Oldfields, where he felt closer to the elements than ever before: the earth, the sky, the dramatic cloud formations he could see from the gallery, the sun, the waters of the sound. "I had never seen the sea until I stepped on to the front gallery," he wrote one day. "I was like this year's bird, born in the mountains. I had never seen the sea!" The very landscape invited one to draw: "The unending line of the horizon was broken by a bird's wings. A line on which to play heavenly music of vertical pine trees, cows, lighthouses and islands. And sight that was almost sound. A white bird lighting on a wharf post." Among his first discoveries were the domestic and barnyard animals: the sad, scrawny cows that wandered through the broken fences and gates onto the lawn, moving their heads to inaudible music; the noisy guinea hens; chickens and turkeys; cats (for him the most mystical of animals); the pelicans that posed on the pilings of the pier; the swaybacked horse, Jim, who pulled the wagon in which he gathered firewood with the children; the fiddler crabs who waved their arms in obeisance to the sun or celebrated the retreat of the tide (scientists were quite *wrong*, he insisted, when they said those arm movements were something "sexual," merely a mating ritual). Sissy sensed that, after his long period of silence and detachment, the "Alienado" (as he titled one of his self-portraits) was finding his way back to life, and that he was doing so through animals. "Holes in heaven are the birds, dogs, cats through which man may pass," he wrote on the back of a watercolor. He added, a little later: "Animals always act intelligently. . . . If a man could literally be guided by animals without losing his will or his manhood, he would act intelligently."

Almost anything he saw—trees, plants, insects—seemed to awaken wonder, and both his drawings and his writings, from those early days at Oldfields, reveal a rediscovered love of the creation: the "continuous gift of fire;
the heavenly gift of rain . . . the gorgeous carpets spread for my delight each
Fall." Language, too, was returning, and often he found time to record—in
word or image—moments of pure lyrical beauty. For him, time seemed to
move more slowly. It drifted by, in Sissy's words, "in the fine dreamy fashion
of childhood years." He would disappear for an entire morning, clipboard in
hand, pausing in the midday heat by one of the pools he called nullahs, where
he could soak himself, sit in the mud, and meditate.

> Today I cut bean poles. . . . The little ferns were particularly beautiful. Then,
> when I was hot, I found a deep black pool and bathed. The reflections were
> beautiful—sequences of purple and different greens and black. I decided that
> black was not a color, should not be considered with colors; that the colors all
> belong to the sense of sight, but black belongs to some sixth sense. I bathed
> my head and when I raised it I realized Medusa: the little trickles of water
> became alive and crawled down over my face. I've felt the same, or something
> like it, with raindrops, each drop became a live being without body as soon as
> it touched me. I brought the beanpoles home and planted them in the garden,
> not in the beans but in the peas, and cultivated with the plow (I'm beginning
> to think that all forms are created by the sun as it moves to the west).

He thought often of the Psalms, and so did Sissy—she, praying for
strength, and he, praising God for the creation. "It is not enough to love it,"
Bob reminded himself, with a new sense of certainty. "You must show that
you love it or it will change. Love plants and animals. Plant gardens and show
the animals that you love them. If you like good weather, a blue sky and trees
and flowers, show it. These things are yours. Play with and enjoy them. Cows,
trees, and the birds! They want to be admired and loved. Establish a relationship with the general order of things. Evolution, if there is such a thing, did
not take place over a period of thousands of years. It is literally happening in
this very second."

Perhaps to express that sense of gratitude, he began a series of "calendar
drawings"—first in ink, later in watercolor—in which he captures his daily
activities and typical seasonal phenomena. Each stylized vignette is framed in
a box with the date written just under the margin in the lower left corner,
although it seems obvious that he worked on distinct series of them from

Muse

about 1941 to 1943, drawing dozens at a time, thinking back over all he had done or seen during the preceding period. Like a modern *Très Riches Heures*, the calendar drawings "consecrate" times and places, plants and animals, or turn daily activities into memorable or "typical" episodes, forming an idealized "life of Walter Anderson," born from a returning sense of self: he has gained sufficient distance from his problems to see himself as "protagonist," as the "subject" of a life. A few of the drawings commemorate an event in his daily existence: some glowing oranges, for example, signal the number of days he had been on a fruit diet; scenes of carpentry show his progress on a guest house. Works and days: he plows the garden, catches crabs, goes to the dentist, or swims off the Oldfields pier. He was living his own sort of Virgilian *Georgics*, relishing every aspect of life on a coastal farm. It isn't enough to plow the land, he advises the city dweller in a note; you must *dance* as you plow in order for things to grow. And, to escape the city entirely, you must "dance your own music," and not some "square-dance sanctioned by the gods." His, however, was a Hindu muse, not a Virgilian one. Time and again he drew a figure reminiscent of Sarasvati, Hindu goddess of learning and music. He portrays her not with the musical instrument she holds in traditional renditions, but with a bucket of paint in one hand and a brush in the other, in flowing robes flecked with stylized raindrops. Around the upper body of the goddess, suggesting wings, are a pair of mallards in flight. Wavy lines—currents of water—rise from her head. The figure advances toward the viewer, and in several of these drawings he sketches a compass rose and the letters NW, an allusion to the northwesterly winds (preceded by rain) that had always given him ideal conditions for artistic creation, or, as Sissy put it, a "strange exultation or exaltation" when "sky and air seem swept of all impurities" and the heart swells with hope.

Part of the "recovery" Sissy had noticed at Oldfields was that, for all his rapture over his new surroundings, her husband no longer lived entirely in the present; there was an awareness, now, of economic realities and of his own future. Shortly after moving in with her and the children, he had decided to produce a new series of figurines to sell at Shearwater. In December 1941 a local newspaper announced that they would portray "life along the Gulf. . . . There will be travelers, oystermen, shrimpers, all with their proper gear." Days after Pearl Harbor, the reporter found the idea of the three brothers, "working quietly in a natural setting to produce beauty" was "a tonic in this war-torn world." But unlike the widgets Bob had toiled over earlier—the figurines of blacks, pirates, and football players—production of the new series was to take place entirely at Oldfields. Over the objections of Mr. Grinstead, and perhaps of Sissy, he built a wood-burning kiln in the old carriage house, a large building just south of the main house with three bedrooms and a big bay for carriages or cars. He drew the kiln design from that of a great Renaissance Italian maker of majolica, Cipriano Piccolpasso, and fired it for the first time one day in February 1942, when the earth was coming to life after the family's first winter at Oldfields. A sluggish, blind old water moccasin was basking in the sun, and sparrows twittered in two cedar trees planted, long ago, for Pat and Sissy when they were born. Little white and pink asters dotted the meadow, and there were violets in the sheltered spots. Sissy felt that the first firing was "a happening of magnitude." She recorded it in her journal, and Bob in a calendar drawing. All day they fed the kiln "a fairly slim diet of fat pine" and watched the smoke coming from its vents, black at first, and then much paler. The sun sank into the sound and later, in the moonlight, flanked by two of their cats, Webb and One-Eye, they peeked through a watch hole in the kiln and saw a clear, "diamond-pure atmosphere." It was a joyful moment. They longed for the presence of the family, especially Peter, to observe and advise. They cut off the fuel after twelve hours, cooled the ware for a day, and removed the first figurine. But their joy was short-lived. One of the calendar drawings, dated December 23, perhaps from that same year, shows Mr. Grinstead's old carriage house in flames, with onlookers who raise their arms in mock horror as they stare at the conflagration. There were no fire engines in Gautier, and the old building burned to the ground. Sissy felt it was a devastating loss, not only for her father and her—the carriage house had been a part of her childhood—but also for him:

> A few pieces from that unlucky kiln are still extant. Of course, they did not come out as they were planned. He had made them in slip without glaze, and the strange alchemy of the firing had turned the natural clay color a smoky gray and the red a rich chocolate, while surface was hard, almost vitrified. Most of the figures belonged to the farm—cows, horses, ducks, guinea hens, a plowman, a corn harvester. A few figures belonged to the sea—a magnificent schooner, an oyster opener in his skiff, a fisherman, and a strange little standing lute-player. Most of them he dumped over the bluff.

Within days, however, he was redesigning his prodigious flower and vegetable garden, using the bricks from the kiln to line it with pathways, and

Unloading the Kiln at Oldfields (calendar drawing), c. 1942

bringing Oldfields very close to self-sufficiency at a time when Ocean Springs and Biloxi were, like the rest of wartime America, subject to food rationing. "We would live to perfection with no outside contacts right now," Sissy wrote in her journal in May 1942. "Today's products included more milk and cream than we know what to do with, about five quarts, twenty-one eggs . . . a half bushel beans, a half pound butter, two quarts buttermilk, potatoes ad lib, crabs ad lib, blackberries, honey, squash . . ."

Her creativity seemed to awaken along with his. Her desire to write was stronger than ever, though the form was indistinct, blurred by the host of daily chores that began early each morning. She filled a notebook with stories for Billy and Mary and wrote poems for them, some illustrated by Bob:

The rain in winter has a sound
quite different from the rain in spring.
It falls directly on the ground,
nor stops for anything.
In spring, in summer and in fall
you hardly hear the rain at all.

She planned an ambitious novel, "in tapestry form," about life on the coast. But caring for two grown men who, in different ways, "were having trouble with their minds," was exhausting, and she had the "dreadful feeling of being alone at the center." When she thought of her daily routine, she wondered where she could possibly find more time to write. She had Robert to help with Mr. Grinstead, and Suzy to help with the cooking and cleaning. The Yocum family helped care for the animals. It was the responsibility that overwhelmed her, and there was no one to share it with. Up at seven; breakfast and dish-washing; attending to chickens and cow; picking vegetables or crabbing; cleaning the house; swimming with the children; lunch; rest with children; supper; gardening, chickens, pig, the cow again; putting Billy and Mary to bed; reading and writing with Bob; and falling into bed herself, exhausted, at nine-thirty or ten. "If dog, cat or whatnot is sick or needs cleaning, bathing, *me*. If screens need attention, *me*. If trash needs burning, cans burying, *me*." Despite that routine, she was writing poetry more steadily than ever. Fiction, too, occurred to her, in scenes or conversations that "came into [her] head from someplace," she didn't know where. "Each day should contain its measure of creative effort, or at least mental effort, or just plain 'letting the imagination run wild,'" she wrote. For Bob's thirty-ninth birthday, on September 29, 1942, she offered him these verses, an enumeration of all that he most loved:

These things are most for you.
North-west days.
Horn Island ways,
Music and dancing too.
All winged and flying things,
beauty of line

Pine Trees, c. 1943

and scent of pine,
each joyful bird that sings,
the whitest beach, the bluest sky,
the gentlest rain,
the frog's refrain,
at night, the heron's cry
and in the heavens' height
each burning star—

all these most are
yours through the lover's right.
I cannot give the things you now possess,
so for your birthday take my fond caress.

She had never ceased to admire his sensuous love of life and his gentleness with nature, but wondered, as she had so often before, why he had never guessed what she wanted. A little "tenderness. Just a little." "Wonderful word, tenderness," she wrote in her journal. "Linger over it. It goes with caress and has much to do with love, less with passion. It connotes sympathy and under-standing and thoughtfulness. Respect, too. For one who is tender is gentle, and gentleness asks leave. I would give and receive it, so help me God." In some ways, the first year at Oldfields had been a difficult one for her, with the profound sadness of a miscarriage and the weariness, caused by severe bleed-ing, she had felt ever since. Some verses, illustrated by Bob, describe her "emptiness." Bitterly, she reproached him for his inability to acknowledge her anger and depression:

I tremble with my emptiness.
All my insides are gone
and I am hollow like a shell,
or like a dried, deserted well.
My anger left me bitter,
my anger did me drain,
my anger, like a river,
was swollen with the rain.
You raised some levees round it,
you tried to shut it in,
I made a cut-off through the wood
to let my anger in.
You should have been the quiet sea,
receiving both my hurt and me.

If he had felt any sympathy, he hadn't shown it. "To My Love," she had titled the birthday poem. But there were constant reminders that they thought of love in two entirely different ways. For him it was a "universal lan-guage," like birdsong, a force of nature, "a constant thing like fire or water," always there, sustaining all creation, transcending the relationship of any two people: "*amor che move il sol e anche le stelle.*" Love had nothing to do with "you and me." It was the spiritual acumen that allowed him to peer into nature: "Without love, man is blind. Aided by the light of love, man may see through a stone wall." Love could even be applied to color: "Blue may be identified with the reception of love; red and yellow with the giving of love; and green with the result." For Sissy, it was "being able to be the other so completely that nothing he can

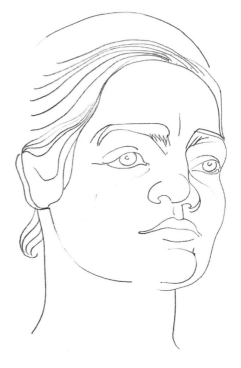

Sissy, c. 1943

do can hurt you [and] you cannot hurt him." To her, perfect love meant that "one mind could not differ from the other in the expression of its love." If Bob's idea of love was a state of heightened awareness of the beauty and bounty of nature, hers lay in the possibility of two souls becoming one, in intimate communion with God. "All that they did—even to the sex act, especially that—would be done through and for Him. The male could not dominate the female. There could be no 'against will,' no 'shame.'" With Bob, there was no such "intimate communion"—not the kind she wanted. He could live without it. And at times the natural world triumphed over physical desire: "I have no new desires. All mine are shared by thousands of people: for a woman's breasts, for [a] man's shoulder. Strangely, I have almost the same feeling for both. Which would probably disappear in a trip to the mountains."

At Oldfields, despite their fundamentally different views of love and desire, Sissy had given him the most precious of gifts: a freedom greater than he had known in many years. For her, that freedom seemed elusive. Burdened by her responsibilities—for him, her father, and the children—it was difficult for her not to feel envy, even resentment.

PERSPECTIVES

One of the things Sissy worried less about now was Bob's relationship with Billy and Mary. He had become a father—a generous, impatient, unconventional father—leading them on excursions to the beach and sharing his enthusiasm for birds, wildflowers, and arrowheading. On a hot summer day, when they were tired from walking, the three of them would plunge into the water and he would teach the children how to attract fish: if they put their mouths at the level of the water and blew gently, minnows would nibble at their lips. On the bluff at Oldfields, the three of them played wild games of hide-and-seek with their own improbable "Indian" identities: Billy became "Balboa"—why, no one knew—and Mary, "Imogene." He "signaled his whereabouts with bird sounds." On their walks he often drifted away behind a bird, dragonfly, or rare moth, but they knew that, unlike Sissy, he would never wait for them or pick them up and carry them. And yet, he could be incredibly attentive. When Mary was composing her first little poems, he sat on the gallery listening to her, writing down her every word, making her feel that nothing mattered more to him. "Gently!" he would tell her as he lifted her up to see a bird's nest or showed her some baby animal. The admonition reappears in a special Valentine's Day card.

In the fall of 1943, Sissy discovered that she was pregnant again. Remembering his denial, a couple of years earlier, that Billy and Mary were really his children, she waited as long as possible to tell him, dreading his reaction. To her immense relief, he covered her with kisses and announced: "He will be Leif." Leif, for Leif Eriksson. Absent for the birth of his first two children, he

Billy and Mary Swimming

had accepted them—Sissy once said—"like rather fascinating bits of human-ity that happened to be there." But by now nothing interested him more than birth and development, and he followed all of the details of Sissy's pregnancy, at least until April, when he sailed away to North Key in the Chandeleurs to join the pelicans that were nesting there. When he realized Sissy must be about to give birth, he cut off his visit and sailed through a storm back to Old-fields, but found only Mr. Grinstead and Robert, who told him that Sissy had already left for the hospital in Ocean Springs. He pedaled to Shearwater on his bike and fell exhausted into a chair at the Barn, until his mother prodded him awake and the two of them raced to the hospital. It was a girl—seven pounds, nine ounces, with a "terrible temper"—but the name was to remain. Leif! Less than a month after she was born, even before the umbilical cord was healed, he carried her down to the beach and danced with her in the water.

At Oldfields Sissy learned to accept—even to respect—his peculiar way of caring for the children. Once, when she was away in New Orleans, Billy devel-oped such severe stomach pains that Bob emerged from his attic studio and declared that he needed to be taken immediately to a doctor. He drove him to Ocean Springs, one hand on the child and the other on the wheel, but the

If you should find a little fairy.
Knocking at your door my Mary.
Treat her gently, gently please.
When she drops down on her knees
She's holding out my heart to you

Valentine's Day card for Mary

doctor's office was closed and he hurried across the bridge to the hospital in Biloxi. A doctor poked and probed, drew a blood sample and asked for permission to operate: it looked like appendicitis.

Disgusted with needles and poking hands, Bob picked up his son, made his way past the doctors, who predicted the worst of consequences, and stopped the car by Davis Bayou, one of the nullahs where he had always found refreshment and renewal. Billy was burning up with fever and barely conscious, but Bob lowered him carefully into the shallow water and sat with him, fanned by the breeze, until the sun sank into the water. He told Sissy later that he had not prayed. "It was deeper than that," she remembered him saying. "I think that Billy and I became one with the time and the place and with whatever beneficent genie presides over nullahs. Presently he opened those huge green eyes of his and smiled at me." When they got home to Oldfields, he bathed his son, dressed him in a nightgown, gave him a bottle—the only time he ever fed a baby—and fell into bed, exhausted.

To the delight of Billy and Mary, he often turned the house into a theater. One Christmas Eve, when Sissy had ordered Indian costumes for Billy and Mary, he made them tepees out of burlap feed sacks and painted them with Indian symbols, gathered holly, pine saplings, and smilax, and transformed the cold central hallway into an Indian camp. He made bamboo stars and candle-holders with real candles for the tree (and fell asleep in the dining room while the tree and part of the mantelpiece caught on fire). When he read to Mary and Billy from *The Odyssey*, he made them a five-foot model of Ulysses' boat, carved from a log, with rowers and oars that moved. He made dolls for Mary—he turned a cypress knee into a likeness of Sissy—and in summer 1943 he treated them to a puppet show about the rhythms of life in the "cut-over lands," where the timber companies had clear-cut the first-growth pines: a sacred spot for both Bob and Sissy. To her, they were a symbol of faith, accept-ance, and renewal. Years later, Mary remembered how her mother's sadness over the cutting of the trees, among the last virgin pines on the coast, gave way to a joy in the transformation that followed the loggers and their oxen.

> She believed that the cutting of the trees somehow altered the surface drainage and caused a wetland. As the ravaged earth, newly opened to the sun and to the drenching rain, began to heal, plants appeared that had not grown there before. Long golden grasses of the pine savannah waved across the cutover land, replacing the long-leaf pineneedled carpet of the lost forest.
>
> Pale gold, the grass was a perfect foil for the jewel-like collection of life, both flora and fauna, which miraculously appeared beside the road. . . . Plants share this boggy world with assorted dragonflies, spiders, grasshoppers, bee-tles, wasps in wild red and blue, marvelously dressed frogs, crawfish and tur-tles. My father brought me here when I was very young . . . at a time in his life when his difficulties with other people seemed insurmountable. When I look at his angry drawings of the destroyed forest and then at the joyful musical celebrations of the varied forms he found in the bog, I understand a verse I found among his writings:

> *But if thou canst not love thy friends,*
> *thou still mayst love thy foe.*

For he hath brought thee low
and taught thy ear to know
the voice of growing grass.

In the puppet play he devised, what mattered to him was the counterpoint of flora and fauna. He wanted to experiment with "synchronized puppetry": "to time the leap of a frog with the blooming of a flower. . . . A whole symphony could be built up in the same way." A host of "characters" from the cutover lands were cut from beaverboard and vividly painted: turtles, frogs, pitcher plants, skinks, moths, beetles, the sun, stars. In the attic, he constructed an ingenious system of ropes, fishing line, and pulleys to work the figures, some of which were six feet tall. From behind a stage he beat the drum and played music on a homemade bamboo instrument, narrated the story, and worked the intricate machinery. Somehow, a moth emerged from its cocoon, a seed sprouted and grew, and a plant produced a flower. Skinks rustled, ran and stopped, beetles went cr-r-rk, cr-r-r-r-k, and a chorus of frogs greeted the rising sun: Up-urrr-*UP*! Up-urr-*UP*! All this in harmony with the "other cycle" of the sun, moon, and stars. There were repeat performances until the summer heat drove everyone but him from the attic.

One of the underlying tensions at Oldfields was Bob's uneasy relationship with Billie Grinstead. For years, the two had detested each other. They were temperamental opposites—Bob, passionate and impulsive, and his father-in-law, deliberate in thought and movement, slower still from the effects of arteriosclerosis. For Grinstead, Bob would always be the Diogenes who entered his home with muddy feet, the mad artist whose "widgets" had failed to support his daughter. Bob could not abide his father-in-law's stodgy sense of decorum, his illness, and his total dependence on Sissy and Robert, who dressed him in his seersucker suit and Harvard tie and took him out onto the gallery or the lawn, where he sat smoking the cheroots that Sissy substituted for the big cigars he had always preferred. The thought that Grinstead was supporting Sissy, him, and the three children, and that Sissy not only cared for but also "relied" on her father, made matters still worse. For both of them, family meals were an ordeal, and one evening at supper, when all was "quiet and peaceful," Bob picked up a pancake and flung it across the table, hitting his father-in-law in the eye. "Is it fair to ask Daddy to go on living in the same house with Bob?" Sissy asked herself in her journal. "Is it fair to let the chil-

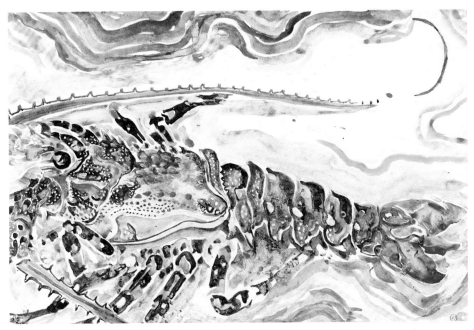

Chinese Lobster, 1949
Watercolor on paper, 8½ x 13 in.

Mardi Gras, New Orleans, c. 1962
Watercolor on paper, 8½ x 11 in.

Mary Anderson, 1952
Watercolor on paper,
11 x 8½ in.

Portrait of Young Woman
(*Patricia Anderson Findeisen*),
c. 1954
Watercolor on paper,
11 x 8½ in.

New Orleans, c. 1943
Watercolor on paper, six sheets each
25 x 19 in.

Horn Island, c. 1960
Oil on plywood panel, 25 x 60 in.

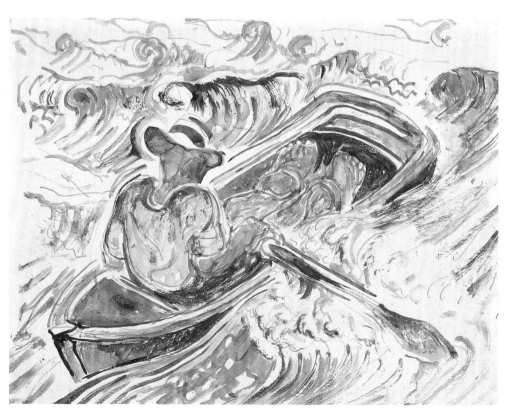

Walter Rowing His Boat, c. 1955
Watercolor on paper, 8½ x 11 in.

Grackles, c. 1960
Watercolor on paper, 8½ x 11 in.

Owl, c. 1960
Watercolor on paper, 8½ x 11 in.

Stone Crab, dated Oct. 9, 1951
Watercolor on paper, 8½ x 11 in.

Waves, c. 1955
Watercolor on paper, 8½ x 11 in.

Coots and Waves, c. 1961
Watercolor on paper, 11 x 8½ in.

Red-Head Duck, c. 1955
Watercolor on paper,
11 x 8½ in.

Baby Herons, c. 1960
Watercolor on paper, 8½ x 11 in.

Two Birds in a Tree Plate, c. 1955
Ceramics with underglaze decoration
Thrown by Peter Anderson, decorated by Walter Anderson

Purple Gallinules, c. 1960
Watercolor on paper, 8½ x 11 in.

Dead Red-Head Duck, c. 1955
Watercolor on paper,
11 x 8½ in.

Duck Bowl, c. 1953
Ceramic, 3¼ x 10 x 10 in.

Green Heron, c. 1960
Watercolor on paper, 8½ x 11 in.

Racoon, c. 1960
Watercolor on paper, 8½ x 11 in.

Reflections in a Bull-Rush Pool, c. 1960
Watercolor on paper, 11 x 8½ in.

Baby Bird, c. 1960
Watercolor on paper, 8½ x 11 in.

Goldenrod on Horn Island, c. 1955
Watercolor on paper, 8½ x 11 in.

Rowing at Night, c. 1960
Watercolor on paper, 8½ x 11 in.

Chesty Horse, designed c. 1935, decorated c. 1950
Ceramic, 13½ x 4½ x 14 in.

Sea, Earth and Sky Vase, c. 1934
Ceramic, 12 x 7 x 7 in.
Thrown by Peter Anderson,
decorated by Walter Anderson

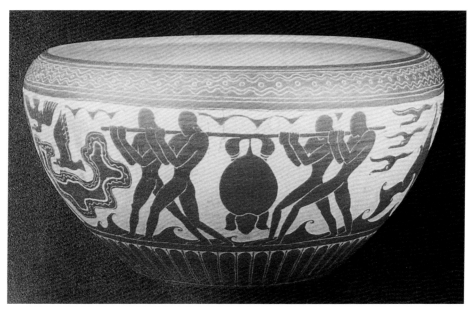

Harvesting the Sea Bowl, c. 1934
Ceramic, 7½ x 14½ x 14½ in.
Thrown by Peter Anderson, sgraffito decoration by Walter Anderson

Southeast corner of "Little Room" Mural, c. 1951–53
The Cottage at Shearwater
Oil on wood

Northwest corner of "Little Room" Mural, c. 1951–53
The Cottage at Shearwater
Oil on wood

Self-Portrait, c. 1955
Watercolor on paper,
11 x 8½ in.

The Islander, 2001
Christopher Inglis Stebly (Walter Anderson's grandson)
Hand-colored block print,
21 x 13½ in.

dren in for the fear and nervous tension that goes with that kind of craziness—lack of any right feeling or control? No it isn't." It was "incredible," she
added angrily, that "an artist, a person of supreme sensitivity, should be so
impervious to others, so soaked in self." And what "self" was there, anyway?
"It could be big-time—universal—and he lets himself melt away doing little
blockprints that probably won't even sell—and I feel guilty—not he." As
always, she reminded herself that he was ill, and that what he needed was "the
constant protection of a wall of prayer."

"God in Bob, God over Bob, God through God," was her mantra, an "affirmation of his worth, his safety, his right action," a reminder that the Divinity
was in his person, that it poured out of him to others, and that it was his protection. For a few years now, she had been meeting once a week with a prayer
group. At least once she brought in a Mrs. Johnson, a healer associated with
author and inspirational speaker Glenn Clark, one who visited "enmeshed
individuals who lacked the power to get themselves out of their own predica-
ments." Sissy found her "wonderful, full of compassion," and hoped she could
help Bob. Sitting one day on a log on the beach with the two of them, Mrs.
Johnson described the perfect family. Years later, Sissy remembered the
exchange.

"The first family is the Human Family under God the Father . . ."

"No," Bob answered. "The family of living creatures!"

A smile crossed his lips. He was about to revise an earlier thought.

"Look. . . . See those fiddler crabs? You *think* you're witnessing an act of
worship. But you're wrong. The scientists are right. See the claws raised in
obeisance to the sun? Actually it is an act of sexual invitation. The big-clawed
are the males and they are showing off for those insignificant little females.
It's a mating ritual."

Moments later, he got up, bowed, raised his arm "in fiddler-like salute" and
began pushing his sailboat over the mudflats. *His* religion, he said later, was
"work," not "mass hysteria." "Of what value to the individuals concerned is a
large religious movement—jehad or cathedral building, if there is no determined objective and the motive power depends largely on mass hysteria? Is it
not of more value to the aforementioned individual to put in one day of serious work with a definite object? For one man who will do a day's work there
are ten thousand who would go into a religious war or help build a cathedral.
Work: an activity which requires the use of all of the faculties of man."

Seldom did he attend church. Once he went with his mother and Pat to hear Glenn Clark in Mobile, and one Sunday he accompanied Sissy and the children to St. Pierre's Episcopal, in Gautier, the little wooden chapel where they had married. This time he had his clipboard with him and in the middle of the service he rose from their pew, went to the door, and began to draw. What he dreamed of, he told her later, was to enliven the church with murals. On one wall he would portray St. Peter—patron of the church—and on the other, St. John, in honor of its first pastor, John Chipman, departed friend of Billie Grinstead. He would work for free, he said. But the congregation said no. Paints were expensive, the murals were likely to be too "modern," and the congregation had no desire to indulge the "crazy artist" who sparred over religion and theology whenever the pastor came on his rounds to Oldfields, and who couldn't sit still through the only service he had attended since his wedding. Besides, a local legend was at stake. On one of the walls a spot of mildew had morphed into an effigy of Chipman.

He had been dreaming of murals for over a decade, and since the day he had moved into Oldfields, probably long before, he had regarded its high, smooth walls as an ideal space for them. But to his father-in-law those walls were sacred. Decades earlier, Billie and Marjorie Grinstead had had them restored to their antebellum splendor, finding the best plasterer on the coast to tint the plaster a creamy pink that stood out elegantly against the black woodwork. Murals? It was bad enough to listen to Bob's movements in the attic—"never meant to be lived in"—and to worry whether the plaster would crack under the strain. But "a painter," Bob wrote, "always gets what he wants." By the mid-forties he had found his way back into the world of color, and thousands of sketches had prepared him for something sweeping and summative. If he could not paint directly on the walls, he would paint watercolors on large sheets of paper, combine them into a mural and fasten them to the walls with tape or thumbtacks.

An undated note records his intentions:

Sequence in pattern
change
dominance of color
a certain motive
and above all a main theme (*one*)
As the beginning of the world or the tree of life.

Mary, Billy, John, and Leif

A theme? *One?* Anything would do. The "beginning of the world" was wherever he looked. "Nativity at the Barn," spring plowing, doves and pine trees, the Oldfields garden, the glory of a peacock or rooster, the sun-dews, pitcher plants and wood lilies of the cutover lands. In a series of watercolors done on nineteen-by-twenty-four-inch charcoal paper, each animal or plant is bathed in a golden aura, as though seen in the early-morning sunlight of the first day of creation, before man has grown accustomed to his surroundings. The "aura" makes the ordinary appear miraculous, drawing out the numinous, divine qualities of matter and bringing creation into the present. Idealized objects multiply into series and are arranged in horizontal bands, as in Egyptian relief. One object—sheep, pitcher plant, cow, pine, or pig—becomes a sequence, a "musical" alleluia to the abundance of nature. The *one* becomes the many, and vice versa, brought into "harmony" by the repetition of the Best-Maugard motifs: the s-curves and straight lines of trees or the semicircles of cow horns or sheep's legs. "The idea," Bob wrote, "is to relate calves to oak trees, and heaven knows it's a difficult thing enough to do." In a note he expresses the idea more fully: "The sheep grazed at right angles but kept getting closer. They stopped with heads up, then started, ran away, then stopped. Then, strung out in a line, walked determinedly westward—then stopped and started, all in perfect harmony with the interrupted lines of pine trees behind them. Animals always move in relation to their surroundings.

Cow, c. 1945

Harmony is not just a word. It is literally true." There is unity, also, in the use of color. The primary colors capture a world: the blue of the figures, the lemon-yellow aura which seeps into their forms, the warmth of subtle reds. The intended effect is that of a visual "symphony." They "compose well," Bob sometimes said of his subjects, or "they compose well with themselves," and the musical nuance was not lost on him.

A little later, he began another remarkable series (now known as the "Trunk Paintings"), using poster paints from the five-and-ten on long strips of wallpaper, nineteen inches wide and up to twenty feet in length, with bold free-flowing lines. Here, too, the figures are edged with an "aura"—not pale or transparent yellow as in the earlier paintings, but iridescent. This second series—farm scenes and fairy tales—prepared him for a remarkable corpus of linoleum block prints. One day, after returning from the five-and-dime in Biloxi, Bob told Sissy he was disgusted by the poor quality of the art people hung in their homes, particularly in their children's rooms. What he wanted to make were huge, colorful prints that could be hung vertically like scrolls or horizontally like friezes or "overmantels" and sold at the Pottery at reasonable prices: his own answer to the abstruseness of modern art. "If we are to develop a common language of forms in art, it must be through the decorative," he wrote in 1947. With the war drawing to a close, stores in Biloxi were selling surplus "battleship linoleum," thicker than the ordinary kind, with heavy burlap backing. He bought rolls of it, stretched it out on the floor in the attic, and carved so rapidly and assuredly that he did not pause to print one block before going on to the next. Huge mounds of linoleum shavings showered down the attic stairs. He inked the blocks, laid long strips of wall-paper on top of them and printed them by pressing them with a roller: a piece of sewer pipe filled with sand. He colored each print by hand, working with bold, swift strokes, and the showroom at Shearwater was soon glowing with fables and fairy tales, scenes from the *Arabian Nights*, *Mother Goose*, Grimm, Perrault, and Andersen, Arthurian legend, and *Aesop's Fables*. Like the Best-Maugard motifs, the tales themselves were a "common language," a primer of the imagination. An art historian has called them the first body of oversized prints ever made by an American artist.

Additional evidence of his interest in a common imaginative heritage had been coming to life each night in the long dining room at Oldfields. He slept little, almost not at all, and often when Sissy got up in the middle of the night she would find him at the table reading. As he turned the pages with his left hand, he used his right to sketch what he was reading about. Around him, pen-and-ink or crayon drawings spilled from the table onto the wide pine floorboards. Sissy would collect them each morning, tie them in bundles, and toss them upstairs to the attic. No wartime "blackout" for him! The lights were on, shutters and curtains were thrown open to the night air, and government-imposed precautions were flouted. There were *no* German U-boats in the gulf, he told her; none, at least, near Gautier, Mississippi. "At first I spent quite a lot of time with him, reading aloud," Sissy remembered later.

> But gradually I became persona non grata. The dining room where he worked was at one end of the 85-foot house. I think he felt sufficiently removed from the rest of us. In the early evening, I would make a pot of coffee, leaving it in the pantry for him. Whenever I went out to see what was going on, he was so absorbed that he didn't even notice, and became much annoyed if I became obtrusive with "it's past bedtime" and such. Sometimes in the very early morning, when he was just stopping, I would catch him quietly feeding a tea-spoon [of] coffee to a couple of very large oak-tree cockroaches who seemed to be his pets, and he would laugh, gently but pointedly, when I objected—life seemed to be one long struggle against cockroaches. He said they were his "familiars." The illustrating seemed, certainly, to take the place of any interest in more usual things such as sex. Often we would hear him singing Beethoven's *Seventh Symphony* or the *Emperor Concerto*; he often worked to his own or someone else's music.

Over a period of several years, in nearly ten thousand sketches—all of them on typewriter paper—he brought to life some of his favorite books: Pope's translation of Homer's *Iliad*, Coleridge's "Rime of the Ancient Mariner," *Alice in Wonderland*, *Hamlet*, *Paradise Lost* and *Paradise Regained*, *Faust*, the works of Ossian, *Don Quixote*, Bulfinch's *Legends of Charlemagne*, and Darwin's *Voyage of the Beagle*. For some titles, such as *Don Quixote* and *Paradise Lost*, he did two or three series, each executed in a distinctly different style. The sketches were "outline drawings," animations rather than illustrations: attempts to savor more fully the written word and to bring word and image, his two great loves, into the closest possible relationship. There is no evidence that they were meant to be shared with anyone. As the editor of these drawings, Redding Sugg, Jr., has observed, some form rapid sequences and produce the effect of an animated film, with touches of droll humor. Some plate designs, done during the same period, attempt to capture the same world of voyage and discovery.

Of all the figures he drew during his reading, one of his most beloved was Don Quixote. What Cervantes's novel shows (he says in a note) is that the "way or road is the important thing," and that an "object is important because it gives direction, not a thing to be claimed." The "road to Dulcinea" was what "made" the book. What must have attracted him, also, to Cervantes's "alienado," were the novel's ironic contrast of individual "madness" and collective "sanity" and, above all, Cervantes's humorism and gentle skepticism: his notion that the truth of a situation or the identity of an object—windmill, steed, or golden helmet—depends upon one's perspective. "Beware by whom you are called sane," Bob once wrote, in silent homage to the seventeenth-century Spaniard whose birthday he believed he shared. It was a sense of perspective he was beginning to apply both to nature and to his relations with others. In reaction to the anthropocentric, increasingly mechanistic world of the 1940s, he was beginning to imagine a universal "symphony" where different "points of view" and strata of life form a counterpoint that can be heard by anyone attentive enough to listen, although, of course, the symphony would never be "realized" at all without the artist. The idea of multiple worlds—within humanity, within each man, within nature—occurs frequently in his own writing, as does the imaginative leap into the worlds of others: the realm, say, of a turtle or frog or cat. This, too, was a turning outward, away from self-destruction.

> Every form in nature—cat, dog, pig, rat—have all had worlds made for them.
> Despise them as you—as man—will, each one has owned his world. So that

for the turtle, crawling low upon the earth and bearing the burden of his shell, the flowers were made, stars brought close and hung just above his head to fill the space between the blades of grass. The cat walks delicately, winding serpent-like between invisible obstacles, planting its four feet in the openings and flat places, not disturbing a leaf. The patient turtle will bore its way through thick grass for hours, to be rewarded with the sight of a star swaying from a tall stalk above its head, leg after leg, approaching a young plant, green and tender, brought up by the rain and the warmth of spring. He pauses, neck outstretched, listening, while the rain falls on his plated shell. The music dies away. He stretches out his neck and snaps off the young plant, close to the ground and crunches it between his jaws. Wheels begin to turn within him. The small eye gleams. He walks again . . .

At Oldfields, Walter Anderson's imaginative voyages—into literature or into the world of nature—whetted his appetite for real ones. The pastorale at Oldfields was interrupted by sailing trips to the islands; a trip by train to New York and Philadelphia, in fall 1942; another trip, on a new bike, to New Orleans in 1943; and a long trip, also by bicycle, down the Old Spanish Trail into the hill country of west Texas, to draw the landscape. In Philadelphia and New York, he had hoped to visit places where he might sell his block prints or interest people in his wallpaper designs. Instead, he feasted his eyes on the Chinese things at the University Museum in Philadelphia and on the Egyptian rooms at the Metropolitan in New York, and "tried drawing what I admired as an expression of appreciation." A model of Deir el-Bahri and a pink granite statue of Hatshepsut filled him with the longing to descend the Nile, perhaps in a canoe, as he had once descended the Mississippi. At the Metropolitan he paused before the Coptic textiles, "things from Cyprus and Crete," Etruscan art, early Greek figures, and Mesopotamian pottery. He decided that Epstein's *Woman and Child* was a "work of genius" and was "struck by the fact that medieval armor looked very much like Negro sculpture." Crossing Central Park to his old stomping grounds, the American Museum of Natural History, he took in Mayan art, drew skeletons, and went to the planetarium, where he "made the acquaintance of Gould's Belt and the Southern Cross." He saw other "heavenly things"—little sea animals that looked like snowflakes reproduced in glass—and drew the Alaskan Indian artifacts, with a "cunning little girl" doing her own drawings beside him.

Wartime New York was exhilarating, and there was a certain enjoyable tension in the atmosphere. He sat on a fire hydrant in Times Square, drawing the "heavenly crowds," and rode a bus up Fifth Avenue into the midst of a Navy

Day parade. At night, in the cold October air, "the windows were frosted, and the people had shifting auras of color from the red and green and blue neon signs" on the sidewalk. Crossing the Williamsburg Bridge to Brooklyn, he stared down into the river, "green with white seagulls and little boats blowing smoke into the fog." On the flat roofs of the houses around the bridge, little boys were "playing with their pigeons. One boy would throw a bird out into the air, and it would circle once and come right back like a toy."

> I bought paper and went up on the west end of [the] Bridge and drew people until I was ordered off by a policeman and taken to the precinct station, where my registration card was examined and copied. I was told at the desk to notify the policeman in charge of the bridge each time I went up. But outside I was told to get permission from the War Department. I wasn't sure about that, so asked another policeman, who told me to go to the Customs Office. I think there is a general feeling that anyone drawing might be a spy. So I don't think I'll draw again for a while.

Months later, he traveled to New Orleans, rising at midnight at Oldfields and pedaling his way down the coast. He stopped to swim off the Biloxi beach among "wonderful big illuminated jellyfish" that glowed in the phosphorus. When it began to rain, he took refuge in a culvert, and swam into an old drainage canal that had "grown up with all sorts of water plants—water lilies, arrowhead and other things." He swam again in the Pearl River, bobbing around in the water hyacinths, and reached the city around dawn, rolling up Elysian Fields Avenue past "tourist courts, hot dog stands, [and] beer-drinking places." In the city he searched the stores for a camp stool he could sit on while he drew the crowds, but found none ("either people have stopped sitting or stopped camping"). He bought a packing crate instead, and sketched on Canal Street, had a "wash and shave" in Audubon Park, and went to sleep on the levee. Army jeeps whizzed by in the night, on the alert for saboteurs. One morning he drew a group of black children sitting on logs, ready to go swimming. "They were beautiful. It was an experience I won't forget—to find pure beauty isolated so close to the mixture of the city carried you into another world." He drew tennis players and found a quiet place "and ate supper of bread and oranges, and watched fishermen and swans and the lights come on and shine reflected in the water." He drew the crowds and architectural detail of the business section, all very "stimulating."

Then, while I was drawing, I became conscious of a large pair of feet out of the corner of my eye. Raising my head the feet became a large blue police-man, and beside him was another. They questioned me and apparently were not satisfied with my answers, and when they found out I was not carrying my draft registration card . . . I was put in a car and holding my bicycle on the running board was taken to the first precinct station. I was again kept from telephoning, and told that my case was for the FBI.

The situation was more serious than he realized at first, and he spent the night in jail, sitting glumly on a bench while the police waited for a teletype from the registration board in Ocean Springs. In court, the next day, he sat among "rows of prisoners" and "a colored girl who held her head beautifully poised," and heard his case dismissed. Annette, who had been notified by telegram, came to the jail to get him, and took immediate objection to his shorts—she "insisted on pants." They went off to buy him clothes, and then to the Delgado Museum, where they listened to "heavenly movies of birds, the song being given contemporaneously with the picture." Annette turned the trip into a round of visits to friends and relatives, among them James Gowan-loch, of the department of conservation, an expert on snake bites and friend of the family who had helped spring Bob from jail. The day before his return, alone, to Ocean Springs, Bob went back to the levee, and had the "pleasure of telling the [same] policeman" who had arrested him that Gowanloch had asked him "to draw the whooping crane, a rare bird."

During the war years, Sissy struggled to get him to carry his registration card. Because he was strong and young (though unfit for the military), he was asked for it wherever he went. Once, on a voyage from Oldfields to the Chan-deleurs, he sailed into a storm off the tip of Horn Island. It was a foggy night, and his boat capsized in the turbulent waters. He swam against the tide toward the beach, fighting for his life, and when he staggered exhausted onto the shore, he wondered whether he was dreaming. Through the fog of Horn Island came a small locomotive. Dogs—German shepherds—sniffed at him, and soldiers handcuffed him and led him to a sort of barracks and asked him for his registration card. It was in his boat, he told them, and the boat was lost somewhere out in the gulf. When they towed it to shore, they found it in the garbage can where he carried his supplies; Sissy had tossed it in before his departure. He continued on to the Chandeleurs, with a damaged boat and no food at all—it had been washed overboard—wondering why Horn Island had

Wedding of the Cat Princess from Madame D'Aulnoy's *The White Cat, c. 1945*

been placed off-limits to civilians. But the story was just beginning. Sissy remembered that on the Chandeleurs his boat drifted away from the beach, and he was "marooned" for days.

He was fond of the walks he called "progresses," and another of his memorable voyages from Oldfields was a walking trip into the country northwest of Gautier, in late December of 1943, in search of the Mississippi sandhill crane: a huge archaic-looking bird, four feet tall with a six-foot wingspan. It wasn't long before he heard cowbells mingling with the strange call of the cranes: "something between bells and brass horns." There were eight of them, "walking along with their heads just below the horizon . . . one of the most heavenly sights" he had ever seen. They fled while he was drawing them, but the next day "a strange and secret thing happened," one which he would remember forever:

> I felt I needed a sign that the birds still loved me, and so I thought, "If only one of you will come a little closer I will know," and at once a hermit thrush came and sat on a stump a few feet from me, and a woodpecker with a red head came and lit on a trunk and put its head into the hole. Then I suddenly knew the meaning of love, and felt "my love has come to me," and knew that love meant having an object to love, and not reception; [no] amount of reception could possibly give understanding in the same way.

Mary Anderson Pickard noted, years later, that during the Oldfields years her father "mythologized" the birds and animals around him, awakening and maintaining a sense of wonder, and that he achieved what Joseph Campbell once described as "a sanctification of the local landscape." This trip was no exception. As he waded across bayous, emerged from a nullah "feeling like a god," and tramped the fields and country roads, shifting his heavy blanket roll from one shoulder to another, he imagined that the animals and birds he encountered "had all been at the crucifying of Christ." A thrush—the very thrush he was looking at—had terrified the Roman soldiers. A woodpecker had poked his beak into Christ's side to get his red head. Every animal he saw—a sheep he recognized from a previous meeting or some "incredible fox squirrels playing on a tree, with orange bellies, black faces and white ears"— partook, somehow, of the archetypal or ancient. He looked at a crane or cow or cat, and thought of Egypt, and once again, art came together with nature, and the past came into the present.

No creature was more mysterious to him, more beloved, or more imbued with myth and fable than the cat, friend of witches and stars, "thou who car- ryest the sun for a head, a serpent for a tail, and for feet four flowers which follow thee wherever thou dost go." The upper and lower worlds of cats were perfectly reconciled, he wrote, unlike those of "struggling, mistaken beings"

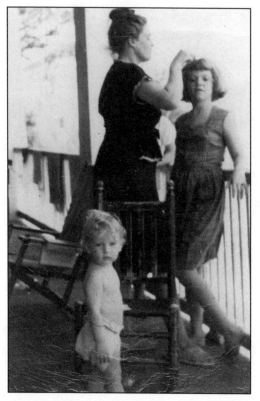

Sissy, Mary, and John on the gallery at Oldfields, 1948

like dogs and men. Oldfields was crawling with cats—not only Webb and One-Eye and their brood ("dependents or tutelary deities," he didn't know which) but also Anderson, a foul-smelling bedraggled female kitten who appeared on the doorstep one night infested with blowflies and suffering from dysentery. After Sissy nursed Anderson back to health, she followed Bob everywhere, and he drew her obsessively. Once she snapped at a piece of shrimp hanging from Billy's fishing pole, and Bob removed the fish hook embedded in her mouth, working as skillfully as a surgeon and making Sissy feel, both for Bob and for the stoical Anderson, who lay quiet and still, "the admiration one feels for heroes." The stillness and attentiveness of cats was, in fact, one reason he loved them. In a story he wrote for Billy and Mary, it is a cat—perhaps Anderson—who teaches a young boy "how to move gracefully, without making any noise. . . . And how all movement is to invisible music, although only a few people hear it. It comes from the sun and the wind and the movement of water and a running rabbit and a crowing cock, and together it is like a part of a great symphony. The longer we listen and the quieter we are, the more we hear of it, and when we do, we are part of the music, instead of an unwelcome interruption."

From 1941 to 1945, he brought to life thousands of cats, conjuring them up from the s-curves of Best-Maugard, along with block prints of Robinson, "Dick Whittington's Cat," "The White Cat" of Madame d'Aulnoy, and Puss in Boots. In the *Summa Artis* and at the Metropolitan Museum of Art he admired Egyptian cats. He remembered the cats of the Mayas, imagined Krishna moving through his garden accompanied by a pair of cats, and cele-

Sissy and Leif, Oldfields, c. 1945

brated the dreams of his own cat, asleep by the fire: "Many talk of heaven and hell and of the evils angels and devils devise for each other. I have seen a cat asleep by the fire creating new worlds (none of the sweetest) for both angels and devils." Proud of his "sympathetic understanding of cat nature," he guessed at their language. You could tell a great deal by a single meow: "I love you very much, but I think you might have given me a little of that last bowl of cereal." He loved the way cats "save face" among humans, and wrote of one: "She could suddenly pretend to be a kitten and run up a tree, and then pretend that she couldn't get down without losing face. But she could not return affection as it was given. She either had to show an unrequited love or a cool aloofness, but to those whose understanding was inferior she would occasionally hint that it was the dignity of the house she was considering, and not a personal dislike." When he looked at a cat, he marveled at how much man had sacrificed "in order to grow into a man." He had surrendered wings to the birds and flight, and fur and grace to the cats, and "beauty of coloring and stability of place to the flowers, and what he had left he had to divide with a wife and children, if he had any."

It was that notion of "dividing" his life—among his art, his travels, his family and, presumably, his cats—that brought an end to the years at Oldfields. By December 1946, when Sissy was pregnant with their fourth child, the two of them had already drifted apart. In a note found among his papers, he writes, almost certainly to Sissy, "The point is that although my unhappiness does make you suffer, that is my life and vitality. My happiness or loss of consciousness—which is what most people mean by happiness—makes you happy and cheerful. You can't turn back. You must be alive through consciousness . . ."

The baby, John Grinstead Anderson, was born on March 12. Two months later, after describing his birth and development, Sissy remarked: "I am at a low ebb. Feel guilty about Bob. We have separated. I can't figure out the right. Am trying to ask God." Eventually, she decided to clean up his studio in the attic.

> The puppets hung wearily from their fishing twine. The last bursts of linoleum chips lay at the head of the stairs. Clay scraps, plaster scraps, drawings . . . I sat on the edge of the old workbench and began to gather up scraps of paper. Most of them had writing on them, bits of poetry, bits of wisdom. I did try to bundle things into old trunks. . . . Suddenly, in the closeness of the attic, a horrible depression descended upon me. I was utterly unable to go on. I could not even get down the attic steps. I sat on the top step and slowly bumped myself to the bottom. I went straight to bed, and did not tackle the attic again for about ten years. There were many circumstances, but the real reason was of course reluctance—the holding back from final things that plagues so many lives.

He, too, was holding back from finality. When they separated, he had gone to live in the Cottage at Shearwater. But for a time, he would cycle at night to Oldfields to be with her, riding along the narrow highway between Ocean Springs and Gautier, at risk from passing cars, until a sniggering policeman asked Pat to tell her sister to "move to Ocean Springs before we pick him up in a basket." And then, in the fall of 1947 a hurricane with winds of up to 160 miles an hour roared down the coast, and wreaked havoc on the house and grounds. For Sissy, who was there alone with her children and father during some of the storm, it was a terrifying experience. Even before the storm started, one could hear the boom of the surf on Horn Island, seven miles out in the sound. The waters rose to the top of the bluff—twenty feet—and the waves flung sea spray over the house. As the bluff began to crumble, cows and barnyard animals were swept away. Peering through cracks in the shutters, Sissy saw huge live oaks turned on their side between the house and the water, and feared that the house, too, was about to collapse. With the wind howling outside, and Suzy kneeling in prayer in the pantry, three-year-old Leif danced excitedly from room to room, crying, "Over the bluff we go!"

When Bob came, days later, and saw the devastation, he told Sissy how sorry he was not to have been there to help. She simply stared at him. "Why?" she asked bitterly. She hadn't expected more. She had spent the summer taking courses for a provisional teachers licence, and that September, she began teaching second grade in Pascagoula, feeling "both terrified and exhilarated . . . terrified because I was so shy and had spent so many of the last years in a sort of seclusion," and thrilled because she had taken an important step toward independence and was doing something she had always wanted to. Months later, in February 1948, Billie Grinstead died. It comforted Sissy to think that he had spent the last years of his life in a place he had always loved, but with his death her life reached another turning point. Oldfields was no place for a "single" woman living alone with four children. Years later she remembered that "with no man present at night" she had to "fight off visitors." In the fall, she took the children back to Ocean Springs and began teaching first grade there. With Bob living in the Cottage, she found a house in town. They were renting, but to Sissy it felt like a place of her own.

THE ISLANDER

From the bluff at Oldfields, on a clear day, one could look out over the sound to Horn Island, faintly visible on the horizon. The island was as intimate and beloved a part of Sissy's childhood as the great house itself. Often she had sailed there for the day with her parents and their friends. She and Pat would race across the point to the gulf side, hunting for shells while her mother and grandmother came along slowly behind them under their parasols. There were wild ponies back then, and Pat would climb onto one of them and ride it until it tumbled her into a bush or onto the soft white sand. At mealtime, the Grinsteads and their friends would arrange their chairs in the shade of some huge pine. They were precious memories: the scent of rosemary, the tablecloths dappled with shade, the gradual shifting of chairs to keep ahead of the sun.

Years later, during their courtship, Bob had dreamed of sharing the island with her. They would live on "palmetto, cabbage and ghost crabs, with an occasional salad of morning glory leaves." They would stay awake on moonlit nights, catch turtles, and float in the surf, looking up at the stars. But during the years at Oldfields, Bob had begun to make the island his own. In one of her poems, Sissy watches "weary-eyed" while his white sail vanishes behind the curtain of the rain and reappears in a circle of sunlight, making her long to follow him, "to find green water and the sun, / whiteness and brightness, salt, and air unbreathed."

Another poem, found among *his* papers, might well have been addressed to her:

Raindrops, c. 1945

Leave the land to the beasts that toil.
Leave the land to the men of the soil.
Leave the tree and dance with me
over the deep and dark blue sea.
"I can't," said the leaf. "I'm tied to the tree."

In a note probably written during his last years at Oldfields, he had summarized his indecision: "They have tried to keep me from going where I could paint without them. So shall I go where I can paint without them? Or shall I go where I can paint only with them? Or shall I stay where I can paint partly with them and partly without them?" By the late 1940s, he had made up his mind. Horn Island was becoming the principal object of his love. It was no longer an imaginary space where he could be alone with her, but one where, for the first time in his life, he could be entirely alone with nature, completely immersed in the present, with no need to look back. "Nostalgia, whether it is born of effort or memory, is a trap," he wrote, "and only definite knowledge is of any earthly use in defeating it. It is the undertow after the wave has broken on the beach, and unless man can be fish, bird, beast as well as man, he may not escape." As he began traveling more frequently to the island, and staying for longer periods—from ten days to two weeks at a time—Sissy realized its psychological importance to him. Like any island, it was an image of wholeness. The long, white sliver of sand, brush, and pine might as well have been a perfect orb; it was a world unto itself, a fully apprehensible microcosm where he could bring together art and nature. "Adam in a hat—not a high hat," he once called himself. His arduous Garden of Eden was crawling with serpents, but there was no longer a place for Eve. At times, he had the overwhelming sense of being alone at the center of creation, like a ringmaster in some celestial circus: "A heavenly morning and a heavenly place: a sandpiper taking a bath, a purple peep running along the shore [despite] sumptuary laws!, mullet jumping, wind blowing, clouds moving, two great blue herons, mallard, dogris, gallinule."

Visible both from Oldfields and from the highest ground at Shearwater, Horn Island lies seven miles south of Oldfields and ten miles from Ocean Springs, bounded on the north by the placid waters of the Mississippi Sound, to the west by Ship Island, to the east by Horn Island Pass, and to the south by the rougher surf of the Gulf of Mexico. Twelve to thirteen miles long, three-quarters of a mile across at its widest, it is a sandy carpet of marsh, salt grass, sedge, brush and slash pine, a resting place in spring and fall for birds migrating between North America and South America. Up to sixty inches of rainfall a year feed dozens of ponds and lagoons of every size, although their waters turn brackish and remain that way for weeks when storm winds blow the tides over the beaches. Fringed by bulrushes and teeming with life, the ponds range from two to six feet in depth, with the largest covering over fifty acres. Breezes from the gulf cool the island in summer, but on hot, still days, the white sand can reach 120 degrees and the sunlight—reflected off the sand and glassy water—is blinding. Between June and late October, storms and hurricanes pummel all of the barrier islands, which act as a natural buffer for the Mississippi coast. The winters are mild, with mean temperatures around fifty-three degrees, but occasionally the ponds and even the wet sand have been known to freeze.

Although almost all of Horn Island was privately owned, no one else had lived there for any length of time since 1906, when the keeper of the Horn Island lighthouse and his wife and daughter ignored a hurricane warning and perished in the storm. A single family had lived on the island until the early 1920s, and there were traces of the house—a pillar, bricks, parts of a stove. Occasionally, people came to hunt alligators (they sold the hides in New Orleans) or to haul away the white sand, which was used in glass making and water purification. In 1943, the army came, closing the entire island to civilians, and setting up a testing station for biological warfare. Up to a hundred enlisted men were stationed there, preparing for chemical warfare with botulinum and ricin. In some of America's earliest experiments with weapons of mass destruction, botulin spores were loaded into rockets not much bigger or more complicated than firecrackers, with the goal of infecting rabbits, guinea pigs, and sheep. At one end of the island the army built a barracks, and at the other a lab with an incinerator with a tall, red brick chimney, to dispose of contaminated materials and carcasses of test animals. The U.S. Army Corps of Engineers set about "improving" the place, laying down a narrow-gauge railroad, building docks, a sewage system, a weather station, a basketball court, and an outdoor movie theater, and dumping creosote into all of the island's ponds and lagoons to keep the mosquitoes under control. On another of the barrier islands—on *Cat* Island, ironically—they were teaching German shepherds to recognize and attack Japanese soldiers. Bob had gotten a glimpse of the troops on Horn Island the night he had swum to shore without his identity card. In November 1945, when the war was over, the army departed, and all that remained on Horn Island were the ruins of the huge wooden barracks, the chimney, concrete foundations, and some wooden ties where the railway had been. There was also a path cutting diagonally across the island, where nothing grew. A "military high road," Bob called it, wondering what they had done to annihilate the vegetation.

Both the *Pelican* and the *Dos* were gone now, and he crossed the ten miles to the island by a combination of sailing, rowing, pulling, and pushing through the shallow waters of the sound in a series of leaky wooden boats, ten to twelve feet long, loaded with supplies kept in gunny sacks and a garbage can for his paints and the inexpensive typewriter paper on which he did all of his drawings and watercolors. He sometimes used a blanket for a sail, and

Bob on his way to Horn Island, c. 1950

occasionally, with a following wind, he would open a big umbrella, like the one he and Sissy had used on the Mississippi River, though this time he had cut a "window" in it, and used it as a sort of jib. To his annoyance, people on fishing boats and cabin cruisers sometimes cut their engines and offered him a tow, nearly swamping him in their wake. "Where are you going in that thing," he once heard someone shout in the dark; but he had no interest whatsoever in finding a faster, less primitive way to make the trip. At least twice, when one of his little skiffs came apart, he found another, abandoned on the beach of the island, and caulked the cracks with a heated axe and the lumps of tar he gathered on his walks, though even then the boats leaked, and he had to put down the oars and stop to bail every hundred yards or so.

Because there were no buildings on the island except for the deserted barracks, he would turn the boat over and use it as a shelter against the elements, banking up the sand to keep out mosquitos, flies, and the rats that burrowed in at night, a foot from his head, to search for food or eat his soap. In bad weather there was space enough under the boat to eat, sleep, and cook, write up the log, and even paint, although he discovered that working in the shade sometimes "dirtied" his colors and he preferred painting in the open air, sitting under an umbrella or a tree to shield his sensitive eyes from the glaring light. In cold weather, he built a fire under the boat so that he could cook and keep warm, and he left the sides open so that the wind would carry away most of the smoke; when the wind blew hard at night he would reach for the thwart above his head, to hold the boat against the sand.

The Artist in His Boat, c. 1960

Dinner was rice and whatever happened to emerge from his "larder." He often brought cans of fruits and vegetables from the mainland, but the labels came off in the damp air, turning many of his meals into a surprise. His beach-combing turned up extra little treats: half-empty jars of pickles or peanut butter or pineapple; bananas that fed the entire island when a banana boat out of Gulfport was "whacked" in a storm; this or that mysterious distillation sent to him by the tides: "I found a strange dark bottle with little white shells growing to its neck, and drank from it a rich mixture of rum or some liquor." For water, he walked to an artesian well he called Rabbit Springs. He filled his gallon jugs, and returned to camp with odd things he found along the way that he wanted to paint: "I came home with a feather in my hat, two water bottles slung over my shoulder, one with yellow daisies stuck in it, and a dead trigger fish in one hand and a dead muskrat in the other. My pants were holey and my rescued shirt—red, white, and blue checks."

He knew he was a strange apparition to anyone who happened to see him: the flounderers who came over at night, rabbit hunters, or the families who came from Ocean Springs or Biloxi on the weekends to spend a day on the island. Once, as he was bathing naked in a pool of bulrushes, he heard shots, and spotted a falling grackle and then some human faces. "I got out and met four hunters with shotguns and pistols strapped on. They passed. A natural man suddenly emerging from a pool on a desert island must have been quite a shock, but they didn't smile."

Not a day went by without its surprises. He would awake before dawn, when the morning star was reflected in the wet sand, and make coffee under the boat. "I sit up in bed," he wrote, "move the pillow, and start a little fire, heat the water, and I'm done and ready for the day." The day's activities were woven together unpredictably from love, compulsion, and chance—whatever he encountered on his morning walk. At times he felt compelled to do water-colors or drawings of specific things—for example, the microcosm, dense with life forms, of the sargasso weed on the edge of the tide; the purple shadow of some pine trees; a family of gallinules; some peculiar cloud forma-tions; an alligator gar or toad—but on his way to work he would often run across a dead or wounded fish or bird that required immediate attention, and he would fall to the sand to draw it, or carry it back to camp. Often, when it was impossible to paint on his excursions down the island, he would sketch and take color notes, and do a watercolor under the boat: "I made a drawing of the bitterns nest while the flies stung; later a watercolor under my boat while the rain poured. Such is the life of an artist who prefers nature to art. He really should cultivate his love of art more but feels that will take care of itself as long as it has things to feed upon."

In the logbooks he kept on the island, he often thanks fortune for provid-ing him with an endless stream of "natural objects" to paint, and for washing onto the beach exactly what he needed at this or that moment. He had placed himself in the hands of Providence and found that, for the first time in his life, he was entirely free: "A bleak dawn but the sun has come out. I took a walk and found a much-needed pair of shoes that fit me. Fortune's favorite child. Indeed, if man refuses to allow himself to be distracted—driven wild, mad, sick, raving—he would often realize that he was Fortune's favorite child, and not simply an idle ass with an empty saddle, begging to be ridden and driven. God knows there are plenty willing to ride him—professionals and the virgin youths full of confidence in their own skill."

Life on Horn Island was a test of physical endurance, a battle with the elements, with gnats and mosquitos, and a prickly, painful struggle with the dense vegetation (one could only traverse the island at certain places). He was far from medical attention and there were many risks: drowning, the torment of flies and mosquitos (he was susceptible to anaphylactic shock), cuts, puncture wounds and infections, botulism, forest fires, sudden storms, the deathly threat of cottonmouths and alligators. After his first few visits, his feet had grown tougher than shoe soles—once, he came down with all his weight on a board with two groups of nails, covered by the sand, but none of them even broke the skin: "I was, as Yeats would say, born under a kind star." Another time he was painting and swatting gnats: "I have an open cut on my foot. I thought it was getting along pretty well. I was painting, and it began hurting—Oh lord, it is getting infected. Finally I looked and it was swarming with red ants—getting breakfast—so it is still pretty healthy."

After a long apprenticeship on his Fortunate Isle, he came to take those risks in stride, and began to feel like a midwife at the Creation. No mere onlooker, he felt himself a participant in natural processes, and developed a sense that nature needed the artist—poet or painter—to "realize" itself. "Order is here," he wrote of the island, "but it needs realizing," and to him "realization" had come to mean discovering and giving authoritative form to unities missed by the casual observer. "Realization" was more than a psychological process in the creator; it was, metaphorically at least, a phase of nature itself, by means of which nature—and mankind—achieve a perfection they could not reach on their own. Nature, he believed, was "only too glad to have assistance in establishing order."

"The artist has been content to be the discoverer," he wrote, and to find that art and nature are one. "It is time that he realized that it is *he* who makes them one by the act of art." Readers of Bacon or of Sir Philip Sidney's sixteenth-century *Defense of Poetry* will recognize the concept: art is an imitation of nature, but not a "realistic" one. For Sidney it is art which carries nature to

Pelicans, c. 1948

perfection, creating a brighter, more vivid version of reality. Nature gives us a world of brass; only the poet—in this case, the painter—can give us a golden one. And yet, over the years, this Aristotelian idea of creative mimesis would yield, in the work of Walter Anderson, to an attitude similar to that of Chinese landscape painters influenced by the Taoist tradition. Alongside the "Western" idea of the artist as *maker*, and as perfecter of nature, one also finds the Taoist notion of the artist as medium. The artist's personality, his godlike powers of invention and imitation disappear before (as Otto Fischer once wrote) "the Taoist-inspired endeavor to interpret art as the revelation of Being through a human medium . . . to render visible the Life Force of

Nature." At Oldfields, Walter Anderson had tried to discover universals and, through them, to create an idealized nature. On Horn Island, for the most part, he wanted to let it speak through him: "to regard nature not as something striving to improve or to become but as something which has become and needs only to be observed and appreciated." The "symbolic" art of Oldfields—the search for the archetype—was swept away on Horn Island by an aesthetics of "surprise." Refuting Hambidge, with his Aristotelian advice to anticipate nature rather than copy it, he wrote: "Nature does not like to be anticipated, but loves to surprise; in fact seems to justify itself to man in that way, restoring his youth to him each time, the true fountain of youth." While drawing trees one day, he remarked on their variety: "I suppose eventually I shall reach the archetype; at present, very much the *ex-type*"—meaning that "type" was hard to find amid such eccentricity. "I like the wandering ones—not absolutely freaks but not just the ordinary healthy ones either. There are some wonderfully strange [trees] on Horn Island—years of storm and years of sudden growth, one side retarded and the other growing like a vine."

For him, the first step in "realization" was still, as at Oldfields, the perception of unity, the imaginative leap—akin to metaphorical thought—from one part of nature to another. Often, these perceptions of unity are formal ones, as when the seven motifs appear in unexpected places. Eternity—the seamless continuity of nature—can be found not only in a grain of sand (he loved Blake's poem), but on the legs of a hermit crab: "Yesterday afternoon, I looked at a hermit crab through my magnifying eye glass and saw Best Maugard on [its] front legs." Those motifs made the crab part of a larger whole. The legs of spider crabs held their own surprises: "What makes a day? The discovery that for years I have been doing spider crabs without noticing that their legs are striped has made mine. Incredible that one should enjoy one's own blindness so much." The important thing was to look hard, allow the "facts" to register, and acquire what he liked to call "definite knowledge," without which neither art nor the appreciation of nature would be possible. Facts, he wrote, were "amusing things." Often they led the artist to the perception of an overall design. A number of drawings and watercolors could arise from one particular observation: "It seems that a bullrush is just wide enough for a little green frog to get on the other side of and have one eye on each edge, so that he is completely hidden except for his own eyes and fingers holding on."

Out of the observation of minute particulars came a surprising larger, transcendent unity. "Order out of chaos, in spite of the piled-up driftwood, thrown up anyhow! When analyzed there is an inescapable order about the vertical pines and the wide horizon that makes something of a pile of drift-wood." Often, objects perceived at first as separate coalesce magically into one. The "cloisonne" of a monarch butterfly "becomes" the goldenrod it is resting on; a bird appears inseparable from a tree, forming one epiphanic "image," the basic unit of poetry and painting.

> I looked up into a dead pine [and] saw a young heron climb up, using feet, wings, and the point of its bill. Then it reached a branch and stood, and stretched and stretched, silhouetted against an enormous white cloud. It seemed that with very little effort it would climb the cloud and take the king-dom of heaven by force. God knows it needs taking. I drew it in ecstasy. It was a concentrated image that nothing could take from me. If it was not poetry it was the image asked for by Yeats from which poetry is made. I am a painter, so this morning I did two watercolors of it before I got out of bed. This does not mean that I am going to be content with that one image for the rest of my life. It will generate power in me for a while, then I need another. One image succeeds another with surprising regularity on Horn Island. Whether they could be shared is another matter. People need different things.

One image succeeded another, and each was infinite. "One single beautiful image is practically inexhaustible," he wrote. "Man is a wasteful fool."

Not only line but color brought the creation together into a perceptible, joyous whole. Color could lead from a dead mullet, say, to a peacock: "I did a study of a dead mullet, a peacock sequence. To me the peacock's color begins with the hen and then emerges in its full glory in the cock, but it begins with sameness and monotony and depends on realization to turn into magic."

Another articulative process, closely related to "realization" and mentioned more than once in the Horn Island logs, is "materialization," the sudden sur-prise that occurs when the mind assembles sensory data into a recognizable object, or two objects produce a third. Of an afternoon on the island he writes:

> Materializations occur fairly frequently after standing still for five or ten min-utes. I was suddenly aware that the thing of various parts, spots, times, changes, was one thing: a large long-nosed gar.

> Then, on the way home, a materialization: two bright yellow eyes—one on each side of an elevated beak, with honey-colored stripes leading down from

them and incredible feet grasping with unnecessary competence the dead bulrushes.

I heard a cry, how far away I couldn't tell. I went on then heard it again, from
miles away. Then I looked and [there] materialized before me a loon: strange
values of dark and white against the sand and the strange hot eyes, sometimes
like a coal the reflecting the sky, brown and lilac.

One of the loveliest things I know is to have a flock of white herons materialize suddenly against an ominously dark sky.

Many of the watercolors attempt to suggest the moment of confusion, of
sensory "assemblage" immediately before "materialization"; one stares at the
painting for a few seconds before knowing what, exactly, it represents: hawk,
alligator gar, squirrel hidden in a tree. The effect of materialization—an idea
antagonistic to Hambidge—is to defeat custom, which blinds us to the
beauty of the world, covering it, as De Chirico once said, as though under a
veil. The momentary puzzlement, the visual groping toward unity which
precedes "materialization," sparks wonder, and without wonder art—and
even life—seemed to him hardly worth living. So easy to take things for
granted! "Man's relation to nature is constantly shifting," Bob wrote. "The
flower that he has elevated to the symbol of a great mystery" becomes, from
one day to another, "no more to him than a lot of pink paper wired to
sticks." Nothing—not even a simple blade of grass—seemed too common
or humble to awaken the consciousness of beauty which makes man
"almost equal" to the thing he is observing. In one of the logbooks, he
speaks of frost. "The world was dead. Dead to beauty, dead to pain, dead to
the cold and to the rising sun. But in its death it was beautiful. Each frost-
bitten blade of grass was etherealized into a new and strange existence. The
touch of the cold was the connecting link which made him conscious of
sight and touch. Without this consciousness, he too would have been a
frozen form translated into beauty for the satisfaction of some passive [per-
son.] He knew, and through his sharing in the cold obtained a consciousness which lifted him above the dead plants."

An idea found in the logbooks is that only surprise and wonder—the wonder born of love—can bring man fully alive, making him as "real" as nature,
and restoring his youth. How sad, he thought, that so few people allow themselves to be surprised: man can use his senses, yes, "but his relation to life, to

being, to existence, is so incredibly vague that, to his intelligence, he can barely seem alive."

> Man begins by saying "of course," before any of his senses have a chance to come to his aid with wonder and surprise. The result is that he dies, and his neighbors and friends murmur with the wind, "of course!" The love of bird or shell which might have restored his life flies away, carried by the same wind which has destroyed him. The bird flies, and in that fraction of a second, man and the bird are real. He is not only king, he is man. He is not only man, he is the only man, and that is the only bird, and every feather, every mark, every part of the pattern of his feathers is real, and he, man, exists, and he is almost as beautiful as the thing he sees.

Birth and death, beginnings and endings were especially propitious moments for "materialization" and "realization," and Walter Anderson drew as close to the birth and death of natural things as any painter of his time. Birds, especially, drew him into their cycles of nesting, egg laying, and hatching. For weeks, on one trip, he stalked a family of purple gallinules, hiding behind a spice bush—"the perfect blind," he called it—while the mother fiercely guarded her eggs, rewarding him from time to time by letting him see her rise, "with a view of purple flannel drawers and white petticoats." No courtship, not even his own pursuit of Sissy, could have been more persistent and passionate; he even doffed his old felt hat to avoid frightening his gallinules. Day after day he returned to their nesting spot, far down the island, approaching silently by land or water, staring into the father's eyes, seeing his own reflection—"Cyrano" he called himself—and sympathizing with the object of his affection. "I realized the terrible predicament of the gallinule: if he keeps the back of his head to the enemy he is nearly invisible, but who can keep their heads turned away always, feeling the approach of the deadly enemy? He must turn his head to look, and at once becomes visible because of his red nose." When the eggs hatched, and the parents were away, he approached silently with a forked stick, leaned over the nest from above, and "borrowed" one of the chicks to draw. In fact, he was always "borrowing" young birds and animals, carrying them back to camp, and feeding them in captivity (rice, the minnows he caught in jars and ingenious traps) until he had finished a series of drawings or watercolors and could release them or stealthily return them to their parents. Of a newly hatched green heron he wrote: "The eyes already open—little black oriental slanting pools of ink. It is

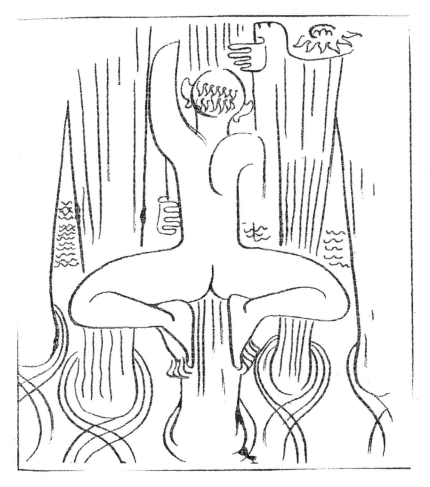

Finding a Nest, c. 1943

dressed in an undergarment of lilac and white—lilac short feathers, white wisps more like hair than feathers." Almost every day he drew dead things— the many he found and a few that died in his absentminded care.

For many species migrating from South America to Canada, Horn Island is the first landfall after many hundreds of miles of open sea. Birds fall from the sky, starving and exhausted, trapped in nets of wind, and wash up on the beach: winter wrens, brown thrashers, purple martins, what he called the "the common casualties" of migration flights. More than once a frog washed in from Pascagoula, clutching a stalk of river grass. The shrimp boats whose lights he saw every night out in the gulf would find strange creatures in their nets, sort them on the deck, and discard them, and these casualties, too, he found on his daily walks. Often, when there was life in them, he tossed them back into the sea, against all odds. One night, under a full moon, in the chill of a north wind, he threw three dozen stranded crabs back into the gulf. "Out you go!" he chanted, while he listened to an imaginary chorus: "Set my people free!" In hundreds, perhaps thousands, of drawings and watercolors, he captured the processes of birth, growth, and fading life.

Audubon once noted that "feathers lose their brilliance almost as rapidly as flesh or skin itself . . . a bird alive is 75% more rich in colors than 24 hours after its death." "Transitional forms" fascinated Walter Anderson, especially the transition from life to death. A dying turtle "identified itself with all the precious substances of the Chinas: old gold, jade, copper red." It was, he said, "impossible to allow all that form and color, that order to go to waste." A ghost crab expired with "strange sequences of color." A drum fish whose eyes had been pecked out by gulls seemed "brutal, strange and terrible in death. I drew it, and tried to do a watercolor." Water hyacinths turned "a strange metallic green in dying" and a dead catfish "had turned purple, its eye pale turquoise blue, fins and mouth old gold." One day he drew the "almost irresistible Portuguese Man o' War": "They are stranded and have apparently resigned themselves. When a wave comes in, magic! What glowing sequences of color, what strange convulsion of form. I drew furiously, as if at a bedside, the last expression of living emotion."

Midwife, veterinarian, and undertaker, he came to see death not as an ending, but as part of a greater unity. "Occasionally a young bird dies and thru some change becomes food for the turtles, and through that eating the island becomes more united than ever," he wrote on the Chandeleurs. When he had buried a pet duck in too shallow a grave, he noticed that "the maggots that have been rising to the surface have fed grackles, blackbirds, rats, and possibly the rabbit. I maintain my position. Nature is not wasteful, although I would have a hard time in an argument. It had better remain an assertion. (The butterfly here stamps its feet.)"

The cycle of life and death became as constant to him as the rhythms of the seasons. Each time he journeyed to the island, he stepped out of linear, "historical" time into a sort of "eternal return" of seasonal events: the nesting, hatching, and migratory movements of birds and butterflies or the merciless winter struggle, of all the island creatures, for food and for survival. It was a "one-dimensional being," Mary Anderson Pickard writes. "The expanses of sky, of sea, the simplicity and complexities of the island, all woven indivisibly together." The minutely observed lives of animals and insects reminded him that on the island, time moved more slowly than on the mainland, depending on the perspective one chose to adopt. Sometimes, thinking of Whitman, he would stop by a lagoon, "intending to loaf and invite my soul." Like Oldfields, the island was a series of worlds within worlds, each living to its own rhythms and inviting contemplation. Of an insect he wrote: "What could be more delectable than to climb a new blade of grass with the dew still on it and spend the morning swinging in the wind? It is true that we must change our entire conception of time to appreciate this. Our time moves so much more rapidly. What would make an eventful life for a cricket might be a slight event in the life of a bird, and not even be noticed by a larger animal walking on two legs."

All of nature lent itself to his sense of multiple perspective: the ant carrying a twig or leaf down a blade of grass, the turtle inching its way forward through the cool grass, the coon making its way down a log toward the water: "I am a coon. All the incredible intoxicating smells of the night began, and man's conceiving, taste, sight, feeling, are nothing. I live through my nose. I look for crawfish because it is expected of me. I follow a log of wood down to the water delicately and like lightning catch the crawfish. But this is separate from my heavenly existence, which is passing in my nose."

There was an immediate reward for what he called "definite knowledge" and for his nonanthropocentric conception of time. Birds and animals became his familiars. A flock of red-winged blackbirds flew to greet him each time they saw his boat approaching. In a place where food was nearly always scarce, he laid out cooked rice for them each night on a long weathered board, and watched them while he had his own supper. "The whole contains all its parts, and there are a good many entertaining parts to the whole," he wrote of his flock.

> I had something like a house warming last night—with birds and animals. I fed the birds rice and the coon prunes, peanut butter, and rice; but the rat may have gotten them. There were about twenty red-winged blackbirds, four grackles, two or three rabbits, one poldeau which wandered in due to the high waves within a few feet of the fire, then turned and wandered out again: an absent-minded guest. The coon, which also ignored the host, ate some rice, looked around for something better, and left. The white-throated sparrow, almost invisible until it moved, and a white grain of rice would disappear.

The scene became so familiar that in the log he often noted simply that he had dinner "with the usual guests." Once, when he had settled down for the night, one of them reminded him noisily that it had not eaten yet, and he crawled out of his blankets to put more rice on the "table."

Animals were not always mere guests, and his relationship to them extended beyond Franciscan tenderness. They were cordial enemies, pets, or—like the gallinules and pelicans—objects of the love that sustained him. "Today a grackle sat on a branch quite close and sang a duet with two voices—one the usual grackle *quexques* [and] the other a treble toodle-oodoodle-ood, in exactly the same tune for about two minutes, all the time looking [me] straight in the face as much as to say, 'You know, you didn't know I could do this.' And I gaped with mouth open."

Some inspired a kind of professional envy, as when he swam around a large lagoon "borrowing" frogs in order to paint them. One day, "two enormous great blue herons flew up. I wondered how they caught their frogs. We were almost rivals, though I bring most of mine back." Still others were helpers. A farmer who had left the island in the early 1920s had raised hogs and they had long ago returned to the wild, feeding on roots, dead fish, turtle eggs, and much else. In winter, Bob would sometimes start awake and see one of the mother sows looming over him like a "black mountain." In summer, they burrowed their way through the stinging, almost impenetrable underbrush to get around the island, and he crawled gratefully through their tunnels, blessing them for their girth and their noisy movements; a duck or gallinule he was stalking might hear him rustling the dry palmettos and take him for a hog, rather than a dangerous biped. With humanity at a safe distance, nothing in nature was alien to him, although he sometimes had to make a conscious effort to rid himself of fear or repugnance. In a lagoon, once, he "swam round in company with a surprisingly tame five-foot alligator, who was very reluctant to submerge. He did finally, and I swam through the bubbles where he had been, with certain qualms from my submerged portions." In the same lagoon, he was pleasantly nibbled by little fish, and thought it "all right, unless they find a sore spot. Then they keep on nibbling, and there's no telling where they will stop. Perhaps they wouldn't stop until you were all gone!" While drawing a toad one day, he saw something out of the corner of his eye. "At my elbow was a dark snake with jowls: a moccasin and a small one. Wishing to get rid of what I consider an unreasonable repugnance to touching snakes, I got a stick and with some difficulty pressed the supposed moccasin to the ground, stick just behind the head; then, slipped my left hand up under the stick and gripped the neck. It was not a moccasin. My relief and disappoint-

Moccasin

ment occurred simultaneously. Grasp the nettle firmly, and it won't bite you. Or will it turn into a Lilly?"

No matter that the moccasins were among the deadliest of creatures. They, too, had their "pride" and there was something courtly in the way he treated them.

> As I crossed to the inner beach following a hog trail, something whispered to me. I looked and saw . . . not a field of daffodils, but a brand-new copperhead. He must have shed as soon as he got out of his hole. I drew him twice. He was squarely in the middle of the path and would not budge, with this giant thing between him and the sun. If he showed his back, down it would come on him. He held his ground. I could go around—pride forbade. I took a long step and walked over him, looking down into a wide open white mouth, like a cottonmouth. Both had saved honor and face: no bad dreams for either of us.

Looking beyond the immediate danger, he could see the "formidable beauty" of the moccasin:

> I spent the morning doing two watercolors: a cactus and [another] from a drawing I made yesterday of the moccasin. His beauty and the form of his

head have changed me. The first drawing was deadly sinister: the worm poi-
soned against the world which trod on it. The second, I began to see the formidable beauty was from the ancient head (no spring lamb, this), something
of stone made from stone, possibly a conglomerate form made from the
organization of several stones, many related to one. Still, I haven't become
fond of it as I did with both the King and the palmetto snake. This thing has
lived on the defensive too long.

Over the years, he adopted, named, and cared for more than a few animals:
Bill the Lizard, Reddy the Duck, Slimy and Eureka (both frogs), a racoon he
called Inky, and a beloved rabbit, Split Ear, who often ate from the board with
the red-winged blackbirds or devoured the core of an apple. Some creatures
traveled with him, precariously, to Ocean Springs and back so that he could
show them to his children: the cecropia moth cocoons that yielded a pair he
called "the Heavenly Twins"; an octopus called Barrel-of-Monkeys; an injured
scaup, Simy, who "made no pretense of liking" him but reminded him of "the
Greek conception of soul: nature and intelligence in one." When one of his
pet racoons died, he felt he had lost something irreplaceable: "Boom-boom-
atum-atum-atum! They are the requiem for little Inky—died partly of good
intentions and partly selfishness on my part. I thought I could fatten him up,
but he was too young. He still needed mother's milk. I saw coon tracks on the
beach this morning. She may have come to tell him goodbye. That much less
charm in the world, so much the loss of magic, the magic which brings the
unreal together with the sordid thing most people call reality." He drew him
in death, over and over, and buried him. "No more pets. I'm wrenched every
time I think of him. He was so independent, which made him so attractive."
But days later, unrepentant, he was pursuing Inky's brother, and Simy II took
the place of Simy I: he is "alive and strong and yet he can't stand up. Feeding
him by force, like Reddy. It's a nuisance, but he's a charming companion. It
will be hard to give him up, but I don't want another accident."

On Horn Island, his yearning to become one with nature became so overwhelming that he could feel himself "becoming" what he was painting, a
transformation brought about by the extreme attentiveness, the "definite
knowledge" acquired through love. The feeling could strike at any time: "I
drew a swarm of flying ants and leaned against a tree to do it, and . . . suddenly the trees behind me moved and I thought and felt that we were one."
Again, the coincidences with Taoist art are striking. In Walter Anderson, as in
the Taoist tradition, the artistic "ego" dissolves, and the painter becomes one

with nature. "When Wen Yü K'o painted bamboo, he perceived only bamboo in front of him and no people; not only did he not see people, but he lost all sensation of his own body, which also became bamboo. He thus became a new being . . . When Han Kan painted horses, he himself became a horse." Even the isolation and concentration of the Chinese artists remind one strongly of the Islander: they were said "to have lived for weeks on end in the mountains and forests, among animals, or even in the water, in order to lose themselves completely in nature. . . . Mi Fei called an oddly shaped rock his brother. . . . Kao K'o-ming (tenth century A.D.) loved darkness and silence; he used to roam about in the wild and spend days on end contemplating the beauty of peaks and woods, oblivious of himself . . ."

"Those who have identified themselves with nature must take the consequences," Bob once wrote. One of those consequences was the dissolution of self and the acceptance of a subsidiary role: "To be a justification to the little black and white ducks. To appreciate the great cumulus clouds and to judge between winter and summer which shall win in the yearly war of the ellipse. To laugh and give reason to the love affairs of the birds, himself vile, and they still happy in that first garden. . . . To count the stars and keep them in their places, to be the servant and slave of all the elements." The artist as "medium," as "interpreter," as midwife, was to concede that "all things exist in themselves, have an integrity of their own: the wind, the grass, and the little animals that move through the grass, regardless of whether my stomach is temporarily upset by the food I have eaten and has affected the sight of my eyes."

There is nothing in his writing to show that he had read about those Taoist painters. A book on Chinese art, which he liked to look at in the 1930s, barely mentions them. Perhaps he had heard of The Way on his travels, or discussed it with Annette, with her lifelong interest in Eastern things. His own theory of influence leaves room for the imagination. "You may think you're being influenced by a person in the same room with you when it is really from a star a thousand miles away. We are really transparent like fish and electric currents pass through us—we are very apt to identify ourselves with that current."

BROOKLYN AND CHINA

In September 1948, Burton Callicott, a young instructor at the Memphis Academy of Fine Arts, was sent to Shearwater for a quick course in pottery—a subject he had to teach that fall. Pat had invited him to board at the Front House. He knew he wouldn't learn much in a week, and as he walked up the quiet path to the Pottery, he felt "pretty much like an interloper," aware, perhaps, that potteries like this one were rare, and that Shearwater wouldn't last for very long in its present form. In fact, that month the chamber of commerce had proposed a bond issue that would allow the Andersons to turn the pottery into Shearwater Crafts: Art Center of the South. Up to 120 employees would mass-produce "art and functional pottery," decorative tile, block-printed textiles, and wallpaper. New buildings were envisioned, including "studio-cabins to house visiting craftsmen who will be 'paying guests,' seeking to improve their techniques through observation of the work of the Andersons."

No sooner had Callicott set foot in the workshop, with its ingenious arrangement of belts, shafts, and motors, than he discovered that Peter Anderson was "not about to waste his time with a beginner." Stationing Callicott at the potter's wheel, Peter gestured toward a supply of clay, flipped on the switch to the wheel, and disappeared for the rest of the day. Sensing trouble, perhaps, Annette sent someone to bring him to the Barn, and the two of them chatted for a long time about "prayer and healing." Callicott was interested in mysticism and philosophy, and they hit it off immediately, despite the difference in age. Later that week, as he stepped again into her dimly lit living room, she introduced him to Bob, who looked tanned and weathered and barely smiled, giving the impression, as Peter had, that he wasn't in the least enthusiastic about meeting him. Callicott stared at his shabbily dressed "fellow artist," and realized that he was there only to please his mother. At Annette's suggestion, he brought out two watercolors—still lifes of melons—and told Callicott that they were his own way of giving thanks for the gifts of nature. A note found among Bob's papers expands on the thought: "Painting still life is one way of paying the debt which we owe to the earth. All the beauty, all the form and our own inadequacy in expressing our gratitude is slightly satisfied by increasing our consciousness of the beauty of fruit, flowers, vegetables, the voluptuous return, gift of an austere mother to her children."

"His words had no hint of falseness," Callicott remembered years later, "and after a few more brief exchanges, he left us." For the next few years, until about 1953, the still life would be one of Bob's preferred genres.

The next morning, Callicott found a gift at his door—a generous mound of potting clay, left there by Bob—but he realized that the Cottage was "strictly off limits" to everyone, except perhaps to Annette, and was too nervous to knock at the door. A newly carved figure, nearly six feet long, lay on the porch: *The Swimmer*, which Bob had carved from an oak tree blown down in the hurricane a year earlier.

Mac and Peter proved more sociable, and one still, windless night, they took Callicott fishing for flounder.

> This consisted of wading in shallow water near shore, pulling a small rowboat. Peter and Mac were armed with unbarbed, smooth steel spears, mounted in the ends of wooden poles. They gave me a net at the end of a long wooden handle with which I was to snare the crabs stirred up by our feet. My batting average was near zero and they eventually took the net from me and netted a good number of crabs. They carried a bright lamp, and by its light searched the sandy bottom through the clear water. Once, when they saw the outline of the hidden flounder they pointed it out to me, but I saw nothing. They would drive the spear through the spot and then pass a hand under the speared flounder, lift it, and throw it in the boat. They got eleven, and I judged by the accounts to others the next day that it was a larger than usual catch.

There was a flounder feast with Pat and Peter, and crabmeat gumbo the next night with Mac and his new wife, Sara, the young woman who had worked at the pottery and, in 1940, had accompanied Sissy and the children to Chicago (a few years earlier, Jackie had run away with another man, and she and Mac had divorced). Annette showed Callicott the houses and gazebos along Front Beach, and somebody drove him to Oldfields, where he saw children frolicking about, snacking on crab legs the way children in Memphis snacked on potato chips. The walls of the great old house were still covered with Bob's huge block prints. A final scene etched itself in his memory. One evening, with a hurricane approaching, Peter sat on the porch of the Front House, overlooking the stormy water, ignoring his family's pleas to get to a safer place, and delightedly pointing out to his visitor "the ways the sea birds, especially the pelicans, weathered the tempest."

All year, Bob had been observing the same phenomenon. Since 1943, perhaps before, he had been visiting a colony of pelicans on North Key in the Chandeleurs, and in 1948 he lived with them for weeks, returning with hundreds of sketches in sepia ink that captured the pelicans in every possible attitude. Drawing them he found that "the proportions of a pelican are as elusive—and at the same time as authoritative—as some of El Greco's figures." Swan, hawk, eagle, "name what bird you will. . . . None of them hold their head with its axis on the center of the earth like that old bird with the fleshy horn."

Mary Anderson Pickard has pointed out that, of all his birds, the pelican was the most important to him. "Beautiful and ugly, dignified and comical, graceful and awkward, fragile yet indomitable, the pelican is a union of opposites reflecting the ambivalence of my father's own nature, and for that reason endlessly fascinating to him." The fruit of his observation was a vivid essay which Annette encouraged him to write and illustrate, in hopes that it would be published in the *Times-Picayune*. It is an outpouring of love not only for the pelicans but for the multiple "strata" of life on the island: the pelicans' domain, in the sweetness of the mangrove swamps, is shared with turtles in their "horizontal world," fiddler crabs, who wave their arms in joy at the retreating tide, and man-o'-war birds, who cast their hieroglyphic shadows over all of them. It is clear from the essay—written with the authority of one who has many years of experience—that he had drawn as close to pelicans as he ever had to any human being.

> After you have lived on the island for a while, there comes a time when you realize that the pelican holds everything for you. It has the song of the thrush, the form and understanding of man, the tenderness and gentleness of the

Pelican, c. 1948

dove, the mystery and dynamic quality of the nightjar, and the potential qualities of all life. In a word, you lose your heart to it. It becomes your child, and
the hope and failure of the world depend upon it. You share in all of its reactions and conditions of life. You awake with it. You feel the change from the
cave of sleep to the beginning of consciousness and desire. You hear its cries
of hunger, with the need to cry to the first mover, the *primum mobile*, the sun
and light of the world, for whatever it is that you need yourself: food, light,
warmth, change.

Patiently, he studied the speech of pelicans, taking notes for a "pelican dictionary of common terms." What surprised him were the number and variety of sounds triggered by a single stimulus. Humans would find that wasteful and irritating, he wrote. But "economy of means" seemed a distinctly human idea. Most enchanting of all were the young, who fed themselves by forcing their beaks down the mothers' throats. "Although this feeding goes on all day it reaches its climax a little before sundown when it turns into a frenzy of orgiastic satisfaction, when both parents and young work themselves into a state of furious anticipation before the act of feeding takes place. No longer does it occur in a desultory way, but over acres of nests and with hundreds of families the same act is occurring. It becomes a ritual, a life feast, to keep life in the young through the darkness until the return of day." He was in a different world. As he swam up a little stream on the island, his sketchbook strapped to the top of his head, the banks were lined with "tiers of pelicans hissing and squawking. I felt a little like Satan returned to his mates from his adventures on earth."

When Burton Callicott returned to Memphis and wrote Annette to thank her for his visit, he told her how sorry he was that an artist of Bob's "power and originality" wasn't "more widely known and exhibited." In fact, that very month, September 1948, the situation had started to change. The chain of events was a complicated one, and those who put it in motion were friends from Memphis. For years, John and Louise Lehman (he was a salesman for Sherwin Williams and she, an amateur painter) had been visiting the Pottery and buying Bob's decorated vases, woodcarvings, rugs, and block prints. In 1948 the Lehmans persuaded Louise Bennett Clark, director of the Brooks Memorial Art Gallery, to put on an exhibition. Practically every piece in the exhibit was purchased by museum curators and collectors, among them an amateur painter from Memphis, Margot Herzog, fashion director of the Cotton Textile Institute, who bought a brightly colored carved cat and several of the fairy-tale scrolls that Bob had begun to produce at Oldfields. In New York Herzog showed them to textile designers and manufacturers and, at Clark's suggestion, to Una E. Johnson, curator of the Print Department at the Brooklyn Museum. Within days, an enthusiastic Johnson wrote to tell Bob that she wanted to do a show at the museum.

Her letter of September 17, 1948, must have been amazing news at Shearwater: "The Brooklyn Museum is very interested in having an exhibition of your work—the block prints, drawings, ceramics, and wood sculpture." Johnson added that several members of the museum staff wanted to purchase scrolls, and asked about the prices of *King Arthur* and *The Three Goats*. In December he sent her a sampling of prints, carvings and decorated pottery. There "would have been more prints," he wrote Johnson, "but my hand has been out of order due to a fall from a bicycle." Although he was "prepared to fill orders . . . it should be understood that the color will only approximate that of the prints shown." As for prices, he hoped she would "be able to reach the people who cannot afford to pay a great deal for works of art, but still have an appetite for beauty and the imaginative world of fairy tales."

Enclosed with the letter was a statement from Bob on the importance of fairy tales as a life force:

> Fairy tales have been used so often as sedatives that it is very usually forgotten that they are also explosion, as the late Mr. Chesterton would have said. These present attempts are by one who feels very strongly that the alternative to the atomic bomb explosion and the annihilation of humanity would be obtained through art in a series of small explosions which are so identified with the life of man that they stimulate, without destroying, life. Although they are told by the people and claimed and possessed by the people, they have a tendency to become all one tale, one solar myth, and whirl back to the sun as the source of all life.

Fairy tales, he added, were a "sacrifice to the sun" and the stars; the stars too "must be satisfied by the tales people tell their children before they go to sleep at night." In their infinite variety, those stories keep us away from "the 'fierce devourer,' the 'owner,' the big house, the center of the storm." They "keep the circle growing, and the variety and number of life in existence," turning the "vortex" into "an engine of life instead of destruction." No doubt, the "center of the storm" alluded to the recent horror of Hiroshima and Nagasaki. In the years since Bob had read Adolfo Best-Maugard (whose motifs are ubiquitous in the block prints) the whirling spiral had turned into a symbol of annihilation.

Johnson, who struggled to understand his handwriting and his thought (the statement goes on, less coherently, for several more pages) used only part of his letter, and sent out news releases with a somewhat cheerier sales pitch of her own: "Bob Anderson executes his gay, animated and colorful scroll prints not only for his own pleasure but for the pleasure of everyone who enjoys or remembers folk tales and fairy tales. His work reflects extensive knowledge of art forms and a keen and refreshing understanding of fantasy. Suitable for almost any informal setting, whether it be a country house, recreational quarters, or a converted old brownstone, they are truly every man's art—to be owned and enjoyed."

Subsequent letters brought another piece of good news. One of New York's leading dealers in interior decoration and American art, Bertha Schaefer, a native of Mississippi, was "anxious to handle Mr. Anderson's work," and would take over some of the prints once the museum show closed. During the years Bob had spent at Oldfields, New York had become a great center of experimental printmaking. Major painters were taking a new interest in silk screen, drypoint, lithograph, and the woodblock. A handful of European artists—Chagall, Ernst, Léger, Lipchitz, Masson, Miró, Tanguy—were making prints at Stanley William Hayter's workshop, Atelier 17, along with Americans like Jackson Pollock and Alice Trumbull Mason. In 1948, Bertha Schaefer's gallery, and others on Fifty-seventh Street, were introducing New Yorkers to the color woodcuts of Louis Schanker, retrospectives of the German Expressionists, the figurative work of Ben-Zion Weinman, and the first prints of Leonard Baskin and Antonio Frasconi. A year earlier, in spring 1947, Johnson had curated the Brooklyn Museum's first National Print Exhibition, featuring works in all the print media. Both she and Bertha Schaefer had played a role in renewing public interest in prints of all kinds, and it looked, for a while, as though Bob might form part of that renaissance. Although *Art News* reported in April 1949 that "the average print dimension is steadily growing, like everything else in the new generation" (Schanker had recently produced a woodcut six feet in length) Bob's linoleum blocks may have been the largest ever done by an American.

Titled *Folk Tale and Fantasy: Modern Scroll Prints in Color*, the museum show ran from May 26 to October 1, 1949, drawing together the pieces sent by Bob and a number of others loaned by Herzog and by the Brooks. Despite his request to offer the prints at reasonable prices—say, $7.50 each—Johnson had priced the smallest at $15 and the larger ones, like *Biloxi Beach*, at $30; she had "never seen block prints so finely executed and of such great dimension." At least one print—*The Cock*—was cut into sections, and the parts were sold separately. Ten prints were sold, and two carved cats, and Johnson reported that she had sold more than from any show the museum had ever done. The scrolls were ingeniously hung over wires, with "the top and bottom . . . rolled up like a Japanese kakinomo." For the most part, the press was silent. The *New York Times* noted that some of the color scrolls—*Sinbad the Sailor, Red Bull of Norway, Flying Cranes*—were "sophisticated enough for serious appreciation by adults." *Art Digest* praised the "imaginative themes . . . brightly colored and deeply delineated. . . .The lightness of subject gives added character to this unusual display, which is further accented by some primitive-type carvings and ceramics."

Late in May, Annette wrote Johnson that her son hoped to visit the exhibition, and it is easy to imagine her urging him to make an appearance in person, not only at the museum but also at the Schaefer gallery. "Success" looked inevitable. "After that Brooklyn show," a friend of Johnson wrote, "your work will be in demand in every market." After years of uncertainty and struggle, the show had been a vindication, at least for Annette. "So much of what I have prayed for is coming true," she wrote in her journal. "Night before last Bob came over and we read part of *Uncle Vanya* by Chekhov. It was beautiful. We read two acts. Then he said goodnight and left, but came back in a minute and kissed me. Then I knew the next morning that he had gone to New Orleans. This morning a postcard, saying he was on a holiday in New Orleans and would write. How happy it made me!"

That day she had been to the Cottage and found some "beautiful watercolors." Hoping, perhaps, to cross paths with her son, she vowed to take them the next day to New Orleans to be mounted. For days after that, he kept her guessing as to where he was headed. From New Orleans to New York, she imagined. But he was soon back at Shearwater for a family dinner at the Barn with Sissy, the children, and Aunt Hulda, talking not of New York galleries but of China and Tibet. Months earlier Annette had given each of her sons two thousand dollars left to them by their aunt Dellie, and on July 18, with the Brooklyn show still in progress and his mother attempting to fill the orders sent by Johnson, he was crossing the Pacific in the back of a Pan Am Clipper, with the intention of traveling across China to Tibet. For years he had wanted to see the murals in Buddhist monasteries.

It was a bad moment for such a trip. China had been ravaged by long years of civil war, Chiang Kai-shek was about to take refuge on Formosa, the United States had cut off its relations with the mainland, and, a day before Bob left home, Russia detonated its first atomic bomb. Major events, but none of them mattered as he flew from San Francisco to Hawaii and took off again for Japan, enjoying the bumpy ride. The plane "leapt and trembled and rose and fell, and I thought of Vayu mounted on his antelope, coming in great leaps from the northwest."

Japan he loved, "even the billboards, which insist on the principle of yang and yin and reconcile heaven and earth, as an advertisement should." In a country ruined by war, the young mothers looked "superb, full of life and authority," and reminded him of Pat. As he looked out the plane window, on his way to Hong Kong, "the pearl divers disported themselves in a sea by Edmund Dulac." Everywhere, there was "incredible color—unbelievable blues and green, with purple and gold of reefs seen through it, and the white of breaking waves streaming into the land. Against all this, the orange bodies of the divers!" Then, in the afternoon, his first glimpse of the mainland. Even before he landed, he was making color notes: "red volcanic rock, purple clumps of houses set at right angles to each other, and the cloisonne of maps. Different shades of green and gold and lilac and pink fitted to the valleys between hills of dark green and blue, with raw red ochers and volcanic red purple. The whole connected and divided by yellow ochre rivers. The shoreline white surf, then sequences of pink lilac, to all of the blues and greens imaginable."

As on all of his trips, he had done a minimum of planning, trusting to fortune and his own good instincts. He kept a logbook, but in the pages that survive he never mentions a map, and his geography seems to have been word-of-mouth: he simply asked people for a list of names of the towns he would encounter between one major city and another, a tricky business since he did not know any Chinese, and "names have strange treatment. There is the name in an American geography, the name given the place by people who know, and the name finally recognized by the people who know and use the place referred to." He sensed that the "farthest certain point on [his] journey," before turning toward Tibet, would be Chongqing, on the Yangtze River, in southwestern Sichuan Province, twelve hundred miles northwest of his starting point in Guangzhou, and he trusted that, between one point and another, things would somehow take care of themselves. Nor did he worry much about lodging. At first he slept in hotels, boardinghouses, the Chinese Travelers, or village inns, but later on, when he began to sleep outdoors, he spent his nights under overhanging rocks, beneath the eaves of a house, beside the road, inside an old corn crib, and, more than once, in a graveyard, "with several strange and lanky cedars providing resting places for my head." Graveyards, it seemed, were "almost the only solid areas of ground not broken up for cultivation of rice."

Man in rickshaw, 1949

The destruction and chaos of the war were still evident. Soldiers crowded the trains and stations, "boys walking like young tigers, with submachine guns under their arms," rifles and cartridge boxes everywhere. And yet, even in places bristling with weapons, he found humor and grace. On the train from Hong Kong to the coastal city of Guangzhou, he sat opposite a "fat Chinese" with a fan, "my introduction to the fan as a symbol of authority. It has a great many uses. It is used by all classes and at all times. I have seen a coolie after carrying a tremendous burden put his foot on his load and with all the grace of a court beauty draw out and unfold his fan and refresh himself—change his world from one of servitude and slavery to one of democracy and equality. A group of people on a hot day fanning themselves in unison are surprisingly like the young pelicans whose throat pouches vibrate together waiting for the day to cool or for their mother to bring food. Fans are carried thrust into belts and brought out when needed."

In Guangzhou, after a long day's journey, no one would cash his traveler's checks, obliging him to retrace the 180 kilometers to Hong Kong. There, he encountered problems with his passport, and had to wait a few more days, so he "took to the hills" and climbed "the nearest mountain," and roamed through the countryside. Describing a strange new fish, he must have felt a little like his favorite explorer, Darwin: "It runs like a skipjack on its tail, but when it comes to a rock it leaves the water and walks one fin in front of another, used alternately until it is high up on the rock. It has goggle eyes, is almost colorless, and is about eight or ten inches in length." Back in Guangzhou, hoping to board a train north for Hangyang, in Hunan Province, he "had [himself] driven miles to a station which didn't exist," barely making it back in time to the real one. In Hangyang, a boy insisted on accompanying him into the hills, where they saw a magnificent fritillary, "which [the boy] frightened by trying to catch it with his hands—I got so annoyed that I sent him home, then went on to the river, and had a bath among millions of little green fish and a green and gold frog watching me from the bank."

On the train again, headed for Kwei Lin, he looked across the compartment at another "stout Chinese," who "slept with his socked feet out of the windows—fortunately there were no tunnels." A farmer with his little son was sitting beside him, and let the child fall asleep with his head on Bob's knee, giving him "the indifferent feeling of an oak tree which lets squirrels run about it." At Kwei Lin he walked through the rocky hills, admiring paving stones set in a curious herringbone pattern, polished by the feet of centuries of travelers, and the stone sculptures beside the road. When it was time to depart for Chongqing, the bus to the airport took him bouncing back over those same hills, and as he daydreamed about their similarity to the hills in old Chinese landscape paintings, his passport bounced out of his pocket and flew out the window ("Fortunately it was seen by the bus following behind, so I got it back"). At Chongqing, no hotel rooms were available, so he stayed for a night at the Canada Mission, and spent another long night on a flight of stone steps leading down to the Yangtze River, amid the "constant passing of people: water carriers, farmers, boatmen"—an oriental version of the levee in New Orleans.

The following morning he made a horrible discovery: for the second time, he had lost the elusive passport. "My hair turned white, perspiration came out on my brow, sorrow and woe were my companions." He filled out forms at the consulate, and resigned himself to weeks of immobility as he waited for a new one. But incredibly, Fortune smiled yet again. "When [the consul] came in to say that the missing passport had been recovered, everyone seemed to share in my happiness." On, then, to Chengdu, the capital of Sichuan Province, where he asked a hotelkeeper for the "names and distances of places" between there and Ya'an. His plans, apparently, were to walk to Ya'an, and then into Tibet following an ancient trading route. The time had come to abandon his suitcases. In preparation, he bought "cans for rice, matches, etc., and a water bottle, none of which I needed, and loaded my two burlap bags, and went to bed after a conversation with the [hotelkeeper] in which I told him he could have my suitcase and its contents if I did not return within one month."

Taking to the open road, he felt an overwhelming sense of freedom: "I walked west. I bought a yellow ear of roasted corn and ate lunch. The road was clear before me. The weeks of argument and coaxing, begging and cunning arrangement were over. It was now simply a matter of endurance, economy, and following a plainly marked road." He jostled along among peasants with carrying-sticks on their shoulders, loaded with buckets of water, baskets of ducks or cats; rickshaws; and "pig carriers"—"these belong to a class by themselves, and so do their pigs, which are of a reddish purple color with black bristles, and either wake and complain with squeals, or slumber shrouded in green leaves lying on their backs in a wheelbarrow and carried by their owner. Besides their strange color, they have form. Dürer would have loved them and drawn each wrinkle and whisker with joy." Occasionally, there were "*ladies* in wheelbarrows, who took the places of the pigs with great dignity and no loss of charm." As he walked, he thought about the political implications of different modes of travel, and decided that nothing could compete with an umbrella and a fan, at least not in the summer: "Man organized, loaded with weapons of war, cooking utensils, preventive medicine, massed into numbers doing the same things in the same ways, against that airy individualist tripping along protected by the sun and rain by his umbrella and from the heat of the road by a fan as graceful as a butterfly's wing and as

Asking Directions, 1949

general in its usefulness as a hand or a new appendage." Poised between those extremes, "the image of the water carrier, with his scales on his back."

The road was as fascinating and unpredictable to Walter Anderson as it ever was for Don Quixote. Men passed on bicycles, exciting his envy, and by the side of the road people displayed fruit and home-baked bread in open shops. Families were cooking their meals in metal containers on a coal fire. When he stopped to eat, crowds gathered round him and watched him feast on cornmeal lumps, rolled in leaves of corn and left to steam. As on Horn Island, his fare was various, "and I almost never knew what it would be next, except that I was sure of getting it"; at times it was enough to hold out one's hands. There were lively villages along the road and much to see: "dogs, pigs, children, chickens, and trays spread with drying yellow corn, red peppers, and a bright cerise stuff which seemed to be a kind of dye." Passing through one village, he met the nightwatchman, "heard his gong first, and then, as I approached the village, saw his light. He was a fearsome sight, with hair and a wide hat and his light and gong."

For several days he traveled toward Ya'an, his starting point for Tibet. When his two burlap bags began to feel too heavy, he shed more belongings, "all the supernumerary things," his "last claim to respectability." Traveling lighter now, he cut through rice fields and bathed in small rivers and canals. When he asked some idlers for the road to Ya'an, they pointed straight ahead, and he followed their directions down a pleasant river until he felt lost and stopped at a village for a cup of tea. "The entire village assembled, and it decided that I should have to return and take the other road." In the morning he walked until it grew too hot, and stopped beside a stream to wash his clothes and get a look at his own bruised body: the right shoulder raw from carrying the burlap bags, a "stone bruise" on the ball of his right foot, and two or three raw places on top. "My left foot was in pretty good shape, but in fixing my pack I cut my finger to the bone and had to bandage it with a piece torn from my shirt. But I made my twenty *li* [ten kilometers] for the day, and camped beside a pond in the rice fields."

As he limped along he thought about the "mechanistic" course on which the world had embarked. If bicycles made him envious, the thought of automobiles reminded him of the folly of progress. It was "growth," not "progress," which mattered. "Automobiles would seem to be a perfectly safe place for the practical evolutionist to enjoy life without serious damage either to himself or his object. But he follows his chosen path, and foot by foot the horrible truth begins to dawn that he is progressing, but not in the right direction, and the question is shall he give up progression or change direction. A child could do either very easily, but so great has grown his sense of responsibility that the evolutionist will probably crack at his post in plain sight of everybody rather than admit that growth is a reasonable and natural thing and progress is not either." On foot, all seemed vivid and surprising. Everywhere, for example, he admired the beauty of the water buffalo, and captured it a series of verbal snapshots: "still figure holding a rope and, at one end of the rope, the perfect form of the [contented] beast"; the "still shadow of a child mounted on the beast"; the "happiness of the beast taking its bath in a tank beside the road."

One night, camping beside a small stream, he found himself surrounded by a miscellaneous crowd of "soldiers, farmers, villagers, [and a] boy, cheerful but curious. They went through my bags, making the money clink and examining everything. I thought the soldiers had a sort of right, and showed them my passport. Later, everyone departed and I slept." Soon he was dreaming of an enormous water buffalo, grazing beside his head, and before long he saw the huge animal hook his bag with his horn and carry it away. When he awakened, all had vanished: bag, money, passport, drawings, and logbook. He had only his blanket, pocket knife, and about a dollar in change, and realized with a shock that his trip was over. He would never reach Tibet. "It was as simple as that."

From then on, the trip began to unravel. He walked back to Chengdu, where friendly people at the university lent him money and helped him straighten out his affairs. The hotelkeeper returned his suitcase, and he caught a plane for Chongqing, where the American vice-consul gave him some of his own clothes and issued a new passport, and Bob wired his mother for money. Then, after receiving her telegram—FUNDS ARE ON THE WAY—he took a DC-3 back to Hong Kong, where he spent several days rewriting the lost logbook and painting watercolors. When the money arrived he discovered it was only enough for passage by ship, and he wrote back and told Annette he wanted to fly. Two days later, on August 20, with his journey nearly at an end, he made a brief excursion to Macao. From the third deck in a rolling boat, he stared at the colors of the old Portuguese colony, bathed in a "general yellow ochre tone" that made an "admirable foil for bright colors placed against it." The "dull purple, cool green, red and blue" of window frames and doors produced "a very modern high-keyed color scheme."

Back in Hong Kong, he discovered that he had overstayed his visa—it expired on August 25—and was ordered to report to the police. And finally, armed with the right visas, he boarded a plane for California and caught the Sunset Limited from Los Angeles to New Orleans, arriving at Shearwater on September 11, 1949, the same way he had begun the two-month trip: by bicycle. "Had a flat tire on my way home," he said to Sissy, by way of greeting. Annette invited the entire family to the Barn, and celebrated his return with ice cream and cake. With Billy, Mary, and Leif sitting on the stairs, he read from the logbooks he had rewritten in Hong Kong, and Annette couldn't help telling him "how well he had spoken." Days later he wrote to Una Johnson, thanking her for her efforts at the Brooklyn Museum, adding that "China is a strange and incredible place to an American who has not learned to accept resignation as the chief virtue."

It had been a life-changing trip, toward a level of self-reliance and simplicity that transcended even his life on Horn Island. Abandoning himself to the open road, feeling a little like Darwin or Doughty, he had shed one layer of baggage after another, and had come out fine on the other side. His drawings and watercolors had vanished, along with his other belongings, but there had been a notable change in his painting. As he sat in Hong Kong, waiting for Annette's cable, he painted crabs, fish, and lobsters he bought in the marketplace. Never before had watercolors been so obedient to him. Years later, his daughter Mary, a watercolorist herself, described the change that had come over his painting and his thought:

> Before he visited China it seems to me his watercolors on typing paper—the only affordable, available, easily transportable vehicle for his chosen (albeit again dictated by circumstance) medium—were attempts to use the paint as it is meant to be used: wet and loose and translucent. But the typing paper would wrinkle and the paint would puddle on the smooth surface. He conveyed appearances but without his later brilliant control of nuance and contrasts of positive and negative space. Nor had he found a means for fine detail, delineation or texture. Painting wet on typing paper was a one-touch process. I believe he was using the watercolor as he'd been taught, following the old rules, techniques, even, while using paper not meant to be painted on. He was still confined by his technical training and, perhaps, by the old rules of propriety and manners of his upbringing.
>
> In China, far from home, help, family, school, he first knew real freedom. He was outside bounds and the experience for all its discomforts, bad teeth, aching feet, no food, was intoxicating (as evidenced by his log).
>
> He used materials available to him—a child's paintbox, perhaps, and what paper he could find—but with them achieved the impossible.
>
> No longer contained even by the given properties of his tools, he transcended them. For the first time he worked with complete confidence, combining his gifts, his skills with the potent drive of sharpened undistracted concentration. The resultant images are alive with sensual spirituality. "How strange," he would later marvel, "how incredible, is the relationship between matter and spirit."
>
> I believe that in Hong Kong, whether because he was free from any dominant mode, because of his limitation of means, his sensory deprivation—lack

of food, regular sleep, pain with teeth, feet, exhaustion—coupled with sensory stimulation—the newness of China/ its ancient richness of culture—new sounds, sights, smells, tastes—he was somehow propelled into fully high gear.

For the first time he may have experienced the ultimate bliss of his power, discovered the satisfying sustenance of painting, while recognizing the freedom of physical and material limitation.

Perhaps he realized then what would lead to his chosen island —that limitation could provide the strengthening discipline through which he would find fulfillment in creative intimacy with nature.

In the sweeping landscapes of China, he had thought, as he often had at Oldfields and on Horn Island, about the relation of art and nature. Back at Shearwater, in a handwritten collection of his favorite poems, he reread Wallace Stevens's poem "Anecdote of the Jar," which begins, "I placed a jar in Tennessee," about the way a human artifact organizes the space around it and takes dominion over its natural surroundings. In China, he had confirmed this: "An imitation Greek temple, an architectural form of any kind, placed on a desert island would have an extraordinary effect upon nature. An arch, decorated and painted in bright colors with symbols and placed at the entrance of a Chinese village would establish a relationship between the people of the village and nature which would affect every blade of rice planted near that village. Primitive or more or less primitive people are in a better position to relate art to nature than a larger society with a constant flux of changing valuation and appreciation."

He began experimenting with the same phenomenon at Shearwater. The recent hurricane had blown down a number of enormous trees. He had already carved *The Swimmer*, seen by Burton Callicott, and he was now creating a group of painted wooden sculptures in celebration of the Mississippi. A huge blue river figure, titled *The River* or *Father Mississippi*, stood at the center of the group—a masculine version of the "Sarasvati" muse he had drawn so frequently at Oldfields. The flowing lines of the river's tributaries went downward into his head like veins or antlers. Affixed to either shoulder were two ducks giving the appearance of wings. To the left was a deer, and to the right a possum, a crane, and another bird. All of these figures stood on a huge slab of oak—the waters of the river, carved in low relief with fishes. It was his first large-scale effort at outdoor sculpture, and probably dates from the same period as the draft of an eight-page hymn to the river, inspired, perhaps, by Babylonian epic. Left in the woods for many years, the colors faded

Father Mississippi, c. 1950

and the statues rotted away: another reminder that to him art was a ceaseless process of creation, without much thought for the fruits of that process. Today only the deer remains.

That summer reverberations from the Brooklyn Museum exhibit brought new opportunities. Alonzo Lansford, former editor at *Art Digest* and now director of the Delgado Museum in New Orleans, had been conspiring with Annette about a one-man show of her son's work. And in late July 1949, while Bob was still in China, Lura Beam, an associate with the American Association of University Women, had written to the director of the AAUW to propose a traveling exhibition. The AAUW had been putting on art exhibitions since 1938, she wrote, but had done little to identify new talent. They had done shows of children's art, regional annuals, and some group exhibitions by consecrated painters, but had never truly "discovered" anyone. What she had long been looking for was a new "painter or sculptor of broad appeal in that he reveals our buried American life, so able technically that he has a significant future, and yet young enough to be able to tie up his work on a year's circuit, probably without sales." Until she had seen the work of Walter Anderson, she had never found "all [these] elements together," for "the national trend in art just now is toward abstraction." Anderson was worth taking a chance on: he had "originality, and something to say; control of the necessary techniques; emotional stability, making it likely that the work will continue" and the ability to communicate with "the American Community." She had first seen Anderson's block prints in a storage room at the Brooklyn Museum, before that show opened. The Andersons' enthusiastic promoter Louise Lehman had told her of the variety of Bob's work, and in March 1950 Beam wrote to Pat asking her to assemble and send to her "a fairly comprehensible sample of Walter Anderson—watercolors, prints, line drawings, rugs, pottery, wood-carving," together with photos of Shearwater and biographical information. Although she had liked the Brooklyn prints, she was unwilling to commit to the rest of the work before seeing it; the prints had a strong sense of place, but "some might well be too regionally derived to 'take' outside the South." In November 1949, Pat responded, hoping to broaden the show to include the work of all three brothers: "Walter is of an amazing versatility and most certainly has the most wonderful originality and remarkable control of all techniques. He has done thousands of the prints you saw in Brooklyn, most beautiful watercolors, line drawings, and wood carvings. Mrs. Lehman, a very good friend and admirer of all of the Andersons, felt that possibly a show of the work of all three brothers might be done, and would appeal to the general public. If you, after reading this letter, feel the same thing, we would cooperate in every way to make the exhibit comprehensive of the work of all three."

But both Lehman and Beam held to their original idea. "All three of the Anderson men are very gifted," Lehman confided to Beam, "but Walter is the genius of the family. I have known many capable artists, who are nationally known and have achieved financial success, but Walter Anderson is the only living genius I have ever had the privilege of knowing and seeing at work. He works with the fervor of Van Gogh, night and day for weeks until he accomplishes an idea. He goes on trips to the swamps and to islands inhabited by birds alone and goes through all kinds of deprivations to paint certain birds. He makes literally thousands of line drawings and water colors of these birds, until he feels that he thoroughly knows them. He is constantly experimenting with new mediums, like making carved animals from tree limbs blown down by the hurricane of a couple of years ago. He has designed and made rugs at night, as well as the prints you saw at Brooklyn. This, all in addition to his regular pottery work with the family."

In September 1950, the AAUW exhibit opened at the Brooks Memorial Art Gallery in Memphis, with the block prints mounted on cloth and hung like

Oriental scrolls. Over the next two years sixty pieces—fairy-tale block prints, woodcarvings, large and small watercolors, and line drawings in sepia ink— toured twenty cities in Mississippi, Minnesota, New Hampshire, Tennessee, Alabama, and Oklahoma. At some of these venues, pottery accompanied the graphic works. When the tour came to an end, one of the pelican drawings joined another circulating AAUW exhibition, *Contemporary American Drawing*, at the Whitney Museum of American Art. Annette must have been thrilled to see her son's work heading a list of better-known exhibitors, from "pioneer modernists" like Gaston Lachaise, Georgia O'Keeffe, and Lyonel Feininger to the "Romantic realism" of Thomas Hart Benton and Rockwell Kent. In the publicity for the show, Hermon More, director of the Whitney, grouped Bob with "younger artists" like Milton Avery, whose "decorative drawings are distorted for greater expressiveness."

On the AAUW's tour, sales were meager. At the opening in Memphis, Louise Lehman had the feeling that "many, many watercolors and line drawings as well as scrolls could be sold on the spot if they could be delivered immediately," and she wrote Bob and his mother to remind them of the "psychology of selling." But the Andersons took their time about filling orders, and sometimes simply ignored them altogether. Two months after the opening, an AAUW administrator advised Beam to stop taking orders. The Andersons were "hopeless."

> It looks like there is NO NEED to attempt any special sales program in regard to the show. Louise Lehman says that Walter Anderson couldn't find half of the blocks to reprint the "Noah's Ar[k]" when the orders came in from Memphis. . . . The story was, he guessed he had thrown it away!!! Louise Clark thinks they are so irresponsible down there that NO money should go in advance on any orders . . . just let everything be C.O.D. . . . From all I can gather, the family cannot come to any agreements among themselves. Mama seems to favor Walter because he is the "odd" one of the family. . . . She will NOT let Mac or Peter handle any of the details of the business or make decisions. Walter will not let Mac handle the business . . . and often does not even let MAMA in on his business. Mama did not even know what pictures he sent you and was grieved when she found out what he sent, as it is NOT his best work. Certain pieces are Walter's favorites and he will NOT let them out. So Mama in her eighties tries to act as business agent, mediator, etc., and she is just NOT capable of handling volume business. Louise tells me that Walter now lives alone in his home, that his wife and four children have moved in with Mama because the children bother Walter.

Whether or not Bob kept his favorite pieces to himself, the show was a critical success. In the Memphis *Press-Scimitar*, in September 1950, Mary Allie Taylor praised the painted wood carvings, "a number of cats in different positions, giraffes, roosters, a squirrel, a Greek warrior, an Egyptian mermaid, the Frog Prince and a Pegasus." Guy Northrop, an art critic for the *Commercial Appeal*, pulled out all the stops, and wrote the first serious review that Bob had ever received. "A genius is amongst us," he wrote.

> [Genius] is found, in the case of Anderson, in his watercolors. They are the most original and exciting works in this medium to be found in America since the rise of John Marin. But there is no comparison with Marin, or with any other painter. The Anderson watercolors are from the brush of an individual giant, a man for whom painting is a safety-valve on a teeming, creative imaginative mind, a mind peopled with the legend of childhood, with the fish, fowl and crustaceans of the Gulf Coast, and the freshness of a morning sun on dew-dampened plants. These are paintings in which line is minor, color is major. Like a Japanese poem, they are brief, lyrical, but so all-encompassing of the nature of life and death it frightens you. Their glittering colors are like raindrops on a window when the sun follows a storm. Without the least distortion of form, and with utmost respect for reality, Anderson surpasses the great abstractions of the Arthur Dove–Georgia O'Keeffe school, and stands as tall as Marin but on different terrains.

Lovingly, Northrop made his way through the exhibit. There were watercolors with titles as simple as specimen tags: *Road, Dogwood, Oak Trees, Cucumber-Tree Magnolia, Lilies, Chinese Crab, Japanese Shrimp*—"a clever arrangement of four flesh-toned shrimps that is abstract yet real as life on second look." There were still lifes—the "voluptuous return" of still lifes—three white onions by a battered old shoe, four oranges, and a grapefruit surrounded by oyster shells, where the artist showed "complete control of texture . . . giving you a sense of feeling through sight, almost [making] you taste the juices." And "tree scenes slightly Japanese in technique," alongside larger watercolors where Anderson had turned to "myth, legend and fairy stories with the same luminous color but with more freedom of brush strokes. "There are Irish leprechauns, battling to protect their pot of gold, a 'Chinese Nightingale' inspired by a Vachel Lindsay poem, 'The Cat Turned into a Woman and Back into a Cat,' and four studies for a linoleum block print-watercolor version of 'Sleeping Beauty,' six feet by 18 inches."

Northrop wondered whether the "unforgettable tones and hues" of the watercolors had been inspired by the recent trip to China. Some had, while others predated the trip. When his article was reprinted in the Ocean Springs newspaper, it was impossible for Ocean Springs to ignore Bob's art. Sissy showed the clipping to the children, and the local Planters Club—the town's closest thing to a group of "society" women—arranged for a three-day exhibition of the AAUW show at the newly built Community Center on Washington Avenue. Some ceramics, too fragile for the tour, would be brought over from Shearwater. Tea was served each afternoon by Bob's protecting deities: Pat, Sissy, Mac's wife, Sara, and Annette. A few nights before the opening, Annette went to the Cottage to see him.

> Last night, went down to Bob's. I went intending to listen. I told him that I remembered what he had said—that I was different this year. "How?" I asked. He said, "You have gone into your cave." . . . I wondered what he meant. "How?" I asked again. "Is *this* your cave?" "Oh, no," he said. "This is a palace. I do not go into my cave. In my cave there is a monster." I did not know what to say. At home again, I thought I should have said, "Turn on the light, and you will see there is no monster." The exhibition is trying for him and me. Too much.

She wondered what "monster" he was referring to. One of the more beneficent demons hidden in his "cave" was the thought of the murals he had never been able to paint. When he went to the exhibition and saw the clean, white stucco walls of the Community Center, he knew he had a space where, finally, he could reconcile public and private. His personal vision would be revealed, once more, to the community.

COMMUNITY CENTER

The town of Ocean Springs had long been planning to build a community center, but in the aftermath of the 1947 hurricane, when so many buildings needed repairs, funding had been hard to come by. At town meetings, other more pressing needs were mentioned. The town's only policeman was using his own car. The road to the seafood plant needed to be paved. Finally, a bond was floated and ordinary citizens raised funds through bake sales, fish fries, and pancake suppers. It was a community movement, and Bob wanted to share, somehow, in the collective accomplishment. Ground was broken, and by the time he returned from China, the building was nearing completion. It was a modest cinder block box, dignified by a formal entrance, with some columns and lunette windows. To the people of Ocean Springs, it was the fulfillment of a dream: a place for "healthful, wholesome supervised recreation" for the young, and for civic organizations, wedding receptions, art shows, Mardi Gras balls, concerts, and dance recitals. At the dedication, on October 31, 1950, the Honorable Bill Colmer—"Congressman Bill"— reminded his audience that little Ocean Springs could help tip the balance between two antagonistic ideologies: "on one side that for which we stand, freedom and understanding; on the other, that dominated by Communism." His listeners sang "America the Beautiful," accompanied by the high school band. It was Halloween, and the ladies from the Planters Club, who were organizing Bob's "homecoming" exhibition, had adorned the new building with "smilax, bamboo, and various greeneries, interspersed with witches and goblins." After the ceremony, the fire department put on a masquerade dance, and Pee-Wee and His Lazy River Boys supplied music. A bank president donned an apron for a charity bake sale and bingo, and Marshall Miller, the town's only policeman, drifted by in his new cruiser.

It must have been a few months later, in January or February 1951, perhaps around the time of his AAUW exhibition, that Bob asked his friend Fred Moran, president of the Community Center and of the Jackson County Board of Supervisors, whether he might be allowed to paint the center's 250 feet of wall space with a mural. For many years he had been thinking about public art, and the chance to do another mural in Ocean Springs mattered much more to him than his recent success in New York. In a note to himself, he recorded some initial ideas, conventional enough to please even Rowan, his old nemesis at the PWAP: "using prominent citizens with action from the daily life of the community. A street scene, using the two sides of the room as different sides of a street, enforcing the idea of unity and a common idea of harmony and world consciousness through the development of a unit (the small town) as a center of growth." Or perhaps a "decorative and suggestive map-like mural with the different points of interest emphasized in bright colors." He thought, also, of something historical, combining past and present: "The landing of Bienville on one side, and the future development of the town on the other." But those early ideas yielded to another, better one that related the local to the universal. In a note, he reminded himself that "when the individual consciousness was at its highest, there were city states and not the large unwieldy forms of republic or empires which tend to come between the individual and the world in which he lives." For him, Ocean Springs was analogous to one of those "city states." Local symbols, the "natural forms" of a particular spot, put one in touch with "world consciousness." And in the 1950s, towns like his were losing their genius loci. "Originality is identified with place," he wrote, "and if the people of a place lose their sense of consciousness and polarity or their relation with both fire and air, the traveler moves in and possesses that place." Months earlier he had written to Lura Beam: "I have a very strong feeling of place in an artist's life, and that place is identified and related to other places by the natural forms which grow there." Mississippi, in particular, seemed to be "at the mercy of any car that passes through it." Tourists were "trying to destroy it, although their own life as Americans depend[ed] upon keeping its own character."

One thing he wanted to avoid was political propaganda. Ben Shahn's *Jersey Homesteads* murals, done in the late 1930s, had taught him that "propaganda is no good. . . . In a mural supposed to show why it was good to have emi-grants, showing [Albert] Einstein and [Charles] Steinmetz coming down the gangplank of a steamer, you couldn't help looking at the things that came with them." The eye was apt to wander, certain elements escaped the mural-ist's control, "and even in that mural, there was a female devil carrying a poor wizened little imp, and four numbered criminals hiding behind the leonine and magnificent Einstein. So if you want to help a cause, don't use propa-ganda." There were no local "natural forms" in the mural by Shahn. In his own, he would paint all the ones he best loved—those he had drawn and painted so constantly at Oldfields and on Horn Island: the typical flora and fauna of the coast. Politics, however, would not be entirely absent. An entire wall of his mural would commemorate Ocean Springs as the site of the land-ing, in 1699, of the French explorer Pierre Le Moyne, Sieur d'Iberville, an honor the town had long disputed with neighboring Biloxi and had com-memorated since 1939 in an annual pageant.

Two questions that needed to be resolved were the matter of payment and the degree of community participation in the project. He had nothing but pity, he once wrote, for the artist who "turns desperately to money not because he needs it but simply to justify himself to his neighbor," and he told Moran he would do the mural for a token sum: one dollar. He had thought, also, about how to involve the community—it was, after all, a collective proj-ect. "The expression of art," he wrote, "is in direct ratio to the will spirit—the number of people participating." The Chinese were like that, he said, with an admirable need for "impersonality." In their religious paintings, "one crew would prepare the wall, the next would do the drawing, the next would put on the color. Then they could all come back and enjoy the painting." In a let-ter from 1948, probably never mailed, to a university professor who was col-lecting ideas for the Community Center, he writes of the importance of the participation of others:

> The thing to do would be to find out how many artists would be willing to work for a nominal sum, just enough to commit the council to the act, and to sharing in the blame for the act, and to show that the town set a value on aes-thetic property. The artist would enroll all those who were interested and felt that they would take part in the work. He would state certain fundamentals of design, motives, spaces. The first effort would probably be more disciplinary than expressive of personal emotion, and would give people an opportunity to find out what liberty and what constrictions would be needed for working together on one project. As most artists have occupations, it might have to be

done in the evenings and in spare time, unless the town were willing to feed and lodge them during that period while they were at work.

The subjects for the work could be discussed and settled between the council and the people to do the work. Probably, it would be best if the subjects were chosen as much as possible by the people of the town, so that the manner of the execution could be left entirely to the artists undertaking the work.

Some movement like this is vitally needed to reestablish the relation of art to the people and to let the people of America realize the value of the esthetic as they have already realized the value of definite knowledge.

Community participation was an idea that had been tried out during the Depression, not without success, on WPA murals throughout the United States. But there were no artists in Ocean Springs who could help him. Sissy heard him consider the involvement of local children. But none came forward—perhaps, she thought, because parents did not want their sons and daughters working alongside the "mad artist," or perhaps because few people besides Moran supposed that the work would be worth preserving.

By the middle of February 1951, he was ready to begin. In an encouraging letter, his friend Moran offered "any assistance you may need, such as scaffolds, primer coat, etc." and noted with satisfaction that "this will do more to fix the landing of D'Iberville at Ocean Springs, as well as mark Ocean Springs as the home of Bob Anderson and Shearwater Pottery, than anything I know." Enclosed was a warrant for one dollar and official authorization from the mayor and five aldermen, whom Moran had somehow persuaded to sign. There had been some last-minute discussion of the medium. Bob had thought of fresco painting—for the past few years, he had been reading up on techniques in the Middle Ages and in fifteenth-century Italy—but the building was new, the contractor was reluctant, and he resigned himself to oil-based paint, which he bought from a store in Gulfport. The walls were twelve feet high, but the scaffolding never materialized either; he used an ordinary stepladder, dragging it from one place to another.

In late February or early March, he laid a "ground" over the grainy white cement stucco and—when it would not dry and harden enough to take the paint—removed it, and applied another coat. He did his preliminary sketches in gold paint, and to his great frustration, it dribbled. As the first recognizable shapes appeared, people began to stop by to watch him, but he was easily distracted by their comments, and took to working at night when the place was closed, consulting only with the man in Gulfport who sold him his

Painting the Community Center mural, April 1951

paints. "The advantage the spectator has over the painter," he wrote with a touch of irony, "is that he can usually insist on color and the tree, while the painter usually has to insist on the paint—and often, on the money with which to buy paint." How strange, "that the artist should have no standards, and be constantly trying to live up to other people's standards."

Down the ninety-foot-long south wall, the surface of which was interrupted by windows and doors, he portrayed the landing of Iberville on the Front Beach in Ocean Springs, the presumed site of Fort Maurepas. Deer Island is shown in the background, and the waters of the sound come alive with diving pelicans, shearwaters, and ducks. Three brightly painted Biloxi Indians—one playing a drum, another a flute, and the third holding a turtle and a Cherokee rose—receive the French explorer, who looks uncannily similar to Moran as he kneels and plants the blue French flag, with its fleurs-de-lis. Five mustachioed men with muskets and a Catholic priest with a crucifix observe him, as Iberville's crew ties a small boat to the shore. Standing jauntily in the boat, easily recognizable in his grey felt hat (the only item of modern apparel), is Walter Anderson, with mustache and a stubbly blond beard. Reds and blues prevail—the skins and blue tattoos of the Indians, and the colors of the conquerors' clothing and hats—in homage to France.

On the east wall was a stage. To the north side of it, Bob painted a rising sun, surrounded by rain clouds, and on the south side, a rose. "I don't know whether Ocean Springs has a flower or symbol," he remarked, apropos of the rose, "but somebody painted a rose on the town's black water tower, and I

Self-portrait from Community Center mural, 1951

took them at their word." What the swirling flower suggests, however, is the compass rose of old maps and wind charts. He had thought of the wind as a symbol of Ocean Springs and Mississippi: "I, who live in a state which prefers the wind to a tomato . . ."

Along the north wall, he painted what he called, somewhat mysteriously, the "Seven Climates," not in the modern sense of meteorological zones, but in the ancient and early modern one—from Hipparchus to Mandeville—of "a belt of the earth's surface contained between two given parallels of latitude." Ocean Springs would be a sort of microcosm, containing all of them. Each of the "climates" had a corresponding celestial body—Jupiter, Saturn, Mars, the sun, Venus, Mercury, and the moon, although for the sun he would substitute Uranus, and he arranges the planets, as Anne R. King has noticed, "from nearest to farthest from the sun, beginning with Mercury and ending with Uranus." He must also have been aware of the doctrine of the seven planetary spheres, with their different tones, producing a celestial music.

His first intentions are recorded in a brief note:

Possibilities
Diaperson [sic]—Whitman's poem. The union of art and nature (man's passage through the influence of the different planets to earth) applied to the local setting using local conditions.

The allusion was to Walt Whitman's "Proud Music of the Sea Storm," from *Leaves of Grass,* a celestial dream-vision celebrating music, from "Earth's own diapason / Of winds and woods and mighty ocean waves" (a music well known to Bob) to the song, dance, and orchestral music of all nations. It was natural to think of Whitman, not only because many of his poems have a cosmic, mural-like scope, but because Bob shared with Whitman a sense of the physicality of things, his love of wandering through nature, and an idea of America's unrealized possibilities. In an undated note he writes: "Mr. Whitman, be my aid—friend of the wind I also am. And an intimate of the brilliant nor'wester. The seductive sou'easter. The green easter and the changeable west wind. America did not flower then. Perhaps it never will. Perhaps there will be nothing but leaves [of grass]."

As for Whitman's "Proud Music . . . ," the "symphony" of nature and its "realization" by the artist had been a major theme of Bob's writing since the years at Oldfields. The mention of "man's passage" through the planets, is a reference, probably gleaned from some secondary source, to an idea popularized by Macrobius, the fifth-century Roman philosopher: that at birth the soul descends from heaven to earth through the seven planetary spheres, absorbing specific moral qualities from each, and storing them up for development in earthly life. In the end, he decided on something else: to associate each planet with a different season. In portraying each of them, he would have the opportunity to show the flora and fauna typical of the coast at different times of year. Some thirty plants and trees and forty insects, fish, and animals, many of them listed in preliminary notes, all of them typical of the coast, found their way into the mural. The diversity of subject matter— human and natural history, the planets and the passage of the seasons, the local and the mythological, the abundance of "natural forms"—posed a problem of unity as difficult as that faced by Whitman in his parallelistic, mural-like enumerations. How to hold it all together? One unifying element, besides color, was the decoration of the frames of doors and windows, brightly painted in a common idiom, the geometric motifs of Best-Maugard, all of which reappear in the mural itself, with charming lapses in symmetry. The entire mural, especially the north wall, with its gods and planets, was a reverberant study in motion: natural forms swept up in the great "spiral" or "vortex"—source of all life—celebrated by Hambidge, by Best-Maugard, and by Whitman. Waves and birds, stars and wind: everything is in motion.

In late April, Louise Lehman saw the work in progress, and felt "overwhelmed," and in June, Guy Northrop, the young critic from Memphis who had proclaimed Walter Anderson a "genius," came to Ocean Springs with his new wife, Miriam, and interviewed him in the Community Center. After three months of work, he "had the entire mural fully sketched in with color, and much of the detail work was there," Northrop wrote. "But he was hesitant to predict when he [would] be through. Several months, maybe a couple of years." Northrop was charmed by his dignity and independence, and noted his "scorn for acclaim."

> It was typical of him that when his paints ran low recently, he should mount his bicycle at daybreak and pedal sixteen miles west to Gulfport to purchase new supplies. Employees of the paint store found him waiting at the door when they opened. When they had helped him lash his heavy load to the bicycle they watched him pedal away, back the long sixteen miles. Although there are cars and trucks in the family, he does not drive, nor does he ask others to

run his errands. When I called on him, Anderson was high on a scaffold, painting a flight of pelicans. My wife and I were introduced to him by his mother, who then left. Alone with us, the artist climbed down from his roost, wiped his hand on paint-smeared brown pants, and greeted us.

Proudly, politely, Bob led his visitor through the "Seven Climates." In the first, some birds perch on a sweet gum tree, with its blazing autumn foliage, circled by scuppernong grapes. Under it are two turtles and, drawn by the grapes, a red fox. To the right, symbolizing winter, are a pin oak, bathed in blue moonlight, and animals associated with the night and the moon: opossum, luna moth, owl, flying squirrel, and a blue cat. Constellations appear on fields of blue, as though through openings in the clouds. All this, presided over by the moon, was to have "the lightness of a Christmas card." Next comes Mercury, symbolized by a stout magnolia, standing, with palmettos, in the swamp and accompanied by a coon, squirrels, herons, and other birds. Bob told Northrop he had conjured up Venus from Whitman's poem "The Dalliance of the Eagles." Male and female gyrate in a venereal spiral powerful enough to sweep birds and fish from the waves beneath, with love seen as a natural force, moving not only "the sun and the other stars," but pulling the water into its orbit. The eagles' claws are "interlocked," as in the Whitman poem:

> The rushing amorous contact high in space together,
> The clinching interlocking claws, a living, fierce, gyrating wheel,
> Four beating wings, two beaks, a swirling mass tight grappling,
> In tumbling turning clustering loops, straight downward falling,
> Till o'er the river pois'd, the twain yet one, a moment's lull,
> A motionless still balance in the air . . .

Mars follows. "Not too terrible," he told Northrop. "Not a God of war, but identified with Spring and the mating season." And not the "mating" itself, but amorous competition worthy of Mars. Beneath a flowering dogwood tree, two iridescent stags lock horns, in a scene reminiscent of medieval tapestry. Their horns blend gracefully with the lines of the dogwood and of the native azaleas like the ones he had been caring for, for many years, at Shearwater. The swirling motion of Venus continues in Jupiter, who exercises his dominion over the heavens, bringing rain and pulling the ducks and other birds into his swirling movement: an allusion, as Gautier has noticed, to the hurricane season of late summer and fall. It is a "whirlwind," he told Northrop. "It lifts the birds, the grass is raised, everything becomes animated, but Jupiter remains in place." Next comes Saturn, depicted as a bluish black bear—then thought to be extinct on the coast—climbing a live oak. Bob explained that he was "pawing for honey and eating bees, too, in his hasty greed. This is the mythological Saturn (bear) who devoured his children (bees), in the Golden Age." A woodpecker perches on the tree, and on the forest floor are toadstools, ferns, pipewort, and an abundance of other plants and flowers. Finally, a "questionable God" called Herschel, whom he said he had come across in his reading. He had imagined Herschel—symbol of Uranus—as an alligator, he told Northrop, "a not too ominous, almost comical creature" crawling through the pinewood. A lightning bolt parts the clouds, threatening a stand of loblolly pine, putting blue jays to flight. "As best he could explain this inspiration, it came from a time when he almost stumbled across an alligator while wading in a bayou, paused quietly to let it decide whether he was friend or foe, and breathed a sigh of relief when it called him friend and slithered away."

The tour was over, and that night Annette organized a dinner on the gallery of the Front House for the critic who had written so glowingly about her son. She had read Northrop's first article, about the AAUW exhibition, and had told herself that such recognition would help Bob—"it should help everything." But Bob had told her, a little later, that he "did not want appreciation—he had always been too much appreciated." And he was reluctant, now, to attend the dinner. "At six, I went down to remind him," Annette wrote. "He said he could not come. Later, from the Front House I went down to ask him to reconsider. Close to his house I stopped. I would ask again. I hoped, and turned back. Before I had gone far I heard him behind me. He would come, he said. He came, and was funny and nice."

As the summer went on, the Community Center mural began to draw comments, and not all were favorable. Except for Northrop's article, the newspapers ignored it completely. No ceremony marked its completion, no letter of thanks arrived from the Community Center or town government. A friend of Sissy, who had been elected to the position of town clerk, confided, years later, that someone had come up to her and said: "Now I helped get you elected. The first thing I want you to do is get me enough nice white paint to cover that crap in the Community Center."

Exhausted by his long labor of love, wounded by the town's indifference, Bob stopped before finishing the mural to his own satisfaction, though few, today, would call it incomplete. In July, he began a much smaller mural in the

Walter Anderson, c. 1951

bar of a dude ranch in Gulf Hills. According to Sissy, it was done in a "decorative manner somewhat in the style of a Georgia O'Keeffe," too "wild" for a golf course and dude ranch. Another artist was asked to paint over it, and, eventually, the building burned to the ground. There is an ironic note, found on the back of one of his watercolors from the 1950s: "The admirable spirit of the people of Ocean Springs is shown in their salutation to the rising sun each morning: 'We accept it!'" Even "acceptance" would take time, though barely a year after he had finished working on them someone guessed in the local newspaper that the murals—for which he had charged one dollar—were already valued at a hundred thousand dollars, and that visitors from all over the country had come to see them.

September brought a new exhibition of prints, large and small watercolors, and Shearwater pottery in the Lauren Rogers Museum of Art, housed in an old Georgian mansion in Laurel, Mississippi. A preview of the show noted that "while many in Laurel know the pottery, few if any know the extraordinary originality in design and color of Walter Anderson." Pat drove Annette and Bob up to see it. There was "silence and love" on the ride north, Annette noted in her journal. An intelligent reviewer for the *Laurel Leader-Call*, Walter Watkins, was charmed by all three Andersons, not least by Annette, with her "unerring eye for fine design . . . ear for poetry, and a too generous heart for business." Bob's nonceramic art, he wrote, was "only beginning to be known," but he was deeply impressed with his sly sense of humor, his "remarkable grasp of everyday objects" and "sense of instinctive balance." The larger watercolors "promised much," especially his sea turtles and pelican, with "many bands of decorative color like a halo round the pelican."

> I suspect that Anderson has for awhile turned away from the smaller water-colors simply because he has already done all he wants in this dimension. Here, his sure grasp of space and distribution of color shows perhaps early experience designing pottery with its small confined surfaces. Always there is instinctive balance. In many every inch is filled yet never crowded. You will notice that several seem unfinished at top or side. With so intense a painter, I cannot believe this incompleteness is laziness or boredom with the design. Most probably, he stops at the very point where intuition tells him the best balance is reached. The separating bands of white between the brilliant patches of color (achieved on typewriter paper!) are essential. These [are] extraordinary paintings.

The flowers of Georgia O'Keeffe, the depth and color pattern of Cézanne, the intricacy of Persian prints were comparisons that came readily to the reviewer's mind. Two weeks after the article appeared, on September 29, Bob celebrated his forty-eighth birthday, surrounded by his family and dreaming of another adventure: an unconventional bicycle trip. He had been paid $150 for the Gulf Hills mural, and he wanted to see the orchids and butterflies of Costa Rica.

"*No* is the concentric," he wrote that fall. "The man who stays at home and says 'no' implies that he has done all those things, said all those things—and perhaps he ha[s]." Better, he thought, to be an eccentric: "You should not go in one direction like an automobile, but in five like a star." There was a practical aspect to that, too: "A man who runs in one direction may be caught by anyone, but a man that runs in three directions can't be caught."

He took special pleasure in seeing things from the air, where the earth looked like "the back of some animal," and "materialization" and simile pulled together sea, earth, and sky. Over Belize, little cumulus clouds "herded together like a flock of sheep." Fields turned to corduroy, and the freshly ploughed earth was like the wake of a boat until "three pale spots at one end" of the boat made him realize that men were plowing with oxen. An erupting volcano reminded him of a pineapple, and its wisps of smoke, carried north by the wind, made "a succession of cumulus pillows, like the smoke from a train." The shadow of the airplane "suddenly appeared in the center of a rainbow," and the rainbow "became double."

In San José he found a boardinghouse and celebrated his arrival by dancing to the radio with the innkeeper's large family. He bought a bike for a huge sum of money—sixty dollars—and took to the road in search of new flowers, birds, insects, and interesting people. For over a week he drew plants and landscapes: lupines, orchids, the view of a harbor. He remembered some Spanish from his days of translating the *Summa Artis*, and everywhere, people seemed friendly. The "Spanish are intelligent and kind and rather melancholy," he wrote. "The Indian has form which is in some way associated with nature: a volcano which may blow the top off at any moment." Though he didn't look much like a tourist, people did him little favors. One family let him sleep on their front porch, and gave him "a pillow, and water to wash with, and bananas and oranges and breakfast in the morning." A highway crew gave him a lift on the back of their truck. A little boy climbed a tree for him to get an orchid which he had seen growing in enclosed places, without daring to trespass, and another boy transmitted a dinner invitation from his father ("I was tired, and begged off"). He had bought a shirt that was too small for him and one night at supper in his boardinghouse, the buttons flew off. A "bevy of señoras" sewed them on again. "I am degenerating," he sighed. "There was a time when I would have sewed them on for myself!" In the countryside, he was charmed by the sound of rushing water. Tropical rain interrupted his drawing, but he was grateful for the luxuriant plants, some of which were entirely new to him, though most had "family relations in the north." He returned to Ocean Springs with specimens he had purchased or dug himself—thirty-nine orchids, fifteen succulents, one tree fern—none of them destined to survive.

It was his last trip abroad and when he returned, his life fell back into the pattern it had had since he left Oldfields. His work at Shearwater, where he was responsible for decorating at least ten pieces per week, gave him just enough money (from $7.50 to $15.00 weekly) to continue with his painting, spend two- or three-week periods on Horn Island and the Chandeleurs, and take a bicycle trip whenever and wherever the spirit moved him. In the spring of 1953, at a moment when he was experimenting with intense color in his own art, he decided to look at paintings by his old teacher, Henry McCarter, and caught the train to Philadelphia to see what he could find. At the Academy, the morning of his arrival, he learned to his great disappointment "that there was no McCarter Museum, and that his paintings had all been given away to his friends." In the afternoon, he spotted his old friend Francis Speight giving a class, and the two of them walked out the parkway to the museum of art to look at some McCarter drawings that were in storage. They had eaten lunch together, and Speight asked Bob whether he wouldn't care to spend the night with his wife and him in Manayunk.

"No," he replied. "I think I had better be getting home."

By the following morning, he was back on his bicycle, rolling through southern Pennsylvania, and that night, a little beyond Elkton, Maryland, he slept in the open, his blanket wrapped around him, trying to keep warm. He cycled over eleven hundred miles back to Ocean Springs, crossing terrain he remembered from fifteen years earlier on his escape from Pratt. As he headed south, spring turned into early summer: "a single day's journey made a noticeable difference in the foliage of the trees." He was pursued by the "hound of heaven," the hounds of farmers, and by Greyhound buses with their "violent but not unmusical tooting." At times, he was forced off the bike by headwinds and hills. It was a rainy, chilly April and, as in China, he slept anywhere he could—in deserted houses and cow sheds, in culverts and ditches, and in sheltered places in the woods, and took no thought for the morrow: "When you take life lightly, the birds know, and come to pick the lice out of your clothes." He had his usual encounter with the authorities; the Virginia State Police stopped him and demanded his social security card. "I had none, but fortunately I had [the logbook] and could show him where I had come from." On a bridge in Virginia, he balked at paying the toll, and asked ironically whether he looked like an automobile. The woman collecting tolls "was all solicitude in a moment, and said no." But he gave in, and paid all further tolls without question: "So much has been done to turn two-lane roads into four-lane that the money is probably needed." Not that he was happy about postwar highway construction. In the heat of Alabama, detours added miles to his trip, and he bridled at the highway department's apologies: *Improvement of Roads Means Progress.* "I have never much cared for that word, and I care less for it now than ever."

The towns were prosperous, "full of life and color, and almost all centered around the grocery store," where grumpy clerks dealt with cheerful customers. "Perhaps someday," he wrote, "there will be a real 'help yourself' grocery store." And a help-yourself diner. At one which advertised the best food in the country, a pretty girl bought him a bowl of soup and crackers. When he praised it, she replied "with her nose in the air, 'It *is* good soup.' None of them wanted their food appreciated by a hungry man. *Any* food would be good to him."

Back on the road he watched the clouds gather and enjoyed the smell of rain on the hot dry road. When the rain cleared, whippoorwills sang duets from both sides of the highway, and farther south, they yielded to chuck-will's-widow, and redheaded woodpeckers who "flirted" with him, flying ahead and lighting on a fencepost or telegraph pole, waiting until he was abreast of them, and flying ahead again. In the early morning, rabbits nibbled on the dewy grass, birds sang, the wind blew, the wheels turned, and he thought once more of the "symphony" of nature. What amazed him was all that nature owed to man and to art.

> To know that every movement you make is related to the movements of the pine trees in the wind, the movements of a man in a field plowing, the orbit of a star, or the spiral movement of the sun itself. . . . To know that this was done through art—by men, not gods, who named each gesture and posture and assumed each in its correct place and time until they became perfectly related to the movements of the stars . . . is to accept man's inheritance. To deserve it is another thing, but the first step is to acknowledge the debt to those men who have numbered and realized and lived with art. That day follows night as I move and in relation to my movement; that I follow the sun west and make a certain number of revolutions to the earth's and the sun's. To realize that I am keeping time, and therefore am a brother to the wind and sun and every other thing which is consciously in time. That every little movement, each discovery, is part of the heavenly music, and if my ears were functioning properly I would hear not just the wind in the grass, the two or three different rhythms of insects, the piping of a frog, the call of a nightjar, but an orderly and recogniz-able harmony which might or not have been written; that seeing would not mean an isolated explosion stimulating the memory and temporarily waking me out of the day's sleep, but all part of the divine symphony: bird, wave, wind, wind, wave, bird. Then, unless I am at work, I could continue that move-ment, affected by that same wind through movement, warmth, firelight, action. If I am already participating in the day's work, that wind would still be a part of me, but subordinate to the dance in which I was already taking part. Thus, the monotonous turning of a bicycle's wheels would become the part of a village festival, spring plowing, the movement of wind in the grass or the growth of a clump of flowers beside the road.

At home that spring, Annette too had been telling herself how important it was to listen. Not to the "heavenly music" her son had written about, but to other people, especially the family. For the past several years, with her eyesight beginning to fail her, she had been barely able to read or see her own hand-writing clearly. Told that her sight would improve with an operation, she refused, and sometimes told others of a horrifying experience. She was cross-eyed as a little girl, and her perfectionistic father brought an eye doctor to the house to operate on her. She was laid out on the dining room table, and her arms, legs, and head were held in place while a surgeon cut into her eye, without anaesthesia, in a crude operation that could easily have left her blind. Throughout her life she had done exercises to strengthen her vision, but for years she had felt she had always given too much importance to sight, design, and visual beauty of all kinds. "Anyone can draw if he really tries," she liked to say, and people in town still came to her, hoping to learn something about art. Tactfully she criticized their work and wondered how to awaken people to the unnoticed beauty around them. But the whole exercise often felt empty and useless. It was "childish to want always to tell what you know. The man or woman who *listens,* who appraises, who *sees,* who is aware, is one in a thousand." Eyes, perhaps, were not so important, "and it is only my eyes that have been trained." How wrong she had been—since the time she was a girl—to value line and color and design above all else, to judge the gift, and not the feelings and intentions of the giver. She thought of Swedenborg, and his "*spiritual* sight" and "spiritual hearing" and of Thoreau in his own moment of enlightenment:

> I hearing get, who had but ears,
> And sight, who had but eyes before,
> I moments live, who lived but years,
> And truth discern, who knew but learning's lore.

No, neither sight nor hearing nor simple "learning" could lead one to truth. "Bird lovers can hear the faintest chirp and the bird that makes it, but bird lovers are not the best people in the world. It must help to listen for bird notes, but after all that cannot be enough." All people, she thought, liked to sum themselves up in a single thought, or capture the "routine of life" in a single motto. *Sans Dieu, rien,* was the one that accompanied her great-grandfather, Samuel Jarvis Peters. Her mother had spoken of "hope with head and heart." Her husband's motto, she couldn't remember, though she had once designed a gravestone for him with the Andersons' emblem: a live oak and the words "Stand Sure." Long ago, over the fireplace in her tiny room in the Barn—a fireplace Peter had built for her—she had written some lines from Shaemas O Sheel:

He whom a dream hath possessed
Knoweth no more of doubting. . . .

Those words had guided her for years. But perhaps a better motto would be *to listen*. A few years earlier, she had made it a New Year's resolution. "To listen! That will be my study for the year. To read the Bible every day. To listen will mean to be still, even when I am alone." Bob had told her that he didn't listen either, not to other people. There was a poem they both liked, "The Goat Paths," by James Stephens, that spoke of finding peace—the goats went down crooked paths, "cropping here and cropping there," to a "deeper quietude":

If I were as wise as they,
I would stray apart and brood,
I would beat a hidden way
Through the quiet heather spray
To a sunny solitude.

Both of them—mother and son—sought that "quietude" in nature, and both reached beyond nature for something spiritual and transcendent. One hot, still summer afternoon Annette sat outside the Barn, listening to the buzz of a single cicada and some hammering from across the marsh. She would take a bath . . .

> . . . a swim, everyone calls it here. It was not even a good wetting. The water was warm and very shallow, but you could lie on your back and see above the pines and cedars of the shore the great white cumulus clouds of summer making the sky so much more important than the land or the quiet sea. A fish's soft mouth nibbled at my finger on the sand. Coming back to land, some malicious imps of the sea bottom sucked down each foot into the malodorous mud, holding on tightly to each canvas rope-soled shoe. On shore again, the army of fiddlers moved together slowly, away, at my approach. I saw all the beauty and wonder of sky and sea without emotion because I had not taken the time to free my mind of care. . . . I still carried my burdens as if I had not found the way to turn them into wings.

Sitting in the Barn with her cats and kittens, listening to the radio or reading the Bible, arranging the wildflowers that Peter always brought to decorate the showroom, she sometimes felt unutterably lonely. The Pottery was a magnet for interesting people from faraway places, and often she crossed the path to the showroom, "tacking," her sons said, "like a sailboat in a headwind" (sometimes they followed her, imitating her movements). She yearned as much for intelligent conversation as for "quietude." In the family no one seemed to have the time to talk to her. Sissy and the grandchildren kept her company—a year after they had left Oldfields, she had invited them to live with her in the Barn, and she had always wanted to build them a house on the place—but there never seemed to be anyone with whom she could converse about art or ideas, poetry or religion. "This place closes one up," Pat said once of Shearwater, "in spite of being a kind of heaven." For many years, Pat had seen to it that both Bob and her mother-in-law got a good hot meal every day at the Front House. She had never missed a day. But whom to tell about the books that she liked? Only with Bob—when he was happy—could she share the things she clipped from magazines or newspapers, the "healing light" she read about in Agnes Sanford, the news and politics she heard on the radio from Norman Thomas or Martin Agronsky. Sometimes, when he was happy, he would go to the Barn to read to her and kiss her goodnight. Peter and Mac had drifted away from her long ago. Peter could be charming—they ate together, and sometimes at night the two of them played chess—but often he treated her badly. Not that she blamed him; she knew what a strain he and Pat were under at the Pottery. The labor of producing "utilitarian ware" was stifling the artist in him. It had been too long, she thought, since he had experimented with new glazes. Mac was doing wonderful work—over the years some of his carved vases had been featured along with those of his brothers at the Robineau exhibitions, and he was beginning to receive commissions for panels and murals—but he had shocked Annette by taking a full-time job in Ocean Springs, in 1952. He and Sara had two children now, and after years of dealing with the problems of Bob and Peter, they were trying to give them as normal a childhood as possible. Sissy, too, came home exhausted from her first-grade classes. They were all in her prayers, but Annette prayed hardest for Bob, often with the sense that she had failed him.

"HALF VILLAIN, HALF FOOL"

Never again did Bob attempt a public mural. For the next fifteen years, he kept to himself in the Cottage, drawing, painting, writing, and decorating pottery, making occasional bicycle trips and staying for ever-longer periods on Horn Island. Pat and Annette arranged for exhibitions of his work at Newcomb and at galleries around the state but, for the most part, public response was muted or obtuse. "His watercolors are not so much paintings per se," one reviewer wrote, "but integrated patterns to be used as wall decorations." If he cared about the lack of public recognition, he seldom complained. "The artist lives between assistance and opposition and is first overwhelmed by one and then both together—then is reduced to the ranks and is told that the gods help those who help themselves. So that he usually ends up living almost entirely on stolen fruit."

At times, to relieve some inner tension, he would punch his fist through a windowpane in the Cottage and it would often be Sissy who bandaged his bleeding hands and asked him what was the matter. On one occasion, she found him lying on the bed sobbing disconsolately, and he told her how he missed their life at Oldfields. Decades later, she tried to recall what he had said:

Do you remember how it was? Especially supper time and the sleepy children and the good food. Things we had raised, picked and now were eating? Do you remember the night Mary played Cinderella with Billy for prince and decided she would rather have me? Do you remember tiny Leif dancing around the table because she was the fairy? I thought my heart would melt

Don Quixote and Sancho, c. 1945

out of my chest with the joy of it. I believed with all my soul that we were all
a part of earth's highest good. Oh why did I have to ruin it for you, for the
children, most of all for me?

She had always been careful not to criticize him to the children and to
remind them that he was a special person who could not be expected to live
like everyone else. Mary remembers that they "saw him only at his inclination,

and that wasn't often. On those increasingly rare occasions when our comings and goings did coincide, I was expected to treat him with respectful affection. 'Give your father a kiss, Mary,' my grandmother would say when I burst in from school on one of his infrequent visits to the Barn. I think it was as awkward for him as it was for me."

He would sometimes pay the children to pose for him, an experience they dreaded, for it meant a long spell of sitting still. Sometimes Sissy would use a story to ease them through sad or awkward moments. She was a marvelous storyteller, Leif remembers, and "her stories were so shiningly adventurous, the characters so real, that we could hardly miss the absent father figure. We were a family . . . and everything was fine." Both Peter and Mac helped give them that feeling. Looking back, years later, Billy remembered gratefully how Peter and Pat took the place of his absent father, taking him on trips in the *Patricia*, a twenty-six-foot boat Peter had built for family excursions, and John remembered his uncle's patience as he helped him build a pirogue. For all four of Bob's children, Mac (who had found his own way as painter and potter) was a steady, calming presence; as a child, Mary wished she could live inside one of his tranquil landscapes. "Nobody really lacked for a father, or a brother, or a sister," John remarked, many years later. "There were so many role models around." And yet, it disturbed the children to hear their father breaking glass or dancing by himself in the Cottage at night, no matter how often such things occurred. "I forget that he is my Daddy," Leif wrote in her memoirs, restating her childhood feelings.

> He doesn't feel like someone's Daddy; he feels strange and distant. I sure wish I couldn't hear him dancing in the night. The music from his radio is loud, not pretty music, and his feet are pounding on the floor. You can't forget that he's there, or that he's drinking . . . probably. . . . My brother, Billy, turns the television louder, but it doesn't help. In the daytime, when I see him coming, I try to hide. I'm not sure why I do this, just, I don't feel good; even how he smells is weird. . . . Maybe I still love him, but I can't remember hugs and kisses, or nice words. Somewhere inside, maybe, from long ago. . . . I guess my father's like a character in a book; he is dramatic. But it is difficult to live real close to someone in a book. It is unreal. You go through motions, and you wish that you were somewhere else; perhaps in another book.

At times, in the 1950s, all four children were fearful; sometimes they were simply embarrassed, and looked the other way when they saw him riding around Ocean Springs on his rusty bicycle, with his "ancient and strangely colored shirts and trousers, his broken sometimes mismatched shoes on sockless feet, [and] the inimitable felt hat shaped by weather and use." It occurred to Leif that it must have wounded him to know that his children were afraid of him: "My daddy can pet snakes; so if we find one, we go tell him . . . and we get to see him stroke its scaly back. We laugh and scoot away, just like the snake. I think that Daddy must be lonely, if he knows that nearly everyone is scared of him. Perhaps he is a little like the snake, and mostly hides so he won't have to feel their fear. He is so different from the others, and I think I understand, almost. I think I may be different too."

There were better moments, especially when the children grew older. For Billy's birthday one year, Bob presented him with a beautiful brass ship's lantern he had found on Horn Island, wrapping it in brown paper from the showroom the way he wrapped all of his gifts. And when Billy married Carolyn Rose Fournier and the two of them wanted to build a house on the grounds at Shearwater, Bob gave them a piece of his land overlooking the water, though he flew into a rage and nearly took back the gift when he spotted them clearing the undergrowth. Without realizing it, they were hacking away at some rare, late-blooming wild azaleas. To Bob, it felt like murder. Not only were they rare, but he had for years marveled over the "suffusion of color" on grey, cloudy days when "several bushes of brilliantly colored azaleas [are] in juxtaposition."

When he returned from his trips to the island, tanned and strong, with a two- or three-week growth of beard, he looked happy and eager to share his stories and return to his work. But the transition from the solitude of the island to a town even as small as Ocean Springs was always a hard one, and he must have felt—as he did sometimes on the island—like a hermit crab, "without the protecting shell." Within a couple of days after his return the sociability and the healthy glow were gone, and he retreated back into the Cottage. Once, on the island, he had found "a flight of ship's stairs," and, incredibly, had rowed them all the way back to Shearwater in his tiny boat— they "would be a great help to Mother in getting into my house." But he had not installed them; instead, he let the Cherokee rose cover his door. In Ocean Springs more than a few parents warned their own children to keep away from "that crazy Bob Anderson," who pedaled wobbily down East Beach Drive or Washington Avenue, on his way to buy supplies or "borrow" a game hen, a turkey, or some numinous vegetables to take home and paint. Like Peter, he seems to have been unusually sensitive to alcohol, and although he drank little or none on Horn Island and on his bicycle trips, in the Cottage, beginning around 1953, he would start sipping beer or wine at noon, and go on drinking and smoking all afternoon. When drunk, he would break glass or furniture, tossing some of it out the door. When the family gave him a refrigerator for the Cottage it appeared the next morning in the marsh; he had somehow gotten his arms around it and carried it there by himself, astonishing everyone by his strength. When he left on one of his trips to the island, Annette would have the place repaired and cleaned. On his way to the workshop, Peter would see his brother on the screened porch of the Cottage, taking in the day, and would tell their mother, "We have to find something for Bobby to do." Years later, Sissy recalled that, for all its misgivings, the town was "protective" of him. "No one in Ocean Springs would sell whisky to him," Sissy wrote, "but there were stores where he could pick up wine as easily as rice. . . . I remember one night the patrol car stopped in front of the house. I went out to see what had happened, heart in mouth. The kind policeman called out, 'He's all right. We just wanted you to know we just put him to bed. We found him in a ditch with his bicycle on top of him, but he's all right.' And he was. It was only when he had hard liquor or even wine that there were truly bad effects."

Once, in the showroom, after he had asked Pat to lend him a little money for wine, she asked him, as she often did, "Don't you realize you're the greatest living American artist?" He looked at her seriously for a moment and replied: "Sometimes I think I am great." And, then, Sissy remembers, the sparkle left his eye. "Sometimes I'm just a no-good bum. All I want is six bits until pay day. And I don't want anyone's judgment." Despite the unspeakable turmoil he had sometimes caused at Shearwater, Pat had never stopped caring for him or believing in his genius. It wasn't often that he sat down with the family for lunch at the Front House, but she made him feel he was welcome there, and when he didn't come, she left him a good meal on the steps of the Cottage.

He had given up hope, long ago, of ever forming part of the "tribal council." "The worst of a small community," he wrote, "is that any attempt at seeing clearly will be considered a personal insult." Nor would his family ever understand his motives—or he, theirs. In a bitter note to himself, he writes that he has been "living like an Indian."

Almost everything I've done has been like taking the scalps of an enemy, the enemy being people who share the same interests and therefore are potential

Pigs, c. 1943

friends. A certain number of scalps make a coup. If I make enough coups, I am given a place at the Council and may share in the pipe of peace. To one who has done what they wanted to do—honestly believing that what they were doing and trying to do was for the general good—it comes as a shock to find that everyone—particularly one's family and those who have reason to believe that they know one best—all think that what one has done was done from purely selfish motives.

As for his social status as an outcast, a "bum," it wasn't the way he perceived himself. "One can belong to society without agreeing with it," he wrote. "One of the conditions of [belonging to] society may be that the man does not agree with it—at least that he has the right to disagree with it as a criminal has not. Perhaps the criminal has the better chance of reaching heaven first." He was as ready as anyone to intervene, sometimes quixotically, when he saw an injustice. Once, in the 1950s, he noticed a holdup in progress at a gas station on Bell Fontaine Point, and wrestled with an armed intruder until authorities could be called. And one day, riding his bike from Oldfields to Ocean Springs, he saw a car parked by the side of the road and heard terrible sounds of fighting. A man was beating a woman. "As he went by on his bicycle, he reached his fist in and popped the man," Sissy remembered. Both of them—man and wife—came after him angrily, and he had to be rescued by a neighbor who was watching from his house.

Particularly distasteful to him was his inability to make enough money to help the family. It was Sissy, not he, who was supporting the children. Years earlier, a little after he moved out of Oldfields, he had applied for a job as a draftsman at Ingalls Shipbuilding, where Mac had worked during the war years, but they had no use for him. Later, he cycled the long miles to Hattiesburg to apply for a position as an art teacher at the University of Southern Mississippi. No luck there either, though perhaps it was just as well: "If the average man realized the amount of energy, the amount of work he did in simply repeating going to work morning after morning, he would soon be appalled and would probably stop doing it. . . . Man apparently lives the life of some sort of draught animal as soon as he begins to work. Put his back into it, he feels the traces tighten—the world begins to breathe again—the chariot of the sun is once again in motion, only it isn't a chariot at all, it's the terrible truck of doom. . . ." Peter continued to pay him ten dollars a week for the decoration of at least ten pots, with the understanding that he would work at home in the Cottage: when he was drinking, no one wanted him around the Pottery. When he returned from three or four weeks on the island, he did his best to make up for the work he had missed. "He tried. He really tried," Pat recalled years later. "Sometimes he would work three days straight, right through the nights, to get his forty [monthly] pieces done. But sometimes he didn't finish . . . and then we'd find a note in the Pottery cashbox: 'IOU, $20, Bo[b].'"

"In my cave is a monster," he had once told his mother, adding, in a note to himself, "Man is a cave from which all sorts of strange things come. Strange beasts, gold, stones, and even another man." "We are half of ourselves always," he wrote. "There seems to be another half to what we do. Sometimes it's a beast or a bird, sometimes a man." Worried about his solitary way of life, Annette had a telephone installed in the Cottage, so that they could call one another if either of them needed to, but before long he tore it from the wall. One night, in July 1955, Billy burst into the Front House, summoning Peter from his sup-

per to the Barn. When he arrived, together with his twenty-year-old son
Michael, he came upon a scene no one in the family would ever forget. Annette
was lying in her bed, with Bob standing over her. Her face was bloody and she
was barely conscious. She had been having a severe migraine headache, and
had asked Sissy to call Bob, who suffered, like her, from migraines, and who
had often attended to her lovingly at such moments: he would "sit by the bed,
soothe her head with a scented cloth, and hold the basin for her." This time he
came at once, but as he brushed by Sissy on the path, she smelled alcohol on
his breath and feared the worst; she knew he had been drinking and was feeling very tense. She describes the scene in *Approaching the Magic Hour*:

> When I reached the Barn, I heard his voice, a frightening voice, coming from
> Mère's room. It was unnaturally controlled and icy with anger. By the time I
> ran into the room, he was raining blows on her face. I heard him hissing
> through his teeth, "This is one headache I am really going to cure . . ."
>   "Bob, stop that! You're hurting your mother!"
>   I was trying to pull him off. I succeeded only because he turned on me. He
> crashed his fist into my mouth, shoved and pushed me out of the room,
> knocked me down, and closed the door, locking it.

Michael watched as his father grabbed Bob and threw him to the floor of
the living room. Annette, who was almost ninety, secluded herself until her
wounds healed and her black eye disappeared. "She refused to be seen," Sissy
wrote. "People might infer what had happened. I think she was still saying, if
only to herself, 'Bobby is Bobby.'" From her journals, though she never mentions the incident, it is clear that she quickly forgave him, praying that God
would make him "entirely himself." Weeks later, on Labor Day weekend, 1955,
after a second violent incident set off by "beer and a pint of whisky," Annette
called a prominent psychoanalyst in New Orleans—Henry H. W. Miles—and
asked for help. Miles contacted a fellow psychiatrist, Edward H. Knight, and
Bob was taken in an ambulance to DePaul Sanatorium in New Orleans and
treated by Knight from September 4 to September 24. Sissy accompanied him
to the hospital, but said she could not miss classes and returned to Ocean
Springs, leaving Pat and Annette to explain his history to the doctors. Bob was
an "artistic genius," both women insisted, but they "differed considerably on
certain aspects of his emotional problem." For Pat, he was "anti-social"—
unable to make friends, with a longstanding hostility to his mother: he felt he
had been "pushed into everything" by her, and could not forgive her for hav-

ing hospitalized him in the past. Annette pointed out that "prior to [his] emotional disturbance he was 'delightful company'" and that even now, he loved to talk. She would concede only that he was "unusual" and "different," and told the doctors she was making arrangements to send him to the Menninger Clinic, in Topeka, Kansas. Crudely, a nurse wrote up his case: "Long history of seclusive, bizarre, exoteric [*sic*] behavior—never really rational. Very intellectual and mystic. Paints quite well. No normal social or vocational contacts." The diagnosis was "schizophrenic reaction, paranoid type," a term taken from the American Psychiatric Association's 1952 *Diagnostic and Statistical Manual,* where all types of schizophrenia were designated as "reactions" (partly in response to Adolf Meyer's holistic view that disorders were biopsychosocial responses to specific stressors in the environment). "Schizophrenic reaction, paranoid" deonoted "autistic, unrealistic thinking, with mental content composed chiefly of delusions of persecution, and/or of grandeur, ideas of reference, and often hallucinations. . . . It is often characterized by unpredictable behavior, with a fairly constant attitude of hostility and aggression. . . . There may be an expansive delusional system of omnipotence, genius, or special ability." In this case, there were ideas of reference. What seemed to trigger the drunken attack on Annette was a short story by Aldous Huxley in the *Atlantic Monthly*: the patient had "interpreted [it] as saying: 'If you did not shoot ducks, you should kill your mother.'" Thorazine and Equanil—an antipsychotic drug and an antianxiety agent—were administered, and after a few days in the hospital, Bob was painting a portrait of one of the nurses and asking permission to go to the zoo to paint, as he had since he was a little boy, though he "didn't press the matter" when Knight said no. A decade later, Sissy remembered that during his stay—probably in occupational therapy—he devoted himself to doing sketches and watercolors of nurses, attendants, and fellow patients. "I do not think any artist has ever been more sought after, any portraitist in more constant demand. Almost all the portraits were given to the sitters. When I went to bring [him] home, he was surrounded by admirers, many of whom followed him out to the car." In the months that followed, Annette did her best to get him back to a doctor. At her urging, in June 1956—nine months after his hospitalization—Knight warned him that it was "very important . . . to continue your occasional visits here":

> You have a nervous difficulty that will periodically get to be too much for
> you. I may be able to help you ward off the ups and downs by judicious use of

medication and counseling. It would be extremely unwise for you to remove yourself from medical guidance. Regardless of your attitude toward medical matters, you are human and subject to human frailties. Therefore, I would strongly and urgently advise you to come down to New Orleans at least once a month. . . . Unless you place yourself under medical care, you will inevitably gravitate toward further hospitalization. I am sorry to use this threatening tone, but your work and yourself are too valuable to risk by inadequate care or negligence. I hope you will understand my intentions and call here for an appointment.

At DePaul, he had told Knight that he "despised hospitals," and that "none of them had ever done him any good." By fall, Knight's warning about further hospitalization was fulfilled: after another episode of violence, the details of which are now lost, he was hospitalized for a week (December 16–22, 1956) at Mobile Infirmary. This time, Sissy remembers, he was kept in closer confinement. He was back at Shearwater for Christmas, and two days later, headed back to the island, the first of seven long trips he made that year, perhaps, in part, to remove himself from the possibility of harming others.

To Sissy it seemed that, at some point, as he grew older, his desire for self-destruction had been transmuted into a cheerful, unshakable belief that he was protected by Providence. In a note found among his papers, he writes: "Suppose you felt that you were in the grip of fate; that, like Sinbad, you were destined to be shipwrecked; 'that it was written.' Suppose you turned it into pattern, made a dance of it and were shipwrecked six times to music in your own dance. You would have used fate for your own purpose and turned it into art."

Of real shipwrecks there were more than a few. All three women—Sissy, Annette, and Pat—worried about him on his trips to the island, sometimes in stormy weather, in flimsy, leaky boats never more than ten or twelve feet long. In 1956, months after Knight warned him about further hospitalization and a little before he was hospitalized in Mobile, a pogy boat in the gulf spotted a disabled skiff and, behind it, barely visible in the mist, a bobbing head.

"Can we pick you up?"

"No, thank you," he said, his teeth chattering. "I'll make it to North Key."

"You ain't goin' to make it in this cold. We'll just have to pick you up."

He had been swimming and pushing the boat for three hours, and had gotten to within a mile of his destination, thirty-five miles from the mainland. He would come aboard, he said, only if they promised to pick up his boat. In the darkness just before dawn, they pried his fingers from its stern, hauled him from the icy water, wrapped him in blankets, and carried him to the warmth of the engine room. Meanwhile, his boat drifted away. A helicopter came to take him to Keesler Air Force Base. But his pleasure over his first helicopter ride—and his first sight of the island from the air—turned to anger when he realized they had not retrieved his skiff. "They *promised*," he sputtered indignantly when Sissy went to pick him up. In the infirmary at Keesler, he told her that he had fallen asleep at night somewhere in the shipping channel; without running lights, he had been invisible. A tugboat pushing a string of barges had caught him off guard, capsizing the boat in its wake, and sending the mast straight to the bottom. Peeling off his heavy jacket, he swam in the darkness, through wind and choppy water, grabbed the stern of his boat and started kicking hard. Weeks later, the captain of a Biloxi tour boat walked into the Shearwater Pottery Showroom with an aluminum binder of sodden drawings and watercolors. An old fisherman had found it on the beach somewhere in the Chandeleurs.

On another occasion, in the strong undertow at the western end of Horn Island, his boat tipped over and drifted away from him. Whirled about by the current, he realized he was about to drown. "Then he relaxed, let himself go, and his foot touched bottom, where no bottom existed. He insisted that a new spit, as narrow as a needle, had formed." Once, when he capsized off Bell Fontaine Point, a shrimp boat picked him up and "trawled" for his things. He watched his trousers tumble onto the deck along with a net full of shrimp and fish, and recovered everything but a precious Indian bead—Sissy had found it during their arrowheading days and he had worn it for years like a talisman around his neck—and a copy of one of his favorite books, *The Collected Poems of W. B. Yeats*. When he was gone for too long, or there was a hurricane warning, someone would call the air force base and the Coast Guard. In 1961, in the days before Hurricane Carla—a category-four storm that took fifty lives—an air force plane dropped a note that landed near him on the beach: "For Walter I. Anderson. Your brother [Peter] suggested you return home immediately due to the hurricane."

"In this day of the machine age, even a one-mile row is considered an incredible feat," Bob wrote, and the family wondered how to persuade him to change his way of getting to the island. Once, he returned from Sears, Roebuck with a 7.5 horsepower Elgin motor, and tried to attach it to the back of one of his little boats. When he yanked on the cord to start it for the first time, the motor fell off and sank to the muddy bottom of the bayou. He carried it back to the porch of the Cottage, and, years later, when Billy asked him for permission to use it, they found that the engine had been ruined by the mud and water. "The difficulty of keeping up with our inventions!" Bob wrote. "An Indian would have bad tools and very poor seed, and yet would make it grow. Man's intelligence seems to pass with the development of conveniences." He added that "one of the great mistakes of modern times is to confuse eagles with aeroplanes."

"The world of man is far away and so is man," Bob wrote gratefully one summer day on the island. "How pleasant without him!" But people were not always as distant as he would have liked. Over the years he had grown accustomed to being awakened by voices at night and to having people bang on the bottom of his overturned boat ("a hollow tree to a hound contains a mystery"). Flounderers, hunters, and weekend campers amused themselves by scaring the hermit out of his shell. He wondered whether they envied him for his freedom. Not all visitors were hostile. Once two little boys made him an "object of charity," and asked, "Can't we get you something?" Some campers gave him a perch rod and some suntan lotion, in return for his autograph: "probably the first and last time I'll ever be asked for it." Sometimes he responded to intrusions with a drawing or watercolor. When the captain of a party-fishing boat trained his binoculars on "the strange native on the beach," the native stared back and drew the "ensemble . . . which built up beautifully: the wide horizon, the hull of the boat, the fishermen with rods up and out, the lower roof of cabin, the upper roof, the turret, the captain, the triangle of the captain's arms up with the binoculars, above him the wireless mast, and above it all the sun, almost overhead."

More often, though, visitors were a menace. The crack of a rifle or the sight of frog spearers filled his mind with "frightened gallinules and slaughtered bullfrogs," a silencing of the amphibian orchestra. The birds he stalked silently, with pencil and clipboard, would vanish for hours or days, and there would be new dead things on the beach. One group of vandals shot up his water jugs, and one day, on his way back from bathing in a lagoon he found his camp being looted by a man and three boys. They had tilted the boat onto its side, and were ripping out the middle thwart to get at what lay underneath. With "a strange mixture of methodical procedure and the most monkey-like curiosity," they stole some of his paint and a barlow knife, heaved his anchor halfway up a sand dune, and scattered his cans of food. He slapped the man in the face, and made him apologize. On another occasion, when two people pounded on the boat, he came out swearing and warned the larger one—a "virtuous and self-righteous hoodlum"—to remove his glasses. Always the pained question: why didn't they leave him alone? "I hope the fools keep away. There are lots of ways of having fun without bothering other people." He had chosen, quite deliberately, to live on the edge of society, but even there, people would not leave him to himself. Toward the end of his life, a band of hunters shot Split Ear—the rabbit he had shared his meals with—and tossed the body, riddled with buckshot, into his camp.

There were other dangers that Sissy and Pat and Annette worried about whenever he was away for a long time. He was allergic to bee stings, and at Shearwater they had twice seen him unconscious, in a state of anaphylactic shock, before an injection of epinephrine revived him. His courteous detente with water moccasins came to an end one spring afternoon when he reached his left hand into a bittern's nest just over his head. He was making his grand rounds of birds' nests—bitterns, grackles, green herons, gallinules—enjoying the sacred mystery ("The outpouring of life must find expression in the egg"). A sharp pain shot through him, and he realized he had been bitten by a snake: what kind, he didn't know. He hurried back to camp for a knife, but managed to draw little blood. With his hand beginning to swell, he remembered the desperate journey of the narrator of *Green Mansions* after he was bitten by a coral snake. Suspecting that movement would help him, too, he walked five miles, sat down by one of his island landmarks—the leaning tree—and applied compresses. Night fell, and he built a fire. The following day, he was strong enough to write up the log:

> I used big wood and kept up the compress[es] when the moon went down. Then I lay by the fire with my bed in the warmth and slept until my wood began to go out. Then I started a fire in another place, then decided my old place was better. While I was asleep the wind picked up and I think changed a little. The grass caught fire. There were cactus, so I had to go all the way back to camp for my shoes. The fire had a good start. The wind was northeast and drove the fire in a lane to the southwest. I kept on the side, beating it out in the thin places until dawn. Then I went under the boat and slept for about two hours. At dawn I did more fire fighting until I thought it was under control, but I became sick with diarrhea and vomiting and was so weak that I could hardly move. I retired under the boat and let the fire burn. I slept a good deal, taking baths to cool off and am much better this evening. A party of six outboards are camped near, so if I do have a relapse I can go in with them.

Bob and Peter, Christmas at the Front House, 1955

The log comes to an end on those words. Two boys in one of the outboards hurried him, nearly unconscious, blackened by the fire, back home to Sissy, and she took him to Dr. Schmidt, who told him that the snake had delivered only half of its venom; one of its fangs had pierced the ring finger of his left hand and the other had landed between fingers. As for the theory he had deduced from *Green Mansions*, no—his exertion had only spread the venom more efficiently, and he was lucky to be alive. Sissy and the children kept him in bed for a week, and a joke went around Ocean Springs. Bob Anderson had survived a bite by a moccasin. Yes, and the snake had survived, too! For the rest of his life, he was unable to fully use his left hand, but reported he bore no animosity toward snakes. "How many times have I *not* been bitten by snakes, times beyond counting I expect." Something always warned him not to put his foot down. He made it clear, in a whimsical note to himself, that he would not be set back by minor injuries: "To cure an injured toe, either dance to an accompaniment of heavenly music or put a spot of some rare pigment—malachite or turquoise—so that the discolored purple flesh assumes the color of twilight or that period of the day associated with change!"

One of the last long bike trips that he made was in December 1960. Sissy felt a pang of jealousy when she found a note on the Cottage door—"Gone South. Back with the Birds"—and realized he was probably on his way to visit

Grapefruits, 1960

Frank Baisden, who had bought a grapefruit grove and a house near Vero Beach, seven hundred miles from Ocean Springs.

It was cold and windy in the Florida panhandle—he needed a "double pair of socks" to keep his hands warm—but the weather improved as he reached the eastern coast and pedaled south, down a road parallel to the stream of cars on the main highway. On his side road it was "still and sunny and quiet, with migrating birds—yellow-throat sparrows, thrush, red-bellied woodpeckers and the feeling of others: perhaps Rima is hiding in the bushes." As always, travel by bike took his mind off other troubles. "The wheels are turning again. A bicycle seems to leave no room for other evils, or goods for that matter. It is an inclusive and exclusive wheel." Baisden and his wife, Kay, were on their way out to dinner when "Voltaire"—their nickname for Walter—pulled up like some strange Candide in front of their house. Kay was shocked by his rugged, unkempt look. When they returned, after dark, he told them he would not trouble them for a bed. It was raining, and he had already set up camp in the sand under the porch, enchanted by his "white couch" and the view of the grapefruit trees, the huge golden fruit glowing in the light from the house. In the morning he did watercolors of them, and over the next few days helped the Baisdens pick fruit and pack Christmas boxes. For a week he ate breakfast with them and in the evenings went inside and sat with them by the fire. Baisden brought out his recent work, and the two drew and painted together, as they had done so long ago at the Pennsylvania Academy: grapefruits and oranges, a wharf, some turkey buzzards that unnerved and delighted him. Baisden thought them beautiful, and when Bob was gone, he took some drawings of birds to the ornithologist and wildlife photographer Allan Cruickshank, who had written a big book entitled *Birds Around New York City*. He and his wife were "charming people," Baisden reported two months later, "but fairly well congealed into the purely ornithological mould; that is, they are feather-number conscious, and prefer each feather to be drawn around with an engraved line. Yet they were quite rightly impressed by your drawings, and suggested that we contact the head of the Florida Audubon Society about an exhibition. Meanwhile, we have sent a sample collection of 10 of your drawings to a friend in Washington, D.C., who has connections at the Smithsonian." The Baisdens' faith in his work—and in him— must have seemed an ineffable luxury. When he wrote to thank them for their hospitality, Kay replied: "You were our Christmas present: the unexpected, the surprise, and the rewarding qualities of your nature are all in the meaning of Christmas, and whatever we might be able to do about your watercolors is because of the belief in their worth. Everyone we have shown them to, even people who are not interested in birds or know very little about painting, are impressed."

They had mentioned a friend at the Smithsonian who might be willing to organize a traveling show, but as always, Bob had his mind on other things. When he got back to Ocean Springs, he caught up on his plates and vases and hurried back to his Island. It was February, and he wanted to see the wintering ducks. His red-winged blackbirds—he counted thirty-one of them—flew out noisily to meet him and he gave them bread to snack on while he cooked their rice. Even in winter, there was human mischief: "Two men came in an outboard yesterday and stole my log. One of them yanked up the cover to my boat and looked to see what I had. They probably have some official position, but they have no right to steal my private papers without telling me about it. They should lose their job if they have responsible positions. It's the second time it's been done. They took some pants too last time." A few days later, someone stole his food, "all that was in the sacks." As always, the island offered its own generous compensation, and animals gave him better company than people. A "Philosophic Goose," his mind on other matters, let Bob walk behind him drawing, hissing if he came too close. Porpoises and seagulls cavorted around the western tip, and the beach was strewn magically with starfish. The tides brought him a half-empty bottle of wine, a huge dead turtle, and a dead gannet, which he carried away to draw. A flock of thirty or forty redheads put their heads over their shoulders and fell "so sound asleep" that he was able to sketch them from different angles. He turned up some emergency rations, stashed on a previous trip, and the Philosophic Goose followed him under the boat for a snack, the two of them feasting on chocolate and crackers while the goose posed for his portrait. "So they have stolen my food, have they?!"

Almost every month that year Pat saw him collect his wages at the showroom, pedal to the store for ten or fifteen dollars' worth of provisions, and return to the ongoing "drama" of an island that had become a part of his very being. "The Islander," he called himself. There were birds and animals he remembered, and who seemed to remember *him*—he had observed three or four generations of the same family—and he knew he had become as much, perhaps more, a part of island life as the birds who rested there before flying north. Nature, he wrote, "bore no grudge" for the animals he had taken into captivity or had absentmindedly—"half villain" and *worse*, "half fool!"—allowed to die. "I survived the terrors of the sea, and saw the red sun go down to come to this place to paint. All nature appreciates my courage and love. (It *is* a kind of love and has united to make me happy and alive in this place.) The rabbits, the blackbirds, all the birds . . . even the old sow with her litter instead of charging me led her children past in a parade."

In April, he made an unusually rough crossing, rowing hard through the "wolves teeth" of the waves. The seabirds looked famished, pushing in from the Chandeleurs against a forty-mile-per-hour wind. Young male orioles opened their beaks to sing, but the wind forced their songs back into their throats. "A little green heron took shelter among the dunes near my fire. I found a heavenly water snake on the beach (inside) this morning, poor jack-anapes. He seemed exhausted with his swim. He had probably come all the way from the Pascagoula. I had landed in the same condition yesterday. The birds are flying in exhausted, so we are a sorry lot." In May, revisiting his gallinules, he worried one of the females would "scold" him for having bor-rowed one of her chicks the year before. As he bathed in a lagoon, two little purple peeps flew past his head, six or eight times, "before I realized—too late!—that they were trying to use my head for a dead stump." A beautiful five-barred skink ate the dead roaches in his coffee cup. A catbird shared an apple with him, but could not be persuaded to come closer than three or four feet. A man he had drawn earlier came back in the same boat and trained his binoculars on the islander, and again the scene "composed" beautifully in a drawing: "a pyramid at sea!" And so on, into another summer. July brought its heat and gnats. Up and down the island he "ran the gauntlet of flies," grate-ful for a can of Flit he had found on the beach. Sudden rushes of mullet darted toward the shore, visible for miles in the clear water, or whipped the water into one of Best-Maugard's spirals. Bulrushes withered in the blazing sun, and he spent hours "composing" their dead, bent-down stalks with the dragonflies that alighted on them. He bathed in the bulrush pools, and "a strange and pretty thing happened. I saw two small mosquito hawks—the kind that look like costume jewelry—coupled. I drew them. I was standing in water up to my shoulders, and another dragon fly, not of the same species, came and lit on the corner of my note book. It was a new kind to me, a mix-ture of lilac green and blue and gave me quite a shock." In early October 1964, poldeau and dogris "posed obligingly," one day after another. Once again, as it always had, the island gathered round him like a celestial circus:

> Green-headed Mallard drake climbs out on log and preens itself while small flocks of Dogris and Black Ducks dash backward and forward behind me, light-ing and getting up in the most delightful way. I draw violently from my bush. I leave almost sated, and push on to pick up my dropped sheets. Then, on the way past the Little Hole, I see again the emerald-green flash of the Mallard

head. He has seen something too, and during the five or ten minutes I wait, he does not move a feather. A perfect picture of *what*? "Me, imperturbable!" I yield, and depart the way I had come, crouching so as not to disturb him.

When his year on the island came to an end, in late October, he felt "like roy-alty: gold all around, white sand as a foil. Red sumac and the palmettos are pouring out a crop of fruit. The goldenrod swarms with Monarch butterflies which gorge themselves, hanging like some strange jeweled pendent to the stalk."

Months later, hungry for the city, he made one of his last bicycle trips, into New Orleans, at Mardi Gras time. A nightmarish feeling comes from his watercolors of the crowds and the revelers on floats. A new style of watercolor had been developing, much looser and less carefully drawn, the colors applied more heavily, and a more insistent use of blues and purples and blacks. A large oil painting, done about the same time, catches the same sinister feeling: black figures with umbrellas, like ghoulish inquisitors, are outlined by street-lamps and traffic lights. True art, he had once written, "consists in spreading wide the intervals so that the imagination may fill the space between the trees." Since the beginning of his career, his art had been a dialectic of narrow-ing those intervals and spreading them wide, and for the last few years he had been in a "wide" period, drawing and painting things more broadly and loosely, using his brush to suggest the thick outlines he had once drawn so carefully in pencil.

"Different people need different things," he had written once, wondering whether his images of the island would ever interest others. His watercolors were "private," he said, and for the most part, he kept them to himself, culling his work periodically. "Don't let *anyone* see what you are doing until you go as far as you can," his mother had written him long ago, when he was still at the Academy, adding some of her favorite words from scripture: "'If thine eye be single, thy whole body shall be full of light.' It means getting ahead like a river between high banks." Around 1960, perhaps when he was visiting Bais-den in Florida, his daughter Mary was lying in bed recovering from an oper-ation, and Pat handed her some watercolors Bob had wadded up and used to light the fire in the Cottage. She had found them in the fireplace, and the edges were singed. "See if you can smooth them out," she said. "It will give you something to do." Pat, Sissy, and Annette had seen some of the work he had done on Horn Island, but there were few people outside Shearwater, besides

Baisden, with whom he ever wanted to share them. One exception was Margaret Sidney, the daughter of Annette's brother Jimmy, to whom Bob felt strongly attracted. One day he presented her with ten or twelve of his most exquisite watercolors. She told him that they were beautiful and that she couldn't possibly accept such a magnificent and valuable gift. Stung by her rejection, he took them back to his Cottage and burned them.

Another notable exception was Norman Cameron, who, as a young resident, had treated him at Phipps and had followed his progress through Henry and Ellen Mead. In 1960, when Cameron and his wife, Jean, also a psychiatrist, spent time at Shearwater and stayed in Bob's studio, Pat led him down the path to the Cottage and knocked at the door, unsure how her brother-in-law would receive them: "Bob! You have a visitor." No doubt, she was hoping for some professional insight; Cameron was the author of a huge book on personality development, required reading at universities all over the country. What struck him at first—after more than twenty years—was Bob's "tremendously deep voice" and "his dignity," traits he shared with Peter. "There was only one chair in his main room, and he insisted that I take it," Cameron remembered. The two began to talk, Bob circling around him in his old hat, telling him of his life on the island, giving Cameron the feeling that he was "testing him out." That day he was "*especially* clear and interesting." A year later, after Henry Mead died, Bob wrote Ellen to console her, reminding her that her husband had come into his life "at a critical time." Moved by the letter (now lost), Ellen sent it to Cameron, who was amazed.

> Professionally, [Bob's letter] confirms other experiences that *I* have had with persons who are or have been in an inner turmoil and yet have written and spoken with the most thoughtful, judicious words, demonstrating the difference between what goes on (in all of us) beneath the surface: the kind of thing that we meet with over and over, again and again, in dreams and in the occasional flash of intuition or madness. He is one of those rare souls . . . Marañón spoke of Goya as not mad, though his murals of his last years *are* mad, but "un hombre especial," as if that took care of the whole thing. In a way, I guess it does.

Ellen had sent him one of Bob's pelicans, either a watercolor or a ceramic piece, and in thanking her, Cameron called it the "work of a genius." She had written him about her excitement over one of Bob's Horn Island logs, and Cameron wished it would "find its way into print. This kind of elemental thing is balm these days. If you were 'moved to the quick' by it, it must have great human, and in that sense literary, merit." Sissy, too, must have been touched by Bob's letter of condolence. From Easton, Maryland, where she was helping Ellen close down the house she had lived in with Mead, she wrote Bob: "You're the only one I haven't written to, not because I haven't been thinking about you, but because I thought of you on Horn Island where letters wouldn't do as much good as just thoughts. I've got a system by which I sort of think I keep in contact. . . . I'm always thinking of you, whenever I enjoy anything. I suppose it comes of the old days when you taught me how to be happy looking at a flower or what not, and I do love you with a special kind of love."

When the Camerons returned again in 1962, Ellen had moved into a house on Lovers Lane in Ocean Springs. She took them to Oldfields, and showed him the old house where she had spent so many years as a child. Years after the hurricane, a team of workmen from Jackson had rolled the house back from the eroding shoreline. For a while, in the mid-1950s, Mary and Sissy had run a summer camp there. But by 1961, unable to pay the taxes and the maintenance, and fearing fire and vandalism, Pat and Sissy had sold Oldfields to an local entrepreneur. Going through it now was a haunting experience for Cameron: the setting sun, the huge old live oak beside the house, "the cold penetrating as soon as the sun began to set . . . the boozy-looking caretaker with his dog. The empty rooms, with their loose electric wires against the ceiling." Ellen entertained them with Christmas and New Year's parties, and Bob and Norman had another long talk—on China, on art (Cameron had recently started to dabble in oils and watercolors), and on Cameron's work at Yale's child development center and kindergarten.

"Little children, not yet spoiled by the impression of life in society, give me the same thrill that you get from your Horn Island creatures," Cameron said.

"I have never found one that did," Bob answered. "Perhaps Leif, when she was first born." Listening to Peter on pottery and Bob on art, Cameron found that the two of them had "an equanimity about them which is nothing short of extraordinary." Before long, the unthinkable happened: Bob showed Cameron some of his watercolors—he was painting turkeys, posing them in the sink in the Cottage. He also gave him a Christmas present (Edgar Snow's *Red Star Over China*), and invited him to accompany him to the island. The next day, over tea, Sissy stared affectionately at Cameron in his tweed jacket, tie, and spectacles and lectured him about the hardships he would face as a

Bob with Norman Cameron, c. 1962

guest in Bob's primitive camp. He was sixty-four years old, and most of his stomach had been removed in an operation the year before.

"Are you really that jealous?" Cameron asked, proud that Bob hadn't taken him for an "unemotional intellectual" and aware that no one but Sissy and he had ever received such an invitation. For the rest of his life, he regretted not accepting it. Having seen Bob's drawings, he told Ellen he wished "he'd just give me an armload to bring up [to New Haven] so I could sit and pore over them before sending them back to him. But I know he just won't let any of them go."

When the Camerons returned to Shearwater in 1964, Annette was drifting toward death. Bob spent much of that fall on the island, but Pat was there to care for her, and recorded her final days. She was nearly blind now. It was like "living in a hole," she said. She could see only on a slant, and identified people "by their legs." Her prodigious memory was in ruins. "Some days she waited for her late husband to come home, but he was not much in her consciousness. She remembered her daughters-in-law, but forgot most of the grandchildren and all of their children. She loved her father and thought of what he had said and did, and adored her mother, and loved her sister, Dellie, and often asked when Jimmy, her brother, would be home. Sometimes she went to her piano and played, and at others she lay completely at rest, her eyes closed." Some mornings she would awaken and imagine she was in the fam-

ily house on Broadway, in New Orleans. A little after her ninety-sixth birthday, she was hospitalized with pneumonia and Bob asked Sissy to accompany
him to her bedside. She did so reluctantly, remembering how his father's
death, decades earlier, had helped to precipitate his nervous breakdown. This
time she was surprised by his calm detachment. Sitting beside her bed, he
made one sketch after another of his dying mother, and Sissy realized that he
had been prepared for the moment by his familiarity with death on the island.
On January 25, 1964, Annette gave a "small sighing smile" and was gone. A few
days later, Bob's cousin Margaret Sidney—Annette's niece—wrote him a
moving letter of condolence, remembering Annette's "courage and clear good
sense." "Talking with her," she wrote, "was such a revitalizing joy." "A letter
from the gods," Bob wrote on the bottom of it. He stayed for the funeral and
sailed away days later, in early February, on his little boat, leaving others to
deal with her meager estate. One night that spring he went to Sissy at the
Barn, and they walked to Peter's pier and lay down under a sky full of shooting stars.

"Souls," she remembered him saying. "Mother told me that when I was a
little boy. . . . Did you think I didn't care [about her]? In a way, I didn't,
because I felt that it was time. Life, you know, is like light. It is continuous. It
is our eyes that seek beginnings and endings. I was trying to find an ending
with my pencil, but all I found was that there was no ending."

FINAL VOYAGE

The boat in which he made his last trips to Horn Island was a green plywood skiff he found on the outer beach, laid out "in parts, just as a dressmaker would lay out the parts of a dress before sewing them together." When he had carried it piece by piece back to camp and assembled it, it was eighteen inches deep, four feet across, and ten feet long, light enough to push over the mudflats when the northwesters had swept the tides miles out into the sound. Later, he found more pieces of plywood and improvised "a forecastle and a poop" to keep himself from being swamped.

By the time he made those last trips, the modern world was closing in on him. One night he peered into the sky, saw a beautiful silver streak of light, "four fingers south of Cassiopeia's chair," and recognized it as a satellite. "I also saw what I took to be my first guided missile—no wings, no appendages of any kind that I could see. It flew fast over my head then began to climb and soon disappeared." Gazing toward the mainland from the inner beach on a clear day, he could see the huge cranes of Ingalls Shipyard, where they were building nuclear submarines and colossal oil rigs the newspapers proudly called "floating islands of steel and machinery," over three hundred feet high and even more than that in length and width. Even those rigs would be dwarfed by the "fully automated" container ships Ingalls was planning to build; each of them was to contain twenty thousand tons of steel and would be longer than a ninety-story building. All this was visible from his own little shipyard on the beach.

Rowing to Horn Island, c. 1964

The island itself was changing—it was a wildlife refuge now, and more protected than it had ever been, but one day he returned to camp and found surveyors marking trees with splashes of bright yellow paint and putting up stakes, as if they were dividing the area into building lots. "Here all sorts of improvements are in motion," he wrote one day on the mainland, "which usually seems to mean cutting down trees and rooting up the earth with bulldozers. A channel goes out from the breakwater about a quarter of a mile, which sounds as though they expected big boats." In the early 1960s, tourism was down, and there was talk in the newspapers of linking some of the barrier islands by causeway, beginning with a bridge from Biloxi to Ship Island. There would be fifteen bridges in all. "Little use is being made of [the islands]," someone complained at a hearing. "For the most part they are uninhabited." All along the coast, development was beginning to affect the wildlife. By the late 1950s Bob noticed that his beloved pelicans were growing more and more rare, and that they were laying thin- or soft-shelled eggs that did not hatch. In 1933, the year of Bob's marriage, an ornithologist had reported twenty-three hundred pelican nests on North Island in the Chandeleurs. Thirty years later, they had dwindled to two hundred pairs with a total of about a hundred nestlings. By the "silent spring" of the early 1960s they had disappeared both from Louisiana (except from car license plates and the state seal) and from the Mississippi River, a phenomenon Bob attributed correctly to pollutants and pesticides. On one of his last trips to the island, he had noticed an increase in numbers: "Seventeen in one flock!"

There were changes, too, in the society of mainland Mississippi, though he slipped away to his island without recording his thoughts on them. When one looks back on them now, his last trips form a counterpoint to the prejudice and racial hatred of a state in turmoil. In a single brief note to himself, a res-olution—"Offer to teach drawing in a colored school!"—he reacted to the apartheid around him. Long ago, after the Community Center mural, he had given up on "politics" and had decided to follow his *own* law: "The law that is made by society is slow and clumsy, and tied down by expediency. The law you make from your own experience of good can outstrip any law made [only] for convenience or expediency. The law you make yourself will gradu-ally, as you develop, approach the general good, and [a time comes] that you recognize that your law and the general good are one."

In August 1964, a fateful moment for Mississippi, he was back on the island, fighting the heat and glare from the sand, observing the life of an "aquarium," a "new world," that the tides had placed on his "front doorstep." A huge, rotten fallen pine, "like fruit cake to fish, entirely porous with worm holes," had pent up the water, and it was rippling with life. Crabs and parula shells, a sheepshead fish, and a baby alligator distracted him from his newly hatched gallinules or baby green herons. Toward the shipyards of Pascagoula, there were "phenomenal cloud risings," like the hand of a giant, growing fin-gers. From a thousand feet in the air, a man-o'-war bird sprayed him with white guano: "I felt honored." Once again the world of man—and of his fam-ily—vanished beyond the horizon. In one of his logs, months earlier, he had written without comment: "The other day coming home from the West Point I met Billy and his new wife; the first time since he has been married." From the tone of his greeting, they knew he did not wish to be disturbed.

During the final year of his life, he made six more trips to the island, begin-ning in January, when the sand crusted with ice and he snuggled inside a lean-to he had thrown together with plywood on the inner beach, drinking tea and reading *Doctor Zhivago*: "I have wind shields fore and aft with a fat pine fire between. The wind howls overhead and rattles the palmetto leaves. The Her-ring Gulls drift slowly past at right angles to the wind." By March, fish hawks were rising and falling in their mating dance, "piping their own music—one of the signs of spring on Horn Island"—and he himself "jumped a purple gallinule—almost as if I had a date with it." Ecstatic grackles, "a little crazy," were being "forced into nest building by their wives," and he found the first eggs of the season. April brought its wave of migratory birds—on one of his walks he counted fifty-two different species—and for nearly a month he peered into nests, some "beautifully made," and spent hours watching birds from his "blind," a spicebush beside a lily pond. A little green heron gave a "truly villainous performance in 'The Dagger with Wings,' terrifying all the little fish in sight" until "its mate flew over [and] it gave a squawk, forgot the little fish, and followed her." At breakfast one morning, a coon took food from his hand—the first time that had ever happened: "literally it took it with its paw, then ate." Never had he felt so close to birds and animals, or written about them with such "definite knowledge" and affection, nor had he ever had such a vivid sense of the "strange and transient unity" of things. That summer, with the island as "dry as a bleached bone" and the blowing sand stinging his face, he stood awaiting rain. "With the birds and the strong wind and the clouds casting moving shadows and the white wave caps and the dark rain squalls on the horizon and growing cumulus thunder heads that changed every minute, it was a dramatic effect of strong contrast, the glare of the white sand at one end and the dark shadows on the water, with the white star set in a black widow's peak on the forehead of each tern. There was light in everything. No lost places disappearing without definition. Everything needed to be considered in relating the parts to the strange and transient unity."

In September, during hurricane season, he set aside his work at the Pottery and returned again to the island. After a string of halcyon days, there was a "gory sunrise," an "intense vermillion against a turquoise blue sky." Strong winds began to blow, and the tides began eating chunks out of the outside beach, forcing him to choose "suitable trees to tie to if the water kept on rising." And rise it did, sending him wading, chest-deep in water, with his boat tied to his waist, to a high dune, where he turned over the green skiff, and "slept well until time for coffee." At Shearwater, as the storm—Hurricane Betsy—began to crank up its seventy-to-ninety-mile-per-hour winds and eight-to-ten-foot storm surge, someone asked the Coast Guard to search for Bob, though Sissy doubted they would ever persuade him to leave the island. She pictured him in some leafy refuge, or under his boat, laughing at the cutter tossed about by the storm, and she was right—he was relishing every aspect of one of the worst storms the coast had ever experienced. "Never has there been a more respectable hurricane, provided with all the portents, predictions, omens, etc. etc. The awful sunrise—no one could fail to take a warn-

ing from it—the hovering black spirit bird (man o' war)—only one—
(comme il faut)." As for the Coast Guard cutter, it took him completely by
surprise. He stared at it from under his boat, where he had kept a fire going
to keep warm: "A large Coast Guard boat appeared!—going to and fro in front
of my camp—large boat, but there were large seas lifting her up and down;
she finally went off, her running lights showing in the water."

When he emerged the next morning, and the waves had flattened into
churning, dirty brown water, he looked out with amazement on his island.
"My camp was gone—the place where I had nested snugly for years—was
gone, simply sliced off by the waves." All of the beaches had been flattened to
sea level. The enormous old sow whose paths he had followed for years
through the brush had drowned, and the pine trees and plants were turning
brown from the salt spray. The whole eastern point of the island had disappeared, and the tides had left only the highest dunes in place. A line of pine
trees that had stood back far from the beach was now only feet from the water.
The beach was littered with trash that had washed over from Louisiana. A
lagoon had grown wide enough to cut the island in two, "with a quicksand at
either end to catch the unwary traveler." There was no more access to Rabbit
Springs, with its fresh water. In the midst of destruction, he found beauty:
"Never have I seen more ravishing jewelry than shone in the foam cast up on
the beach in thin broken pieces quivering with the slightest breath of air so
that all the colors scintillated with the movement—half a mile of Sinbad's valley of jewels, with no deadly serpents to guard them, yours for the possessing—no one to dispute your ownership, no one to claim prior right, no jealous person to claim more or bigger or better ones."

When he sailed back to Ocean Springs, he barely stopped at Shearwater. He
told Sissy that he had a new theory about the origin of hurricanes—he had
felt sand in the sultry atmosphere after the storm, and suspected that storms
like the one he had just experienced were spawned in the Sahara. Within a day
or two he was back on his bicycle, headed for New Orleans to ask Nash
Roberts, a meteorologist there, to allow him to consult his weather charts. He
camped, as he always had, on the levee, not far from the family homestead,
amid refuse left there by the storm. While he was eating his breakfast the next
morning, he felt something observing him, parted the grass, and stared at one
of the most vividly colored birds he had ever seen, some sort of exotic pheas-
ant. He handed it a bread crumb and saw that it was ravenously hungry. The
same had happened on the island: "fascinating to feel that eyes are watching

Self-portrait, c. 1962

you, then find the bird or animal that possesses them." Other beady, hungry eyes were peering at him through the grass, and he realized that they were tropical birds that had escaped from the storm-battered aviaries in the zoo. He did watercolors of them, and a month later, on another trip, painted and drew the zoo animals and lingered in the shipyards: "The indifferent workmen"

managed to repair barges damaged by the storm "without showing the slightest interest in any of them—there would be the helmets lowered over the face,
then the bright flash of peacock blue light, the shower of orange sparks."

A little later, at the beginning of November 1965, he stopped Peter's daughter Patricia on the path at Shearwater, told her he was spitting up blood, and
asked her what to do. "I don't know," she answered, surprised that he hadn't
told Sissy. Sissy was living now in the studio, and on Sunday, November 14, as
she sat there talking with Leif, he came through the door and asked her to take
him to the doctor. Just like *him*, Sissy thought, to ask for a doctor on a Sunday. She had no idea that he had been ill—a sign, she thought, of how badly
they communicated with one another—and he explained that for a long
while he had been feeling pain in his chest and coughing up blood. On one of
his trips that summer he had lifted a big sack of apples into a tree, to keep
them away from the hogs, and had fallen to the ground with a strange, stab-
bing sensation. One day he had noted, with disbelief and indignation, that he
couldn't even ride his bicycle over the crest of the harbor bridge near Shearwater. Mary, too, had noticed something wrong. Recently she had seen her
father rolling the bicycle instead of riding it.

Frank Schmidt examined him in the hospital in Ocean Springs, and told
him gently that he probably had lung cancer, and would have to be admitted
to the hospital in New Orleans as soon as a room was available. Schmidt's son,
Frank Schmidt, Jr., was associated with Baptist Hospital, in his first year as a
thoracic surgeon, and seemed the ideal person to care for him. Like his father,
Schmitty felt affection and admiration for the Andersons, and had a vivid
sense of their peculiarities. Dr. Frank, Sr., was the soul of discretion and never
talked about his patients, but as a young man, before going away to college,
his son had spent enough time at Shearwater and Oldfields to know something of the man whom he was about to treat. Like Bob, he was a sailor, and
the two of them had often crossed paths in the gulf—he on his catboat, and
Bob in a tiny "pulling skiff." He had often marveled that anyone could make
it to Horn Island so often and so bravely, in such a craft. Often, Schmidt had
seen him pedaling through Ocean Springs, though Bob had never returned
his greetings. And once, perhaps in 1943, while Schmidt's mother was driving him and a couple of friends to New Orleans for Mardi Gras, they had
spotted Bob biking down the highway. That, too, had struck him as extraordinary. People did ride bicycles around Ocean Springs, but no one but Bob
Anderson biked the ninety miles to the city. But the Andersons had always

been one of a kind. Annette, too, had an odd way of getting about: almost into her nineties, when someone had taken away her keys, she had wheeled about town in the Pottery pickup, grinding the gears and overruling the normal flow of traffic. To Schmidt, the whole family seemed unusual, "artistic," "different." One day, as a boy, he had gone to Shearwater to play and it had begun to rain, prompting somebody—perhaps Mary—to suggest that everyone stay inside and do "some sort of modern dance."

For the next two days Bob lay resting at the Front House. Pat had suggested hot baths and had asked him to come. There had never been hot water in the Cottage, and years earlier a pipe had burst, so that there was no running water at all. He had been bringing it in from a faucet in the yard. On Monday or Tuesday, he lay on the grass outside his old studio, enjoying the clear fall weather, and called Sissy to show her a purple hairstreak butterfly resting on the goldenrod. For the most part, she remembered, he kept his thoughts to himself, "singularly uninterested in things around him." That Monday Leif had given birth to a daughter, but he did not go to see her. When Sissy went to the Cottage door, he told her he was busy sorting his watercolors and drawings. He had filled a box with provisions, as though wavering between entering the hospital or returning to the island.

On Wednesday, November 17, he packed some clothes and books into a battered old paper suitcase he had brought back from Hong Kong, and Sissy drove him to New Orleans. It had been a warm fall, and the sweet, heavy scent of honeysuckle came through the windows as they sped along the Honey Island Causeway toward the city. Unable to speak without coughing up blood, he closed his eyes and listened to Sissy reminisce about other trips and other times. She knew he felt trapped, stricken like one of the lead-poisoned ducks he had found on Horn Island: "When we got to the outskirts of town, he raised up rather suddenly and put his hand to the door handle. I had an awful moment and slowed the car. He reached over and patted my hand, as if to say 'I won't jump out.'" He wanted to stop and have dinner at a roadside diner: vegetable soup and crackers and milk, which he got down with difficulty.

As he signed himself into Baptist, he smiled at her and said that for once he was entering a hospital on his own volition. He insisted at first that he would pay his own bills. "Mother has money," he said, forgetting, for a second, that she was gone. Finally, he allowed Sissy to present her insurance card. No sooner had he settled into a double room on the sixth floor than it became

clear to the staff that this man—in hospital gown and wide-brimmed hat—
was a somewhat unusual patient. "The Rebel," one of the nurses called him,
shaking her head when he requested wine. It was merely to soothe his cough,
he said. Told that wine was against the rules at Baptist, and offered cough
syrup instead, he started to climb angrily out of bed, sending things clatter-
ing to the floor. Somebody sent for Dr. Schmidt, who decided immediately to
prescribe it. There was no point in making his patient any more uncomfort-
able than he was already.

During Bob's first days in the hospital, Schmidt led him to the stairwell,
asked him to run up and down the stairs, and satisfied himself that despite his
chronic bronchitis, his sixty-three-year-old patient was strong enough to
recover from an operation. On Thursday, November 18, after a bronchoscopy,
Sissy left for Ocean Springs; she had to teach the next day. When she returned
on Saturday morning, Schmidt gave her the bad news: the tests had revealed
a malignant tumor in Bob's left lung, and it would have to be removed immediately. She found her husband on the sundeck of the hospital, block in hand,
busily sketching, pursing his lips in the way he always had, though the bronchoscopy had left him unable to whistle or hum. Hurricane Betsy had ripped
some of the slate tiles from the roofs of nearby houses, and he was looking
across Esplanade Avenue, drawing the roofers, who were almost at eye level as
they went about their repairs. He also drew patients—a sick child in its
mother's arms and an old man in a wheelchair. Looking down the avenue, relishing the special light of New Orleans, Sissy wondered whether he was glad
to be "home." She handed him a picture of the new baby and he looked at it
and sighed: "Life!" As he waited for the operation to remove the tumor, he lay
in bed, his hat pulled down over his eyes, and asked her to read from a book
someone had sent—the newly published autobiography of Edith Sitwell. One
day, when Sissy got up to go to the cafeteria, she left the book, but not the hat,
within reach on his bed. She was going through the door when his roommate
called her back: "The hat! Give him the hat, Mrs. Anderson. He can't read
without his hat."

Pat and Peter came in with Sissy on the day of the operation, Tuesday,
November 23. While he was emerging from sedation, the three of them went
to see Dick and Virginia McConnell and when they returned to the hospital
in the afternoon, Schmidt told them that Bob had had a heart stoppage. He
had been able to revive him and do "a quick tracheotomy," and had placed

him on a breathing machine. When the tube came out a few days later, he told a nurse that he needed exercise, and wanted to get up and walk. She asked him not to rush things, and he lay in bed, pedaling his legs above his head, lickety-split. A few days later, he was strong enough to sit in a wheelchair and enjoy his meals. Told that the danger was past, and that he would soon be going home, he shook his head, as if to say no. He knew that Sissy would want to be with Leif and Moira, her two-week-old baby. "Go home," he told her on Saturday. "You have done your duty."

When Mac drove her back to the hospital on Tuesday, November 30, she found a group of people around his bed, and realized something had gone wrong. That morning he had collapsed on his way to the bathroom, and he was now unconscious, kept alive by the respirator. He died at 4:50 that evening. The autopsy, performed by Dr. Schmidt and his associate Henry Reichard Kahle, revealed that death had been caused by a blood clot in the left pulmonary artery. If there was any consolation, Schmidt told Sissy, it was that the autopsy had shown that the tumor had metastasized to the left adrenal gland: "it would certainly have grown and proved that [his] condition was not curable."

He had spent his last conscious hours sitting on his bed, watching a particularly beautiful sunset, until the last light left the sky. One of the nurses remembered him saying that he would have liked to paint it, or that he had painted many in the course of his life. Years earlier on Horn Island he had written: "It is approaching the magic hour before sunset when all things are related."

His body was sent by train to Ocean Springs, and a memorial service was held the next day in St. John's Episcopal Church. In a gentle rain, he was buried beside the graves of Annette and Walter and Marjorie and Billie Grinstead in the family plot in Evergreen Cemetery. It is a peaceful spot, with cedars and magnolias, on a slope overlooking Fort Bayou. The woods were beautiful across the marsh and the smooth grey water. The entire family was present, and a host of McConnell relatives had come from New Orleans. As the minister consigned Bob's ashes to the dust, he was interrupted by a raucous laugh, and then another, and another—the cry of a bird, flying up from the marsh below. Sissy and the children looked at one another, nervously at first, "with lifted eyebrows," each wondering if others were thinking the same thing. "We all knew the voice of the little rail," Sissy wrote, "but it seemed perfectly plausible that Bob had entered into a feathered body to use its voice for

Work table at the Cottage

a few minutes, to deny the finality of any grave. As the service ended, the rail flew off down the bayou, and we said to ourselves, 'There he goes!'"

Days after the burial, Sissy entered the Cottage to put his things in order. It felt as though a storm had passed through and the building were returning to the elements. A chinaberry tree, felled by the hurricane, had crashed though the bathroom wall, and rain was coming through the roof. Vines poked gently through broken windows and curling rusty screens, and baby mice nestled in the pocket of one of his shirts. Everywhere, in the midst of destruction and decay, were signs of his incessant creation. Drawings, water-colors, and writings were piled in grocery boxes or lay ankle-deep on the wide pine floorboards, thick as fallen leaves. There were carved wooden animals, sketchbooks, scrolled-up prints, decorated vases that had not yet been fired, designs for furniture and pottery, and notes and illustrations inspired by his readings. Into an old cabinet once used for storing bread, he had tossed many of the logs he had kept on the island. As Sissy bundled things together and swept out the place, she felt a twinge of irony. For years the family had worried about his solitude and the waste of his talent.

Around the Cottage lay the relics of his uneasy life. She gazed at the objects he had brought back from his trips to the island: conch shells and driftwood, the precious junk brought to him by the tides, glass orbs from Japanese fishing nets, the tiny bones of birds, a rod of glass made by lightning hitting sand. Hanging on the wall was the skull of the giant sea turtle whose death had haunted him.

There was a padlock on the door of the little room they had added almost thirty years earlier as a nursery for Mary, after Bob's return from Phipps. Pat came from the showroom to help her open it. Neither had been inside for several years. Prying the lock from the doorframe, they opened the door and were astonished by what they found. "The creation at sunrise!" Pat murmured, lifting her eyes from the paint-spattered floor to the eastern wall. He had covered all four walls and the back of the door with a mural more beautiful than any they had ever seen—a radiant hymn to light and to the beauty of one day on the coast, beginning on the east wall with sunrise and continuing around the room through noon, sunset, and night. Working in solitude, without a word to anyone, he had painted his own vision of nirvana, including all of the birds and animals he most loved—creeping things and flying fowl, all things bright and beautiful. On the east wall, a fiery rooster heralded the dawn, a flock of goats came to the sunrise, and cranes rose toward the light. On the south wall, fish, birds, and animals basked in the midday heat. To the west, the sun set on a flock of shearwaters and a cat departed on its nightly rounds. The north wall was painted with moths. Dividing the room into east and west was a pallid muse figure representing the Mississippi River and its tributaries, and on the ceiling, a huge, hieratic zinnia, "most explosive and illuminating of flowers." There were windows on three sides of the room, and he had planned the mural so that the sun from outside would fall upon each wall at the right moment every day, the light and shadow in the mural interacting with the light from outside, a reminder of his belief that nature could only "realize" itself fully through art.

Under one of the windows was a box of papers Sissy carried back to her house and set down beside her bed. Going through it, weeks later, she found a page she associated at once with the mural. In his own hand, he had copied Psalm 104, giving thanks, as he had done on the pine wallboards of the little

The green skiff

room, to a Creator who covers himself with light "as with a garment." Like the psalm, the mural was a hymn of gratitude and an affirmation of the "strange and transient unity" of all created things.

> *Man goeth forth unto his work*
> *And to his labor until the evening.*
> *O Lord, how manifold are thy works!*
> *In wisdom hast thou made them all:*
> *The earth is full of thy riches.*

NOTES

AAA—Walter Inglis Anderson papers, microfilm reels 4867–4872, Archives of American Art, Smithsonian Institution

AGA—Agnes Grinstead Anderson

AGA/Gilley interviews—Agnes Grinstead Anderson, interviews with Joan Gilley, spring and summer 1990

AMcCA—Annette McConnell Anderson

Approaching—Agnes Grinstead Anderson, *Approaching the Magic Hour: Memories of Walter Anderson*

DC—Christopher Maurer with María Estrella Iglesias, *Dreaming in Clay on the Coast of Mississippi: Love and Art at Shearwater*

GWA—George Walter Anderson

HIL—Walter Inglis Anderson, *The Horn Island Logs*

JMcCA—James McConnell Anderson

JXCOT—*Jackson County Times*, Ocean Springs, Mississippi

McConnell Papers—Papers of James McConnell, Manuscript Department, Tulane University Library

Memoirs Ms1—Autograph manuscript of the memoirs of Agnes Grinstead Anderson, 1967–1968

Memoirs Ms2—Typewritten manuscript of the memoirs of Agnes Grinstead Anderson, October 1975–December 1979, prepared by AGA

Memoirs Ms3—Typewritten manuscript of the memoirs of Agnes Grinstead Anderson, prepared by Mary Brister, with autograph corrections by Brister and AGA, ca. 1984 (preliminary draft of *Approaching the Magic Hour: Memories of Walter Anderson*)

Meyer Papers—Papers of Adolf Meyer, Confidential Correspondence and Medical Records (restricted), Alan Mason Chesney Medical Archives, Johns Hopkins Medical Institutions

NARA—National Archives and Records Administration

PA—Peter Anderson

PA Phipps—Medical records of Peter Anderson, Medical Records, Johns Hopkins University Hospital

PGA—Patricia Grinstead Anderson

pm—Postmark on envelope of undated letter

WAMA—Walter Anderson Museum of Art, Ocean Springs, Mississippi

WIAA—Walter Inglis Anderson Archives, Ocean Springs, Mississippi, Family of Walter Anderson

WIA Pratt—Medical records of Walter Inglis Anderson, Medical Records, Sheppard Pratt Hospital

WIA Phipps—Medical records of Walter Inglis Anderson, Medical Records, Johns Hopkins University Hospital

WIA Whitfield—Medical records of Walter Inglis Anderson, Medical Records, Mississippi State Hospital, Whitfield, Mississippi

INTRODUCTION

"Man begins by saying of course*"*: HIL, 82.

"the sordid thing most people call reality": HIL, 150.

"The artist lives between assistance and opposition": Unpublished fragment, WIAA.

"not a product but a process": Patti Carr Black, *Art in Mississippi, 1720–1980*, 199.

"in order to realize the beauty of man": Unpublished fragment, WIAA.

"To know that every movement you make": Unpublished fragment, WIAA.

"So much depends on the dominant mode on shore": HIL, 27.

nature *"loves to surprise"*: HIL, 126.

"Moby Dick": HIL, 87.

"A bleak dawn": HIL, 163.

"the joy of imaginative life": Unpublished fragment, WIAA.

"the normal or even fairly normal man": Ibid.

"reestablish the relation of art to the people": From an unpublished letter, dated May 12 [1948], in AAA, IIIb.

"common language of forms": From a sketchbook entry, Oct. 27, 1947, WIAA.

"people who cannot afford to pay a great deal": WIA to Una E. Johnson, Dec. 27, 1948, Brooklyn Museum Archives.

"Those who swear by purity": Unpublished fragment, WIAA.

tales *"which people tell their children"*: Manuscript in the Brooklyn Museum Archives.

"strange and incredible place": WIA to Una E. Johnson, Sept. 1949, Brooklyn Museum Archives.

McKnight on WIA: Backes, 28.

critical reactions of Sozanski and Russell: Patti Carr Black, *Art in Mississippi*, 199.

"places him in the general sphere of Matisse and Picasso": Driscoll, n.p.

critical reactions of Larsen, Simmons, and Pickard: In Patricia Pinson, ed., *The Art of Walter Anderson* 28, 35, and 6.

Approaching the Magic Hour: AGA's memoirs were skillfully edited by Patti Carr Black, who drew on an eighteen-hundred-page manuscript given to her by the author (*Approaching*, xi). The memoirs are a vivid introduction to the life and art of Walter Anderson, but, as poet and storyteller, AGA was so little concerned with chronological, historical "facts" of the sort that interest most biographers that she did not attempt to reconcile the memoirs with her journals and correspondence from her years with WIA. Regarding some incidents in WIA's life, the manuscript includes several contradictory and equally convincing accounts. For this book I have consulted both the published and unpublished versions of the memoirs. Several series of letters which might have cast much light on WIA and which will undoubtedly be of interest to future biographers have not been made available to me: for example, the letters between Patricia Grinstead Anderson, Annette McConnell Anderson, Agnes Grinstead Anderson, and Ellen Mead.

"One single beautiful image is practically inexhaustible": HIL, 29.

TALENT AND TROUBLE

Unless otherwise specified, all correspondence and manuscripts are in the Walter Inglis Anderson Archives (WIAA) in Ocean Springs. There is a microfilm in the Archives of American Art, Smithsonian Institution.

"comical adorable little ruffian": AMcCA notebook, "Boys' Sayings and Doings," undated, probably from about 1909.

GWA promises male babies: Mary Anderson Pickard, "A Personal View," n. p.

Woodward's philosophy of art: All quotations are from an unpublished, undated essay, "Every Day Art," in the Ellsworth Woodward Papers, Manuscript Department, Tulane University Library. On Woodward and Newcomb College, see Bragg, 7–8. An edition of Woodward's writings is long overdue.

industrial pursuits urged by James McConnell: James McConnell to James McConnell, Jr., April 18, 1907, McConnell Papers, Tulane. On his attitude toward Annette's studies, Kendall/Margaret Sidney interview.

Samuel Jarvis Peters: DC, 46.

on AMcCA's social prominence: PA Phipps, case notes, May 8, 1939.

paternal grandfather: McConnell was the son of Alexander McConnell (d. 1832), chief surgeon of the Charity Hospital, and Margaret Nelson (b. Washington, Mississippi, 1803). DC, 310.

"kindly and interested in others": AMcCA, "My Father," unpublished manuscript, WIAA.

life of James McConnell Anderson (1829–1914): I have drawn on various newspaper clippings and biographical manuscripts in the McConnell Papers, among them "Jas. McConnell, Leader at Bar, Dead at 85 Years," New Orleans *Times-Picayune*, undated clipping, and "Jas. McConnell's Will Probated by Judge Monroe," undated clipping, Nov. 1914, New Orleans *Times-Picayune*; "Tulane Obtains Historical Pen," New Orleans *Times-Picayune*, Nov. 16, 1953. For a vivid picture of McConnell as lawyer, see "True Stories of the City's Strenuous Life," New Orleans *Daily Picayune*, April 27, 1902. On his service at St. Paul's Church, New Orleans, *St. Paul's Messenger*, undated clipping, Marjorie A. Ashley archives; see also James McConnell, Esq., *The Ethic Elements in the Character and Laws of Nations. An Oration Delivered April 2, 1855 Before the Alumni Association of the Law Department of the University of Louisiana*, New Orleans, 1855.

"his naturally sanguine temperament": AMcCA, "My Father," unpublished manuscript, WIAA.

Delphine Angelique Blanc in Bouligny and information on Blanc family: AMcCA, unpublished essays in WIAA: "Bouligny," "My Life," "My Mother's School Days," "Days in the Life of Delphine Blanc," "The Childhood of Delphine Blanc," "My Father," "My Mother," ["The Old House"], "Grandpa Blanc." There are several drafts of many of these essays. Cf. Henry Mead, "Summary of Family History," in WIA Phipps April 7, 1937: "Grandmother—died at 51. Had monthly 'floodings' for five years. Healthy woman."

"grande dame," portrait of Delphine Blanc: AMcCA, "My Mother," unpublished manuscript. The painting, attributed to Beaux as early as 1912, is in the collection of James Ashley and Marjorie A. Ashley, Ocean Springs. See "Father of New Orleans Public Schools," New Orleans *Times-Democrat,* July 7, 1912.

war service; escape of James McConnell from Union prison: "Hon. James McConnell," undated manuscript, McConnell Papers and AGA journal, ca. April 1986, undated entry. See also, on the escape of Annette's uncle Benjamin Franklin Peters (d. 1908), "In Memoriam Benjamin Franklin Peters, Private, Orleans Light Horse," McConnell Papers.

"Battle Hymn of the Republic": Mary Anderson Pickard, "A Personal View," n. p.

Newcomb, Tulane, and McConnell: Details in McConnell Papers, Tulane.

Annette's study of art: DC, 310; Mahé, 7. In the extant autobiographical writings, AMcCA never mentions her studies with either Weir or Chase. She exhibited with the Artists' Association of New Orleans (1889–90, 1899) and the Art Association of New Orleans (1907, 1910–11) and had a solo exhibition at the Delgado Museum of Art in 1920. See bibliography in Mahé, 7. There are numerous works in the WIAA and in the family and a program for the 1920 exhibit is in the archives of the New Orleans Museum of Art.

hospitalization of Dellie: John B. Elliott, the McConnell family physician, recommends hospitalization in a letter to James McConnell, Sr., May 28, 1891 (McConnell Papers). See also James McConnell, Sr., to his son, Jan. 2, 1892; Jan. 4, 1893 (Dellie is at an asylum in Wernersville, Pennsylvania); and Feb. 15, 1903 (McConnell Papers); and undated medical summary of Delphine Angelique McConnell at Friends Hospital (admitted Nov. 13, 1900), preserved in WIA Phipps, with the story of the napkin ring, diagnosis, and comments on "morbid sexual tendency." She was removed from Friends by Annette in Oct. 1919. In an agreement signed in 1903, a rough draft of which is in the McConnell Papers, James McConnell pays Friends ten thousand dollars to care for Dellie "for the remainder of her life," giving her "as much liberty as her condition from time to time may warrant." See also the excellent short story, based on conversations around 1976 with Annette's niece, Margaret Neilson McConnell Sidney, by Kathryn Kendall in *Woman Talk* (New Orleans, 1976), 1–5; Kendall/Margaret Sidney interview; and AGA journal, April 11, 1986.

"office habits": James McConnell, Sr., to his son, Sept. 12, 1891 (advising "sober thoughtfulness"); and letter to his son and daughter-in-law, Elizabeth Y. Logan, May 13, 1907, both in McConnell Papers. On Jimmy's debts to his father, James McConnell Anderson to AMcCA, July 9, 1915, McConnell Papers.

midday sex: WIA Phipps, case summary, April 14, 1937: Jimmy "lost his patrimony through lack of energy—procrastination his sister calls it." Also, interview with Cedric Sidney, Dec. 14, 2002.

Henry Emerson Fosdick: Kendall/Margaret Sidney interview.

"I am not a credulous person": AMcCA to James McConnell, Jr., pm Jan. 28, 1927, McConnell Papers.

"Dean" of local chess: Will Branan, "The Dean of Chess Players," and undated, unidentified newspaper clipping ("The Late James McConnell"), McConnell Papers, and John Paul Phillips, "The McConnell Family Notebooks, Part I," in *Chess Archaeology,* www.chessarch.com/excavations/0004_phillips/ca_steinitzgame.shtml. Phillips draws on a notebook "kept by his great-great grandfather, James McConnell" and a letter from Wilhelm Steinitz to James McConnell, Sr., March 2, 1885.

"gentleman of the old school": An undated obituary in the archives of Marjorie A. Ashley says

that McConnell played Morphy at the latter's home in 1849, and lost the evening's play by three games to one; that he had defeated Steinitz, Zukertort, Mackenzie, Pillsbury, and others, and that "his love [for chess] never mastered him. There was nothing neurotic about his devotion . . ."

Annette at Newcomb College: According to Newcomb records, Annette attended Newcomb from 1889 to 1900. Her transcript has not been preserved, but her courses probably included "(third year) water-color painting, harmony and chemistry of color, decorative design, drawing from life, projections of solids and shadows, history of sculpture, pedagogics; (fourth year) oil painting, drawing and painting from life, modeling in clay, casting in plaster of Paris, pen drawing, and history of painting." Shama Farooq to the author, Oct. 3, 1998.

George Walter Anderson ancestors: Obituaries of his uncle George Anderson, ex-M.P. (*The Glasgow Herald*, Nov. 6, 1896), his great-uncle Walter Fergus Anderson (1822–1869) (undated clipping), and his grandfather George Anderson (d. 1863) (undated clipping, *The Fife Herald*) are in the archives of Marjorie Anderson Ashley. The Anderson/Briggs burial plot, with dates of both families, is in Lafayette Cemetery, New Orleans. A passport for father Peter Anderson, "British subject traveling on the Continent and in America" has him entering New Orleans from Matamoros, Mexico, on May 6, 1865 (archives of Marjorie Anderson Ashley).

career of George Walter Anderson (Dec. 4, 1861–Feb. 21, 1937): GWA is listed in the 1881 *Soards' New Orleans City Directory* as a clerk at Anderson and Simpson, with residence at 240 Jackson. He was Secretary-Treasurer of C. B. Fox Co. from about 1901 to 1917 (GWA to his sister Daisy Anderson, Dec. 21, 1901, WIAA) and president and partner in Anderson and Jackson, Inc. (exporters of grain, foodstuffs, and cottonseed products) for another six years, until his retirement in 1923. In the twenties and thirties, he invested, wisely, in land around New Orleans which he hoped to sell to railways and oil companies (correspondence with Colonial Land Company, Ltd., E. B. Rowan, and John I. Glover, 1928–1935, Shearwater Pottery archives).

"Tell him his marriage is a certainty": Sept. 6, 1898, from East Gloucester, Massachusetts.

"Dr. Sinkler . . . , knowing about both families": AMcCA, "Family History," manuscript, Jan. 25, 1954, WIAA. Cf. "Copy of Dr. J[ohn] B. Elliott Opinion" (copy of a letter of May 18, 1891, to James McConnell, McConnell Papers, 156–2–9).

Broadway house: DC, 38–40 and Kendall/Margaret Sidney interview.

"explored the Louisiana marshes": GWA, "On the Greens," "Introduction," Shearwater Pottery archive.

Professor Elliot of Harvard, Mary Treat: "Boys' Sayings and Doings," undated entry. The journals cover 1901 to about 1916.

"there was always something beautiful": Kendall/Margaret Sidney interview.

castor oil: In a letter to Maurice Partridge, Feb. 10, 1939 (PA Phipps), PGA writes: "Mrs. Anderson worried about *everything*, but most that the boys might know 'the wrong kind of people,' keeping them from making *any* friends to a great extent. . . . I read a diary of [Mac's] of about ten years old. He was kept in for playing with unapproved of boys. A huge dose of castor oil was administered by Mamma to do the trick!"

"There is a right way": GWA to Quentin Reynolds, May 18, 1935, Shearwater Pottery archives.

"happy dream" of WIA: "Boys' Sayings and Doings," Dec. 11, 1906.

"fly all about the sky": Ibid., probably March 1908.

"comical little monkey": Ibid., undated.

"more ingenuity and impudence," "works spasmodically": Ibid., Sept. 19, no year; Dec. 19, 1907.

"Bobby is the most adorable": Ibid., undated.

Drawn to things noble and brave: Ibid. (1910?).

Bobby catching minnows: "Boys' Sayings and Doings," June 10, Bay St. Louis, no year.

Finney sisters, Friday story hour: WIA Phipps, "Summary of Past History," April 7, 1937, Dr. H. C. A. Mead: "It was an 'old fashioned school' and the pupils worked hard four days, Friday being devoted to stories told by the school mistress, who seems to have had quite a hold on the children. He has always said since then that these stories meant most to him." The school had been in operation at least since 1898. In *Smith's Business Directory* of that year, a Miss M[argaret?] A. Finney is listed as running a school at 1328 Aline St.

studies at Lusher and Newman: Bob's very satisfactory record at Lusher and Peter's at Isidore Newman are preserved in their student transcripts at the Manlius Pebble Hill School, DeWitt, New York. On Newman, see Olive Andrus, *Isidore Newman School and the Manual Training Movement,* M.A. thesis, Tulane University, and *DC,* 314, note 63.

Annette's studio and painting: DC, 47.

Manlius a "shot in the dark": GWA to AMcCA, July 5, 1915.

barely passing grades: WIA student transcripts at the Manlius Pebble Hill School, DeWitt, New York. Between 1915 and 1918, with six to eight courses per term, WIA received only two final grades above 80. His grades were abysmal in spelling, biology, and French II. Cf. "Morale Rating of Cadet Anderson, W."; ibid.

"four years of prison," "I know what discipline is": WIA Phipps, "Summary of Present Illness," H. C. A. Mead, undated; WIA to AGA, undated, Nov. 1930.

"button unbuttoned" and other offenses: General Regulations for Saint John's School, Manlius, New York, Sept. 1919, archives of Manlius Pebble Hill School.

WIA carries cross in religious processions: WIA Phipps, "Summary of Past History," H. C. A. Mead, April 7, 1937, and "Monday Clinic," May 23, 1938, 4.

special places to go and read and draw; birds' nests: WIA to AMcCA, Aug. 5, 1915, May 12, 1916, and Mary Anderson Pickard, *Birds,* xi, and *A Symphony of Animals,* ix.

WIA keeps rabbit as pet: WIA to AMcCA, pm May 13, 1918.

Annette's purchase of Fairhaven property: DC, 52–61, and note 54, 312.

character of Ocean Springs ca. 1918 and description by L. Sullivan: DC, 58–61.

Peter's letter to Verbeck, 1919: PA to Verbeck, from New Orleans, Aug. 20, 1919. See also PA Phipps, formulation of PA's case, E. Partridge, Dec. 23, 1938: "He was removed from the school because his father had an erroneous idea that he (the father) was dying. There was nothing the matter with him but he wanted to have the children home [and] did not want to send them back. The patient [PA] says the reason was financial, and he did not mind not going back to school." A slightly different version appears in WIA Phipps, case summary, April 14, 1937: "After three years [at Manlius] he and his older brother . . . were withdrawn and summoned home because his father had had a nervous breakdown." Cf. WIA Phipps, case history, May 3, 1937: GWA had a "depressive breakdown . . . in 1918 following financial reverses."

"Please try to get me a job . . .": WIA to GWA, June 25, 1919.

WIA and Peter at Isidore Newman: Transcripts from Isidore Newman School.

"all [his] time in class": WIA to AGA, letter from Whitfield, undated, EDM 41, WIAA. See the evocation of those trips in Memoirs Ms3, chap. 50.

WIA boating accident, 1920: DC, 62–63.

WIA in Provincetown: Mentioned in WIA transcript from New York School of Fine and Applied Art, University Records Office, New York University.

New Orleans Art Association Scholarship: "Minutes", 1921–22, New Orleans Art Assn., New Orleans Museum of Art, archives.

WIA's "tiny little room" like a "hermit's cell": Alice Perkins to AMcCA, Oct. 22, 1922, and WIA to AMcCA, Oct. 15, 1922.

New York School of Fine and Applied Art: The fragment of WIA's school transcript which is still extant (University Records Office, New York University) shows that he entered the school on Sept. 20, 1922, and that he lived at 519 West 123 Street. There are records for only one of his subjects, advertising. Absent 4 ½ times, he received a grade of "D" during his first quarter and "B" during his second. During the third and fourth quarters he was advanced to second-year advertising.

conservatism of Frank Alvah Parsons: Lewis, 26–29.

Problem Method: Jones 141, 355–56.

Hambidge's "dynamic symmetry": Jones, 141, and WIA to AMcCA, pm Jan. 23, 1923, and Feb. 2, 1923 ("The Hambidge shapes are becoming more interesting everyday").

"feminist" and "commercialist" students: WIA to AGA, pm Oct. 8, 1922.

"Depressing" 1923 Independents Exhibition: On the Independents Exhibition, WIA to AMcCA, March 10, 1923. Cf. *International Studio,* March 1923. WIA might have seen Best-Maugard's work in Juan José Tablada, "Mexican Painting of Today," *International Studio,* Jan. 1923, 267–77.

Walter Gropius: Kolocotroni, 301.

museums and exhibitions seen by WIA in New York: WIA to AMcCA, Sept. 25, 1922 (on Sorrolla, Winslow Homer, and Zuloaga's *Carmen, The Bullfighter's Family, The Flagellant,* and lady in black silk); Jan. 6, 1923 (Brooklyn Museum); Feb. 12, 1923 (Eric Hudson, who was featured in William B. McCormack, "Eric Hudson: Marine Painter," *International Studio,* March 1922: 3–6); Feb. 27, 1923 (Russian Inn and Artzybasheff); March 10, 1923 (woodcarvings at Independents Exhibition); March 22, 1923 (seascapes and painting by Moffit, New York Academy of Design); April 24, 1923, May 1, 1923 (Ernst Barlach woodcarvings, featured in Sheldon Cheney, "A Sculptor in Wood," *International Studio,* Sept. 1922, 529–533); Nov. 24, 1922 (Zuloaga at Metropolitan).

American Museum of Natural History: WIA to AMcCA, Oct. 8, 1922. Sketches for the totem poles are in WIA to AMcCA, Nov. 2, 1922.

woodcarvings: WIA to AMcCA, pm Oct. 15, 1922 (totem poles); Nov. 6, 1922; Nov. 16, 1922 (three wooden figures); Nov. 24 and Dec. 13, 1922 (four small figures and bas-relief); Feb. 2, 1923 ("I have gone back to the wood after quite a long interval"); Feb. 7, 1923 (goes back to pirates); Feb. 12, 1926, March 22, 1923 (pirates); April 24, 1923 ("larger edition of the two pirates and chest"); April 3, 1923 ("six pirates and have just finished an old Mammy that I think is the most successful thing I've done"); May 15, 1923 (unable to carve because of cut). On the accident with the chisel, AGA Memiors MS2, n. p.

walk from One Hundred Twenty-fifth St. to Fifth St.: WIA to AMcCA, Oct. 15, 1922.

Dorothy Stockbridge "very pleasant": WIA to AMcCA, Jan. 13, 1923. Cf. Jan 20, 1923 (she reads poetry); Feb. 12, 1923 (helps with stage decorations); Feb. 27, 1923; March 22, 1923 and May 15, 1923 (helps make a garden); April 24, 1923 (play at Drama League); April 17 (dinner). After marrying William Tillett, a university professor, Dorothy Stockbridge Tillett wrote plays, poetry, and detective stories under the pseudonym John Strange. She was the daughter of Louisa Stockbridge (first cousin of George Walter Anderson). In Memoirs Ms2, 1927, 9, Bob tells Sissy of having fallen in love with her.

New Orleans Art Association Scholarship: PAFA records indicate that WIA held this scholarship from fall 1923 to spring 1926. In 1927–28, the scholarship was "not used." A similar scholarship was given by the Artists Association of New Orleans.

move to Fairhaven: Elizabeth Logan McConnell to James McConnell, Jr., from Fairhaven, April 1, 1923.

Peter's kiln, family activities at Fairhaven: DC, 69–71.

AT THE ACADEMY

application form: WIA student transcript, PAFA archives.
thorough knowledge: PAFA catalogues, 1924 through 1928, in PAFA archives.
Stokowski, art and music: Wolanin, 81–82.
"Do Americans want . . . based on Picasso?": Scott, 236. On the effects of the war, see also Diskant, 216.
Debased art: Diskant, 202–207.
opening of Barnes collection: Wolanin, 91.
Thomas Hart Benton: Minutes, Committee on Instruction, June 4, 1923. PAFA Archives.
"I saw a lot of modern painting": WIA to AMcA, pm April 24, 1925. Carles had asked Barnes to open his collection. Disappointed with the PAFA students, Barnes threatened several days later to close the gallery to them unless they received training in "the general psychological principles underlying art expression" (A. C. Barnes to Hugh H. Breckenridge, April 28, 1925; McCarter papers, AAA).
"An art school at its best": Ingersoll, 56.
"Mystery Man": Letter from Frank Baisden to Lewis I. Sharp, Jr., May 6, 1937, WIA Phipps.
Speight at Academy: York, 9–25.
"chicken in a garden": Maryanne Conheim, "The Artist Is in Love," *Philadelphia Inquirer,* undated clipping, PAFA Archives. Cf. York, 9.
"those who went up the Delaware River": Diskant, 209.
"like a Cubist landscape": Speight, 1979, 6. For Speight's paintings of Manayunk, see the biography by York; *Manayunk and Other Places: Paintings and Drawings by Francis Speight; Francis Speight: A Retrospective Exhibition;* and *Francis Speight: An Exhibition of Paintings,* PAFA, 1979.
Baisden record: Student records of Frank Baisden, PAFA Archives. Baisden (born June 17, 1904, in Atlanta, Georgia) entered the Academy in fall 1922 and left in spring 1926. In 1925 he won both the Henry Thouron Prize in Composition and a Cresson scholarship.
"drank a good deal": Baisden to Lewis I. Sharp, Jr., May 6, 1937, WIA Phipps.
"It must be something beyond mere dislike": AMcCA to PA, March 10, 1926. During his later hospitalization at Phipps, one of WIA's doctors, Lewis Thorne, noted at a staff conference, "In 1924 [sic] he had what he described to his family as a nervous breakdown. He was mildly depressed for about three months—not hospitalized." Dates are often given incorrectly in the hospital records. At DePaul, Annette or Pat told doctors that he had had "some sort of breakdown while at the Pennsylvania Academy . . . but she was uncertain of the nature of the condition . . . and could not even estimate patient's age at that time."

"homesick": Baisden to his mother, undated (1925–26?), Barbara Huet archives.

friends at Academy: Conrad Roland studied at the Academy beginning in 1918–1919 (Cheryl Leibold to the author, June 17, 2002). Baisden refers to him often in letters to his family; archives of Barbara Thuet. Leon Karp is mentioned often in Baisden's letters.

Archie Bongé: Student records, Archie Molloy Bongé [*sic*], PAFA Archives. Bongé spent only the Sept.–Dec. semester of 1925 at the Academy. A note on his transcript reads: "good influence in school, but I doubt if he comes back." In 1931, WIA wrote Sissy about Bongé's work. "He showed me what he had done during the summer, and it was pretty bad. Somebody ought to tell him that he is no good and let him try something else. But it won't be me. The worst of seeing that sort of stuff is that it fills you with an insane desire to show how much better you can do it. You see what a conceited ass you have chosen for a husband? Not that this particular case is so bad, because his stuff is terrible, but there have been times . . ." WIA to AGA, pm Oct. 17, 1931.

Cyril Gardner recollections: Interview with the author, Feb. 20, 2002. Cyril Gardner (born Jan. 9, 1907 in Liverpool, England) studied at PAFA from Feb. 1926 to May 1931, and won a Cresson Travelling Scholarship in May 1929. His older brother, Walter Henry Gardner, (born 1902) studied at the Academy from 1921 to 1929. Cyril's wife, Florance Foote, studied there at the same time and won the Henry Thouron Prize in Composition in 1927. Student records, PAFA Archives, and Cheryl Leibold to C. Maurer, Feb. 29, 2002.

McCarter, "very amusing to listen to": WIA to AMcCA, undated.

"Decorative Design and Color Values": Description in "Special Classes, open to All Students Without Extra Charge," circular entitled *Schools of the Pennsylvania Academy of the Fine Arts, One Hundred and Twenty-Second Year,* 1927–1928, 37.

"everything that could possibly have bearing": Frank Baisden to AGA, March 12, 1985.

quotations from Henry B. McCarter: Ingersoll, 63–65, 123, and McCarter Papers, Archives of American Art, autograph mss., including class notes of Hanna Rile Weiman, taken in spring 1929.

"Walter understood this use of warm and cool colors": Frank Baisden to AGA, March 12, 1985. Cf. Baisden's letter to Sugg, quoted in *HIL,* 12–13: under McCarter's influence WIA "enriched his painting . . . by modeling in color from warm to cool or vice versa, by chromatic radiation of light around solid forms, and by allowing outlines to dissolve in light composed of colors, as in Impressionist paintings." Baisden adds that "students were required at times to paint with 'broken color,' in the pointillist manner, 'in order to experiment with rendering light as color, rather than as value or tone.'"

"How to make color vibrate": Class notes, Hanna Rile Weiman, spring 1929, McCarter Papers, AAA.

Carles and plaster cast: Wolanin, 98.

on Carles's teaching: Bill Scott, 29, and Franklin Watkins, quoted in Wolanin, 3.

private instruction from Carles: Another was Quita Brodhead, who remembers the moment in Bill Scott, 27, 29.

correspondence of color and music: Wolanin, 62–63. On Kandinsky's theory of synaesthesia in the arts, see Kevin T. Dann, *Bright Colors Falsely Seen: Synaesthesia and the Modern Search for Transcendental Knowledge* (New Haven, CT: Yale University Press, 1998) and bibliography therein.

McCarter painting chime of bells: Diskant, 24.

Matisse, colors vibrate at twilight: Wolanin, 46.

"color resonance is what you paint pictures with": Scott, 81.

WIA on drawing classes: WIA to AMcCA, Dec. 12, 1924; Jan. 17, 1927. The PAFA faculty agreed on Feb. 27, 1927—too late to affect Bob—that "painting be given more attention in the Schools, and that students be required to qualify in the Still-Life and Saturday Sketch Classes as painters, as well as draftsmen in the Antique Classes, before promotion to the Life and Illustration and Portrait Classes" (minutes of the Committee on Instruction).

"I'll be a draftsman yet!": WIA to AMcCA.

Speight on Garber: Foster, 38.

Skit about Garber: Foster, 38–39.

Speight on Carles's drawing classes: Wolanin, 72.

Portrait of a Girl: WAMA Collection. On the picture's history, see "Art Mates" in Biloxi *Sun Herald,* July 21, 2002. WIA discarded it at the Academy, but C. Gardner removed it from the trash and it hung on the wall of his studio for seventy-five years until he learned, through a newspaper article, of the Walter Anderson Museum of Art and sold the painting to them. The other two paintings, *Composition* and *Still Life,* are reproduced in the PAFA circular for 1928–1929, 70, 87.

"President's Prize" in Packard: PAFA Archives, WIA transcript and minutes of the Committee on Instruction, May 22, 1924, and PAFA circular, 1924–25, 60. The prize was twenty dollars. Six drawings are reproduced in the 1925–1926 circular, 60, and many more are in the WIA Archives.

"going to night class regularly": WIA to AMcCA.

Swedenborgian Church: In a letter to his family (undated but ca. 1926) Baisden describes a "five-day walking trip up the Delaware" with one of the Gardner brothers and several other PAFA students, and a stop at the Swedenborgian Church (Raymond Pitcairn's "Bryn Athyn Cathedral"). B. Thuet archive.

saints, overmantel and "crude" angels: DC, 88, 319.

Pennsylvania Dutch chests: In Nov. 1927, GWA wrote to the New Orleans Arts and Crafts Club that WIA had left him with "two large carved and painted chests," each worth a hundred dollars, which he hoped could be sold in New Orleans. On the *Truhe,* or dower chests, see "Pennsylvania German Painted Chests" in *The Pennsylvania Museum Bulletin,* 21:96 (Oct. 1925), 25 ff., in which the author notes "the similarity in method used by chest painter and maker of sgraffito pottery. In each case the design is *scratched* by some sharp-pointed instrument" (31). Cf. the chest made by WIA (around 1925?) in Sugg, *Painter's Psalm,* 14, and the comment in a letter postmarked March 26, 1927 to AMcCA: "I have been seeing some great [pottery]. It's called scraphito [*sic*]; most of it is Pennsylvania Dutch. Peter probably knows all about it; bowls and pie plates." See also Rubin, 105–107.

lithography: WIA to AMcCA, pm April 24, 1925. No examples survive.

WIA readings: Letters to AMcCA, passim. On the Stevenson letters, WIA to AMcCA, April 18, 1928.

McCarter distaste for art criticism: Ingersoll, 57. On the book WIA refers to as *After Cézanne,* WIA to AMcCA, undated.

attendance at St. Clements: WIA to AMcCA, undated.

"We must lead orderly lives": AMcCA to PA, undated letter, winter 1926.

"Handel, Debussy and Ravel": WIA to AMcCA, pm Feb. 22, 1927.

girl at orchestra: AGA, Memoirs Ms2, 1929, 29–30; 1934, 11.

Bellows exhibition: WIA to AMcCA, pm Nov. 6, 1925. In another letter, undated, he reports on a show by the Art Club of Philadelphia, an exhibition of "sixty paintings by artists from all over the world. Most of them were pretty poor. A lot of them have imitated Zuloaga, nearly all have plagiarized somebody." The 1928 Annual at the Academy was "a little worse than usual and that is saying a good deal. If *that* is self-expression and the aim of all aspiring young art students, I will spend the rest of my life growing cucumbers!" (undated letter).

Isle of Pines: WIA to AMcCA, pm Jan. 18, 1928.

trips by boat to Philadelphia and New Orleans: WIA to AMcCA, undated.

WIA trip across Pennsylvania; canoe trip down Mississippi: Memoirs Ms1, and WIA Phipps, case summary, April 14, 1937, where a doctor states that "instead of wiring for money to return home, he took a job on the Pennsylvania Railroad—laboring—and earned $90 with which he went to Louisville where he purchased a canoe and outfit and paddled home down the Mississippi." Cf. Henry Mead, "Summary of Past History," April 7, 1937: "While on this trip he got an attack of illness from eating corn, so severe he pulled up to the bank and obtained a bottle of Shane's Liniment from a negro, which he drank."

Cresson scholarships: PAFA circular, and agreement signed by WIA, June 22, 1927, PAFA archives, wherein he promises to use the scholarship to "improve [his] education in art," and agrees to "keep a journal" of his travels. If he did keep one, it is no longer extant.

"If I get the scholarship": WIA to AMcCA, April 10, 1926.

Baisden in Trenton; Schuyler Jackson; antique shop: Undated letters from Baisden to his family, 1926, in the archives of Barbara Thuet.

"Briefly, what Orage has said": Munson, 4. C. S. Nott gives a vivid account of both the institute and the New York sessions, 88–124. On the institute, see also *Gurdjieff International Review*, "Special Issue on Le Prieuré" 1:4 (Summer 1998). For a sampling of three question-and-answer sessions from November 1927, see Orage, "Discussion on 'Good and Evil.'" See also Sugg, *HIL*, 13–14.

"[I] had the honor of meeting [Orage]": WIA to AMcCA, pm Jan. 25, 1927.

Cresson, June 1927: The other Cressons for painting in 1927 went to Henry Cooper, Fred Flanigan, Margaret Gest, Vincent McCoy Reader, Dorothy L. Van Loan, and Edith Wood (none of whom had won before) and William H. Ferguson, Lucius Kutchin and Marina Timoshenko (who had won it previously).

travels in France: Two letters from WIA to AMcCA from France are preserved, the first postmarked in Paris, July 25, 1927, and the second dated Aug. 27, 1927. WIA wrote additional comments on the trip in 1939 or 1940, while in Jackson, Mississippi, but only two pages are extant (EDM 45 and EDM46, WIAA). In Memoirs Ms., AGA describes WIA throwing himself down a cliff in the Pyrenees and being cured by a local magus. There is no reference elsewhere to this incident.

visit to Fountainbleau: WIA Phipps, case summary, April 14, 1937, states that WIA "divided his time [in France] between studying architecture and painting, and the Gurdjief Institute." H. C. A. Mead notes in "Summary of Past History" that he went to the institute "where all sorts of strange things were done."

"part of nature, rather than": AGA in Mauda Burton, "Portrait of a Mississippi Artist," *Mississippi* 2:5 (May/June 1984): 14.

"Gothic was not simply a matter": Undated fragment, WIAA.

"art of the caves and the cathedrals": Mary Anderson Pickard, *A Symphony of Animals*, xi.

Toppan Prize: See Committee on Instruction minutes, May 23, 1928. In WIA's transcript from DePaul Sanitorium, Pat or Annette pointed out that "He tried for the prize a second time . . .

and did not win it. . . . Informants state that it was not lack of artistic ability but rather his lack of conformity with school regulations which kept the award from him."

"No one can do their best work": AMcCA to WIA, May 22, 1928.

LIVING ON AIR

Peter at Shearwater: DC, 82–83, 91–92.

tourism and "progress" on the coast: DC, 85–87.

visit by Grinsteads; Peter and Pat: DC, 94–111.

early ceramic pieces by WIA: Documents in the Shearwater Pottery archives mention some of his earliest pieces. Photographs from 1928, probably by the newspaper photographer John Hypolite Coquille, show *Horse and Rider* in *Symphony of Animals,* 55; *Resting Geometric Cat* and *Sitting Geometric Cat* in *Symphony of Animals,* 23; pelican bookends; a horse; and an incised vase. Correspondence mentions crab bookends (Dec. 1928), and in 1929, various pieces: vase incised with pelicans; *Chesty Horse,* which Walter jokingly called "one of Bob's chests—the horsey one"); and a vase with cat and geese.

AGA first impressions of the Andersons: Memoirs Ms1, 61–63 and *Approaching,* 2.

girl at orchestra: Memoirs Ms2, 1929, 29–30; 1934, 11.

engagement: DC, 96, and AMcCA to James McConnell, Jr., Aug. 28, 1929.

"Does fair work . . .": Alumna file and student transcripts of AGA, Schlesinger Library, Radcliffe College.

Institut des Jeunes Filles: PGA scrapbook and unpublished essay on her studies in France, archives of Marjorie Anderson Ashley.

Grinstead's career: A transcript in the archives of Harvard University Law School (HUG 300) shows that Grinstead (April 16, 1864–Feb. 7, 1948) attended Harvard College from 1883 to 1886 and Harvard Law from 1886 to 1888. See also the autobiographical statements in *Harvard Law School Class of 1889. Secretary's Report No. II,* 1892, 14; *Harvard Law School Class of 1889, Secretary's Report No. 3,* 1914, 19–20; *Harvard College Class of 1887 Secretary's Report, No. 5,* 1902, 168; and *Harvard College Class of 1887 Fiftieth Anniversary Report,* 1937, 194–195; and (on Grinstead's management of the Helen Culver estate), Charles Hull Ewing to Helen Culver, Jan. 11, 1908 (University of Illinois, Chicago, Helen Culver Papers, Special Collections). Grinstead describes his work with Culver in Thomas Wakefield Goodspeed, *The University of Chicago Biographical Sketches,* Vol. II (Chicago: University of Chicago Press), 89–90. See also Charles Hull Ewing to Helen Culver, Nov. 1, 1907, Hull House Collection, Special Collections, Library of the University of Illinois, Chicago. For the history of the Grinsteads in the nineteenth and twentieth centuries, see E. H. West to AGA, March 17, 1936, WIAA. On his marriage to Marjorie Hellmuth, see the report in the *Biloxi Daily Herald,* March 1, 1906, and PGA, "To My Grandchildren," archives of Marjorie Anderson Ashley.

history of Oldfields: See W. W. Grinstead vs. The Hull House Association et al. Bill of Complaint, filed Aug. 4, 1920, in the Jackson County Archives, Pascagoula. Grinstead acquired the house and grounds on Nov. 15, 1902.

on Ellen Wassall (1896–1981): See *DC,* 101–102. Published and unpublished songs by Ellen's mother, Grace Wassall, who married the New York lawyer Thomas Chadbourne after Ellen's father was drowned in Lake Michigan in 1909 ("Dr. J. W. Wassall Drowns in Lake," *Chicago Daily Tribune,* Sept. 20, 1909, 1) are in the archives of John G. Anderson, and there is abun-

dant unpublished correspondence regarding the drowning and Ellen's life with the Grinsteads in the archives of Marjorie Anderson Ashley and John G. Anderson.

WIA visits Sissy at Oldfields: Chase; conversation; burned hand; other details of courtship in
AGA, Memoirs Ms1, 64–65, and *Approaching*, 1–6.

*"nicest person in the world . . . pleasant, cheerful, sweet normal sort of person," "no danger," "see
things":* WIA to AGA, pm Dec. 2, 1930; ca. Aug. 30, 1930.

"desperately unhappy," "I like quietness": Memoirs Ms1, 65.

"to see whether I'd mind the heat": WIA to AGA, undated letter, Aug. 1930, *DC*, 113.

"might like somebody else's love better": WIA to AGA, pm Sept. 17, 1930.

"Dear Agnes: I love you": WIA to AGA, undated.

"Dear Bob, You must know": AGA to WIA, pm Aug. 19, 1930.

"I have known what it is to be happy": WIA to AGA, pm Sept. 3, 1930.

"It is impossible for me at any rate": WIA to AGA, pm Oct. 29, 1930.

"When I'm doing mudpies," "Indian god": DC, 118.

"very intense high-keyed colors": WIA to AGA, pm Oct. 27, 1930.

"reaching into the air and grabbing": WIA to AGA, pm Sept. 6, 1930. His slip painting varied in
technique from day to day, he says in a letter pm Oct. 31, 1930.

"Some day I'm going [to] give up everything . . . I'd probably burn out on the first day": WIA to
AGA, pm Nov. 6, 1930, Nov. 19, 1930.

Ellen's book on primitive art, "flitting from one influence to another": WIA to AGA, pm Sept. 5,
Nov. 2, Dec. 2, 1930.

"pretty late Greek": WIA to AGA, undated, "Saturday," 1930.

woodcarving: WIA to AGA, pm Nov. 2, 1930.

African sculpture: WIA to AGA, pm Nov. 21, 1930. One of his favorite books was Paul Guillaume's *Primitive Negro Sculpture* (1926) and he had probably seen African art at the Barnes
Collection, in Philadelphia.

Horn Island/Ocean Springs/cat mural: See WIA to AGA, letters pm Sept. 1, 6, 7, 8, 17, 23, 1930,
pm Oct. 15, 1930. The painting is no longer extant.

"flat color, forms playing against one another": AGA to WIA, pm Sept. 1 and 6, 1930.

"suggest the nicest things": WIA to AGA, undated, "Thursday," pm Sept. 5, 1930.

"We [will] make everything": WIA to AGA, pm Feb. 20, 1932.

imaginary furnishings of house: WIA to AGA, undated letters, ca. Aug. 30, 1930; letter pm Sept.
5, 1930; pm Sept. 17, 1930; pm Nov. 3, 1930; Jan. 11, 1932; Feb. 20, 1932.

WIA's advice to AGA on painting: letters pm Oct. 9, 31, 1930; Nov. 8, 10, 19, 21, 1930.

"wind and water and hot sun," Winslow Homer: WIA to AGA, pm Oct. 15, 1930.

Mayan art at Tulane, La Argentina: Letters pm Nov. 3, Nov. 8, 1930.

Russian dance, music and painting: WIA to AGA, pm Nov. 8, 1930.

opening of Annex, making of figurines: DC, 137–144.

"Potboiler work," "perfectly worthless": WIA Phipps and WIA to AGA, pm Feb. 7, 1932.

"old man of ninety": WIA to AGA, pm Oct. 17, 1931.

"horribly monotonous": WIA to AGA, pm Nov. 1, 1931.

engagement of WIA and AGA: The first reference in the correspondence to the engagement
occurs in WIA to AGA, Oct. 10, 1931, and as Neill, 45, points out, there is a letter from Sissy's
former roommate, Margaret Farnum (1907–1997) dated July 24, 1931, congratulating him on
his recent engagement.

"spilled over everyone": AGA, Memoirs Ms1, 63.

WIA statement of assets: Approaching, 5–6.

"sweet steadying" presence of AGA: WIA to AGA, pm Oct. 23, 1931.

"Contemporary American Ceramics" exhibition and increased production of figurines: DC, 141–43.

"Aren't you proud of yourself?": AGA to WIA, pm Nov. 2, 1931.

"Buried-alive" feeling: WIA to AGA, pm Nov. 14, 1931.

"Machine for the production of widgets"; "I don't want to lead this sort of life": WIA to AGA, pm Nov. 3, 1931; Jan. 14, 1932.

precious stone (WIA gift to AGA): WIA to AGA, pm Jan. 5, 1932.

"It is a rotten feeling": WIA to AGA, pm Dec. 29, 1931.

"I don't think there's a chance in a thousand": AGA to WIA, March 18, 1932.

"Your intended is not a potter": WIA to AGA, pm Jan. 26, 1932.

Mac "never complains": WIA to AGA, pm Oct. 30, 1931.

"a sort of handyman": JMcCA, autobiographical statement, ca. 1990, archives of Sara L. Anderson.

WIA fires wads of clay at wall: DC, 122.

Mac persuades Peter to diversify: JMcCA, autobiographical statement, ca. 1990, archives of Sara L. Anderson.

"abominably lonely": WIA to AGA, pm Jan. 15, 1932.

hooked rug symbolic of "prostrate state": WIA to AGA, pm Jan. 5, 1932.

hunting trip with Archie Bongé: WIA to AGA, undated, probably early Nov. 1931.

WIA imagines trips with Sissy: WIA to AGA, pm Sept. 3, 6, 1930; to Chandeleurs, pm Dec. 31, 1931; to Pascagoula and Bluff Creek, pm Sept. 3, 1930, and Jan. 11, 1932; to Horn Island, Jan. 15, 1932, Feb. 12, 1932; to Florida, Feb. 10, 1932; to New Orleans, Feb. 14, 1932.

"It was probably because I wanted you so much to myself": WIA to AGA, undated letter.

Imagined life on Horn Island: WIA to AGA, pm Sept. 6, 1930; pm Oct. 25, 1931; Jan. 13, 1932; ca. Feb. 1930 (letter no. 40).

"beastly temper," "I'll probably hurt you": WIA to AGA, pm Jan. 21, March 19, 1932.

tales of woe, William Wade Grinstead's breakdown and hospitalization; WIA keeps watch over Grinstead, who runs him out of house: WWG medical records, Sheppard Pratt Hospital, and WIA Phipps, conference of May 12, 1938: "Some sort of altercation occurred between the patient and [Grinstead] in which some sex topics occurred which profoundly shocked the patient." A doctor at Sheppard Pratt notes that at Oldfields, Grinstead "tried several times to jump into the water, looked the house over for a gun and a straight razor which he had hidden, thought he was being black-mailed. He grew angry with his daughter's fiancé [WIA], ran him out of the house" (WWG records, Sheppard Pratt Hospital, June 20, 1932, 1). Cf. 4: "The patient thought [AGA] and her fiance were misbehaving and he had a grudge against them." In Memoirs Ms1, 69, Sissy writes that Bob was "the most patient and soothing of nurses [and] sat up all night, night after night, with him," and that his "devotion to him had been out of this world, especially considering the fact that Daddy had never even tried to conceal the extent of his dislike for Bob," but in PA Phipps (Maurice Partridge, "Statement from Life"), PGA writes that "Bob refused to have anything to do at any time with my father . . . so that after Mr. G. moved to Ocean Springs to be in his own house the entire burden of seeing him and entertaining him fell on us."

"don't be in too much of a hurry": Marjorie Grinstead to AGA, April 10, 1933, and letters of April 25 and 27, John G. Anderson archives. Cf. WWG's Sheppard Pratt records, April 27, 1933, 18–19.

On May 9, when Grinstead was informed by letter of the marriage, he "smiled and said, 'It looks as if the young people have taken things into their own hands.' He seemed much relieved that he was now relieved of the necessity of making any decision on the matter."

WIA at Peter's wedding: AGA, Memoirs Ms3, n.p.

WIA forgets wedding ring: AGA journal, April 29, 1986.

Marriage and honeymoon, Sissy's conversation with Annette: Memoirs Ms1, 83. Sissy mentions her husband's visit to a prostitute in WIA Phipps.

Wedding night and honeymoon; AGA visit to Marjorie Grinstead and WIA visit to Annette: Approaching, 10–13, and interview with Kendall, Jan. 4, 2003, who spoke with Sissy repeatedly in the 1980s, and took careful notes, about her relationship with Bob. In a journal entry, April 29, 1988, AGA writes: "Wedding anniversary day, 55 years ago. . . . I go back in time and as usual, it is Sissy who comes out as a sort of unwilling culprit. How was it possible for me to be so ignorant and so terrified and so unwilling?"

Death of Marjorie Grinstead and viewing at the Cottage: Memoirs Ms1, 100; WWG Sheppard Pratt records, 21.

AFRAID OF THE DARK

Sissy's "afraid of the dark" letter: AGA to WIA, pm March 14, 1932.

"You flatter my ego": WIA to AGA, pm March 17, 1932.

WIA abandons Sissy on bluff: Approaching, 4, where AGA seems to date the incident in 1929. As Neill (230, note) points out, the incident did not occur during AGA's courtship.

"Bob damn it!": Memoirs Ms, 131, and Memoirs Ms2, 1948, 114, where the comment is attributed to two friends, Frank and Virginia Wells. "I likened Walter to Zeus. . . . Did I really think of him as God? I hardly think so; but I was certainly wrapped up in him, and cognizant of the fact that he represented something far superior to the ordinary human herd. I thought of him always as being like Jesus." Cf. ibid., 182.

Sissy "entirely submissive": WIA Phipps, statement by H. C. A. Mead, May 23, 1938, based on an interview with Ellen Wassall and confirmed in her letter to Mead, May 29, 1938, ibid.

Gift of Cottage: The gift was not recorded publicly until Dec. 28, 1948, when Annette deeded WIA the Cottage and surrounding land. Warranty Deed, Jackson County, Mississippi, signed by Mrs. Annette McC. Anderson and George E. Arndt, Notary Public. Copy in WIAA.

furniture and furnishings: Approaching, 14–17.

no children: In WIA Phipps, Sissy says simply that she and WIA "have practiced birth control since marriage." Cf. *Approaching,* 13, where WIA does "not want to bring a child into a world so filled with pain and terror." In Memoirs Ms1, Sissy adds that "gynecologists in Mobile and New Orleans had told me that I would probably not have children because I had an extremely back-tilted uterus." Cf. ibid., 98: "He told me that he would *never* bring a child into the world because the world was hell and life was agony and completely unbearable." Cf. ibid., 194.

"was always connecting tone with color": Approaching, 17.

arrowheading at Graveline: DC, 126–27 (with poem by Annette); AGA untitled journal ("Composition Book," with records of arrowheading, 1932–35, WIAA); Brown 30–33 (on Indian artifacts on Gulf Coast); and "WPA Source Material."

"Art is a mysterious business": Unpublished, WIAA.

moths, butterflies and moth-baiting incident: DC, 153–56.

meeting with William Jacob Holland: AGA Memoirs Ms2, chap. 24.

trip to Florida: AGA Memoirs Ms2, 1934, and WIA to AMcCA, undated.

other excursions: Island trip, *Approaching*, 23–29. One page of Sissy's logbook survives, in
WIAA (incipit: "What journey's end is this. . . ?")

slaying of turtle: *Approaching*, 30–32.

change in woodcarving techniques: AGA/Gilley interview, "Mental Illness."

portrait of Sissy: Memoirs Ms1.

"strong curves, vivid color": Susan C. Larsen, in Patricia Pinson, ed., *The Art of Walter Anderson*, 25.

Sissy's plans to teach, Cousin Julia: AGA/Gilley interview, "Mental Illness."

Weeks Hall: Memoirs Ms2. Hall had attended the Pennsylvania Academy of the Fine Arts from
1913 through 1919, and, like Bob, had won a Cresson Travelling Scholarship.

Bongé/Swetman wedding: "Bongé-Swetman Wedding in Aug.," Biloxi *Daily Herald*, June 2,
1928, 2, and Memoirs Ms2, 1934, 97–102.

Ellen calls the family "queer": WIA Phipps, "Additional Information," H. C. A. Mead, May 23,
1938.

Summer Art Colony: DC, 79–81.

"Just look at you two!": PGA, unpublished manuscript, "To My Grandchildren," archives of
Marjorie Anderson Ashley.

"Clothes, fashion, and shopping board her": Mary Anderson Pickard, "A Personal View," n.p.

Bob brushes off visitors: Memoirs Ms2, xvii.

"the creative act": *Approaching*, 40.

"very, very conventional sort of family": AGA/Gilley interview, "Mental Illness."

"creative side of people": Ibid.

"Real artists are just people"; questions to visitors, DC, 248, AMcCA to WIA, Nov. 11, 1935, WIAA.

Sissy models "Pied Piper": Memoirs Ms2, 1933, 35, 70–71.

Sissy's epic and poem to Bob: Several pages of "Diego" are preserved in WIAA; also, ms. of
poem to Bob.

Sissy's senior thesis: There is a copy in WIAA.

Christmas play: *Approaching*, 44–49; *"Air, Earth, Fire and Water":* Memoirs Ms1, 183. The friend
and Radcliffe classmate was Margaret Farnum Watkins Gilmore (1907–1997).

little theater group: On the Ocean Springs Little Theater Guild, of which Annette was director,
see AGA/Gilley interview, June 7, 1990, and *JXCOT*, Oct. 20, Nov. 10, 1934.

Orozco on murals: Rodríguez, 199.

"The South has no [art] museums or schools": Minutes from the "first meeting of the regional
directors, Feb. 19, 1934," PWAP records, NARA.

"I've spent 50 years in the South": Woodward, 9.

"Therapeutic" past: Marling, 38.

eight muralists, twenty-three easel painters in Woodward's flock: Burt Brown Barker, Regional
Director, 16th District to Edward B. Rowan, Assistant Technical Director, PWAP, March 22,
1934, PWAP, NARA, 121.2.4.

Payment and dates of murals: Artists in the "Southern Zone" were paid $1.00 per hour for
skilled labor and 40 cents for unskilled labor; see *Federal Civil Works Administration Rules
and Regulations No. 10*, Dec. 13, 1933. In Woodward's summary, "Projects in Progress—Sixth
Region—April 14, 1934," he estimates that $89.25 plus $27.00 for labor will be needed to

complete the murals by PA and JMcCA, and that an additional $271.50 will be needed, pre-
sumably for WIA. PWAP, NARA, 121.2.4. On May 8, 1934, when federal funding had run
out, and the Andersons' project was only "a couple of weeks from fulfillment" (Ellsworth
Woodward to Edward Bruce, May 9, 1934), R.W. Neef, Director of Work, Emergency Relief
Administration for the State of Mississippi, wrote to Charles R. Bennett, mayor of Ocean
Springs, asking him to "authorize this work to be continued to completion, with the understanding that your city will honor all necessary payrolls" (NARA, 121.2.4; see also telegram
of May 11, 1934, from Edward Bruce to Ellsworth Woodward, and telegram of May 11, 1934,
from Perry Fellows, Administrative Assistant, FERA, to George B. Power, Director, Mississippi State Board of Public Welfare). Also, AMcCA to WIA, May 10, 1934: "There is news
from Jackson, saying no more money for putting up tiles. So Peter may have to pay for the
labor, or somebody must." Bob's murals were completed by June 9, 1934, date of an article
by Ruth Dyrud (Director of Art, University of Alabama) in *JXCOT*, "An Appreciation of the
Murals in the Local High School Auditorium." See also "Anderson Tiles, School Murals,
Attract Visitors," *Mobile Times*, July 7, 1934. Besides the three Anderson brothers, PWAP
participants from Mississippi included Mary Ethel Dismukes and Dorothy Hopkins, Biloxi;
Marie Hull and Helen M. McGehee, Jackson; Charlotte E. Tibbs, Ocean Springs; Sara Pryor
Dodge and Lalla Walker Lewis, Greenwood; and Betty McArthur, McHenry. On the restora-
tion of the murals in 1989, see "Restoration of Anderson Murals Begins," *Ocean Springs
Record*, Jan. 18, 1989.

Ann Craton: "Local Artists Highly Praised by Officials," *JXCOT*, June 9, 1934. Craton was on a
tour of the South, "seeking to assist the needy artists who were on the relief project [PWAP]
which was discontinued in April. See New Orleans *Morning Tribune*, May 22, 1934; New
Orleans *Item-Tribune*, May 23 and 24, 1934; New Orleans *Times-Picayune*, May 24, 27, 1934.
Clippings in PWAP files, NARA. The tiles were completed—and inspected—by May 9, 1934,
the date of a letter from AMcCA to WIA.

"Ocean Springs: Past and Present": For a discussion and illustrations, see King, 19–39 and
O'Connor, in Pinson, 48–51.

"It is just that kind of curtain": Melrich V. Rosenberg to AMcCA (?), July 8, 1934 (WIAA), and
reply of WIA, Aug. 14, 1934 (Shearwater Pottery archives).

"so much like paradise," "constantly catapulted," "cherry ribbon": Memoirs Ms1, 139.

"it was one tourist camp after another": WIA to AMcCA, undated letter.

Parks and Ellen Mead: Edwards A. Park to Ellen Mead, undated, archives of John G. Anderson.
On Edwards A. Park (d. 1969), see *Pediatrics*, 44:6 (Dec. 1969): 897–901.

"felt more like Joseph or the donkey," Ellen's "marvelous mind": Memoirs Ms1, 141.

driving of Agnes Park: Memoirs Ms1, 142.

"Sissy and I both feel": WIA to AMcCA, undated letter ("Tuesday").

lampshades: Memoirs Ms2, 154–57, and Memoirs Ms3, xxvii. But cf. AGA's letter of Jan. 10, 1933,
to WIA, where she reports on a visit of her own to the Owing Brook Studio. The only surviving example of such a shade is in the WAMA.

birds' nests in city parks: Approaching, 145.

canoe trip: Two contemporary accounts by AGA are extant (WIAA). The first is a meager
record of expenses, position, weather, and some hurried notes, covering May 25 to June 7.
The second, a fuller narrative, covers the same period, including some of the incidents jotted down briefly in the first account. The second narrative, which has unmistakable literary
intentions, is written on the same type of paper used by Sissy and Bob in 1939–1941, and

may date from that period. Years later (judging from the handwriting), WIA wrote a poem (untitled and undated,WIAA) beginning "It was upon a sunny day in May / I first set forth amid the waters grey"), chronicling his own descent of the Ohio and Mississippi rivers. He seems to be referring to the trip he took with Sissy, but there is no mention of her at all. Another poem written about the same time ("Of the river, / of the winding / returning river . . .") celebrates, in Whitmanesque cadences, the Mississippi's battle with the Gulf of Mexico, and the river's love of its "children," the migrating birds (WIAA). Sissy describes the river trip and Bob's idea of water and "feeling" in *Approaching*, 34–41, and there are preliminary versions of the trip (in which there is a slightly different account of his recovery) in Memoirs Ms1, 139–82, and Memoirs Ms2.

portage incident; "no bravos": Memoirs Ms1, 150–51.

"almost, one might say, a sewer": Memoirs Ms1, 173.

Bob in Arkansas hospital: Memoirs Ms1, 179–80.

QUICKSAND

Marie Hull, "grand passion" for Shearwater: See the series of letters between PGA and Marie Hull, 1938, in the Shearwater Pottery archives, and her statement in "Walter Anderson and Family: A Group of Rare Individuals," Jackson *Clarion-Ledger*, July 30, 1967.

Shearwater annual income: "Application for Licence to Engage in Business," 1935–1936, State Tax Commission, Mississippi, account no. 2648/30-251, Shearwater Pottery archives.

"liberal, according to Southern standards": Emmett Hull to Olin Dows, assistant superintendent, Section of Painting and Sculpture, Jan. 30, 1935; NARA. Materials on the Jackson and Indianola murals are in NARA, RG 121, Boxes 55 and 54, respectively.

"$12 a square foot [was] not too much to pay": Olin Dows to Emmett J. Hull, Feb. 2, 1936, NARA. He adds that twenty dollars a square foot was the maximum rate for mural paintings. Marling, 55, mentions some of the expenses involved in doing a mural for the Section: travel to the location; purchase price of canvas, paint, varnish and adhesive; payments to laborers and photographers; postage for mailing sketches, cartoons and snapshots.

"the best artists in the whole Southern region": Olin Dows to W. F. Henderson, April 16, 1935, NARA.

death of Adele ("Daisy") Anderson and smashing of piano: "Civil District Court for the Parish of Orleans, State of Lousiana, Division 'D,' Judgment Putting in Possession Succession of Adele Anderson," No. 211370, May 10, 1935; copy in Shearwater Archives; and Memoirs Ms2, 126–29.

Peter's depression and illness: PA Phipps, "Formulation to the Clinic," Dec. 23, 1938, 5.

WIA work on bird book: Extant sketches include the warbler, nuthatch, woodpeckers, white-throated sparrow, nighthawk, chimney swift, meadowlark, bluejay, sparrow hawk, kingfisher, and yellow-crowned night heron. See *Birds*, xi, 7,12, 21, 51–55, 57–58, and comments by Mary Anderson Pickard, xi. On the book sent by Park, Edwards A. Park to WIA, March 27, 1935. WIA also made use of T. Gilbert Pearson, *Birds of America* (Garden City: Doubleday, 1936), and there is a copy with annotations in the family library.

cartoons by Winter and Long: Winter's statement about his own design is preserved in the NARA archives. Beckham (75) argues that the design altributed by the Committee to Long was not really his. Long, 94, describes his design in his autobiography as "a giant, illusion-ary, robed figure of a judge" brooding over "a melange of figures and scenes . . . represent-ing various features of the judicial and law enforcement systems." On the history of the Jackson mural, see Patti Carr Black, *Art in Mississippi, 1720–1980,* 189–90, the first to draw upon NARA documentation and O'Connor in Pinson, 51–54. Black (190) and O'Connor (52) reproduce an earlier version of this mural.

"very decorative piece of design": Lucille N. Henderson to Olin Dows, Sept. 18, 1935.

negroid figure: a similar objection was raised in Aiken, South Carolina, to a figure of justice portrayed as a "mulatto." See Marling, 64 ff., and (on the representation of blacks in south-ern murals) Beckham, passim.

"high merit as a design": Olin Dows to Lucille N. Henderson, Oct. 5, 1935.

"treatment in another medium, such as the textile": Edward Rowan to WIA, Oct. 1, 1935.

advice from Inslee Hopper: Inslee A. Hopper, assistant superintendent, to WIA, Dec. 12, 1935.

"We feel that the work of No. 1": Lucille Henderson to Inslee Hopper, April 6, 1936, NARA.

"The southern states are apt to bemoan the fact": Emmett Hull to Edward B. Rowan, April 11, 1936, NARA.

"The Section feels that the color and the design": Edward B. Rowan to Lucille Henderson, May 22, 1936, NARA.

acquiescence of Jackson committee: See Beckham, 76–77.

Simkhovitch mural: Simkhovitch had entitled his mural *Pursuits of Life in Mississippi,* and had painted a "Negro singing typical Negro spirituals" and the "present-day life of Negro share-croppers, picking and weighing cotton, with the white man taking account." Years later, at the height of the civil rights movement, these racial stereotypes would become so unbear-able that the painting had to be hidden behind a curtain. See Black, *Art in Mississippi,* 190; "Word Account for the Jackson, Mississippi Court House Mural Painted by Simka Simkhovitch"; "Mural Painting by Simka Simkhovitch: 'Pursuits of Life in Mississippi'"; and B. L. Todd, Jr., Clerk, United States District Court, Jackson, to United States Treasury Department, June 28, 1939, NARA; and Beckham, 200–201.

iris hunting in Lousiana countryside and Cajun picnic: Memoirs Ms1, 186–89, Memoirs Ms2, 133–38, and *Approaching,* 50–52, where the fall and spring trips are telescoped into one.

"The iris is a lilac flower": Unpublished, WIAA.

Frank and Harry Schmidt, treatment for undulant fever: Approaching, 53; Memoirs Ms1, 188–89; Memoirs Ms2, 139–41; and information in Schmidt family archives, Biloxi. Harry Johnson Schmidt (1905–1997) graduated from Tulane Medical School in 1932 and after interning at Mercy Hospital, New Orleans, opened a practice in Convent, Lousiana, where he did his first research on brucellosis, identifying low-grade or chronic infection in humans and cattle. Frank O. Schmidt (1902–1975) practiced medicine in Ocean Springs and Biloxi (Ray L. Bellande to the author, March 12, 2001; Harry J. Schmidt, Jr., to the author, March 22, 2001).

renovation of Cottage: Memoirs Ms2, 131–33; Memoirs Ms3, ch. 33, and Sugg, *A Painter's Psalm,* 5–6.

Robineau Memorial Exhibition: Correspondence from 1935 to 1937 between GWA and Anna Wetherill Olmsted of the Syracuse Museum of Fine Arts, Shearwater Pottery archives. WIA was represented in 1935 by two copper-red carved vases and copper-red male and female figures; in 1936 by "Negro figures" and football players which "received much favorable

comment from . . . visitors" (letter of Helen Durney to WIA, Oct. 21, 1936) and were purchased by the potter R. Guy Cowan, one of the judges (Olmsted to GWA, Oct. 29, 1936).

California Pacific Exposition: Marian B. D'ave, Fine Arts Gallery, City of San Diego, to AMcCA,
April 30, 1936, Shearwater Pottery archives.

"I find to my disgust . . .": GWA to Anna Wetherill Olmstead, Sept. 22, 1936, Shearwater Pottery
archives.

two pencil sketches submitted to Rowan: AGA to Edward B. Rowan, Sept. 24, 1936, NARA.

"abstractions and decorative qualities . . . treatment in another medium, such as the textile":
Edward B. Rowan to AGA, Oct. 1, 1936, NARA.

Rowan's understanding of "decorative" and "factual," Forbes Watson on the factual: Marling,
56–58. See also Mecklenburg, 12–18.

another five sketches: Edward B. Rowan to WIA, Oct. 22, 1936, NARA.

GWA's book on golf: Several versions of GWA's booklet are in the Shearwater Pottery archives,
along with copies of his unanswered letters to Quentin Reynolds of May 18, 1935, and
March 3, 1936. At Phipps, Ellen Mead told WIA's doctors of his plans for publication and his
appointment of a literary executor—a friend of Sissy's. WIA Phipps; see also AGA, interview with John Jones, May 14, 1979.

GWA's belief family was trying to poison him: Memoirs Ms1, 188; Memoirs Ms3, ch. 33.

GWA's will: Copy in WIAA.

Rowan critique of death scene and color sketch: Edward B. Rowan to WIA, Jan. 25, 1937. Rowan
also found problems with the drawing and with WIA's "particular use of color": "It was also
felt that the scale of figures is possibly large for the three panels into which your design is
divided. You have presented an unusual color scheme for this work [and] I want you to be
sure that this palette will prove harmonious in the Indianola Post Office lobby. A point to
which I would like to call your attention deals with the elevation of the child. In a way the
strength of this theme is lost by your particular use of color. In the sketch, brilliant background detracted from the child. I would like for you to submit to this office either a photograph or the actual full-sized cartoon when you have prepared it."

Death of GWA and Bob's reaction: Approaching, 54, and Memoirs Ms1, 191.

WIA not "kind enough" to GWA: N. Cameron, "Admission Note," April 4, 1937, WIA Phipps.

filing of inventory of GWA's estate: Annette filed the inventory of the estate on May 1, 1937; see
Chancery Court, Jackson County, Mississippi, nos. 547 and 5847, "In matter of last will and
testament of GW Anderson," Oct. 8, 1937, and Sept. 24, 1937, WIAA.

"little flare-ups, small explosions": Approaching, 41.

breaking of phonograph records: Approaching, 41–42, Memoirs Ms2, 1934, 94; and Memoirs Ms3,
ch. 33, where Sissy seems to hint at a sexual provocation for the outburst: "For him the end
[of the dance] came with a return to normalcy. What a normalcy! I fell out of terror into
fury. Out of his arms onto the porch."

"As long as your shoes stick out": Memoirs Ms1, 102.

Sissy's dreams: AGA to Adolf Meyer, April 2, 1937, WIA Phipps.

"prolonged and constant fever": AGA, Memoirs Ms2, 143. Scientists agreed, at the time, that
undulant fever sometimes invaded the nervous system, causing occasional delirium, depression, and, rarely, major psychosis. See Charles M. Carpenter and Ruth A. Boak, "The Treatment of Human Brucellosis," *Medicine*, 15 (1936): 103–27, and bibliography cited therein.
Judging from Sissy's description in *Approaching*, the treatment administered to WIA was
therapy with artificially induced fever, which was then somewhat rare.

Baisden visit: Frank Baisden to Lewis I. Sharp, Jr., May 6, 1937, WIA Phipps; Memoirs Ms2, 1933, 37–39, 78–82; Memoirs Ms3, ch. 31, 51.

WIA's breakdown, trip to Mobile, and admission to Phipps: "Formulation to the Clinic," April 14, 1937, WIA Phipps, and Eugene D. Bondurant to Henry Mead, April 12, 1937, WIA Phipps.

THE PHIPPS CLINIC

first days at Phipps: "Formulation to the Clinic," April 14, 1937, WIA Phipps.

release of Delphine (Dellie) McConnell and subsequent life: DC, 177.

"on a personal crusade": Maurice Partridge, "Past History," undated, 2, PA Phipps.

correspondence with Annette: A packet of her letters survives, WIAA.

Adolf Meyer (1866–1950): On Meyer's holistic approach (summarized here) I have quoted from A. Meyer, "Objective Psychology or Psychobiology with Subordination of the Medically Useless Contrast of Mental and Physical," in *Collected Papers,* Vol. III, 38–39; Lidz 322–23; Stephens, "Inpatient," 751; Ebaugh, 335; John R. Neill, 463; Rutter, 1077.

"by and large from things people did": John R. Neill, 463.

"language of madness": Norman Cameron to Ellen Mead, July 25, 1961, archives of John G. Anderson.

Phipps doctors: Biographical files are available on all of them in the Alan Mason Chesney Medical Archives, Johns Hopkins Medical Institutions.

"growing shadow of the psyche": Henry Mead to Adolf Meyer, Nov. 13, 1936, Meyer Papers.

"sensitive, intense married artist," "tremendously impulsive": "Monday Clinic," May 23, 1938, and "Staff Conference," May 8, 1937, 20, WIA Phipps.

"etiological" and "situational" factors: "Staff Conference," May 8, 1937, and "Monday Clinic," May 23, 1938, WIA Phipps.

"We can't really be sure what things count": Louis Sharp, "Staff Conference," May 8, 1937, WIA Phipps.

Diagnosis: On WIA's case history and discharge sheet the final diagnosis is: "Hypothymergasia with homosexual panic and paranoid trends, and ? parergesic features" (WIA Phipps.) The term "parergesic" was used by Wendell Muncie synonymously with "schizophrenic" (see Muncie, 351). That doctors at Phipps were uncertain whether to label WIA "parergesic" is evident from the staff conferences of April 19 and May 23, 1938.

"anything we would look upon . . . homosexual relationship": "Monday Clinic," May 23, 1938, WIA Phipps. He adds, moments later, that there is "not very definite evidence of homosexuality except his fear." In "Staff Conference," April 19, 1938, Henry Mead suddenly blurted out: "He was a straight homosexual at one time." Mead's son remembers him telling him that Bob thought Henry Mead was gay, because of the blue shirt he was wearing (interview with James Mead, June 27, 2002; confirmed by Mead's "Summary of Mental Status," April 5, 1937, WIA Phipps). In "Staff Conference," May 8, 1937, L. Sharp reports: "He had a depression in 1919, following a homosexual episode, the details of which we don't know, but which I am trying to obtain." For Sissy's uncertainty: May 3, 1937, WIA Phipps. In "Staff Conference," April 19, 1938, L. Thorne transforms the experience with Baisden into an excursion to Provincetown. See also WIA Pratt, 4.

second "Fountainebleau case": "Staff Conference," May 8, 1937, and "Staff Conference," May 19, 1938.

"The life is very simple": "Staff Conference," May 8, 1937. The article, by Clifford Sharpe, "The 'Forest Philosophers,'" *New Statesman*, 20:516 (March 3, 1923): 626–27, is reprinted in *Gurd-jieff International Review*, 1:4 (Summer 1998), n.p.

Baisden letter: Frank Baisden to Lewis I. Sharp, Jr., May 6, 1937, WIA Phipps.

"a trait that has remained unchanged": Dr. Lambert, "Monday Clinic," May 23, 1938, WIA Phipps.

WIA's habits at Phipps, removal of pencil: Unless otherwise indicated, my narrative draws on the daily observations provided by WIA's doctors, found in WIA Phipps. On the pencil, Dr. Woodhall, "Operation," Aug. 9, 1937, WIA Phipps.

visit by Sissy: Progress note, July 22–24, 1937, WIA Phipps.

"magic" of water: Unpublished, WIAA.

"a weakness for thermometers": Progress note, Sept. 2, 1937, WIA Phipps.

"You did! Every damned one of you": Progress note, Sept. 7, 1937, WIA Phipps.

"[She] tells me she knows just how he feels": Progress note, A. Leighton, Sept. 29, 30, 1937.

Sissy's thoughts in Baltimore; pregnancy: AGA journals.

"little dream of beauty"; WIA informed of AGA pregnancy: AGA journal, Dec. 12, 1937.

"blissful": AGA journal, Dec. 13, 1937.

"Help me! I haven't lived right": A. Leighton, progress notes, Dec. 25, 1937, WIA Phipps.

"Of course, my first reaction is no": AGA journal, Dec. 21 [?], 1937.

Metrazol treatment: See Max Fink, M.D., "Meduna and the Origins of Convulsive Therapy," *American Journal of Psychiatry* 141:9 (Sept. 1984): 1034–41; L. de Meduna, "New Methods of Medical Treatment of Schizophrenia," *Archives of Neurology and Psychiatry*, 54 (1938): 361–63; L. von Meduna, "The Significance of the Convulsive Reaction During the Insulin and the Cardiazol Therapy of Schizophrenia," *Journal of Nervous and Mental Disease* 87:2 (Feb. 1938): 133–77; Meduna, "General Discussion of the Cardiazol Therapy," *American Journal of Psychiatry* 94: supplement (May 1938): 40–50; Hans H. Reese et al., "The Effect of Induced Metrazol Convulsions on Schizophrenic Patients," *Journal of Nervous and Mental Disease* 87:3 (May 1938): 571–83. Estimates of percentage of patients treated with Metrazol who "recovered or markedly improved" ranged from 32 to 70 between 1938 and 1944; Garfield Tommey, "Therapeutic Fashions in Psychiatry," *American Journal of Psychiatry* 124:6 (Dec. 1967): 99.

Meyer on Metrazol treatments: "Monday Clinic," May 23, 1938, WIA Phipps.

"wished they would find something to help him": AGA journal, Jan. 4, 1938.

WIA reaction to Metrazol: L. Thorne, progress notes, Feb. 10, 1938, WIA Phipps.

"his peculiar attitude toward self-inflicted pain": "Staff Conference," April 19, 1938, 17, WIA Phipps.

drawings: L. Thorne, progress notes, Feb. 10, March 4, 6, 7, April 8, 1938; Dr. Muncie's rounds, March 3, 1938, WIA Phipps. All of the drawings are missing from WIA's records.

"Dear Mother: Your flowers came": WIA to AMcCA, Feb. 2, 1938, WIA Phipps.

Sissy's return to Shearwater: DC, 177–181.

Mac's rammed-earth house: DC, 182–83, and note, 330. His marriage license to Frances Jacqueline House ("Jackie") is dated Sept. 8 and 9, 1937 (Office of the County and Probate Clerk, Garland County, Arkansas).

"In order to hide and quiet fears and sorrows": AGA journal, Feb. 8, 1938.

"funny how, sometimes line after line": AGA journal, Feb. 10, 1938.

"put even the Shearwater in the shade": DC, 184.

"I'm crazy as hell": "Monday Clinic," May 23, 1938.

"Although Mr. Anderson has been with us a year now": "Staff Conference," April 19, 1938; "Monday Clinic," May 23, 1938, WIA Phipps.

how little anyone knew of "what is going on inside": Dr. Rennie, "Staff Conference," April 19, 1938, WIA Phipps.

tested "to some extent what we stand for": "Monday Clinic," May 23, 1938, WIA Phipps.

"distress of the whole ward": "Monday Clinic," May 23, 1938, WIA Phipps.

"When he draws from imagination": L. Thorne, progress notes, March 6, 1938, WIA Phipps.

"no clear indication of any special content": Dr. Muncie, "Staff Conference," April 19, 1938.

"Most [of the drawings] have a cruel look": Dr. Lemkau, "Staff Conference," April 19, 1938.

"She cites as an example": "Additional Information," H. C. A. Mead, May 23, 1938.

Ellen Wassall falls in love with Mead: Memoirs Ms3, ch. 55.

Miss Rochmel: Memoirs Ms3, ch. 56, and journal, Aug. 1981.

WIA rugs: Progress notes, Oct. 11, 1937; June 1, 22, July 25, 1938, WIA Phipps.

WIA kisses attendants: July 17, 18, 1938, WIA Phipps.

"arrange a meeting with a woman": July 19, 1938, WIA Phipps.

Meyer's meeting with WIA: Notation by Meyer, Sept. 21, 1938, WIA Phipps.

"I want to be with you all the time": AGA journal, Sept. 23, 1938.

THANKSGIVING

"possible suicidal and homicidal tendencies" and mutism: Note from Adolf Meyer, Sept. 23, 1938, WIA Phipps; Meyer on Feb. 13, 1939, 20, PA Phipps.

details of train trip, first days at Shearwater: AMcCA to Adolf Meyer, Sept. 28, 1938, Meyer Papers.

"Home, all of us! Bliss and heaven . . . would never have to write": AGA journal, Oct. 4, 1938.

"Yellow butterflies": AGA journal, Oct. 5, 1938.

WIA daily routine: AGA journal, Oct. 1938, and AGA to Adolf Meyer, Oct. 17, 1938, Meyer Papers.

"If he would just put his arms around me": AGA journal, Nov. 23, 1938.

"I don't see [him] enough": AGA journal, Oct. 24, 1938.

"sound policy of non-interference": Adolf Meyer to AGA, Nov. 23, 1938, Meyer Papers.

"part of the time, as if I were not": AGA journal, Oct. 17, 1938.

incident with broken pot at showroom: AGA to Adolf Meyer, Oct. 17, 1938, Meyer Papers.

Peter enamored of apprentice at Pottery: DC, 193, and PA Phipps, passim.

Peter "horrified" at lack of improvement of WIA: Maurice Partridge, "Present Illness. Summary," undated, 3. Cf. "Formulation to the Clinic," Dec. 23, 1938, PA Phipps.

signs of WIA's improvement: AGA to Adolf Meyer, Nov. 30, 1938, Meyer Papers.

"In every way, except seeing other people": AGA to Adolf Meyer, Nov. 21, 1938, Meyer Papers. For the complete text, DC, 191–92.

duck hunting trip: Partridge, "Present Illness. Summary," undated, 4.

"This place is not glad . . . Peter is down in the depths": AGA journal, Nov. 22, 23, 1938.

"the pain might shock [him]": Partridge, "Present Illness. Summary," undated, 4a, PA Phipps.

days preceding PA's admission to Phipps: Partridge, ibid., and "Formulation to the Clinic," Dec. 23, 1938, PA Phipps.

"drowsy and apathetic": Ibid., 5.

"seriously damaged conscience": "Complaint [from Patient]," PA Phipps.

a room "denuded of furniture": "Course in Clinic, Dec. '38–May '39," PA Phipps.

"intolerable to one accustomed to such almost extravagant freedom": Dec. 25, 1938, PA Phipps.

"the very center and climax": "Case Summary," Dec. 23, 1938, 14, PA Phipps.

"an exceedingly vivid picture": Summary, Jan. 17, 1939, 7, PA Phipps.

"quite obviously, one of the most difficult": "Monday Clinic—Fourth Year," Feb. 13, 1939, 18, PA Phipps.

Annette's questions to doctors: PGA to M. Partridge, Jan. 18, 1939.

"There's never any peace in the place": Partridge, "Past History," undated (Jan. 1939?), PA Phipps.

"you're only his wife": Ibid., PA Phipps.

"She appears rather to have overwhelmed": Partridge notes, Jan. 9, 1939, PA Phipps.

"engaged in angry physical combat": Ibid.

"she was such a leader, so lively": Partridge, ibid. and "Past History," undated, PA Phipps.

"sin against amphimixis": "Case Summary," Dec. 23, 1938, PA Phipps.

information learned by Pat in New Orleans: PGA to Maurice Partridge, Feb. 10, 1939, PA Phipps. On James McConnell's gambling, interview with Cedric Sidney, Jan. 16, 2003.

"Why couldn't I have been like Pat?": AGA journal, Dec. 11, 1938.

"I should have lived one hundred years ago": AGA journal, Jan. 18, 1939. For an analysis of this poem, see Neill, 132–33.

"I could weep, now, with her pain and my own": AGA journal, Jan. 23, 1939.

"Why is it always the men?": Ibid. J. Neill, 135, studies AGA's question in the context of women's reaction "in the twenties, thirties, and forties" to 'a world made for men by men.'"

"pretty big strides in the right direction": AGA to Adolf Meyer, Jan. 24, 1939, Meyer Papers.

"There is to be a big pageant here on the Coast": Ibid. AMcCA describes the same poster to Peter in an undated letter: "Here we are rejoicing in a work of Bob's. He has made a large poster for the pottery. It is full [?] and beautiful. It shows the door of the kiln with a figure receiving a turquoise vase from arms reaching from within. A figure below is throwing a piece of pottery. Pat will take a snapshot of it and send it to you. Of course that will not show the beautiful color, orange and blue on a grey white. To have Bob back at work for the Pottery is so wonderful. He is pleased with the poster and I know it will lead at once to more work." Sissy's drawing of the poster is preserved in the Meyer Papers.

cedar birds: AGA to Adolf Meyer, Feb. 14, 1939, Meyer Papers.

"I'm going to heaven": PGA to Partridge, Feb. 12, 1939, PA Phipps.

"I'm terribly afraid I won't be able to": AGA to Adolf Meyer, Feb. 14, 1939, Meyer Papers. See also Memoirs Ms1, 217, and *Approaching*, 75.

"slight ups do NOT make up": AGA journal, Feb. 17, 1939.

WIA encounter with Pat: PGA to Adolf Meyer, Feb. 16, 1939, PA Phipps.

"Music seems to have a decided effect on him": AGA to Adolf Meyer, Feb. 5, 1939, Meyer Papers.

nails, treehouse: AGA, Memoirs Ms1.

WIA sex with AGA: AGA to Adolf Meyer, Feb. 27, 1939.

WIA's admission to Whitfield: Ibid., and PGA to Adolf Meyer, Feb. 26, 1939, Meyer Papers. On Whitfield, see the 1939 (?) pamphlet *The Mississippi State Hospital*, Whitfield, Mississippi, which is illustrated with photographs, and *What Every Attendant Should Know* (copy in Mississippi Department of Archives and History, Jackson).

"He isn't just gifted or talented": Ibid.

"It was a most difficult decision to make": PGA to Adolf Meyer, Feb. 26, 1939, Meyer Papers.

hospitalization at Whitfield: In *Approaching*, 68, a lapse in memory leads AGA to confuse the
  order of WIA's hospitalizations at Phipps, Whitfield, and Sheppard Pratt.

"ARTIST OR SOMETHING"

doctors' observations of WIA on admission: Admissions statement, Feb. 28, 1939, WIA Whitfield.

Sissy visits WIA: AGA to W. E. Clarke, March 14, 1939.

"dementia praecox, catatonic type": W. E. Clarke to AGA, March 7, 1939, WIA Whitfield.

"There are times when he is quiet": Ibid.

"one of the things most confusing and troubling": AGA to W. E. Clarke, March 5, 1939, WIA
  Whitfield.

"mad at the whole world": W. E. Clarke to AGA, March 3, 1939, WIA Whitfield.

escape from Whitfield: "Escape Note," March 31, 1939, WIA Whitfield.

birds drawn in Ivory soap: AGA Memoirs Ms1, 211; *Approaching*, 74; Memoirs Ms2: "Isabel
  Bratton reported with great glee that the morning after the escape the entire hospital gathered around his building to gaze up at the outer walls . . ."

"provided he did not strenuously object": "Escape Note," March 31, 1939, WIA Whitfield.

"to be a good husband and a good father": "Further Review of Psychological State," ca. April 3,
  1939, PA Phipps.

"descriptions of the doctors": AMcCA to PA, Jan. 20, 1939.

"We want the place to be more and more beautiful": AMcCA to PA, Jan. 8, 1939.

"courage and patience and hope": AMcCA to PA, Jan. 20, 1939.

passage from T. S. Eliot: PA Phipps, n.p.

"You're not a little boy": PGA to Theodore Lidz, April 29, 1939, PA Phipps.

WIA return to Shearwater: AMcCA to Adolf Meyer, May 1, 1939, Meyer Papers.

Peter obsessed with returning home by canoe: Partridge note, May 3, 1939, PA Phipps.

"Mrs. A. Sr. is determined": Ibid.

"My mind is a perfect mess": Dr. Cohen, "History," 10, WIA Pratt.

"You can tie me up and take me there": AMcCA to Adolf Meyer, May 18, 1939, Meyer Papers,
  and "History," 10, WIA Pratt.

WIA escape from train and admittance to hospital: Ibid.

"well developed and well nourished male": "Physical Examination," May 5, 1939, WIA Pratt.

"elderly, thin, wiry lady": "Admission Note," May 4, 1939, WIA Pratt.

WIA's statements to doctors: Dr. Cohen, "Mental Examination," May 5, 1939, WWIA Pratt.

"doubts began to crowd back": Note, May 5, 1939, PA Phipps.

"affirmative religious thought": AMcCA to Adolf Meyer, May 7, 1939, PA Phipps.

"He said merely that he had a high regard": Partridge, note, May 8, 1939, PA Phipps.

"deep concern": AMcCA to Adolf Meyer, May 10, 1939.

interruption of pregnancy: Adolf Meyer to AMcCA, May 16, 1939.

"Mère [Annette] and Pat are home": AGA journal, May 30, 1939.

WIA fears for child's sanity: PGA notes contrasting WIA and PA in PA Phipps.

"would have his hands full": "Staff Conference Report," May 9, 1939, WIA Pratt.

"I think he has a chance": Cohen, "Staff Conference Report," May 9, 1939, WIA Pratt.

WIA drawings "not particularly remarkable": Cohen, note, May 7, 1939, WIA Pratt.

mural pencilled on wall: Pembroke, note, May 22, 1939, WIA Pratt.

drawing of hunter: Cohen, note, May 7, 1939, WIA Pratt.

WIA reacts to other patients: Cohen note, May 15, 1939, WIA Pratt.

"sickness was entirely apart from his art": AMcCA to Adolf Meyer, June 19, 1939, Meyer Papers.

WIA escape from Pratt: Murdock, note, July 1, 1939. In *Approaching*, 69–70, AGA confuses this escape with one of Bob's escapes from Whitfield.

Theodore Lidz: Many years later, Lidz and his wife, Ruth, also a psychiatrist, told an interviewer how vividly they remembered the Andersons: "We had these two brothers, one was a potter and the other was an artist who was a member of some crazy cult in Paris. He was as psychotic as could be, and they found an attendant who was willing to sleep in the room with this homicidal man. And he really could keep him under control. I took care of the brother, the potter, who was in an agitated depression. He would jump on his head and hurt himself badly. I listened to him and he told me that he was supporting three families and his mother by running the pottery. He kept insisting: 'I can't stay here, I can't stay in this confined place, I live on a peninsula.' Finally he convinced me, and I talked to Adolf Meyer about it and he said, 'Okay, we'll take a chance.' We let him go home and he did quite well. . . . We went and visited them on our honeymoon, since we had also gotten to know their wives very well. Two lovely women who were both schoolteachers [*sic*] and unfortunately did not know they were marrying two very disturbed men. When we got down to their place in Mississippi, we asked the wives: 'Well, how are things going?' and they said: 'Well, Walter's living up in a tree right now.' He had built the most beautiful house by himself, a real work of art. Another time they told us: 'Well, the last time we saw him he was just rowing out in the Gulf.' The thing that got us most was when they said: 'Well, when we came home we found the boys playing going to the insane asylum.' This was a really crazy family from the patients' mother and father on down." Marx, 259.

"If only the problem of Walter would solve itself": PGA to T. Lidz, July 22, 1939, PA Pratt.

"crouching and running": AGA journal, July 28, 1939.

Pat's discovery: PGA to Lidz, Aug. 6, 1939.

final diagnosis: "Index," 1, PA Phipps.

"carefully included all of [her] letters": Lidz, "Discharge Note," Aug. 18, 1939, PA Phipps.

Pat's description of Peter's return to Shearwater: PGA to Lidz, Aug. 22, 1939, PA Phipps.

Peter's conversation with Pat about Bob: PGA to Lidz, Aug. 20, 1939, PA Phipps.

WIA's appearance after trip: PGA to Lidz, Sept. 4, 1939, PA Phipps.

WIA's return to Whitfield: PGA to Lidz, Oct. 7, 1939, PA Phipps.

"Once again I must swear . . . he will be well": AGA journal, Oct. 18, 1939.

"God damn it all to hell!": AGA journal, Dec. 9, 1939.

WIA picked up and returned to Whitfield: "Application for Admission," Dec. 11, 1939, WIA Whitfield. On his arrest, WIA gave the police a false name, "Albert Hammond."

"source of trouble at all times": Clarke, note, Dec. 12, 1939. In a 1976 interview with John Marshall Alexander, Hayden Campbell compares the Receiving Ward—where appearances were kept up—and the inhumane squalor of other wards (transcript, Mississippi Department of Archives and History). Three other interviews on care of patients at Whitfield are in the archives of the Mississippi Oral History Program, University of Southern Mississippi: vols. 371 and 378 (1991), vol. 401 (1992), and vol. 412 (1992).

AMcCA and WIA move into cottage in Jackson: AGA journal, Dec. 20, 26, 1939.

Mrs. Going: There are several portraits by Bob. AGA interview with John Jones, May 15, 1979.

"When I hadn't written for a long time": WIA to AGA, undated, probably Jan. 1940.

"A nice letter from my darling": AGA journal, Jan. 6, 1940.

"cleansing effect" of writing: HIL, 156.

"getting away in his thoughts": AMcCA to Dr. Denser, Jan. 28, 1940.

"Idea" for dresses: WIA to AGA, Jan. 23, 1940.

"icebergs on the Mississippi": WIA to AGA, Feb. 6, 1940.

"What lovelier home . . .": WIA to AGA, undated, winter 1940.

"A cardinal and a blue jay": WIA to AGA, Feb. 6, 1940.

"I have only a limited amount of money": AMcCA to Dr. Denser, Jan. 28, 1940.

SEPARATION

WIA's return to Shearwater: AGA journal, Feb. 21, 1940.

"a different person": AGA journal, Feb. 27, 1940.

WIA's first days at Shearwater: AGA journal, Feb. 27; March 6, 18; April 24, 28, 1940.

first time family lived together: Neill, 158.

talk of divorce: AGA journal, May 20, 1940.

"just as he made me love him": AGA journal, June 29, 1940.

"get a long view": AGA to WIA, Sept. 5 [?], 1940.

"decisions floated in the air": AGA journal, undated entry (Sept.?), 1940.

"island of peace and sanity": Approaching, 77.

"beautifully taken care of": Memoirs Ms1, 218.

"everlasting fields of [wheat]": AGA to WIA, Aug. 14, 1940.

"politics and war": AGA to WIA, Aug. 3, 1940.

AGA's news of Chicago: AGA letters to WIA, July 24, 29; Aug. 3, 8, 13, 22; Sept. 3.

Pijoan: The surviving parts of the manuscript show that WIA translated from Pijoan's pages on the Egyptians, Assyrians, and ancient Greeks.

"To ignore the art of the past is to refuse one's heritage": Mary Anderson Pickard, *A Symphony of Animals*, xii.

black and white pottery: PGA to Partridge, July 2, 1940.

"We manage some quite exciting tournaments"; "careful way"; "balled out steadily": PGA to Theodore Lidz, Aug. 29, 1940.

alphabet book: In 1975, AGA remembered that the alphabet book was done "in the early forties for Mary and Billy. . . . I was in on a good deal of the carving. Then, suddenly, everything vanished, and not another word about it. It was not until after his death that the blocks turned up, stacked in the bottom of an old chest, and with them, one complete copy, painted by him. The only explanation I have is that he was such a meticulous person about his prints that the [illegible] backwards and must have caused him to abandon the project." AGA to Elizabeth Perry, Jan. 9, 1975, Walter Anderson Papers, deGrummond Children's Literature Collection, University of Southern Mississippi. In the same collection are a copy of the book, colored by Adele Anderson, and a copy of *Robinson: The Pleasant History of an Unusual Cat*, printed from WIA's original linoleum blocks by Shelley Ashley.

"We've always, even in the best days": AGA to WIA, Sept. 5 [?], 1940.

"as we were, the happiest people in the world": Ibid.

WIA trip to Winnetka and comment to Sissy: Approaching, 76.

"So endeth my family treat": AGA journal, Oct. 11, 1940.

"tremendously well in many ways . . . not to spoil it all . . . I must get back to my old affirmative principle": Ibid.

"[He remembered] only the early days": Approaching, 71–72.

trip to Horn Island: AGA journal, Oct. 21, 1940.

throws knife at Sissy: Approaching, 73; AGA/Gilley interview, "Mental Health."

"I have to confess it": AGA journal, Oct. 21, 1940.

"bitter failure": AGA journal, Oct. 29, 1940.

divorce laws: In an interview with Joan Gilley ("Mental Health"), AGA remembers that "you couldn't get a divorce in this state based on a partner's mental illness. It was impossible . . . I went to a lawyer. He said, 'No, no.'"

"like a beast": AGA journal, Nov. 30, 1940.

"You know that I have long since forgiven": AGA to WIA, Nov. 30, 1940.

farms and dude ranches: Elizabeth A. Sarcka, Spring Lake Ranch, to AGA, Nov. 27, 1939, and Arthur Ruggles to Mrs. James L. Gamble, Oct. 24, 1939.

"The place in Vermont sounds like a penal farm": WIA to AGA, Nov. 30, 1940.

"let me see you as soon as you can stand the sight": WIA to AGA, Nov. 29, 1940.

"It's too bad that you can't make the effort": AGA to WIA, "Thursday."

"I've been decorating pots and bow shooting": WIA to AGA, Dec. 16, 1940.

"You ask me to write": AGA to WIA, undated.

"any assurance that you like": WIA to AGA, Dec. 17, 1940.

"I love you. I'm dying of thirst": WIA to AGA, undated.

"I have thought and thought": AGA to WIA, Dec. 19, 1940.

"You must not think that I am staying away only for myself": AGA to WIA, "Saturday."

"Pick up the fragments of your life": AGA journal, Jan. 1, 1940.

"that I may, without losing myself": AGA journal, Jan. 2, 1941.

"What now? . . . Please tell me, God": AGA journal, Jan. 2, 1941.

Roland J. Brown: AGA journal, Jan. 12, 1941.

"asserted that mental illness": Neill, 166.

"He put me down on the bathroom floor": AGA journal, Jan. 13, 1941.

"good tempered and patient . . . much steadier. . . . Very happy, too": AGA journal, 1941, undated.

Sissy visits her father: Memoirs Ms2, 1940, 1–3. Grinstead had been living in Ocean Springs since his discharge from the hospital on Jan. 8, 1935.

"I've bought a car and a cow": Approaching, 82.

GEORGICS

January 1941 trip to Oldfields: There is a handwritten, illustrated account by WIA, and an undated illustrated letter from AGA to AMcCA, Mary, and Billy; both in WIAA. cf. DC, 215–216. In Approaching, 83, AGA wrote, without checking her old journals: "The Oldfields years, as I think of them now, stretched from 1940 to 1948."

"This was my home": Unpublished poem, WIAA; Neill, 176, offers another version.

Poem about terns and pelicans: Several different drafts are in the WIAA.

Annette's babysitting: AGA interview with John Jones, May 14, 1979.

WIA attacks Sissy and Peter: Henry C. A. Mead to Paul Lemkau, April 21, 1941, WIA Phipps.

"I think you will be interested . . . Bob . . . has definitely changed": Ibid.

"The Anderson boys were seen the latter part of March": Ralph C. Hamill to Thomas Rennie, Sept. 8, 1941, PA Phipps.

"Billy and I watched": Mary Anderson Pickard, in WIA, *Robinson,* n.p.

"The beauty of a shell": Unpublished, WIAA.

WIA associates motifs with emotions: Patricia Pinson, "Curator's Statement," *Motifs of Time,* an exhibit at the Walter Anderson Museum of Art, May 23–Sept. 8, 2002. Files of WAMA.

"What do I see when I walk": AGA, small spiral notebook, probably 1941 or 1942, containing prayers and poems, WIAA.

motifs as mantra and crutch: Mary Anderson Pickard, *A Symphony of Animals,* xiv, and Rubin 119.

"in atmospheric phenomena, as in the vortical movement": Best-Maugard, 160. Rubin writes about the use of Best-Maugard motifs in a variety of works by WIA. See also Sugg, *HIL,* 14–16.

"there are constant qualities in art and music": Unpublished, WIAA.

"what has been called by philosophers 'the musical state'": Best-Maugard, 171.

"Art means exactly what the term implies": Hambidge, 142.

"realization of nature's ideal"; artist must "anticipate nature": Unpublished, WIAA.

Clive Bell: Art, 78. Pondering what factor is common to a variety of artworks, from the windows of Chartres to Mexican sculpture to the paintings of Cézanne, Bell concludes that "in each, lines and colours combined in a particular way, certain forms and relations of forms, stir our aesthetic emotions. These relations and combinations of lines and colours, these aesthetically moving forms, I call 'Significant Form'; and 'Significant Form' is the one quality common to all works of visual art."

"The object in being is realization": Unpublished, WIAA.

"The realization of form and space": Mary Anderson Pickard, *Birds,* xiv.

"It was as if I had lost my flower": Unpublished, WIAA.

"I had never seen the sea until I stepped on to the front gallery": Unpublished, WIAA.

"The unending line of the horizon": Unpublished, WIAA.

"continually arriving from some strange place": Mary Anderson Pickard, *Birds,* xiv.

"Holes in heaven are the birds"; "continuous gift of fire": Fragments, WIAA.

"Animals always act intelligently": Mary Anderson Pickard, *A Symphony of Animals,* xvi.

"fine dreamy fashion of childhood years": AGA journal, Nov. 6, 1942.

"Today I cut bean poles": Unpublished, WIAA.

"the continuous gift of fire; the heavenly gift of rain": Unpublished, WIAA.

"It is not enough to love it": Unpublished, WIAA.

calendar drawings: Several series—one in ink and one in watercolor—are extant. Rubin, 105, associates the calendar drawings with "the Germanic works-on-paper folk art called Fraktur."

dance as you plow: Unpublished, WIAA.

Sarasvati and Bob's muse: I am grateful to Mary Anderson Pickard, who is preparing an essay on the subject, for her thoughts on WIA's muse figure.

"a strange exultation or exaltation": AGA, small spiral binder, probably 1941 or 1942, containing prayers and poems, WIAA.

newspaper account of Oldfields figurines: C.A.S., "Shearwater Pottery Is of the Coast Itself, " *The Dixie Gulf Coast Guide,* Dec. 12, 1941, 3.

firing of Oldfields kiln: AGA journal, Feb. 6–12 (1942?), WIAA, and *DC*, 233-34.

"A few pieces from that unlucky kiln": Memoirs Ms1, 228.

"We would live to perfection with no outside contacts": AGA journal, May 18, 1942, WIAA.

"The rain in winter": AGA poem, WIAA.

Sissy's chores at Oldfields and desire to write: AGA journal, May 25, 1942, WIAA. Plans for the novel in journal, Jan. 29, 1944, WIAA.

"Each day should contain . . . creative effort": AGA journal, Oct. 2, 1944(?), WIAA.

Sissy's birthday poem for Bob: Unpublished, WIAA.

"Wonderful word, tenderness": AGA journal, Nov. 5, 1944, WIAA.

"I tremble with my emptiness": Unpublished, WIAA.

Bob and Sissy on love: WIAA, unpublished fragments, WIAA. AGA, small spiral notebook with prayers and poems, probably 1941 or 1942, WIAA.

PERSPECTIVES

Hide and seek with Billy and Mary: Mary Anderson Pickard, *Birds*, viii and interview with John Jones, May 14, 1979; interview with author, Dec. 30, 2002.

"Gently!": Mary Anderson Pickard, *Birds*, viii; interview, Dec. 30, 2002.

Birth of Leif: Approaching, 112–114. AGA to Leif Anderson, May 19, 1974.

Billy and WIA in nullah: Approaching, 93–96.

Indian camp, Ulysses' boat: Approaching, 103–104; Mary Anderson Pickard to the author, undated. Fragments of the boat and Greek warriors are in the WIAA.

puppet play about life in cutover lands: Mary Anderson Pickard, *A Symphony of Animals*, xvii, and interview with John Jones, May 14, 1979. There are numerous autograph notes on the play in the WIAA, and Sissy mentions it in an entry dated "Thursday–June" in her 1942 journal, and "Sunday": "Bob's beaver board puppets in the attic—wonderful. Moths, frogs, turtle, skink. Now to write a fable." A few days later there is the beginning of a synopsis for the play.

Sissy's attitude to cutover lands: There is an unpublished poem on the subject in WIAA.

"She believed that the cutting of the trees": DC, 231–232.

Bob throws pancake at William Wade Grinstead: AGA journal, Nov. 6, 1944, WIAA. Mary Anderson writes of the incident in a short story, "Family Circle," first published in *DC*, 221–230. Interview with John G. Anderson (on Sissy's reliance on WWG), December 2002.

"incredible that an artist": AGA journal, Nov. 6, 1944.

"the constant protection": Ibid.

"God in Bob, God over Bob, God through God": Memoirs Ms2, 1943, 48. The expression occurs more than once—applied to Bob and others—in the 1942–44 journal.

meeting with Mrs. Johnson: Memoirs Ms2, 1943, 47–49.

Bob's "religion" of work: Unpublished, WIAA.

Glenn Clark in Mobile: Neill, 205.

mural at St. Pierre's Episcopal: AGA, Memoirs Ms1, 86–87; Memoirs Ms3, 1941.

plaster walls at Oldfields: AGA interview with Betty Rodgers, August 1985.

a painter "always gets what he wants": Unpublished, WIAA.

"The sheep grazed at right angles": Mary Anderson Pickard, *A Symphony of Animals*, 4.

"Trunk Paintings": So called because they were discovered in 1987 in a trunk brought from

Oldfields. On their discovery, see *DC*, 293; Jerry Kinsler, "Workers Find 116 Paintings," Biloxi *Sun Herald*, Sept. 24, 1987, A-1; Jerry Kinsler, "Artisans Hail Anderson Find," Biloxi *Sun Herald*, Jan. 17, 1988.

linoleum block prints: Approaching, 117, and Thompson, 7.

size of block prints: Thompson, 7, points out that "not until about 1952 did two American artists, Leonard Baskin (b. 1922) and Mauricio Lasansky (b. 1914), begin to produce oversize artists' prints." When Cynthia Rubin, 136–137, interviewed Una Johnson, curator of the print collection at the Brooklyn Museum, in 1993, Johnson said that "to this day she has never seen block prints so finely executed and of such great dimension."

"If we are to develop": Unpublished, from a sketchbook entry, Oct. 27, 1947, WIAA.

illustrations of classics: Sugg, *Illustrations of Epic and Voyage*, xi–xxi, and *Approaching*, 87–88.

"But gradually I became persona non grata": Sugg, introduction to *Illustrations of Epic and Voyage*, xiv. Cf. *Approaching*, 100–101.

Don Quixote: In 1955, Annette and Pat told WIA's doctors at DePaul: "He has read *Don Quixote* many times . . . and has illustrated it many times."

"way or road is the important thing": Unpublished fragment, WIAA.

"Beware by whom you are called sane": Unpublished fragment, WIAA.

"Every form in nature—cat, dog, pig, rat—have all had worlds made for them": Unpublished, WIAA.

train trip to New York and Philadelphia: Unpublished log, WIAA.

new bike: In the WIAA is a permit from the U.S. Office of Price Administration authorizing the purchase of a twenty-one-inch Victory VWIN-21. As justification, WIA lists himself as "Manager of Shearwater Pottery" and adds, "I live in one place, business in other."

excursion to Texas and to New Orleans, 1945: From logs in the WIAA.

encounter with U.S. Army on Horn Island: Approaching, 96–99.

excursion in search of sandhill crane: There is an unpublished account of the trip in the WIAA, with illustrations. See also Mary Anderson Pickard, *Birds*, xv–xvi.

Bob "mythologizes" animals around him: Mary Anderson Pickard, *A Symphony of Animals*, xvi.

Anderson the cat: AGA, Memoirs Ms2, unnumbered pages.

WIA writing on cats: Unpublished fragments, WIAA.

"The point is . . .": Unpublished, WIAA.

"I am at a low ebb": AGA journal, May 16, 1947. Cf. the account of the separation in *Approaching*, 116–127.

"The puppets hung wearily": Memoirs Ms2, n.p.

move back to Ocean Springs: Memoirs Ms1, 296.

1947 hurricane: Approaching, 122–27. There is a handwritten account by PGA in the archives of Marjorie Anderson Ashley.

"both terrified and exhilarated": Memoirs Ms2, 101.

death of William Wade Grinstead: In a petition filed by PGA and AGA on June 9, 1948, they request that they be allowed to draw upon Grinstead's estate (with stocks and bonds estimated between forty thousand and fifty thousand dollars) while the courts are settling it. The reason is that "Agnes Grinstead Anderson teaches school during the scholastic term, but cannot support herself and the four children upon the salary that she receives therefor [and] the work of her husband is such that he is not able to contribute regularly and to the extent to provide all of the necessities for his wife and four children." ("In the Matter of the Last Will and Testament of William W. Grinstead, Deceased, No. 1039, Chancery Court,

County of Jackson Mississippi, Jackson County Archives.") The actual amount came to about thirty-five thousand dollars.
"fight off visitors": Memoirs Ms2, 1947, 100.

THE ISLANDER

"palmetto, cabbage, and ghost crabs": WIA to AGA, pm Aug. 30, 1930.
poems by Sissy and Bob about Horn Island: Unpublished, WIAA.
"They have tried to keep me from going": Unpublished note, WIAA.
"Nostalgia, whether it is born of effort or memory": Unpublished note, WIAA.
"Adam in a hat": HIL, 26.
"A heavenly morning and a heavenly place": Log, F4, WIAA.
history of Horn Island: See Lionel N. Eleuterius, "Historical Background of Horn and Petit Bois Islands," in *Marine Resources and History of the Mississippi Gulf Coast*, vol. II, *Mississippi's Coastal Environment*, 37–41 (copy in Gunter Library, Gulf Coast Research Laboratory, Ocean Springs); and the publications by E. Avery Richmond, who thanks Walter Anderson, with his "expert knowledge of bird life," for helping him update his listing of Horn Island species (1968, 219; cf. 1962, 61, where WIA is listed as "W. H. Anderson"). Over thirty species were sighted by Anderson and reported to Avery.
army testing station on Horn Island: In the National Archives and Records Administration, College Park, Maryland, are over eight thousand pages of reports relating to experiments performed on the island: see Chemical Warfare Service, Bacteriological Warfare Reports, Library Files-ASF Publications, Control Division, Records of Headquarters Army Service Forces, Record Group 160. A memo from W. D. Styer to George W. Merck, Special Consultant to the Secretary of War, dated June 14, 1944, enumerates the facilities erected there: power plants and distribution systems, pipes, wells, two lighting plants, offices, post headquarters, 2960 square feet of living quarters, recreation building, corral area, animal sheds, holding pens, lab building, two warehouses, small arms magazines, thirteen miles of railroad track, two locomotives, twenty cars. On that date there were eleven technical officers, two safety officers and sixty-eight enlisted men. See also *HIL*, 78.
use of Cat Island by U.S. Army: See Gail R. Russell, *Keesler Field: The War Years, 1941–45* (Office of History: Keesler Technical Training Center, Keesler AFB, Mississippi). Article courtesy of Ray L. Bellande.
"military high road": HIL, 213.
combination of sailing, rowing, pulling and pushing: HIL, 137.
banana boat from Gulfport "whacked" in a storm: HIL, 229.
"I found a strange dark bottle": HIL, 157.
"I came home with a feather in my hat": Horn Island log, F5, WIAA.
"I got out and met four hunters with shotguns": Ibid.
"I sit up in bed, move the pillow, and start a little fire": HIL, 129.
"I made a drawing of the bitterns nest": Mary Anderson Pickard, *Voluptuous Return*; HIL, 34.
"A bleak dawn but the sun has come out": HIL, 163.
"I was, as Yeats would say": Log F8B (1964?), WIAA.
"I have an open cut on my foot": HIL, 211.
"Order is here, but it needs realizing": HIL, 113.

"The artist has to be the discoverer": Unpublished, WIAA.

"The Tao-inspired endeavor": Quoted by Kris and Kurtz, 128.

"To regard nature not as something striving to improve": Quoted by Rubin, 127.

"Nature does not like to be anticipated": HIL, 126.

"I suppose eventually I shall reach the archetype": HIL, 151.

"Yesterday afternoon I looked at a hermit crab": HIL, 135.

"What makes a day?": Log, April 16 (SP9), WIAA.

"It seems that a bulrush is just wide enough": HIL, 136, and plate 24.

"Order out of chaos, in spite of the piled-up driftwood": Horn Island log, F5, WIAA.

"I looked up into a dead pine": HIL, 139.

"One single beautiful image is practically inexhaustible": HIL, 29.

"Materializations occur fairly frequently": Log, July 1, 1964 (SM), WIAA. On "materialization," see Sugg, HIL, 36, 143.

"Then, on the way home, a materialization": Unpublished log, undated, WIAA.

"I heard a cry, how far away I couldn't tell": HIL, 88.

"One of the loveliest things I know": HIL, 228.

"Man's relation to nature is constantly shifting": Unpublished fragment, WIAA.

"The world was dead. Dead to beauty": Unpublished, WIAA.

"Nature does not like to be anticipated": Mary Anderson Pickard, *Birds*, xx; HIL, 126.

"I like the wandering ones": HIL, 152.

"but his relation to life": HIL, 82.

"Man begins by saying 'of course,' before any of his senses": DC, 260.

courtship of gallinules: See log beginning June 24, 1964 (SE), WIAA, and Mary Anderson Pickard, *Birds*, xxii.

"I realized the terrible predicament of the gallinule": Log beginning June 24, 1964 (SE), WIAA.

"The eyes already open—little black oriental": Mary Anderson Pickard, *Birds*, xx.

tosses crabs back into sea: HIL, 116.

"Transitional forms": HIL, 98.

WIA tosses crabs into gulf: HIL, 116.

Audubon: quoted by Simmons, in Pinson, 38.

drawings and paintings of dying animals: Log beginning March 10, 1962? (Sp6), WIAA (*turtle*); HIL, 127 (*dead mullet*); 129 (*maggots feeding on Simy*); HIL, 169, and Rubin 168 (*catfish*); Log F8B (*Portuguese man-o'-war*).

"The expanses of sky, of sea": Mary Pickard Anderson, letter to the author, Jan. 9, 2003.

"intending to loaf and invite my soul": Log beginning June 14, 1964 (SE), WIAA.

"Occasionally a young bird dies": "Pelicans," Rubin, 169, 291.

"What could be more delectable than to climb": Mary Anderson Pickard, *A Symphony of Animals*, 20.

"I am a coon": Unpublished, WIAA.

"I had something like a house warming last night": HIL, 187.

"Today a grackle sat on a branch": Log beginning Oct. 6, 1964 (F4), WIAA.

Bob envies blue herons: HIL, 149.

Horn Island hog population: The hogs were introduced to Horn Island in the mid-nineteenth century, and the army tried to remove them in 1943. See Charles R. Brent and Gerald C. Corcoran, "An Environmental Impact Analysis of the Effects of Feral Hogs on the Stability of Horn Island, Mississippi: A Major Island of the Gulf Island National Seashore" (Gulf

Park, Spring 1977) and Edith Bierhorst Back, "Horn Island's 'Exotic' Pigs Puzzle Wilderness Ecologists," Biloxi *Sun Herald*, March 12, 1978, A1 (copies in Gulf Coast Research Station, Ocean Springs), and log, April 16 (SP9), WIAA.

"At my elbow was a dark snake": HIL, 114.

"As I crossed to the inner beach": HIL, 102

"Swam round in company with . . . alligator": Log, April 1965 (SP), WIAA.

"All right, unless they find a sore spot": Log beginning June 24, 1964 (SE), WIAA. But Mary Anderson Pickard remembers: "Daddy thought that if you had a sore, minnows would clean it for you" (letter to the author, Jan. 9, 2003).

"At my elbow was a dark snake with jowls": HIL, 114.

"As I crossed to the inner beach following a hog trail": HIL, 102. Cf. 112–13.

"I spent the morning doing two watercolors": HIL, 132.

"the Greek conception of soul": HIL, 90.

"Boom-boom-atum-atum-atum!": HIL, 150.

"No more pets. I'm wrenched every time I think of him": HIL, 32, 151.

"alive and strong and yet he can't stand up": Log, Jan. 1962 (WK), WIAA.

WIA becomes one with what he paints: Approaching, 38–39; Neill, 237.

"I drew a swarm of flying ants": Unpublished fragment, probably ca. 1940, WIAA.

Taoist painters: Kris and Kurz, 127–29.

"To be a justification to the little black and white ducks": Unpublished log, July 1955, WIAA.

"All things exist in themselves": Unpublished fragment, WIAA.

"You may think you're being influenced": Unpublished fragment, WIAA.

BROOKLYN AND CHINA

Burton Callicott visit to Shearwater: Burton Callicott to the author, April 11, 2001, and letter of September 1948 to AMcCA, WIAA.

proposed expansion of Shearwater: See "New Corporation to Be Organized to Expand Shearwater Pottery," *JXCOT*, Sept. 24, 1948, 1, and subsequent articles Oct. 1, 8; Nov. 19; Dec. 2, 10, 24; Jan. 28; and unsigned contracts of June 5, 1948, between Associated Management Consultants, Gulfport, Mississippi, and the Anderson family (Shearwater Pottery archives). The plan was never carried out.

"Painting still life": Unpublished, WIAA.

The Swimmer: The carving is now in the WAMA.

"The proportions of a pelican are as elusive": Unpublished, WIAA.

swan, hawk, eagle . . . "name what bird you will": Unpublished, WIAA.

"Beautiful and ugly, dignified and comical": Mary Anderson Pickard, *Birds*, xvi.

pelican essay: Published as an appendix in Rubin, 288–298. Meant originally for the New Orleans *Times-Picayune*. See letter from Ray [illegible] of the *Times-Picayune* to AMcCA, dated "Friday" (probably from late 1948 or early 1949), WIAA. The essay was written after the trip described in *HIL*, 62–76.

"Pelican dictionary of common terms": Unpublished, WIAA. A page is reproduced in facsimile in *HIL*, 11.

"Tiers of pelicans hissing and squawking": HIL, 67.

preparations for Brooklyn Museum show: The chain of events is described by Mary Allie Taylor
in "Brooklyn Museum Features Memphis-Discovered Artist," Memphis *Press-Scimitar*, July
1, 1949, and by Rubin, 135–136.

"The Brooklyn Museum is very interested in having an exhibition": Una E. Johnson, Curator,
Department of Prints and Drawings, to WIA, Sept. 17, 1948; Brooklyn Museum Archives.

sampling of prints, carvings, and pottery: The artworks sent to Johnson by WIA on Dec. 28,
1948, included two carved painted cats ($25 apiece); goblets, plates decorated with roosters,
flowers, pelicans and fish; and twenty-five prints, each $7.50: *The White Cat, Jack the Giant
Killer, The Fisherman and the Genie, Mother Goose, Androcles and the Lion, King Arthur
Drawing the Sword from the Rock, The Three Billy Goats Gruff, The Frog Prince, Puss in
Boots, Tiny, The Ugly Duckling, Sinbad, The Four Beasts, The Seven Swans, The Magic
Carpet, The Three Sons* (from the *Arabian Nights*), *Cupid and Psyche, Beauty and the Beast,
Cinderella in the Coach, The Red Bull of Norway, Cinderella Leaving the Dance, Old King
Cole, Woman Who Turned into a Cat,* and *Beauty and the Beast.* On a visit to Shearwater in
April 1949, Johnson seems to have chosen more prints. Thirty scrolls were exhibited (*Brook-
lyn Museum Bulletin* 10:4 [Summer 1949]: 20, with an illustration of *The Cock*). The Brooks
Memorial Art Gallery sent several additional prints, including *Possum Panel, The Four
Beasts, Overmantel of Flowers and Birds, Roll of Flower Prints, Panel of Pitcher Plant Flowers,
Vertical Panel of Birds,* and *Roll of Flying Tern.* Margo Herzog provided additional prints,
fourteen photographs, and a photo from Brooks. Also exhibited were *Biloxi Beach, The
Black Cock, The Pelican Series, Noah's Ark, Bird of War,* [= *Man o' War Bird?*], *Small Gulls,*
and *The Large Pelican.* In a letter of Aug. 24 to Annette, Johnson requests "another copy of
the blue Flying Crane, preferably one that has three repeats on it" (Brooklyn Museum
Archives).

"Would have been more prints, but my hand has been out of order": WIA to Una E. Johnson,
Dec. 27, 1948, Brooklyn Museum Archives.

"Fairy tales have been used so often as sedatives": Manuscript in the Brooklyn Museum
Archives.

"Bob Anderson executes his gay, animated and colorful scroll prints": News release, Brooklyn
Museum Archives.

Bertha Schaefer: Una E. Johnson to Mrs. John Lehman, March 28, 1949, Brooklyn Museum
Archives. Bertha Schaefer to WIA, July 15, 1949, in which she asks for "a group of your
carved animals . . . about six of them in connection with an exhibition of hand-woven textiles which will open here Sept. 15" (Shearwater Pottery archives). Artists featured by Schaefer had ranged from the primitive (handwoven textiles and African masks) to contemporary pottery (Bernard Leach) to modern prints by Sue Fuller, Schanker, Worden Day,
Ben-Zion, Barnet, Hayter, Karl Schrag, Alice Woods, and Oliver Chaffee.

increasing interest in printmaking: See Una Johnson, *American Prints.*

"average print dimension": Margaret Lowengrund, "Field of Graphic Arts. Print Annual," *Art
News,* April 1, 1949.

"never seen block prints so finely executed": Rubin, 137.

sales at Brooklyn Museum exhibition: Una Johnson to WIA, Oct. 27, 1949.

"top and bottom . . . rolled up": Una Johnson to AMcCA, Sept. 1, 1949.

reviews of Brooklyn show: "Walls Decorated by Printed Panels," *New York Times,* May 26, 1949,
37:2; Margaret Lowengrund, "On My Rounds," *Art Digest,* June 1, 1949; "Prints on Scrolls,"

Art Digest, July 1, 1949; "Brooklyn Museum Features Memphis-Discovered Artist," Memphis *Press-Scimitar,* July 1, 1949.

"After that Brooklyn show": Rubin, 142.

"So much of what I had prayed for . . . Night before last": AMcCA journal, June 17, 1949.

China trip and return to Shearwater: I have drawn on the manuscript log, rewritten by WIA after his original logbooks disappeared, and on AGA, *Approaching,* 132–35.

Wallace Stevens poem: There is a handwritten copy of "Anecdote of the Jar" in WIAA.

"An imitation Greek temple, an architectural form": Unpublished, WIAA.

Father Mississippi: See the color photograph in King, 95, fig. 69, and picture and description in Mary Anderson Pickard, *A Symphony of Animals,* xviii. AMcCA seems to be referring to this group, and to its original title in a journal entry of July 4, 1950: "Bob has put up his figures in wood. The River and the animals. It is beautiful." Cf. Aug. 22, 1950: "Yesterday showed Dot Hamill and Margery Baker *The River.* Bob then asked them in to see his watercolors. They were unbelievably beautiful. Pitcher plants." There is a watercolor of *Father Mississippi* in WIAA.

Alonzo Lansford: AMcCA journal, Aug. 3, 1950, and letter from Alonso Lansford to AMcCA, Nov. 2, 1950, about the sale of some pottery, Shearwater Pottery archives.

"fairly comprehensible selection": Lura Beam, Art Associate, AAUW, to PGA, March 8, 1950, WIAA. See also Louise Lehman to PGA, pm April 26, 1950; Louise B. Clark to PGA, Sept. 13, 1950 (about the mounting of the prints and watercolors at the Brooks Memorial Art Gallery), and Louise Lehman to AMcCA and WIA, Sept. 18, 1950 (about the mounting and the opening), WIAA. Also, Rubin, 142–50.

AAUW exhibit: A memo of Aug. 19, 1950, from Lura Beam to an unidentified recipient (probably WIA) lists the graphic works exhibited in *Block Prints, Watercolors, Drawings and Wood Carvings by Walter I. Anderson.* There is another list, with explanations of some of the prints (written by Beam?) in the WIAA. The list resembles closely the one for the Brooklyn Museum show. Among the prints (18" or 19" x 45" to 72") not exhibited in Brooklyn (or exhibited with different titles) were *Sleeping Beauty, Pelican and Waves, Vertical Ducks, Shells, Sinbad and the Roc's Egg, The Pied Piper,* and *Animals.* Watercolors (18" x 25") included *The Chinese Nightingale, The Sleeping Beauty series, I-IV, Golden Hair, The Cake Shop on the Wooden Bridge, The Swineherd and the Princess, The Little Boy and the Rich Old Man, The Cat Turned into a Woman and Back into a Cat, The Frog Demon, The Leprechaun,* and *The Crock of Gold series, I-II.* Smaller watercolors (8 ½" x 11") included *Road, Dogwood, Oak Trees, Gum Tree, Cucumber Tree* (numbers 1–2), *Green Briar, Magnolia, Pitcher Plant* (numbers 1–2), *Cardinal Flower, Lilies, Little Iris, Chinese Crab, Japanese Shrimp, Lobster, Young Pelican,* and three still lifes of plums, citrus fruits, and a shoe with onions. Line drawings in sepia ink (8" x 11") included *Turtle, Mangroves* (numbers 1–2), *Mangroves and Crabs, Pelicans Swimming* (numbers 1–3), *Pelicans, Pelicans on Nest, Pelican with Wings Spread,* and *Pelicans and Terrapin.* The sepia ink drawings were done during the 1948 trip to the Chandeleurs. The small watercolors were sold for twenty-five dollars apiece, and the line drawings for fifteen dollars. When the show opened in Memphis on Sept. 15, Louise B. Clark added some locally owned woodcarvings: a giraffe, *Pegasus,* and *Ox,* owned by the Lehmans (*Ox* was sold later to Dorothea Ward), and "another giraffe and handsome lion owned by the Memphis Art Academy" (Louise Lehman to AMcCA and WIA, Sept. 18, 1950, and Louise Lehman to AMcCA, Nov. 6, 1950, WIAA). There were also roosters, a squirrel, a Greek warrior, an Egyptian mermaid, and a frog prince (Mary Allie Taylor, "Adjectives Smother Work of Mississippi Artist," Memphis *Press-Scimitar*, undated clipping, WIAA with a photograph of the "Pegasus" carving).

Lura Beam letter to AAUW: Lura Beam to N. Louise Moffet, July 28, 1949; Rubin, 143–46; copy in WIAA.

"Walter is of an amazing versatility": PGA to Lura Beam, Nov. 12, 1949; Rubin, 146.

"All three of the Anderson men": Louise Lehman to Lura Beam, Nov. 25, 1949; Rubin, 147.

Contemporary American Drawing *exhibit:* Program, WIAA, dated 1951–52.

"many, many watercolors . . . could be sold on the spot": Louise Lehman to AMcCA and WIA, Sept. 18, 1950, WIAA. Regarding sales, see also Louise Lehman to AMcCA, Nov. 6, 1950; Lura Beam to PGA, Oct. 21, 1950; Dorothea Ward to PGA, April 19, 24, 1951, and reply of PGA, April 30, 1951 (mentioning Ward's acquisition of a watercolor entitled *The Goldfish*, which WIA had "borrowed" from the fountain at the Front House), Shearwater Pottery archives; and Lura Beam to WIA, July 7, 1951, WIAA.

"It looks like there is NO NEED to attempt any special sales program": Dorothea Ward to Lura Beam, Nov. 8, 1950; Rubin, 148–49.

"A genius is amongst us": "Mississippian's Exhibition Now at Brooks Brings Exciting Watercolors," Memphis *Commercial Appeal*, Sept. 17, 1950. The article by Northrop (1923–1978) was reprinted in the *Gulf Coast Times* on Sept. 22, 1950, 1. On Northrop, see "Guy S. Northrop, 55, Man of Many Words, To Be Buried Today," Memphis *Commercial Appeal*, Oct. 7, 1978. See also Guy Northrop, Jr., "Premiere of Anderson Exhibit Set for Saturday at Brooks," untitled clipping, WIAA; "Walter Anderson Art Exhibit at Jackson; To Tour Entire Country," *Gulf Coast Times*, Nov. 8, 1951; "Walter Anderson Exhibit Will Open Here Tuesday," *Jackson Daily News*, Nov. 4, 1951; brief notices in *Putnam County Herald*, Oct. 12, 1950; *Chattanooga Times*, Nov. 7, 20, 26, 1950.

AAUW Showing in Ocean Springs: The exhibition was held in the Community Center January 31–February 2. See Mary Joachim ("Anderson Exhibit Draws Crowd from Many Parts," *Gulf Coast Times*, Feb. 8, 1951, 8), who praises the large watercolor *Sleeping Beauty*, "line drawings in sepia ink," and five watercolors added to the show especially for the occasion; "County's Versatile Artist Shows at Ocean Springs," Pascagoula *Chronicle Star*, Jan. 26, 1951; and unidentified clippings, WIAA, "Ocean Springs Artist Has First Show of Works Before Home Town Crowd" and "Anderson Art Exhibit to Demand Wide Attention."

"Last night, went down to Bob's": AMcCA journal, Jan. 25, 1950, WIAA.

COMMUNITY CENTER

funding for Community Center and dedication: I am grateful to Ray L. Bellande for sending me the following: "Community House Fund Is Undecided," *JXCOT*, May 27, 1948, 1; "Building of New Center Set to Start," *JXCOT*, Nov. 24, 1948, 1; "Community House to Be Ready Soon," *Gulf Coast Times*, May 6, 1949, 1; "Tuesday, Oct. 31 Set as Date for Dedication of Community Center," *Gulf Coast Times*, Oct. 20, 1950, 1; "Final Plans Made for Dedication of Community Center; Colmer to Speak," *Gulf Coast Times*, Oct. 27, 1950, 1; "Colmer Praises Work of O.S. Citizens. . . ," *Gulf Coast Times*, Nov. 2, 1950, 1. The best discussions of the iconography of the murals are those by Francis V. O'Connor (in Pinson) and Anne R. King.

earliest ideas for mural: WIA unpublished two-page manuscript in WIAA, titled "Possibilities," probably from 1950; King, 52.

"When the individual consciousness": Unpublished, WIAA.

"Originality is identified with place": From an unpublished manuscript (beginning "The Jewish genius . . ."), WIAA.

"I have a very strong feeling of place": WIA to Lura Beam, Sept. 4, 1950; Rubiл, 245.

"Originality is identified . . . its own character": Unpublished, WIAA.

"propaganda is no good": Unpublished manuscript, probably from the 1950s, WIAA. The somewhat fanciful reference is to the *Jersey Homesteads* murals of 1937–38.

"turns desperately to money": Unpublished, WIAA.

"The expression of art": Unpublished, WIAA.

"one crew would prepare the wall": Unpublished, WIAA.

"The thing to do . . .": From an unpublished letter, dated May 12 [1948], in AAA, IIIb, "Relations with Public," apparently written in response to a letter published in the *Jackson County Times* in May 1948 by "William R. Allen, Jr., of the Department of Architecture at Texas A. and M., asking that Ocean Springs residents give him their ideas of what would be needed in a Community House to give the greatest benefit to the greatest number of people." See "Community House Plan Is Proposed," *JXCOT*, May 24, 1948, 1, col. 1.

Sissy on participation of children: Approaching, 136; AGA/Joan Gilley interview, "Mental Health."

"any assistance you may need": A. Moran to WIA, Feb. 16, 1951. Reproduced in facsimile in the thesis by Vialet, Appendix A, along with the warrant for one dollar.

earliest work on murals (dribbling paint): During the murals restoration, which began around 1974, the Ocean Springs Art Association did some research on their creation and interviewed Andy Ffloyd, the Gulfport man who sold WIA his art supplies. Ffloyd "was called one day by Walter Anderson and asked to come over and look at a problem. The 'ground' that Walter had put on the walls of the Centre would not harden properly and take the covering paint. So after a study it was decided to remove the ground. Mr. Ffloyd, being a chemist, developed a solution to remove the 'ground.' This worked satisfactorily, and then Walter proceeded painting directly on the stucco. Several times during the work, Walter called on Mr. Ffloyd for various information. There was the matter of the dribbling of the gold or gilt outlying. Walter and Ffloyd agreed that it was 'interesting' and d[idn't] spend a lot of time removing the dribbles. . . . Ffloyd had an extreme fondness for Walter Anderson." See "The involvement of Ocean Springs Art Association, and particularly of Eldon Holmquist in the preservation of the Walter Anderson murals . . . ," undated, probably ca. 1980; copy in WIAA. See also Vialet, 28.

"The advantage the spectator has over the painter"; "How strange": Unpublished, WIAA.

"I don't know whether Ocean Springs has a flower": King, 71. According to Sugg (*Painter's Psalm*, 21), Anderson "is known to have had in mind the Dorothy Perkins roses the town had planted along U.S. Highway 90 in support of a claim to be 'a city of roses.'"

"I, who live in a state which prefers the wind to a tomato": Unpublished, WIAA.

"a belt of the earth's surface": Oxford English Dictionary.

"Possibilities": Unpublished, WIAA.

plants and animals in mural: See the list by WIA in King, 54, fig. 37, and by Vialet, 31.

Iberville as Fred Moran: According to Vialet, Anderson's family found that Iberville looked like Fred Moran and like Father Deignan (a Catholic priest in Ocean Springs), and Iberville's crew contains likenesses of members of the Beaugez family, who had worked at Shearwater; Vialet, 30; King, 55. See the photograph of Moran in King, 58.

planets from nearest to farthest: King, 65.

"Mr. Whitman be my aid": Quoted in King, 67.

Louise Lehman sees murals: Louise Lehman to PGA, May 4, 1951, WIAA. "I shall be looking forward to seeing the finished product. To me, it is good enough as is." Shearwater Pottery archives.

Northrop article:"Town Gets Big Mural for $1 From Gifted Anderson Brush," Memphis *Commercial Appeal*, June 24, 1951, V 10. AGA told her son Johnny that she thought Bob was speaking "largely tongue-in-cheek" (interview with John Anderson, Sept. 1999).

Herschel: As King, 69, has noted, Herschel is probably an allusion to the discoverer of Uranus, Sir William Herschel. A work painted about five years earlier (tempera on wallpaper) entitled *Whirling Spiral with Birds* (King, 56) is similar in design to Jupiter.

dinner for Northrop and wife: "Anderson Dinner Honors Mr. and Mrs. Guy Northrop," *Gulf Coast Times*, June 14, 1951, 9 (courtesy of Ray L. Bellande), and interview with Mrs. Marion Northrop, 2002.

Bob "did not want appreciation": AMcCA journal, June 4, 1951.

"He said he could not come": AMcCA journal, undated entry, June 1951.

"Now I helped get you elected": In *Approaching*, 136–37, Sissy remembers the elected official as a member of the board of aldermen. According to Ray L. Bellande, it is likely that she is referring to Sadie Hodges (1894–1973), then city clerk (conversation of Aug. 11, 2002). See "Mrs. Sadie Hodges Announces for Town Clerk," *Gulf Coast Times*, July 14, 1950.

Gulf Hills mural: "Gulf Hills News," in *Gulf Coast Times*, July 26, 1951, 6, announcing that the mural "covers one entire wall of The Pink Pony"; and AGA, Memoirs Ms1, n.p.; AMcCA journal, July 12, 1951 (WIA announces he will do the mural) and July 17, 1951 (she drives with WIA to Biloxi "for molding of his panel at Gulf Hills"). In Memoirs Ms1, 329, Sissy mentions another "commission": "a scroll or screen for Mrs. Paul McIlheney," a family friend.

"The admirable spirit of the people of Ocean Springs": Mary Anderson Pickard, *A Symphony of Animals*, xix; written on the back of *Cat and Kittens Climbing Stairs.*

murals worth a hundred thousand dollars: A reporter for the *Gulf Coast Times* (Nov. 20, 1952, 1) points out that the Community Center itself is worth forty thousand dollars and that "art critics place a value of over $100,000 on the Anderson murals." See "Ocean Springs Community Center Is Attracting Wide Variety of Events."

Lauren Rogers exhibition and review: See Walter Watkins, "Walter Anderson's Paintings Now at Lauren Rogers Library and Museum of Art Well Worth Seeing," *Laurel Leader-Call*, Sept. 13, 1951, 10; PGA to Walter Watkins, Sept. 4, 12, 1951, and Watkins to PGA, Aug. 5, 31 and Sept. 11, 1951, in the Shearwater Pottery archives. PGA lists the prints exhibited, and the Watkins letter of September 11 contains a detailed description of how they were displayed (there is also a series of photographs in the archives of the LRMA). The long vertical prints were priced from $13.50 to $17.50. Those not listed in earlier exhibitions include the long verticals *Three Musicians, Terns, Seagulls and Fish, Seagull Mosaic,* and *The Cat and the Fiddle*; the short horizontals (priced at $8.50) *Sunflowers, Zinnias, Pine Trees,* and *Flying Herons*; and the horizontals *Gar Fish* and *Ibis Panel*. See also AMcCA journal, July 12, Sept. 27, 1951.

"While many in Laurel": "Lauren Rogers Library and Museum of Art Will Open Season on Sunday," *Laurel Leader-Call*, undated clipping, Shearwater Pottery archives.

"Concentric," "You should not go in one direction": WIA unpublished fragments, WIAA.

Costa Rica trip: From WIA's unpublished journal, passport, plane ticket, and import permit from the U.S. Department of Agriculture (Nov. 1, 1951), all in the WIAA.

trip to Philadelphia and return bike trip to Ocean Springs: From the unpublished log, and anonymous note ("McCarter paintings") in WIAA.

"To know that every movement you make": Unpublished, WIAA.

Annette on sight and insight: AMcCA journal, Jan. 9, 1953.

Annette's bath: AMcCA, unpublished fragment, WIAA.

"This place closes one up": PGA to Partridge, undated, probably early summer 1940, archives of Marjorie Anderson Ashley.

Mac takes full-time job: AMcCA, July 5, 1952, and *DC*, 271.

"HALF VILLAIN, HALF FOOL"

"His watercolors are not so much paintings": From a review of the "paintings, drawings and craftwork" exhibited in Jan. at the little gallery, Newcomb College, New Orleans. Alberta Collier, "The World of Art: Spring Exhibition Is Planned" (*Times-Picayune*, Jan. 23, 1955, sec. 2, 7). The reviewer adds that WIA is "especially successful in portraying animals and birds," that his wall hangings are "interesting but have color too weak for the strength of the designs," and that his pottery "is varied in colors and styles with glazes a little too close to the commercial style to be really fine."

"The artist lives between assistance and opposition": Unpublished, WIAA.

Bob laments wasted opportunity: AGA, undated journal entry, probably 1987.

"On those increasingly rare occasions": Mary Anderson Pickard, *Birds*, ix.

"her stories were so shiningly adventurous": Unpublished portfolio of WIA paintings, with texts by Leif Anderson, in her collection.

John Anderson on uncles Peter and Mac: Interview with the author, Sept. 1999.

"I forget that he is my Daddy": Leif Anderson, *LIFEDANCE*, unpublished memoir.

"ancient and strangely colored shirts": Mary Anderson Pickard, *Birds*, ix. See also her interview with John Jones, transcription, 16.

"My daddy can pet snakes": Leif Anderson, *LIFEDANCE*, unpublished memoir.

clearing wild azaleas: Interview with Billy Anderson, March 22, 2003, and with Carolyn Anderson, March 19, 2003.

"suffusion of color": Unpublished fragment, WIAA. He contrasts this "suffusion" with the notion of "complementary colors": "On clear days in the hour before sunset, when the light is clean but not strong, complementary colors are most apparent. But in painting, the artist should be allowed to choose from either one so as not to be completely tied to a formula."

Bob's transformation on returning from Horn Island: Memoirs Ms1, 348. See also John G. Anderson's observations in *DC*, 263.

Bob's drinking: DePaul Sanitorium records.

refrigerator in marsh: Interview with Frank E. Schmidt, Jr., Feb. 12, 2003.

"I remember one night": Memoirs Ms1, 309–10.

"We have to find something for Bobby to do": Raad Cawthon, "Walter Anderson's Art Featured in *Clarion-Ledger*," *Ocean Springs Record*, Jan. 6, 1983, 9 (interview with AGA).

Ocean Springs "protective" of WIA: AGA, interview with John Jones, May 14, 1979.

"Don't you realize you're the greatest living American artist?": Memoirs Ms1, 376–77.

"The worst of a small community": Unpublished, WIAA.

"Almost everything I've done": Unpublished, WIAA.

"One can belong to society": Unpublished, WIAA.

foiled holdup and incident with man and wife: Interview with John Anderson, Jan. 6, 2003, and
   AGA interview with John Jones, May 14, 1979.

"If the average man realized" Unpublished, WIAA.

"Man apparently lives the life": HIL, 80.

salary at Shearwater: Account books, Shearwater Pottery archives.

"He tried. He really tried": Backes, 30.

"Man is a cave": Unpublished fragment, WIAA.

"We are half of ourselves": Unpublished fragment, WIAA.

beating of Annette: Approaching, 141–43; interview with Michael Anderson, Aug. 2002; and
   DePaul Sanitorium records for WIA, which note, on Sept. 4, 1955 (date of admission) that
   the patient "violently beat wife and mother a month ago while under influence of wine . . .
   admitted to De Paul Hospital per ambulance."

"When I reached the Barn": Approaching, 142. In Memoirs Ms1, 20, AGA writes: "He most frequently attacked his mother—always, apparently, forgetting immediately—never saying,
   'I'm sorry.' He adored her, was closer than most sons. It was strange that she, too, seemed to
   forget his outbursts. At last it was deemed necessary to confine him in a hospital again."

hospitalization at DePaul: Complete records are preserved: case no. B-3239, Sept. 4–24, 1955,
   DePaul medical records. Sissy writes erroneously that "he spent some two months" there.

"I do not think any artist has ever been more sought after": Memoirs Ms1, 310.

"very important to continue . . . occasional visits": Edward H. Knight, M.D., to WIA, June 25,
   1956, WIAA. Knight was affiliated with a group of psychoanalysts called Colomb and Associates, New Orleans, which included Henry O. and Anna C. D. Colomb, Max E. Johnson,
   and William G. Super. Cf. AMcCA journal, June 28, 1956: "Just back from two nights in New
   Orleans."

hospitalization at Mobile Infirmary: Memoirs Ms1, 311, and Mobile Infirmary to the author, Jan.
   22, 2003. Only the dates of admission and discharge, not the records (routinely destroyed
   after twenty-two years), are preserved. Of this stay Sissy writes: "The next hospitalization
   was not so happy. It was occasioned by the same type of out-break against his mother. This
   time he was taken to Mobile and placed in the Psychiatric Ward of City Hospital. The
   atmosphere was entirely different [from that of DePaul]. There was much more the double-
   locked door, bars at the windows bit. He was unhappy except for his talks with his doctor, a
   man who understood and admired him" (Memoirs Ms1, 311).

desire for self-destruction transmuted into belief in providence: Memoirs Ms1, 316–17.

"Suppose you felt that you were in the grip of fate": Unpublished, WIAA.

capsizes off Chandeleur: Approaching, 150–51. More details in Memoirs Ms1, 319–21, and Memoirs Ms2, 1950, 31–34. An undated clipping in the WIAA ("Ocean Springs Artist Rescued
   After Long Swim) refers to a "53-year-old artist," suggesting the incident occurred in 1956.
   Anderson was picked up a mile west of Chandeleur Island lighthouse by a Castiglioli fishing vessel, the *Mississippi,* from Pascagoula, was examined at Keesler, and told the reporter
   "he was feeling none the worse for his experience." Sissy describes the incident in Memoirs
   Ms1.

"Then he relaxed, let himself go, and his foot touched bottom": Memoirs Ms1, 318; *Approaching,*
   150.

Bob capsizes off Bell Fontaine Point: Approaching, 150.

"For Walter I. Anderson": Communication from U.S. Coast Guard Air Detachment, Biloxi,
   Mississippi, Sept. 7, 1961, Shearwater Pottery archives.

"In this day of the machine age": HIL, 80.

buys motor at Sears: Interview with Billy Anderson, March 22, 2003.

"The difficulty of keeping up with our inventions": Unpublished fragment, WIAA.

"One of the great mistakes": Unpublished fragment, WIAA.

"The world of man is far away": HIL, 145.

"A hollow tree to a hound": HIL, 143.

Bob's encounters with others on Horn Island: Log, Aug. 16–19, 1965 (*"frightened gallinules"*); log beginning June 24, 1964 (SE), WIAA: *HIL,* 131 (*"can't we get you something?"*); *HIL,* 132 (*autograph*); *HIL,* 149 (*"self-righteous hoodlum"*); *HIL,* 150; (*lots of ways of having fun*); *HIL,* 117 (*draws "ensemble" of fishing boat*).

"The outpouring of life must find expression in the egg": Mary Anderson Pickard, *Birds,* x.

snake bite: From a Horn Island log, 1961, Sp 8A, WIAA, retold by AGA in *Approaching,* 155–58; more details in Memoirs Ms1, 338–43.

joke about snake bite: Approaching, 158.

"How many times . . .": HIL, 212.

"To cure an injured toe": WIA unpublished fragment, WIAA.

trip to Florida to visit Baisden: From a logbook in the WIAA and Memoirs Ms2, 1960, 50–53. Many of the watercolors (turkey vultures, grapefruit groves, grapefruit, etc.) are still extant.

Allan Cruickshank and wife, "charming people": Frank Baisden to WIA, letter dated Feb. 15, WIAA.

"You were our Christmas present": Kay Baisden to WIA, undated letter, WIAA.

Smithsonian bird exhibition: The exhibition was finally mounted at the Brooks Memorial Art Gallery in Memphis in 1964: *Fledgling Birds by Walter Anderson;* Mary Anderson Pickard, *Birds,* xxi.

trips to Horn Island in Spring 1961: Log Feb. 1961 (WG), April 6, (Sp4), May (Sp5), WIAA.

"Green-headed Mallard drake climbs out on log": Log, Oct., no year (1961?), WIAA.

"like royalty: gold all around": Unpublished log, Oct. 25, 1961, WIAA.

Mardi Gras trip to New Orleans: The paintings were exhibited in 1988. See Roger Green, "Walter Anderson Captures New Orleans," New Orleans *Times-Picayune,* July 1, 1988 (A), and Estill Curtis Pennington.

"Don't let anyone see": AMcCA to WIA, Jan. 16, 1928? WIAA.

Mary smooths out WIA watercolors: Interview with Mary Anderson Pickard, Dec. 31, 2003.

WIA attraction to Margaret Sidney: Interview with Cedric Sidney, Dec. 2002.

Norman Cameron visit to Ocean Springs, 1960: Recalled by Cameron in letters to AGA, Jan. 18 and June 15, 1970, WIAA. On Cameron, see Ralph M. Crowley, M.D., "A Memorial: Norman Alexander Cameron, Ph.D., M.D.," *Journal of the American Academy of Psychoanalysis* 7:3: 468–71, and autobiographical letters, archives of John G. Anderson.

"Professionally, [Bob's letter] confirms other experiences": Norman Cameron to Ellen Mead, July 25, 1961, archives of John G. Anderson.

"You're the only one I haven't written to": AGA to WIA, Winder Point, Easton, Maryland, July 8, 1961, WIAA.

Norman Cameron visit to Ocean Springs, 1962: Norman Cameron to Ellen Mead, Jan. 8, 17, 1963, archives of John G. Anderson. AGA Memoirs Ms3, 1962.

"he'd just give me an armload [of drawings]": Norman Cameron to Ellen Mead, Dec. 8, 1964, archives of John G. Anderson.

Pat remembers Annette's last days: PGA, paraphrase of an undated poem by PGA, "A.McC.A., 1867–1964," archives of Marjorie Anderson Ashley.

"*courage and clear good sense*": Margaret Neilsen McConnell Sidney to WIA, Jan. 28, 1964, WIAA.

"*Souls . . . Mother told me that when I was a little boy*": DC, 280–81.

FINAL VOYAGE

green plywood skiff: HIL, 166, 180, 230. The skiff is now at the WAMA, Ocean Springs.

satellite and "first guided missile": Log beginning Oct. 24, 1961 (F8), WIAA, and HIL, 179.

nuclear submarines, oil rigs, container ships: JXCOT, May 20, Oct. 28, 1965.

stakes and paint in WIA camp: HIL, 169.

"*Here all sorts of improvements*": Unpublished, beginning Feb. 24, 1964 (?) (WA), WIAA. Cf. HIL, 206.

plans to link islands with causeway: "Proposals Given for Developing Offshore Islands," *Ocean Springs News,* Dec. 10, 1964. See also "Hearing Called on Study of Bridges of Islands," *Ocean Springs News,* Dec. 17.

death of pelicans: Bill Thomas, "The Brown Pelican. A Wonderful Bird Indeed—But a Frightening Omen," *Defenders,* 51:6 (Dec. 1976): 363; "The Return of the Brown Pelican," *Louisiana Conservationist* 23:5–6 (May–June 1971), 10–13.

"*Seventeen in one flock!*": HIL, 223; Mary Anderson Pickard, *Birds,* xix. In 1965 he refers to the pelican as a "rare bird" (*HIL,* 214).

"*Offer to teach drawing in a public school!*": Unpublished, WIAA.

"*The law that is made by society*": Unpublished, WIAA.

trips in 1964 to Horn Island: From logs, July 1, 1964 (SM), and Aug. 16–29, 1964.

encounter with Billy and "new wife": Interview with Billy Anderson, March 22, 2003.

1965 trips: HIL, 177 ("*wind shields*"), 192 (*fish hawks*), 193 (*gallinules* and *grackles*), 196 (*fifty-two species*), 202 ("*Dagger with Wings*"), 196 (*coon*), 217 ("*bleached bone*"), 218 ("*With the birds*"), 230 ("*intense vermillion*"), 231 ("*suitable trees to tie to*"), 231 ("*slept well*").

"*some leafy refuge*": Approaching, 159.

WIA and Hurricane Betsy: One of the earliest accounts of how WIA weathered the storm is by E. Avery Richmond (1968), 221, who may have heard it from WIA himself. See also HIL, 230–34. The story that WIA "tied himself to a tree," which appears in many accounts, beginning in Backes, is apocryphal. For the account given here, HIL, 231 ("*Never has there been*"), 231 ("*A large coast guard boat*"), 231 ("*my camp was gone*"), 231–234 (*changes in island*), 232 ("*Never have I seen*").

trip to New Orleans: Approaching, 160–61.

"*Fascinating to feel*": HIL, 214.

"*spreading wide the intervals*": Voluptuous Return, plate 15.

trip to shipyard: HIL, 236.

encounter with Patricia Findeisen: Interview, Jan. 3, 2003. Sissy had moved into the studio to allow Patricia and her family to live at the Barn.

tells Sissy about coughing up blood: Approaching, 161; Memoirs Ms1, 349; AGA journal, Feb. 28, March 21, 1986. On sack of apples, HIL, 215.

Mary on father's illness: Interview with John Jones, May 14, 1979.

account of trip to New Orleans and treatment at Baptist Hospital: Approaching, 162–71, and Memoirs Ms1; AGA journal, Feb. 28, March 1, 1986; interview with Frank E. Schmidt, Jr.,

Feb. 12, 2003; incomplete records (including a letter from Schmidt to AGA about the autopsy) on WIA at Baptist, WIAA.

"It is approaching the magic hour": HIL, 73, and *Approaching,* between xi and 1; *HIL,* 35.

funeral: Approaching, 172–73.

discovery of the "Little Room" mural: The best account is given by Sugg, *A Painter's Psalm,* 3–22. AGA describes the discovery in *Approaching,* 174–75, and PGA in her interview of 1968, in which she points out that the family underestimated the abundance of WIA's work: "We never had any idea that he was doing all of the painting that he did." The little room now forms part of the Walter Anderson Museum of Art in Ocean Springs.

WORKS CITED

(* indicates works in WIA's personal library)

Ashe, William C. "Reconnaisance Report of the Proposed Horn Island National Wildlife Refuge," National Archives and Records Administration.

Anderson, Agnes Grinstead. *Approaching the Magic Hour: Memories of Walter Anderson.* Edited by Patti Carr Black. Jackson: University Press of Mississippi, 1995.

———. "Hellmuth-Grinstead Family," in Rodgers, *The History of Jackson County,* 234–35.

———. "Walter Anderson: The Man, The Artist." *The Southern Quarterly* 24 (Fall–Winter 1985): 170–94.

———. Interview with John Jones, May 15, 1979, Mississippi Department of Archives and History.

———. Interview with Betty Rodgers, August 1985, Oral History Collection, Pascagoula Public Library.

Anderson, Annette McConnell. *Possums and Other Verse.* Gulfport, privately printed, s.a.

Anderson, Leif. *LIFEDANCE.* Unpublished memoir.

Anderson, Patricia Grinstead. Interview, Picayune, Mississippi, 1968. Archives of the Walter Anderson Museum of Art.

Anderson, Walter Inglis. *An Alphabet.* Jackson: University Press of Mississippi, 1984.

———. *Birds.* Jackson: University Press of Mississippi, 1990.

———. *The Horn Island Logs of Walter Inglis Anderson.* Edited by Redding S. Sugg, Jr. Rev. ed., Jackson: University Press of Mississippi, 1985.

———. *The Magic Carpet and Other Tales.* Retold by Ellen Douglas, illustrations by Walter Anderson. Jackson: University Press of Mississippi, 1987.

———. *Realizations of the Islander.* Selections of Paintings and Essay by John Paul Driscoll. Walter Anderson Estate, 1985 (catalogue of an exhibition at the Pennsylvania Academy of the Fine Arts, 1985).

———. *Robinson: The Pleasant History of an Unusual Cat.* Jackson: University Press of Mississippi, 1982.

———. *A Symphony of Animals.* Jackson: University Press of Mississippi, 1996.

———. *Walls of Light.* See Anne R. King.

———. *Walter Anderson's Illustrations of Epic and Voyage.* Edited and with an introduction by Redding S. Sugg, Jr. Carbondale and Edwardsville: Southern Illinois University Press; London and Amsterdam: Feffer & Simmons, 1980.

——— (illustrator). Lewis Carroll. *Anderson's Alice: Walter Anderson Illustrates Alice's Adventures in Wonderland.* With a foreword by Mary Anderson Pickard. Jackson: University Press of Mississippi, 1983.

———. *Walter Inglis Anderson Papers, ca. 1915–1960.* Reels 4867–4872, Archives of American Art, Smithsonian Institution.

Andrus, Olive P. "Isidore Newman School and the Manual Training Movement." M.A. thesis, Tulane University, 1938.

Backes, Clarus. "Artist in the Eye of a Hurricane." *Chicago Tribune Magazine,* August 17, 1969, 26–31.

*Ball, Katherine M. *Decorative Motifs of Oriental Art.* London: John Lane, The Bodley Head Ltd./New York: Dodd, Mead and Company, 1927.

Beckham, Sue Bridwell. *Depression Post Office Murals and Southern Culture: A Gentle Reconstruction.* Baton Rouge and London: Louisiana State University Press, 1989.

Bell, Clive. *Art.* London: Chatto and Windus, 1915.

*Best-Maugard, Adolfo. *A Method for Creative Design.* New York and London: Alfred A. Knopf, 1927.

Black, Patti Carr. *Art in Mississippi, 1720–1980.* Jackson: University Press of Mississippi in association with the Mississippi Historical Society and the Mississippi Department of Archives and History, 1998.

———. "Introduction" in AGA, *Approaching the Magic Hour,* vi–xi.

Blossfeldt, Karl. *Art Forms in Nature: Examples from the Plant World Photographed Direct from Nature.* Introduction by Karl Nierendorf. New York: E. Weyhe, 1929.

*———. *Urformen der Kunst: Photographische Pflanzenbilder.* Berlin: Verlag Ernst Wasmuth, n.d.

*———. *Wundergarten der Natur: Neue Bilddokumente Schöner Pflanzenformen.* Berlin: Verlag für Kunst Wissenschaft, 1932.

Bragg, Jean Moore, and Susan Saward. *The Newcomb Style: Newcomb College Arts & Crafts and Art Pottery Collector's Guide.* New Orleans: Jean Bragg Gallery, 2002.

Burton, Mauda Kaiser. "Portraitist of Nature." *Horizon* 25 (March 1982): 41–48.

———. "Portrait of a Mississippi Artist." *Mississippi* 2 (May–June 1984): 10–19, 86–92.

Brister, Mary, and Marie Hull. "Walter Anderson and Family: A Group of Rare Individuals." *Clarion-Ledger/Jackson Daily News* (Jackson, Miss.), July 30, 1967, D2.

*Brown, Calvin S. *Archaeology of Mississippi.* With a new introduction by Philip Phillips. AMS Press/Peabody Museum of Archaeology and Ethnology, Harvard University, 1973 (first edition, 1926).

Canis, Wayne F., William J. Neal, Orrin H. Pilkey, Jr., and Orrin H. Pilkey, Sr. *Living with the Alabama Shore.* Durham, NC: Duke University Press, 1985.

Carey, Rita Katherine. "Samuel Jarvis Peters." *Louisiana Historical Quarterly* 30:2 (April 1947): 439–80.

Carney, Margaret. *Charles Fergus Binns. The Father of American Studio Ceramics.* New York: Hudson Hills Press, 1999.

Chadbourne, Thomas L. *The Autobiography of Thomas L. Chadbourne.* Edited by Charles C. Goetsch and Margaret L. Shivers. New York: Oceana Publications, 1985.

Charbonnet, Grace. "The Anderson Story . . . Splendor in Mississippi." *The Delta Review* 3 (November–December 1966): 40–43, 57–58.

Clark, Garth, Robert A. Ellison, and Eugene Hecht. *The Mad Potter of Biloxi: The Art and Life of George E. Ohr.* New York: Abbeville, 1989.

*Cohn, William. *Chinese Art.* London: The Studio Ltd., 1930.

Crowfoot, A. H. *This Dreamer: Life of Isaac Hellmuth, Second Bishop of Huron.* Vancouver: Copp Clark Publishing, 1963.

Diskant, Carolyn. "Modernism at the Pennsylvania Academy, 1910–1940." In *This Academy: The Pennsylvania Academy of the Fine Arts, 1805–1976. A Special Bicentennial Exhibition.* Philadelphia, 1976.

Driscoll, John Paul. See Walter Anderson, *Realizations of the Islander.*

Ebaugh, Franklin G. "Adolf Meyer: A Tribute from Home." *American Journal of Psychiatry* 123:3 (September 1966): 334–36.

*Fechheimer, Hedwig. *Kleinplastik der Agypter.* Berlin: Bruno Cassirer Verlag, 1921.

Foster, Kathleen A. *Daniel Garber 1880–1958.* Catalogue from an exhibition at the Pennsylvania Academy of the Fine Arts, 1980.

Funderburk, Brent. "Man Is a Cave." In *Interior Images: The Influence of Prehistoric Cave Art in France on the Work of Walter Inglis Anderson.* Catalogue of a show at the Walter Anderson Museum of Art, August 17–November 10, 1996.

Funk and Wagnalls Standard Dictionary of Mythology and Legend. Edited by Maria Leach and Jerome Fried. 2 vols. New York: Funk & Wagnalls Company, 1949, 1950.

Gilbert, Bil. "Stalking the Blue Bear: The Fine Art of Walter Anderson." *Smithsonian* 25:7 (October 1994): 108–18.

Goings, Kenneth W. *Mammy and Uncle Mose: Black Collectibles and American Stereotyping (Blacks in the Diaspora).* Bloomington: Indiana University Press, 1994.

*Guillaume, Paul, and Thomas Munro. *Primitive Negro Sculpture.* New York: Harcourt, Brace & Company, 1926.

Hall, Doris, and Burdell Hall. "Shearwater: Southern Pottery of Sheer Beauty." *American Clay Exchange* 6:9 (June 15, 1986): 7, 8, 12; "A Shearwater Experience," 6:11 (July 1986): 3–4; "George Walter and Annette McConnell Anderson's Legacy," 6:15 (September 30, 1986): 9–11; "Shearwater's Figurines," 6:16 (October 15, 1986): 3–5.

*Hambidge, Jay. *Dynamic Symmetry: The Greek Vase.* New Haven, CT, New York City, Yale University Press, 1920 (third printing, 1941).

———. *The Parthenon and Other Greek Temples: Their Dynamic Symmetry.* New Haven: Yale University Press, 1924.

*Holland, William Jacob. *The Butterfly Book. A Popular Guide to a Knowledge of the Butterflies of North America.* Garden City, NY: Doubleday, Page & Co., 1916.

*———. *The Moth Book. A Popular Guide to a Knowledge of the Moths of North America.* New York: Doubleday, Page & Co., 1903.

Hull, Marie. See Mary Brister.

Hurlburt, Laurance P. *The Mexican Muralists in the United States.* Albuquerque: University of New Mexico Press, 1989.

*Ingersoll, R. Sturgiss. *Henry McCarter.* Cambridge, MA: The Riverside Press (privately printed), 1944.

Jamison, Kay Redfield. *Touched with Fire: Manic Depressive Illness and the Artistic Temperament.* New York: Free Press, 1996.

Johnson, Una E. *American Prints and Printmakers: A Chronicle of Over 400 Artists and Their Prints from 1900 to the Present.* Garden City, NY: Doubleday, 1980.

Jones, Marjorie F. *A History of the Parsons School of Design, 1896–1966.* Ph.D. dissertation, New York University, 1968.

Kendall. "Interview with Margaret Neilson McConnell Sidney (1900–1992), Niece of A.M.A., on Feb. 3, 1975," manuscript, Kendall's archives.

King, Anne R. *Walls of Light: The Murals of Walter Anderson.* Jackson: University Press of Mississippi and the Walter Anderson Museum of Art, 1999.

Kolocotroni, Vassiliki, Jane Goldman, and Olga Taxidou, eds. *Modernism: An Anthology of Sources and Documents.* Chicago: The University of Chicago Press, 1998.

Kris, Ernst, and Otto Kurz. *Legend, Myth, and Magic in the Image of the Artist: A Historical Experiment.* New Haven: Yale University Press, 1979.

Larsen, Susan C. "The Seeker Becomes a Seer: 'My Eye Is Strange to Thee.'" In Pinson, 17–29.

Lewis, Adam. *Van Day Truex: The Man Who Defined Twentieth-Century Taste and Style.* New York: Viking Studio, 2001.

Lidz, Theodore. "Adolf Meyer and the Development of American Psychiatry." *American Journal of Psychiatry,* 123:3 (September 1966): 320–33.

———. "Conversation Piece." See Otto Marx.

Long, Frank W. *Confessions of a Depression Muralist.* Columbia: University of Missouri Press, 1997.

Lytal, Bill (producer). *Shearwater Pottery* (video, 27 minutes). Clinton, MS: Mississippi College, 1978.

Mahé, John A. II, and Rosanne McCaffrey, eds. *Encyclopedia of New Orleans Artists 1717–1918.* New Orleans: Historic New Orleans Collection, 1987.

Marling, Karal Ann. *Wall-to-Wall America: A Cultural History of Post-Office Murals in the Great Depression.* Minneapolis: University of Minnesota Press, 1982.

Marx, Otto. "Conversation Piece. Adolf Meyer and Psychiatric Training at the Phipps Clinic. An Interview with Theodore Lidz." *History of Psychiatry,* IV (1993): 245–69.

Maurer, Christopher, with María Estrella Iglesias. *Dreaming in Clay on the Coast of Mississippi: Love and Art at Shearwater.* New York: Doubleday, 2001.

McConnell, James. *The Ethic Elements in the Character and Laws of Nations.* Oration of 1855 delivered to the Alumni Association of the Law Department of the University of Louisiana. New Orleans, 1855.

Mecklenburg, Virginia. *The Public as Patron: A History of the Treasury Department Mural Program Illustrated with Paintings from the Collection of the University of Maryland Art Gallery.* College Park: University of Maryland Art Gallery, 1979.

Meyer, Adolf. *Collected Papers,* Vol. II, *Psychiatry.* Introduction by David K. Henderson. Baltimore: The Johns Hopkins Press, 1951.

———. *Collected Papers,* Vol. III, *Medical Teaching.* Introduction by Franklin G. Ebaugh. Baltimore: The Johns Hopkins Press, 1951.

———. *Collected Papers,* Vol. IV, *Mental Hygiene.* Introduction by Alexander H. Leighton. Baltimore: The Johns Hopkins Press, 1952.

Mitchell, S. Weir. *Lectures: Diseases of the Nervous System Especially in Women.* Philadelphia: Henry C. Lea's Son & Co., 1881.

Muncie, Wendell. *Psychobiology and Psychiatry. A Textbook of Normal and Abnormal Human Behavior.* St. Louis: C.V. Mosby Co., 1939.

Munson, Gorham. "Black Sheep Philosophers: Gurdjieff–Ouspensky–Orage." *Gurdjieff International Review,* 1:3 (Spring 1998): 1–7.

Neil, Scott R. *Walter Inglis Anderson (1903–1965), A Bibliography*. Privately printed. De Land, FL, 1982.

Neill, John R. "Adolf Meyer and American Psychiatry Today." *American Journal of Psychiatry*, 137:4 (April 1980): 460–64.

Neill, Josephine Haley. "Fear of Flying: The Early Poetry of Agnes Grinstead Anderson." *The Southern Review*, 37:3–4 (Summer 1999): 238–54.

———. *Stretching the Boundaries: The Writing of Agnes Grinstead Anderson*. Ph.D. dissertation, University of Mississippi, 1998.

Nott, C. S. *Teachings of Gurdjieff: An Account of Some Years with G. I. Gurdjieff and A. R. Orage in New York and at Fontainebleau-Avon*. London: Routledge & Kegan Paul, 1961.

O'Connor, Francis V., ed. *Art for the Millions: Essays from the 1930s by Artists and Administrators of the WPA Federal Art Project*. Boston: New York Graphic Society, 1975.

———. "The Murals of Walter Anderson: An Encompassing Vision." In Pinson, 47–63.

Orage, A. R. "Discussion on 'Good and Evil' with A. R. Orage." *Gurdjieff International Review*, 1:3 (Spring 1998); 1:4 (Summer 1998); 2:1 (Fall 1998).

Parsons, Frank Alvah, and William M. Oden. "The New York School of Fine and Applied Art." *School Arts Magazine* (Worcester) 22 (June 1923): 600–604.

Pasquine, Ruth. *The Politics of Redemption: Dynamic Symmetry, Theosophy, and Swedenborgianism in the Art of Emil Bisttram (1895–1976)*. 2 vols. Ph.D. dissertation, City University of New York, 2000.

Pennington, Estill Curtis. "Walter Anderson in New Orleans." *Arts Quarterly* (New Orleans Museum of Art), (July/August/September 1988): 5–9.

Pessin, L. J., and T. D. Burleigh. "Notes on the Forest Biology of Horn Island, Mississippi." *Ecology*, 22:1 (January 1941): 70–79.

Pickard, Mary Anderson. "The Birds of Walter Anderson," in WIA, *Birds*.

———. "Incidents in the Life of Walter Anderson." Talk given at the Pass Christian, Mississippi, Historical Society, March 10, 1986. Copy in Walter Anderson Museum of Art.

———. "Interior Images: The Influence of Prehistoric Cave Art in France on the Work of Walter Inglis Anderson." Catalogue, Walter Anderson Museum of Art, August 17–November 10, 1996.

———. Interview with John Jones, May 14, 1979, Mississippi Department of Archives and History (Mary Anderson Stebly.)

———. "Introduction," in WIA, *A Symphony of Animals*.

———. "A Personal View of Annette McConnell Anderson, December 16, 1867–January 25, 1964." *Motif* (Walter Anderson Museum of Art), Summer 1994.

———. *The Voluptuous Return: Still Life by Walter Anderson*. Foreword by Patti Carr Black. Ocean Springs: Family of Walter Anderson, 1999.

*Pijoan, José. *Summa Artis. Historia general del arte. Vol. I. Arte de los pueblos aborígenes*, primera edición. Bilbao/Madrid/Barcelona: Espasa-Calpe, S.A., 2nd edition, 1933.

*———. *Summa Artis. Historia general del arte. Vol. II. Arte del Asia occidental. Sumeria-Babilonia-Asiria-Hititia-Fenicia-Persia-Partia-Sasania-Escitia*. Bilbao/Madrid/Barcelona, 1931.

*——— *Summa Artis. Historia general del arte. Vol. III. El arte egipcio hasta la conquista romana*. Bilbao/Madrid/Barcelona, 1932.

*———. *Summa Artis. Historia general del arte. Vol. IV. El arte griego hasta la toma de Corinto por los romanos 146 A.J.C.* Bilbao/Madrid/Barcelona, 1932.

Pinson, Patricia, ed. *The Art of Walter Anderson*. Jackson: University Press of Mississippi, 2003.

Poesch, Jesse. *Newcomb Pottery: An Enterprise for Southern Women, 1895–1940*. Exton, PA: Schiffer Publishing, 1984.

Richmond, E. Avery. *The Flora and Fauna of Horn Island, Mississippi*. Ocean Springs: Gulf Coast Research Reports, 1: 2 (1962): 59–106.

———. *A Supplement to the Fauna and Flora of Horn Island, Mississippi*. Ocean Springs: Gulf Coast Research Reports, 2: 3 (1968): 213–54.

Rodgers, Betty C., ed. *The History of Jackson County, Mississippi*. Pascagoula, MS: Jackson County Genealogical Society, 1989.

———. "Lewis Sha-Oldfields," in *The History of Jackson County, Mississippi*.

Rodríguez, Antonio. *A History of Mexican Mural Painting*. New York: GP Putnam's, 1969.

Rubin, Cynthia Elyce. *Natural Forms: The Horn Island Logs and Watercolors of Walter Inglis Anderson (1903–1965)*. Ph.D. dissertation, New York University, 1995.

———. "Walter Inglis Anderson." *Country Folk Art* (December 1995): 91–92.

Rudloe, Jack. "The Nature of a Painter." *Natural History* (February 1900): 62–68.

Rutter, Michael. "Meyerian Pychobiology, Personality Development, and the Role of Life Experiences." *American Journal of Psychiatry*, 143:9 (September 1986): 1077–87.

Scott, Bill. "Quita Brodhead. New Horizons for a New Century." *Pennsylvania Heritage. Quarterly of the Pennsylvania Historical and Museum Commission and the Pennsylvania Heritage Society*, 27:2 (Spring 2001): 25–31.

Scott, Wilford Wildes. *The Artistic Vanguard in Philadelphia, 1905–1920*. Ph.D. dissertation, University of Delaware, 1983.

Simmons, Linda Crocker. "Walter Anderson and the American Tradition of Nature Painting." In Pinson, 31–45.

*Smith, Simon Harcourt. *Babylonian Art*. London: Bouverie House, Ernest Benn Ltd., 1928.

Speight, Francis. *Francis Speight. An Exhibition of Paintings Organized by the School of the Pennsylvania Academy of the Fine Arts, March 29–April 27, 1979*. Introduction by Evan Turner. Philadelphia: PAFA, 1979.

———. *Francis Speight. A Retrospective Exhibition. February 16–March 26, 1961*. Raleigh: North Carolina Museum of Art, 1961.

———. *Manayunk and Other Places: Paintings and Drawings by Francis Speight. A Retrospective Exhibition Organized by The Pennsylvania State University*. University Park, PA: Museum of Art, The Pennsylvania State University, 1974.

Stephens, Joseph H., et al. "Inpatient Diagnoses during Adolf Meyer's Tenure as Director of the Henry Phipps Psychiatric Clinic, 1913–1940." *Journal of Nervous and Mental Disease*, 174:12 (1986): 747–51.

———. "Long-Term Follow-up of Patients Hospitalized for Schizophrenia, 1913 to 1940." *The Journal of Nervous and Mental Disease*, 185:12 (December 1997): 715–21.

Sugg, Redding S., Jr. *A Painter's Psalm: The Mural from Walter Anderson's Cottage*. Rev. ed., Jackson: University Press of Mississippi, 1992.

Sullivan, Charles L. *Hurricanes of the Mississippi Gulf Coast*. Biloxi: Gulf Publishing, 1986.

Sullivan, Louis. *The Autobiography of an Idea*. New York: Dover Publications, 1956.

Taylor, Joshua C. "To Be Modern." *Pennsylvania Academy Moderns 1910–1940*. Washington: Smithsonian Institution Press/ National Collection of Fine Arts, 1975.

Thompson, Carole E. *An American Master: Walter Anderson of Mississippi*. Memphis: Memphis Brooks Museum of Art, 1988.

———. "Walter Anderson: Prints from Mississippi." *Print Collectors Newsletter* (May–June 1989).

Vialet, Aimée Gautier. *Walter I. Anderson: Murals of the Ocean Springs Community Center*. M.A. thesis, Louisiana State University, 1973.

Walter, Elizabeth Mitchell. *Jay Hambidge and the Development of the Theory of Dynamic Symmetry, 1902–1920*. Ph.D. dissertation, University of Georgia, 1978.

Wolanin, Barbara A. *Arthur B. Carles (1882–1952) Painting with Color*. Philadelphia: Pennsylvania Academy of the Fine Arts, 1983.

Woodward, Ellsworth. "Advice to South." *The Art Digest* (December 1, 1935): 9.

WPA Source Material for Mississippi. History Jackson County, Vol. XXX. Compiled by State-Wide Historical Research Project. Susie V. Powell, State Supervisor. Jackson, 1937.

York, Maurice. *The Privilege to Paint: The Lives of Francis Speight and Sarah Blakeslee*. Greenville (North Carolina) Museum of Art, 2002.

ILLUSTRATION CREDITS

BLACK AND WHITE ILLUSTRATIONS

COLOR PLATES

Leif Anderson, collection of Leif Anderson

Child, collection of Mary Anderson Pickard

Mr. Boots, the Family of Walter Anderson

Ocean Springs: Past and Present (*The Chase*), the City of Ocean Springs, Mississippi, photograph by Kevin Berne

Sun, the City of Ocean Springs, Mississippi, photograph by John Lawrence

Man on Horse, the Family of Walter Anderson, photograph by Owen Murphy

James McConnell Anderson (Mac), collection of Sara Anderson

Hunter Plate, the Family of Walter Anderson, photograph by Owen Murphy

Don Quixote, collection of Mary Anderson Pickard

Jockeys Riding Horses, the Family of Walter Anderson

Watermelon Eaters, the Family of Walter Anderson

Vase with Horses, the Family of Walter Anderson, photograph by Owen Murphy

Horse Plate, collection of Marjorie Anderson Ashley, photograph by Owen Murphy

Long Necked Horse, the Family of Walter Anderson

The Artist Painting Oranges, the Family of Walter Anderson, photograph by Owen Murphy

Broken Red Pot, Walter Anderson Museum of Art, 97.3.1, photograph by Kevin Berne

Road to Oldfields, Walter Anderson Museum of Art, 89.3.1, photograph by Kevin Berne

Sheep and Pine Trees, the Family of Walter Anderson

Cat Teapot, the Family of Walter Anderson

Turkey, the Family of Walter Anderson

Blue Cat Vase, collection of Shearwater Pottery

Man and Goat Vase, collection of Shearwater Pottery

Non-Competitive, the Family of Walter Anderson

Man Making Music with Cows, the Family of Walter Anderson

Pepper Plant, Walter Anderson Museum of Art, 00.1.1, photograph by Owen Murphy

Orange Fast, the Family of Walter Anderson

Rotten Pumpkin, private collection

Chinese Lobster, the Family of Walter Anderson, photograph by Kevin Berne

Mardi Gras, New Orleans, the Family of Walter Anderson, photograph by Kevin Berne

Mary Anderson, collection of Mary Anderson Pickard

Portrait of Young Woman, Walter Anderson Museum of Art, 75.1.1, photograph by Kevin Berne

New Orleans, collections of Joan Gilley, María Estrella Iglesias, Scott Shows, and the Family of Walter Anderson, photograph by John Lawrence

Horn Island, collection of John G. Anderson

Walter Rowing His Boat, the Family of Walter Anderson

Waves, private collection, photograph by Kevin Berne

Grackles, the Family of Walter Anderson

Coots and Waves, the Family of Walter Anderson, photograph by Kevin Berne

Owl, Walter Anderson Museum of Art, 97.1.1, photograph by Kevin Berne

Stone Crab, the Family of Walter Anderson, photograph by Kevin Berne

Red-Head Duck, the Family of Walter Anderson

Purple Gallinules, private collection

Baby Herons, the Family of Walter Anderson

Dead Red-Head Duck, the Family of Walter Anderson

Two Birds in a Tree Plate, the Family of Walter Anderson

Green Heron, the Family of Walter Anderson

Racoon, the Family of Walter Anderson

Reflections in a Bull-Rush Pool, private collection, photograph by Kevin Berne

Baby Bird, private collection

Goldenrod on Horn Island, the Family of Walter Anderson, photograph by Kevin Berne

Rowing at Night, Walter Anderson Museum of Art

Harvesting the Sea Bowl, the Family of Walter Anderson, photograph by Kevin Berne

Chesty Horse, collection of Louise Lehman, photograph by Kevin Berne

Sea, Earth and Sky Vase, Walter Anderson Museum of Art, 95.4.1, gift of Mr. and Mrs. Gerald Maples, dedicated to Frances Wynn Maples, photograph by Kevin Berne

Duck Bowl, collection of Maria Estrella Iglesias

Northwest corner of the "Little Room" Mural, Walter Anderson Museum of Art, photograph by John Lawrence

Southeast corner of the "Little Room" Mural, Walter Anderson Museum of Art, photograph by John Lawrence

Self-Portrait, the Family of Walter Anderson

The Islander, private collection

INDEX